THE AVALON CHRONICLES

VOLUME ONE

ONCE IN A BLUE MOON

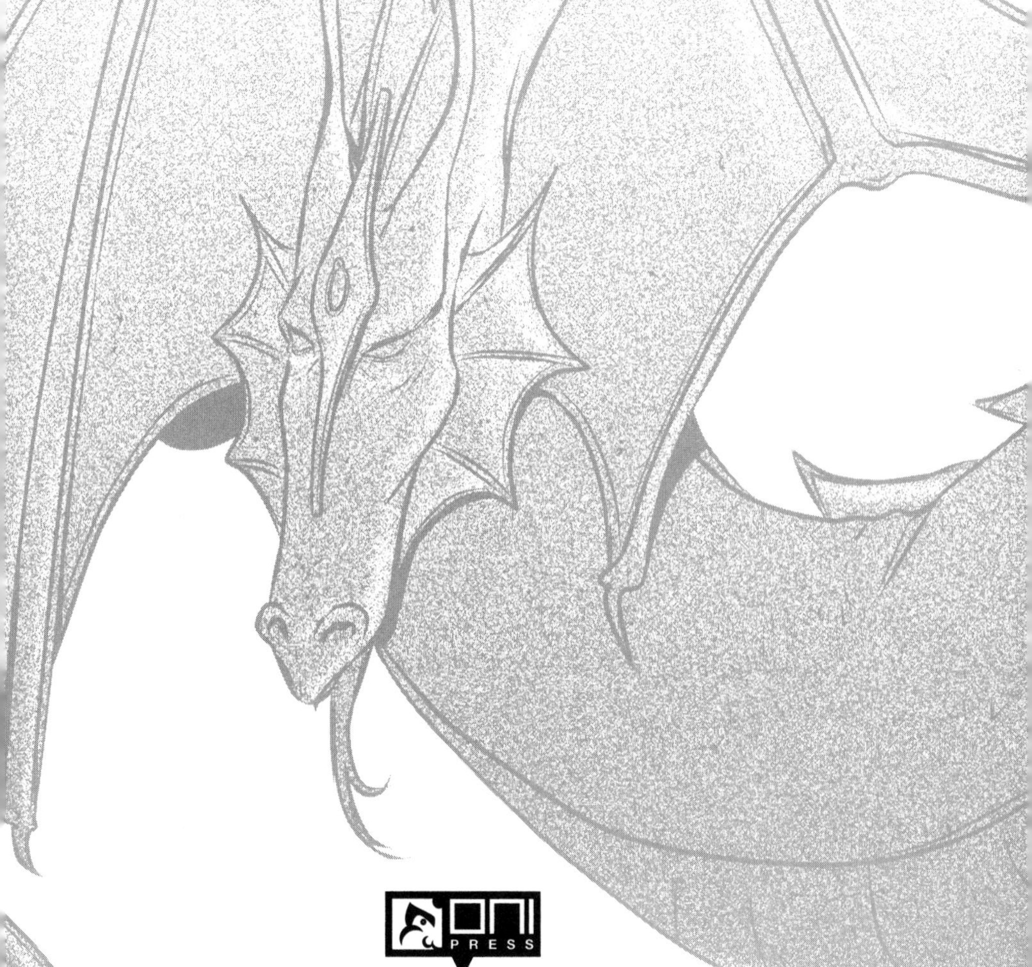

AN ONI PRESS PUBLICATION

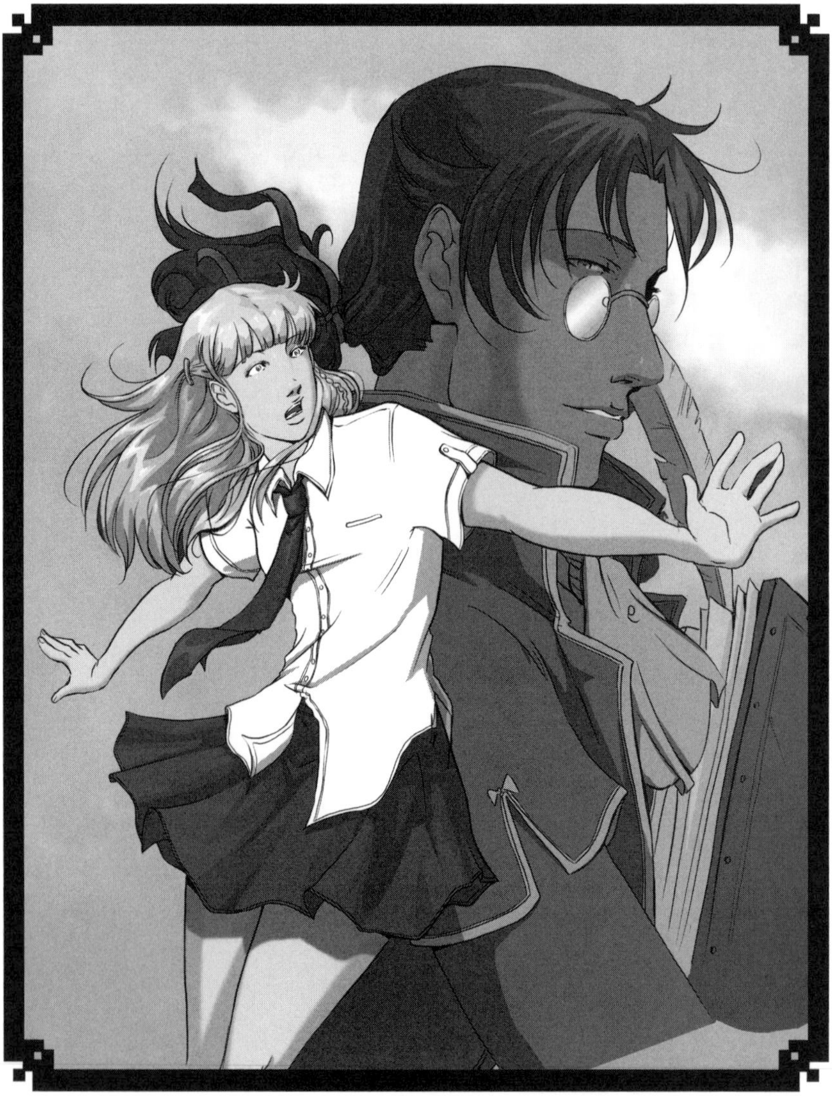

I

THE AVALON
VOLUME ONE
CHRONICLES
ONCE IN A BLUE MOON

WRITTEN BY
NUNZIO DEFILIPPIS
& CHRISTINA WEIR

ILLUSTRATED BY
EMMA VIECELI

LETTERED BY
DOUGLAS E. SHERWOOD

COVER COLORED BY
DAN JACKSON

DESIGNED BY
KEITH WOOD

EDITED BY
JILL BEATON

ONI PRESS, INC.

JOE NOZEMACK • PUBLISHER

JAMES LUCAS JONES • EDITOR IN CHIEF

CORY CASONI • MARKETING DIRECTOR

KEITH WOOD • ART DIRECTOR

GEORGE ROHAC • OPERATIONS DIRECTOR

JILL BEATON • EDITOR

CHARLIE CHU • EDITOR

TROY LOOK • DIGITAL PREPRESS LEAD

THE AVALON
VOLUME ONE
CHRONICLES

ONCE IN A BLUE MOON

The Avalon Chronicles: Once in a Blue Moon, March 2012.
Published by Oni Press, Inc. 1305 SE Martin Luther King Jr. Blvd.,
Suite A, Portland, OR 97214. The Avalon Chronicles is ™ & © 2012
Nunzio DeFilippis, Christina Weir, and Emma Vieceli. All rights
reserved. Unless otherwise specified, all other material © 2012 Oni
Press, Inc. Oni Press logo and icon ™ & © 2012 Oni Press, Inc. Oni
Press logo and icon artwork created by Keith A. Wood. The events,
institutions, and characters presented in this book are fictional. Any
resemblance to actual persons, living or dead, is purely coincidental.
No portion of this publication may be reproduced, by any means,
without the express written permission of the copyright holders.

1305 SE MARTIN LUTHER KING JR. BLVD.
SUITE A
PORTLAND, OR 97214

WWW.ONIPRESS.COM

FIRST EDITION: MARCH 2012
ISBN: 978-1-934964-75-0

LIBRARY OF CONGRESS CONTROL NUMBER: 2011933168

1 3 5 7 9 10 8 6 4 2

PRINTED IN USA

Chapter 1

ONCE UPON A TIME...

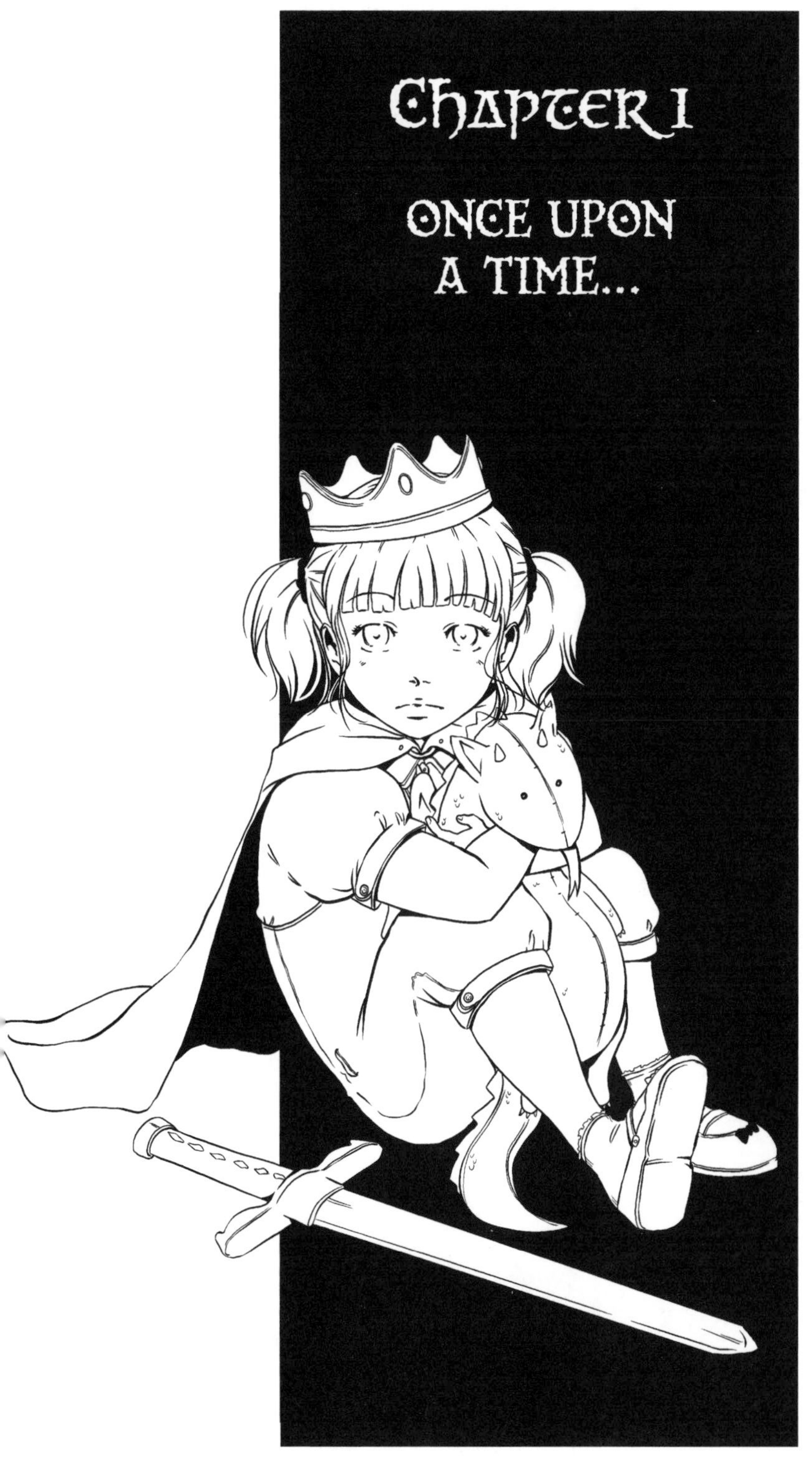

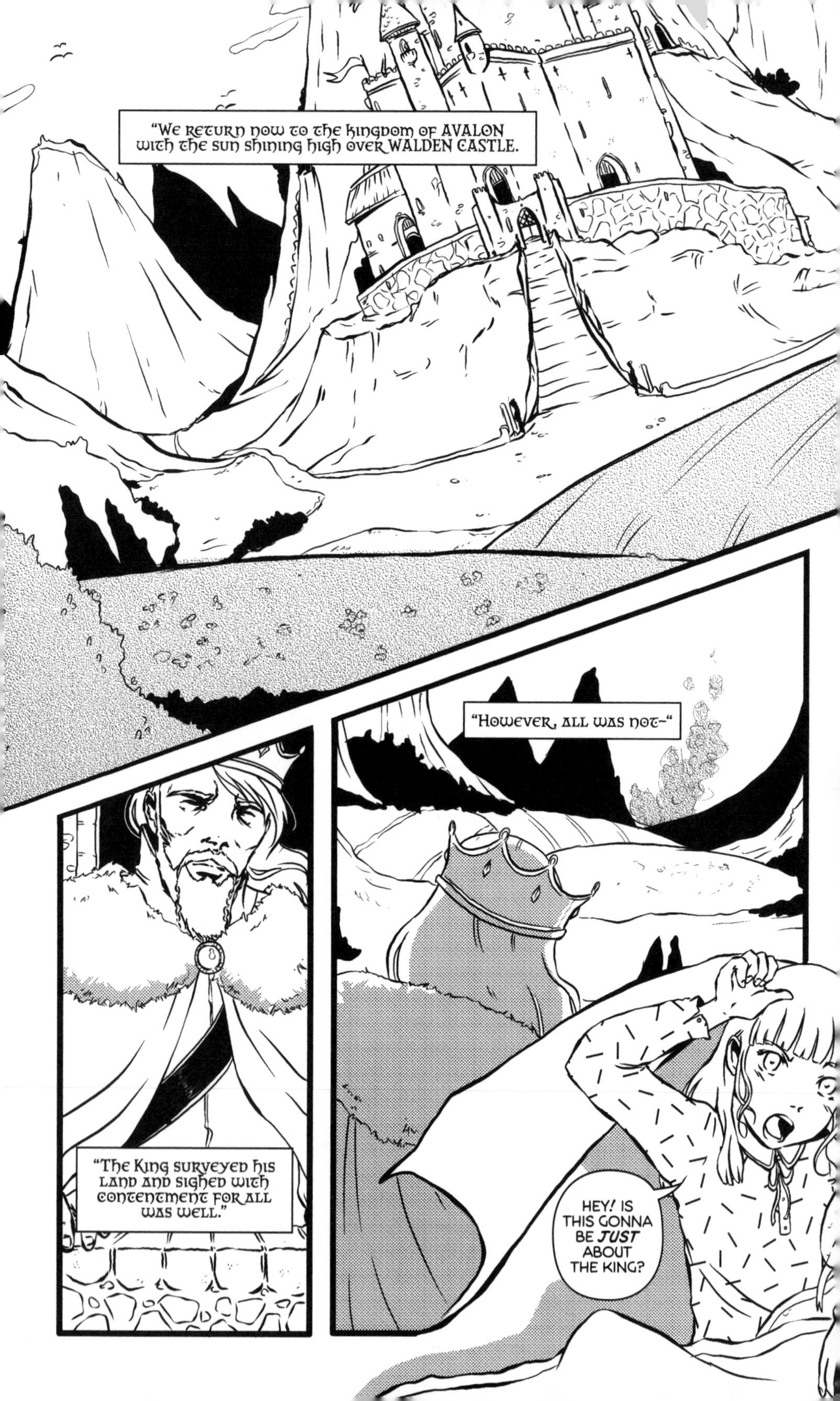
"We return now to the kingdom of AVALON with the sun shining high over WALDEN CASTLE.
"The King surveyed his land and sighed with contentment for all was well."
"However, all was not~"
HEY! IS THIS GONNA BE JUST ABOUT THE KING?

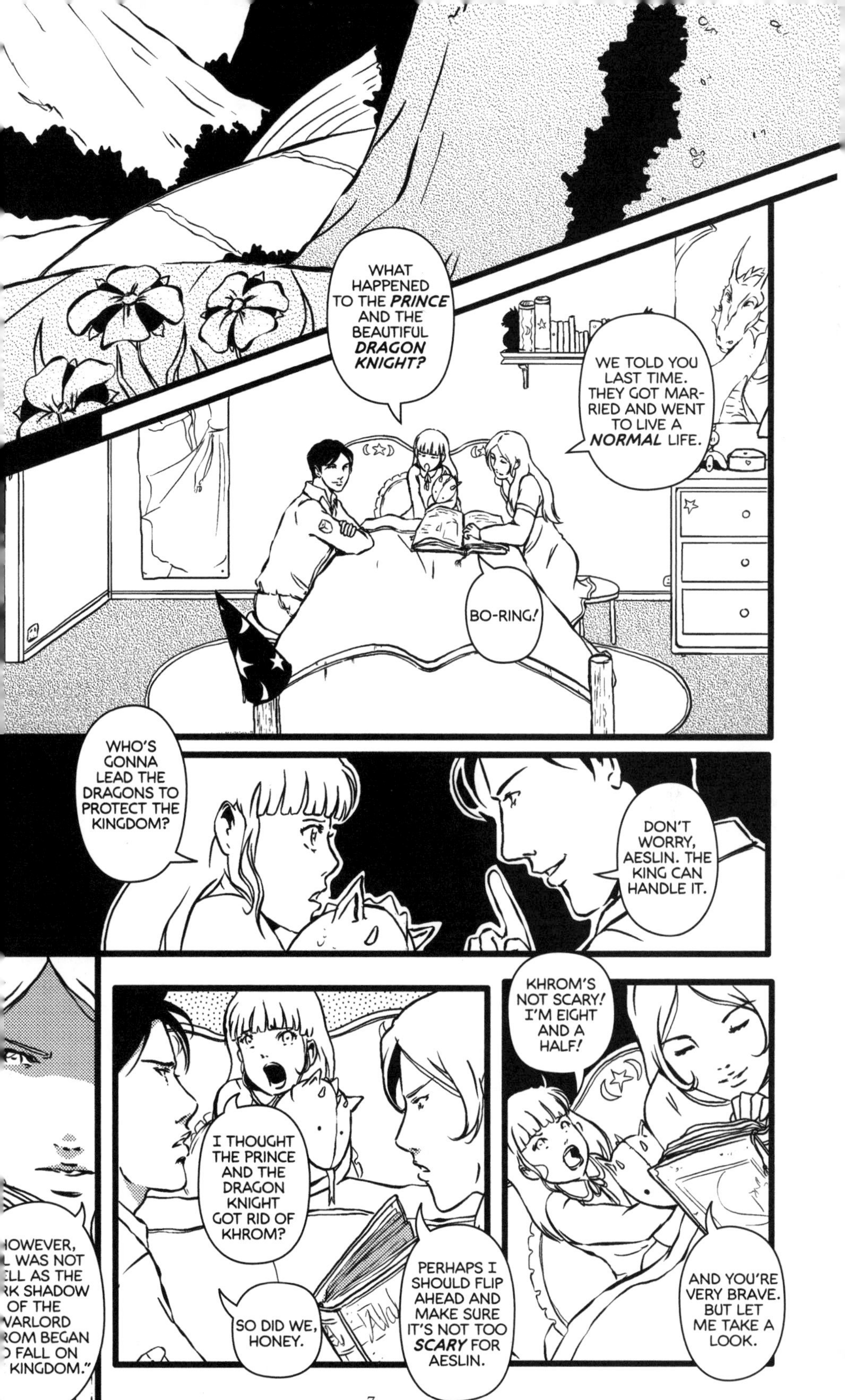

WHAT HAPPENED TO THE *PRINCE* AND THE BEAUTIFUL *DRAGON KNIGHT?*
WE TOLD YOU LAST TIME. THEY GOT MAR-RIED AND WENT TO LIVE A *NORMAL* LIFE.
BO-RING!
WHO'S GONNA LEAD THE DRAGONS TO PROTECT THE KINGDOM?
DON'T WORRY, AESLIN. THE KING CAN HANDLE IT.
OWEVER, L WAS NOT ELL AS THE RK SHADOW OF THE WARLORD ROM BEGAN FALL ON KINGDOM."
I THOUGHT THE PRINCE AND THE DRAGON KNIGHT GOT RID OF KHROM?
SO DID WE, HONEY.
PERHAPS I SHOULD FLIP AHEAD AND MAKE SURE IT'S NOT TOO *SCARY* FOR AESLIN.
KHROM'S NOT SCARY! I'M EIGHT AND A HALF!
AND YOU'RE VERY BRAVE. BUT LET ME TAKE A LOOK.

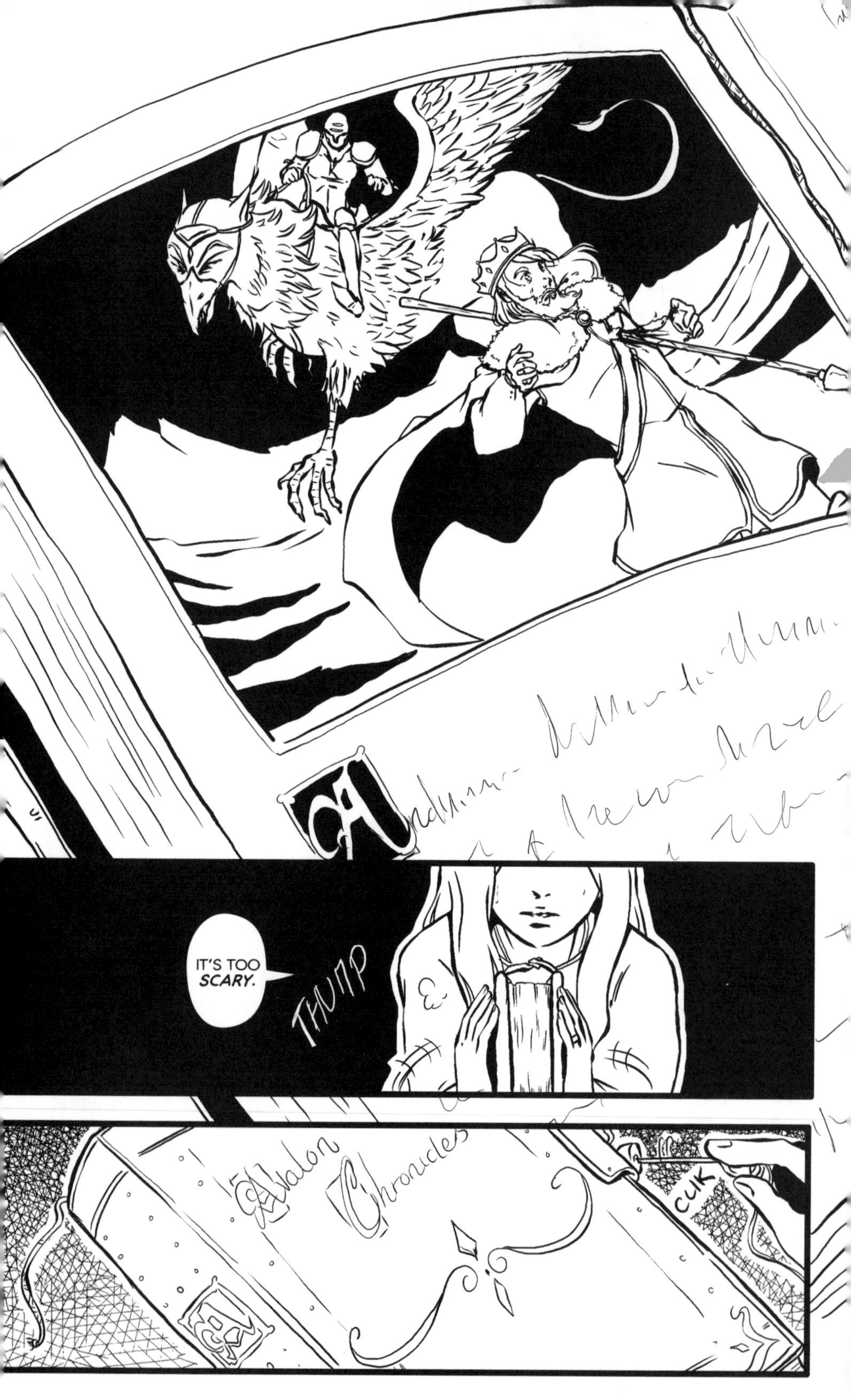
IT'S TOO SCARY.
THUMP
Avalon Chronicles
CLIK

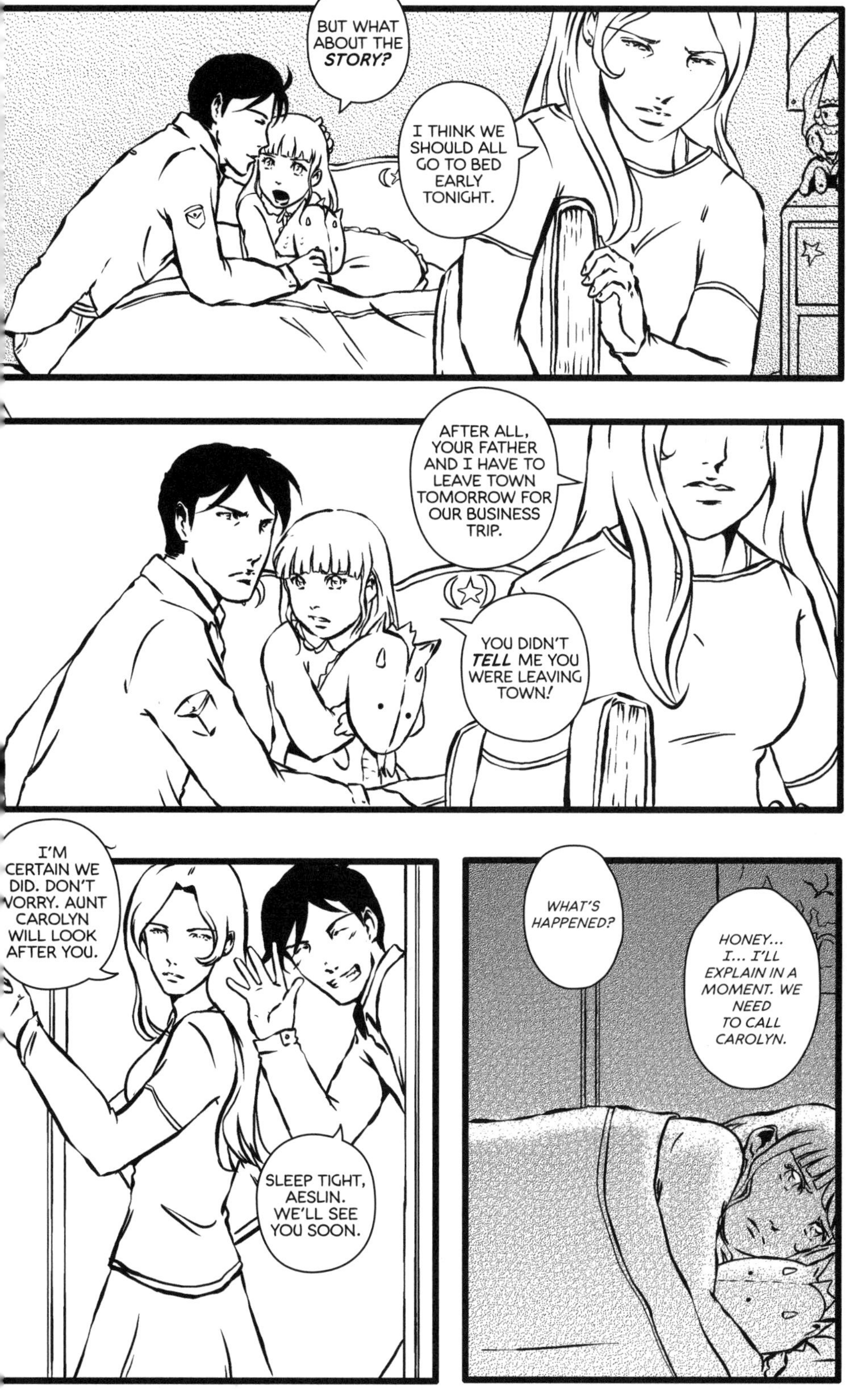
BUT WHAT ABOUT THE *STORY?*
I THINK WE SHOULD ALL GO TO BED EARLY TONIGHT.
AFTER ALL, YOUR FATHER AND I HAVE TO LEAVE TOWN TOMORROW FOR OUR BUSINESS TRIP.
YOU DIDN'T ***TELL*** ME YOU WERE LEAVING TOWN!
I'M CERTAIN WE DID. DON'T WORRY. AUNT CAROLYN WILL LOOK AFTER YOU.
SLEEP TIGHT, AESLIN. WE'LL SEE YOU SOON.
WHAT'S HAPPENED?
HONEY... I... I'LL EXPLAIN IN A MOMENT. WE NEED TO CALL CAROLYN.

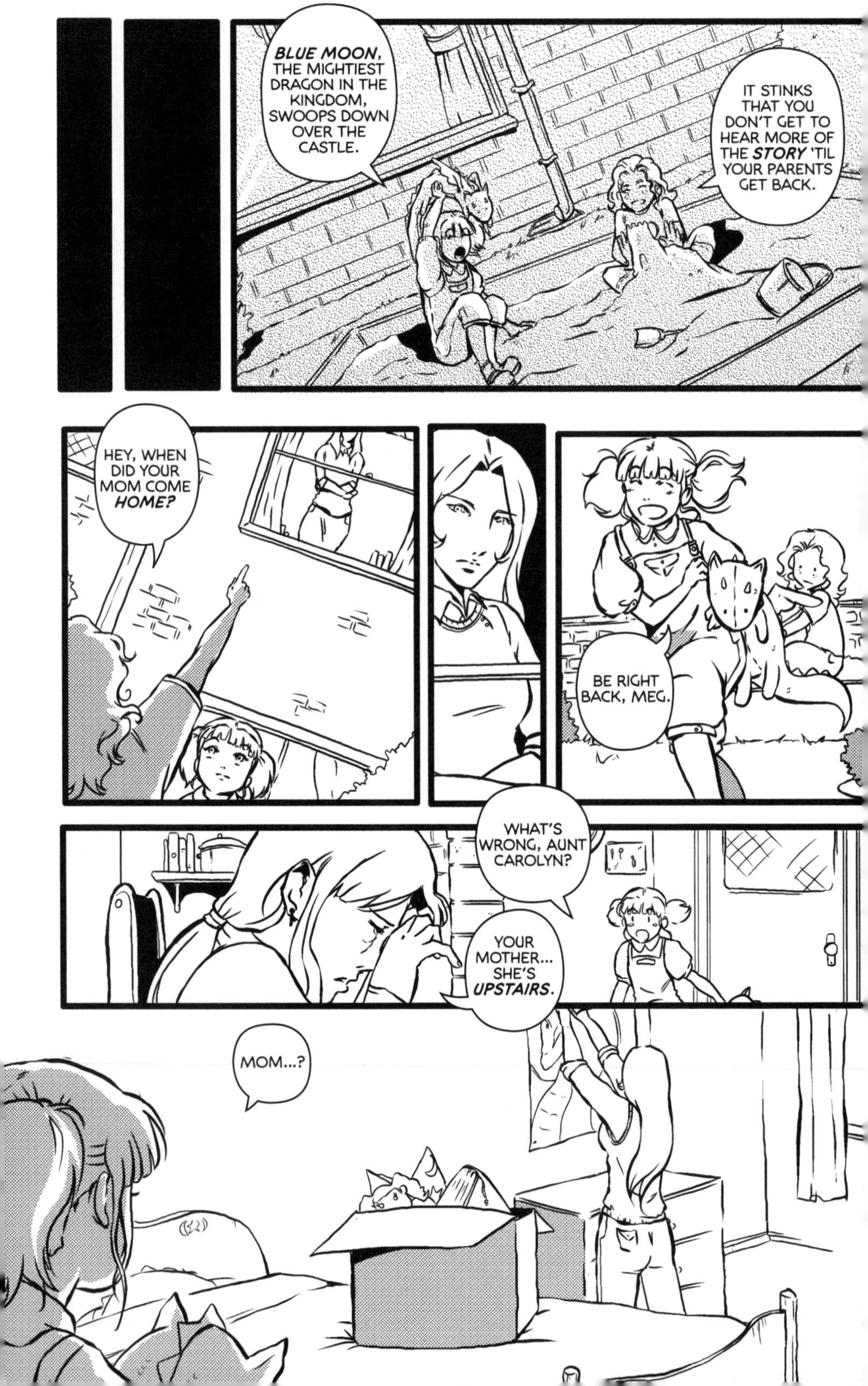
BLUE MOON, THE MIGHTIEST DRAGON IN THE KINGDOM, SWOOPS DOWN OVER THE CASTLE.
IT STINKS THAT YOU DON'T GET TO HEAR MORE OF THE STORY 'TIL YOUR PARENTS GET BACK.
HEY, WHEN DID YOUR MOM COME HOME?
BE RIGHT BACK, MEG.
WHAT'S WRONG, AUNT CAROLYN?
YOUR MOTHER... SHE'S UPSTAIRS.
MOM...?

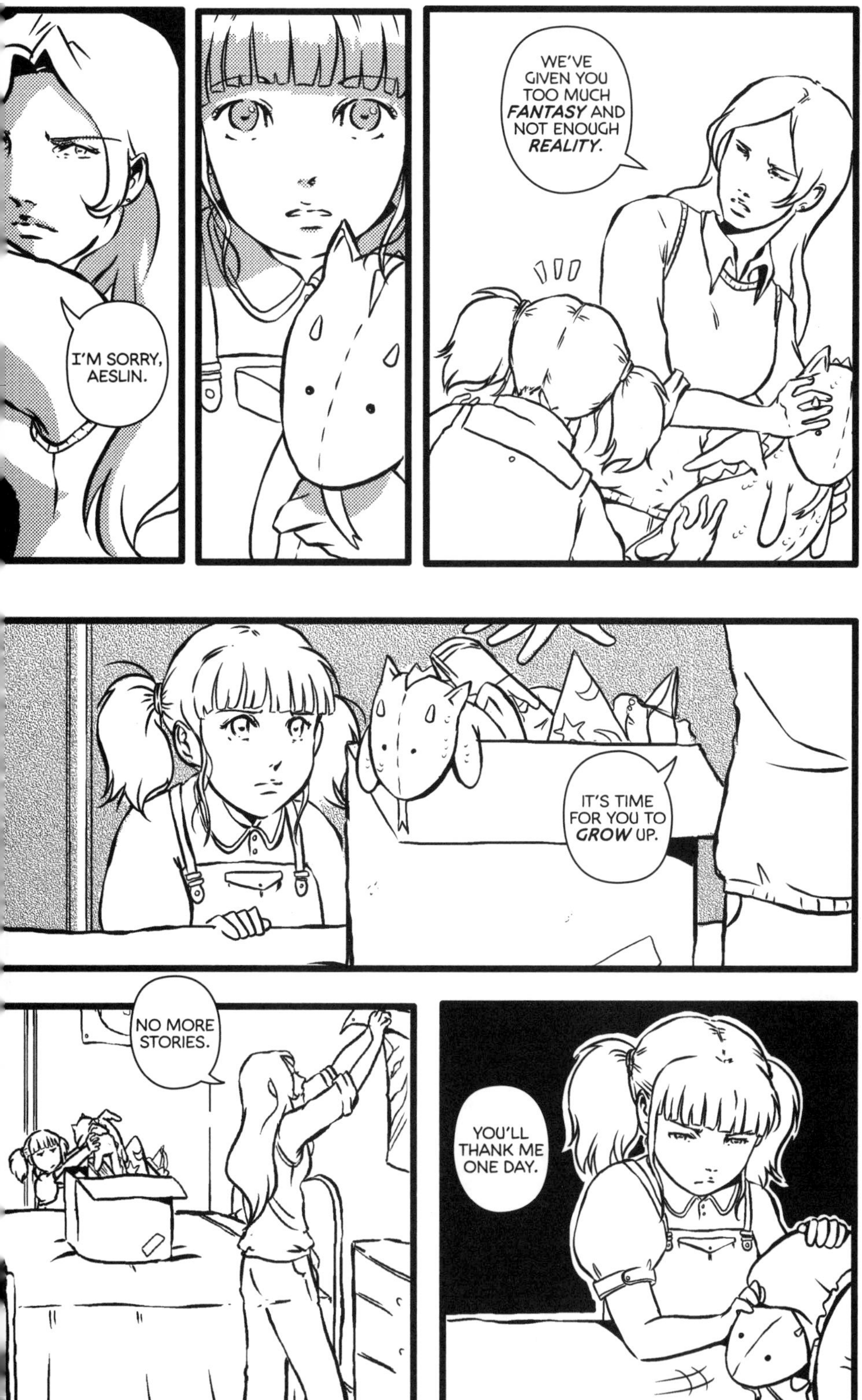
I'M SORRY, AESLIN.
WE'VE GIVEN YOU TOO MUCH FANTASY AND NOT ENOUGH REALITY.
IT'S TIME FOR YOU TO GROW UP.
NO MORE STORIES.
YOU'LL THANK ME ONE DAY.

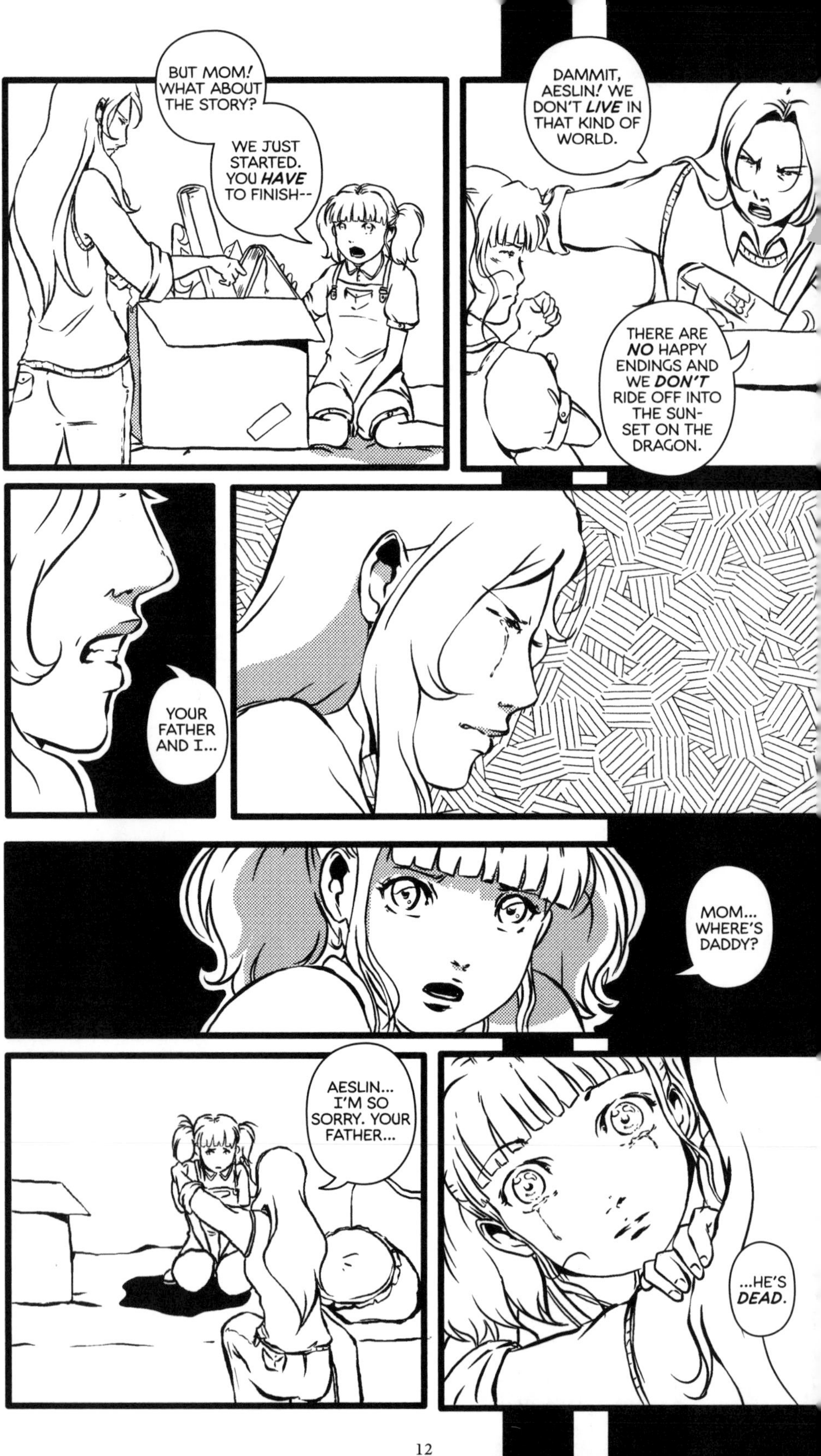
BUT MOM! WHAT ABOUT THE STORY?
WE JUST STARTED. YOU HAVE TO FINISH--
DAMMIT, AESLIN! WE DON'T LIVE IN THAT KIND OF WORLD.
THERE ARE NO HAPPY ENDINGS AND WE DON'T RIDE OFF INTO THE SUN-SET ON THE DRAGON.
YOUR FATHER AND I...
MOM... WHERE'S DADDY?
AESLIN... I'M SO SORRY. YOUR FATHER...
...HE'S DEAD.

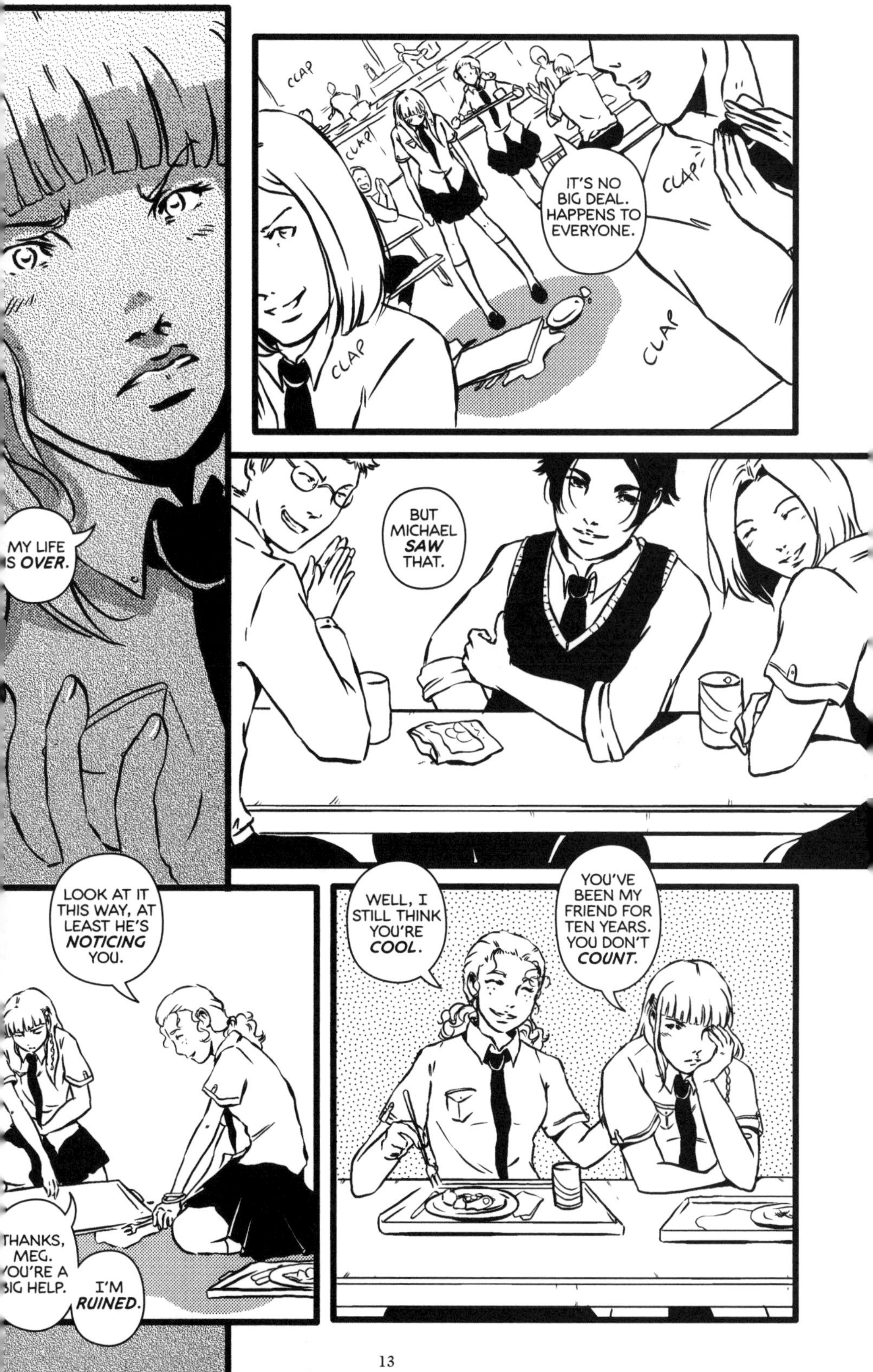
CLAP
CLAP
IT'S NO BIG DEAL. HAPPENS TO EVERYONE.
CLAP
CLAP
CLAP
MY LIFE IS OVER.
BUT MICHAEL SAW THAT.
LOOK AT IT THIS WAY, AT LEAST HE'S NOTICING YOU.
THANKS, MEG. YOU'RE A BIG HELP.
I'M RUINED.
WELL, I STILL THINK YOU'RE COOL.
YOU'VE BEEN MY FRIEND FOR TEN YEARS. YOU DON'T COUNT.

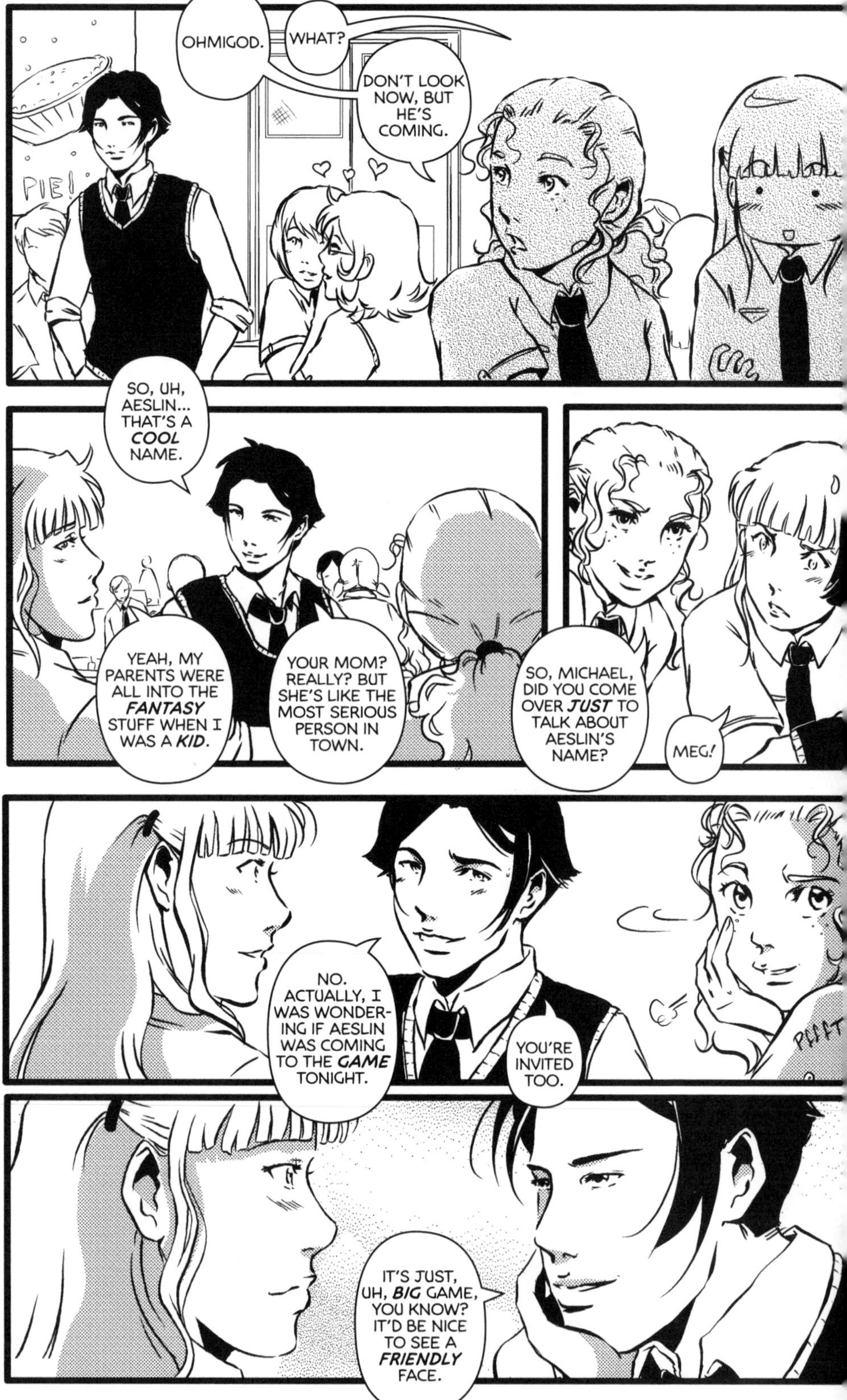
PIE!
OHMIGOD.
WHAT?
DON'T LOOK NOW, BUT HE'S COMING.
SO, UH, AESLIN... THAT'S A *COOL* NAME.
YEAH, MY PARENTS WERE ALL INTO THE *FANTASY* STUFF WHEN I WAS A *KID*.
YOUR MOM? REALLY? BUT SHE'S LIKE THE MOST SERIOUS PERSON IN TOWN.
SO, MICHAEL, DID YOU COME OVER *JUST* TO TALK ABOUT AESLIN'S NAME?
MEG!
NO. ACTUALLY, I WAS WONDERING IF AESLIN WAS COMING TO THE *GAME* TONIGHT.
YOU'RE INVITED TOO.
IT'S JUST, UH, *BIG* GAME, YOU KNOW? IT'D BE NICE TO SEE A *FRIENDLY* FACE.

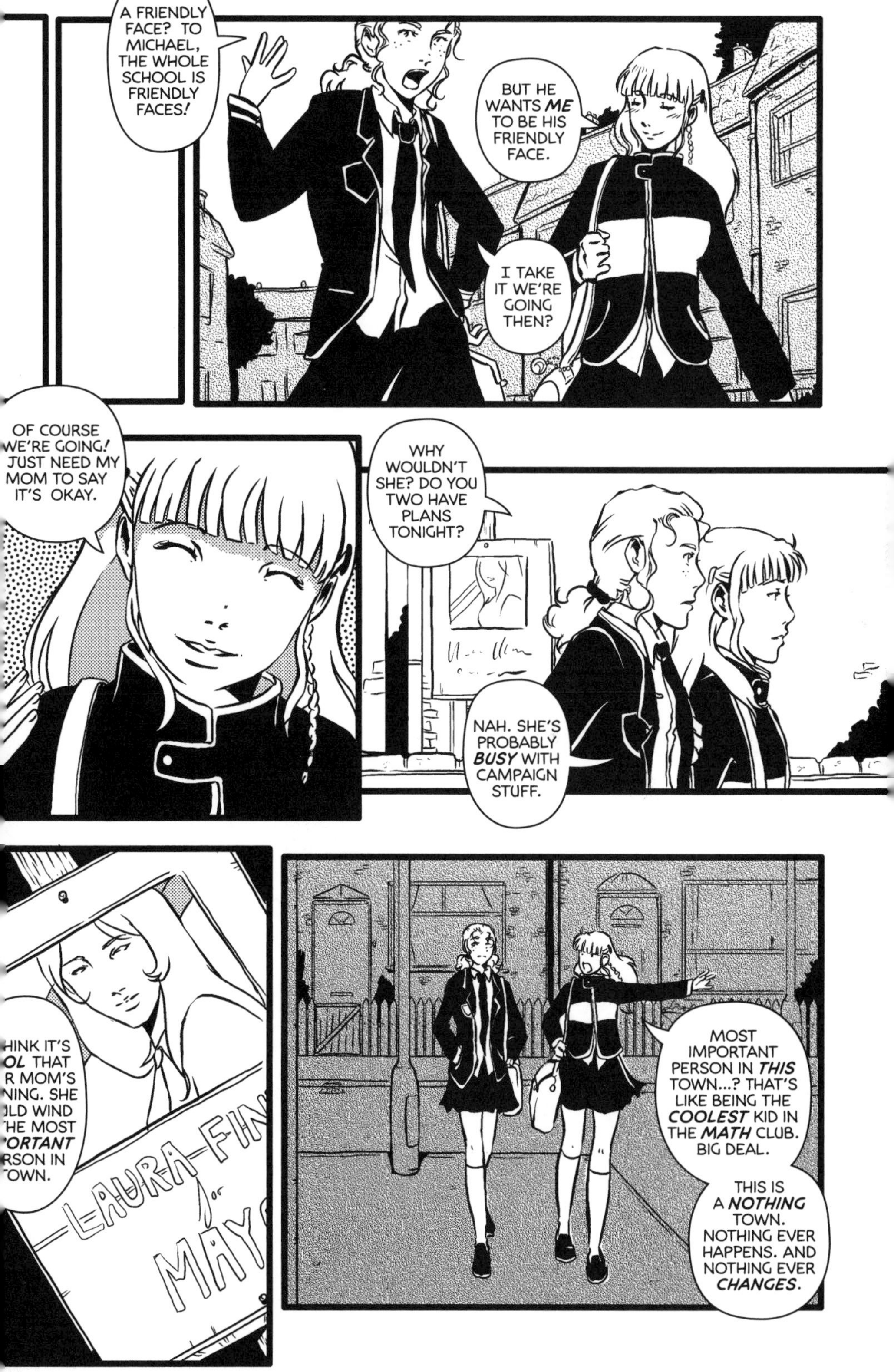
A FRIENDLY FACE? TO MICHAEL, THE WHOLE SCHOOL IS FRIENDLY FACES!
BUT HE WANTS ME TO BE HIS FRIENDLY FACE.
I TAKE IT WE'RE GOING THEN?
OF COURSE WE'RE GOING! JUST NEED MY MOM TO SAY IT'S OKAY.
WHY WOULDN'T SHE? DO YOU TWO HAVE PLANS TONIGHT?
NAH. SHE'S PROBABLY BUSY WITH CAMPAIGN STUFF.
HINK IT'S OL THAT R MOM'S NING. SHE ULD WIND THE MOST ORTANT RSON IN TOWN.
LAURA FIN
for
MAY
MOST IMPORTANT PERSON IN THIS TOWN...? THAT'S LIKE BEING THE COOLEST KID IN THE MATH CLUB. BIG DEAL.
THIS IS A NOTHING TOWN. NOTHING EVER HAPPENS. AND NOTHING EVER CHANGES.

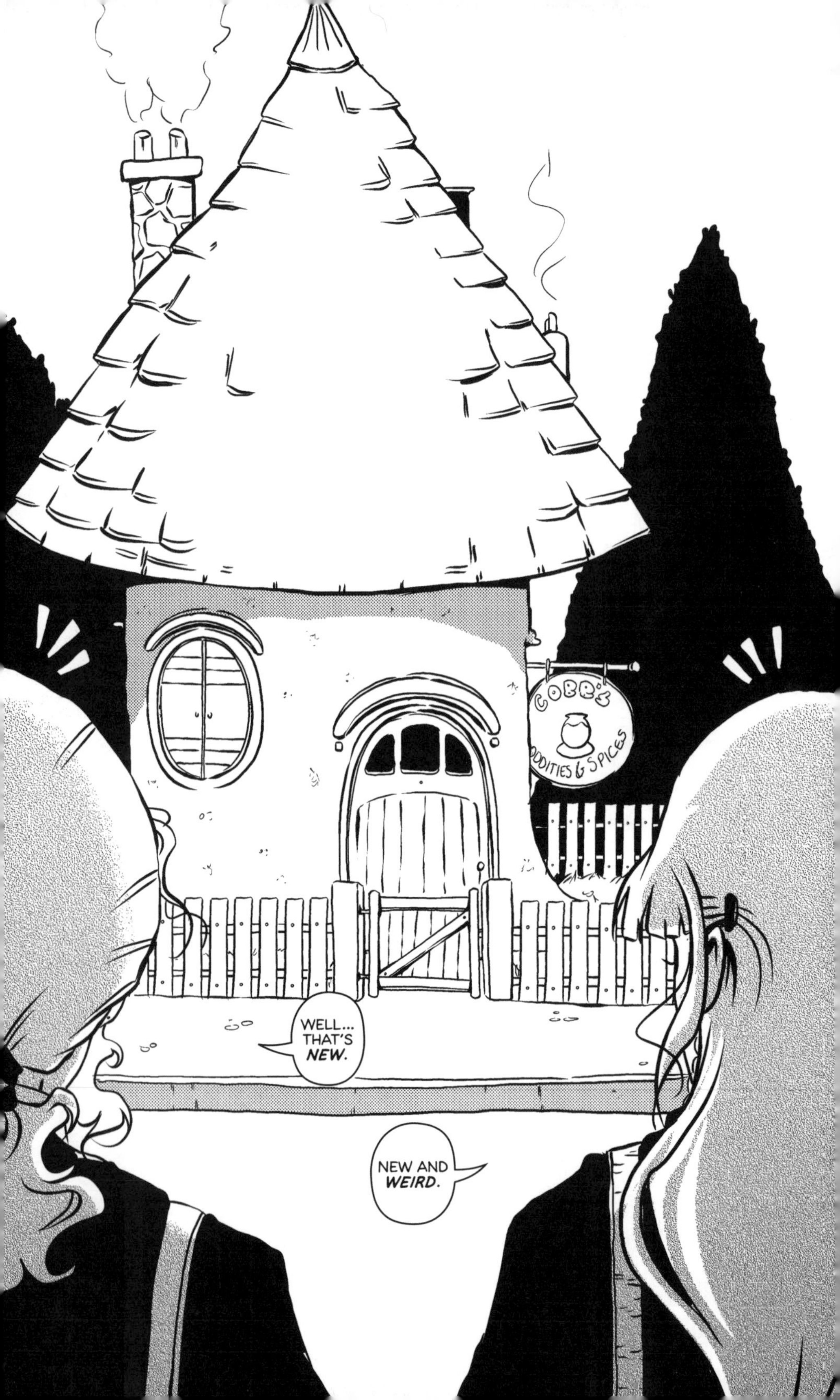

GOBB'S
ODDITIES & SPICES
WELL... THAT'S *NEW*.
NEW AND *WEIRD*.

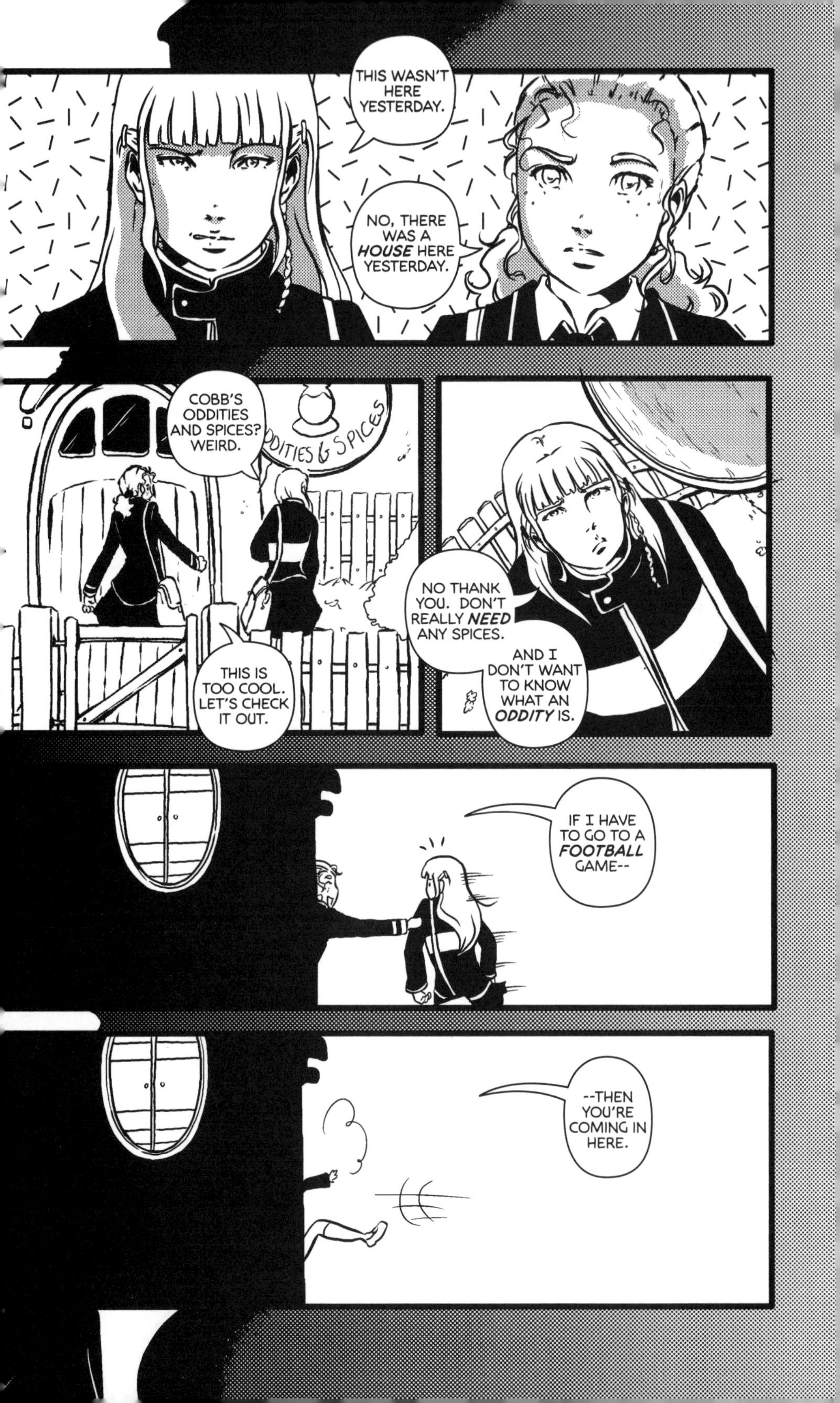
THIS WASN'T HERE YESTERDAY.
NO, THERE WAS A *HOUSE* HERE YESTERDAY.
COBB'S ODDITIES AND SPICES? WEIRD.
ODDITIES & SPICES
THIS IS TOO COOL. LET'S CHECK IT OUT.
NO THANK YOU. DON'T REALLY *NEED* ANY SPICES.
AND I DON'T WANT TO KNOW WHAT AN *ODDITY* IS.
IF I HAVE TO GO TO A *FOOTBALL* GAME--
--THEN YOU'RE COMING IN HERE.

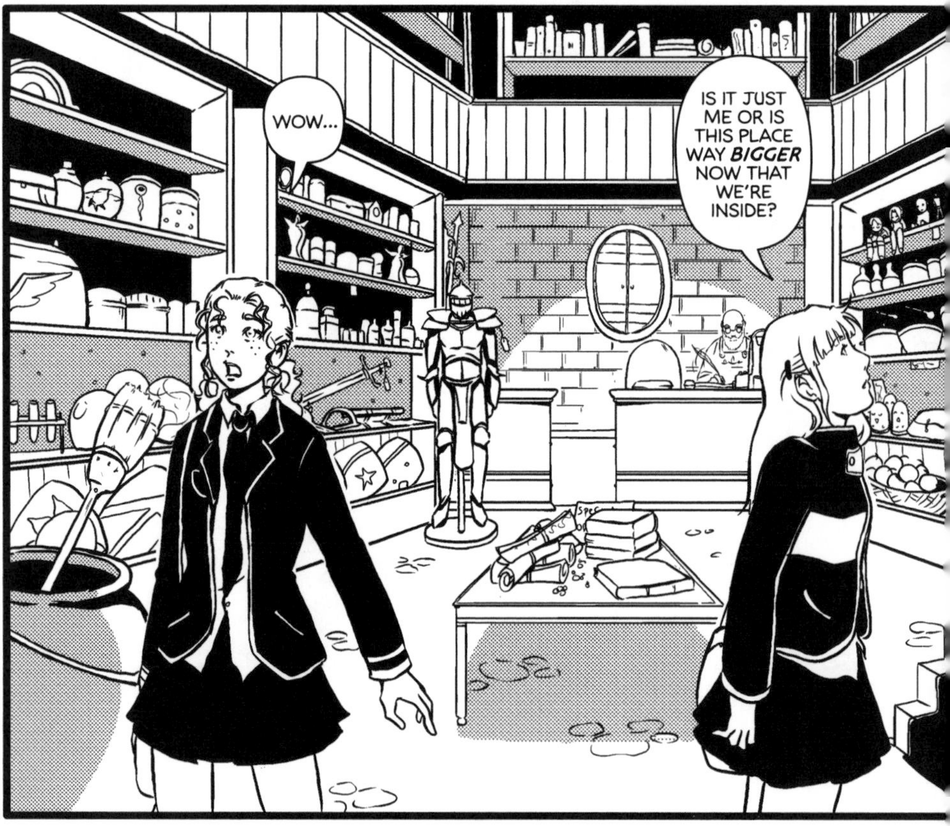
WOW...
IS IT JUST ME OR IS THIS PLACE WAY *BIGGER* NOW THAT WE'RE INSIDE?

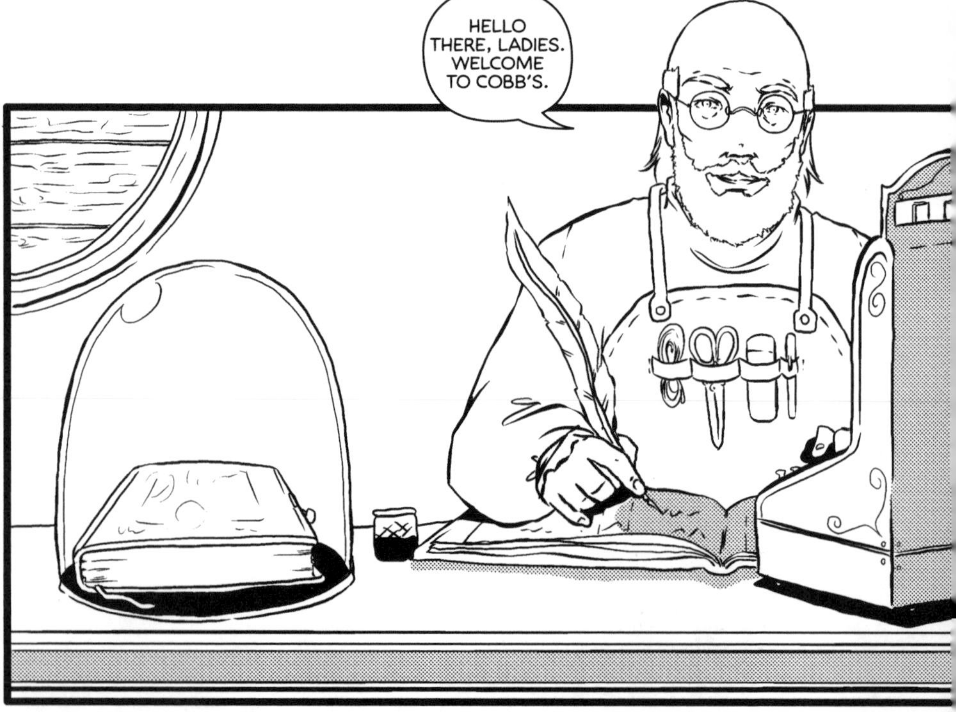
HELLO THERE, LADIES. WELCOME TO COBB'S.

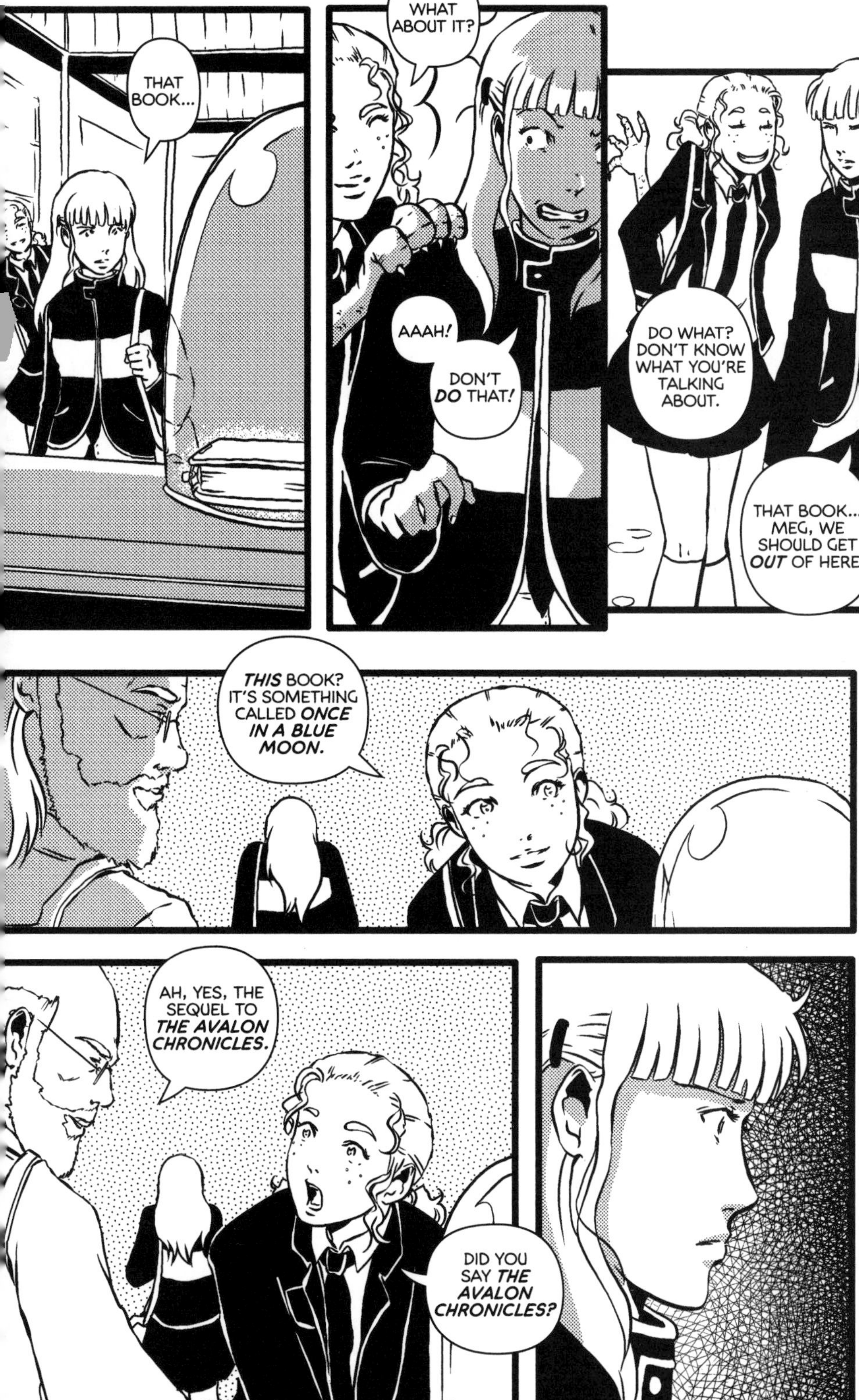
THAT BOOK...
WHAT ABOUT IT?
AAAH!
DON'T DO THAT!
DO WHAT? DON'T KNOW WHAT YOU'RE TALKING ABOUT.
THAT BOOK... MEG, WE SHOULD GET OUT OF HERE.
THIS BOOK? IT'S SOMETHING CALLED ONCE IN A BLUE MOON.
AH, YES, THE SEQUEL TO THE AVALON CHRONICLES.
DID YOU SAY THE AVALON CHRONICLES?

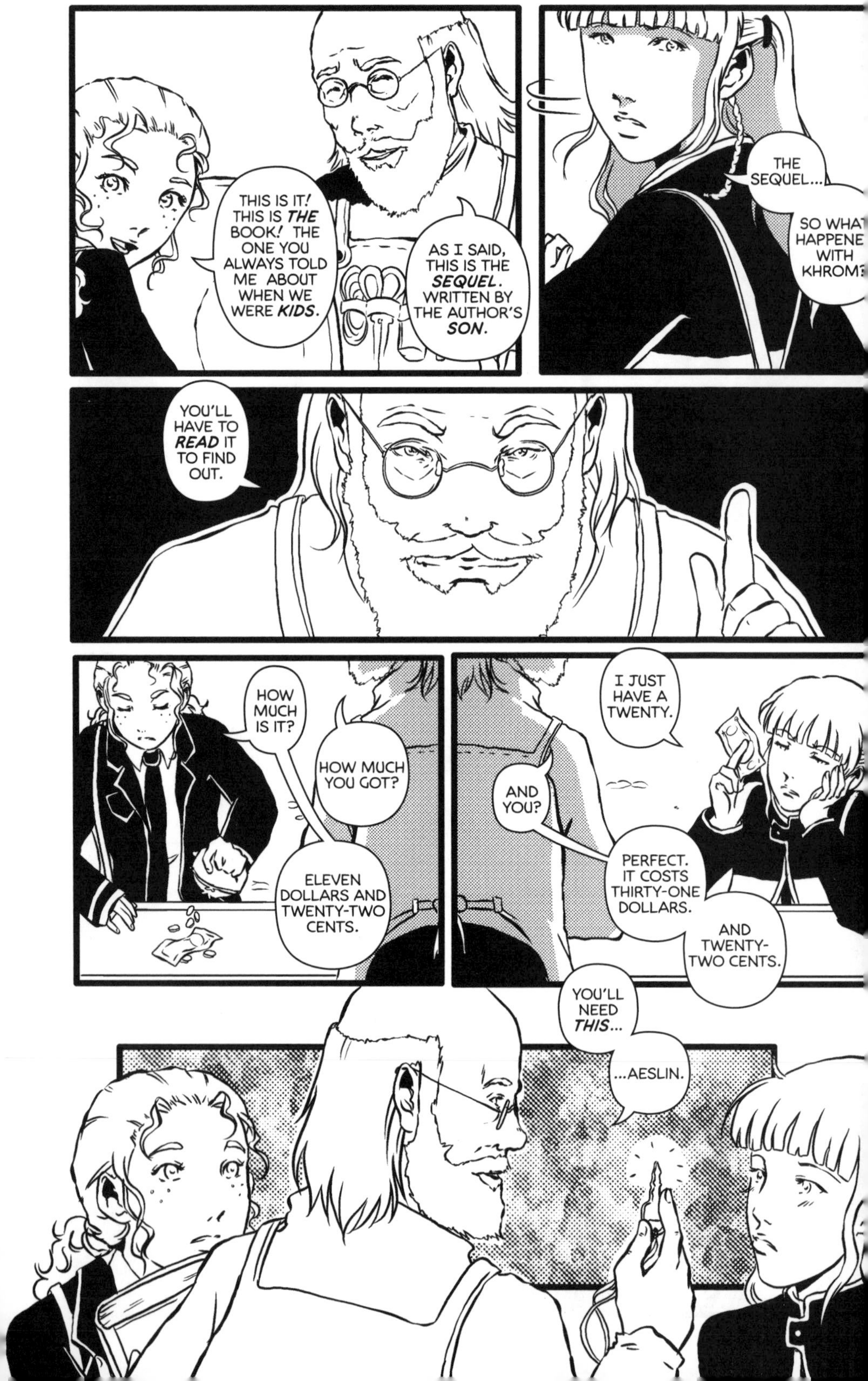
THIS IS IT! THIS IS THE BOOK! THE ONE YOU ALWAYS TOLD ME ABOUT WHEN WE WERE KIDS.
AS I SAID, THIS IS THE SEQUEL. WRITTEN BY THE AUTHOR'S SON.
THE SEQUEL...
SO WHAT HAPPENE WITH KHROM?
YOU'LL HAVE TO READ IT TO FIND OUT.
HOW MUCH IS IT?
HOW MUCH YOU GOT?
ELEVEN DOLLARS AND TWENTY-TWO CENTS.
I JUST HAVE A TWENTY.
AND YOU?
PERFECT. IT COSTS THIRTY-ONE DOLLARS.
AND TWENTY-TWO CENTS.
YOU'LL NEED THIS...
...AESLIN.

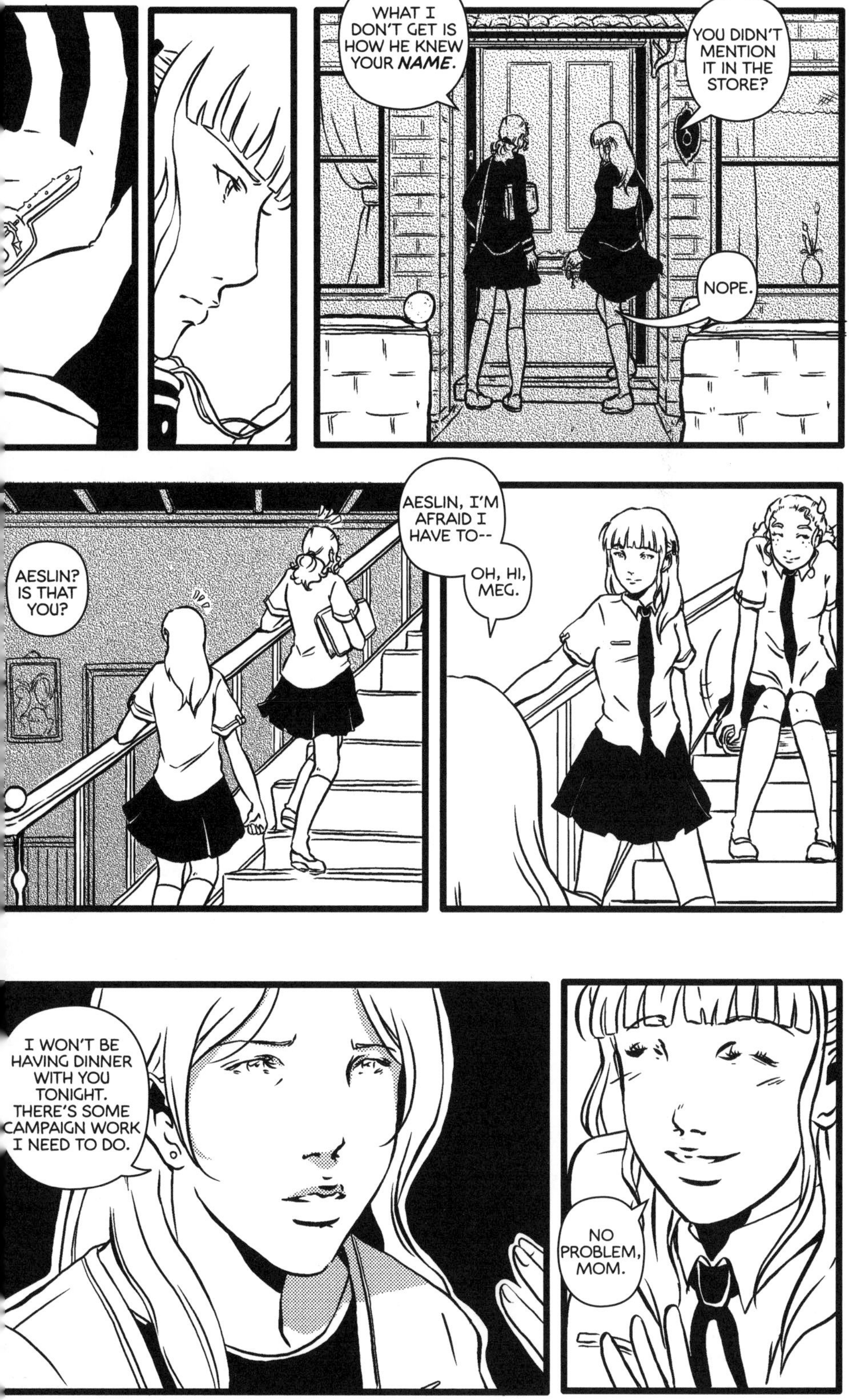
WHAT I DON'T GET IS HOW HE KNEW YOUR *NAME*.
YOU DIDN'T MENTION IT IN THE STORE?
NOPE.
AESLIN? IS THAT YOU?
AESLIN, I'M AFRAID I HAVE TO--
OH, HI, MEG.
I WON'T BE HAVING DINNER WITH YOU TONIGHT. THERE'S SOME CAMPAIGN WORK I NEED TO DO.
NO PROBLEM, MOM.

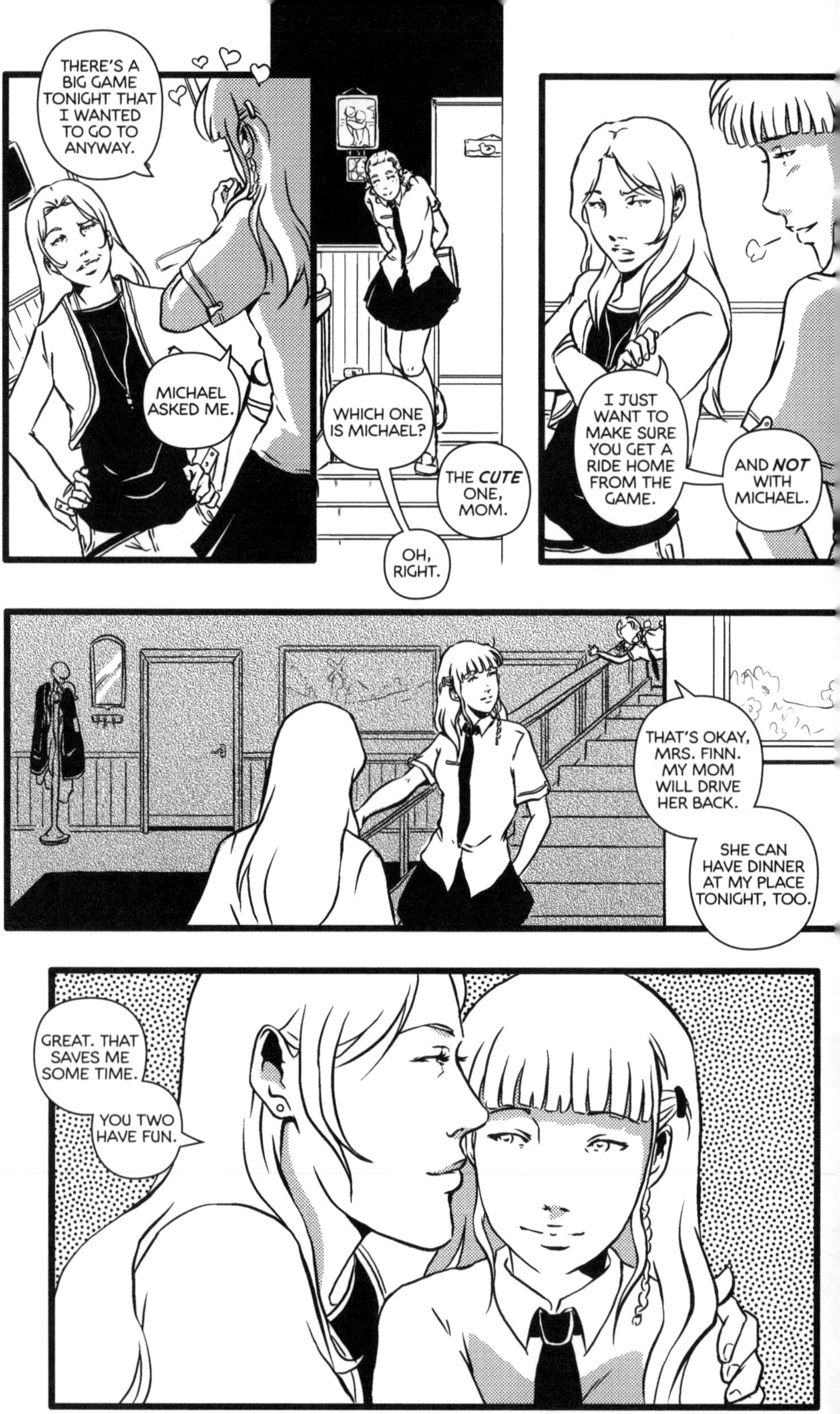
THERE'S A BIG GAME TONIGHT THAT I WANTED TO GO TO ANYWAY.
MICHAEL ASKED ME.
WHICH ONE IS MICHAEL?
THE CUTE ONE, MOM.
OH, RIGHT.
I JUST WANT TO MAKE SURE YOU GET A RIDE HOME FROM THE GAME.
AND NOT WITH MICHAEL.
THAT'S OKAY, MRS. FINN. MY MOM WILL DRIVE HER BACK.
SHE CAN HAVE DINNER AT MY PLACE TONIGHT, TOO.
GREAT. THAT SAVES ME SOME TIME.
YOU TWO HAVE FUN.

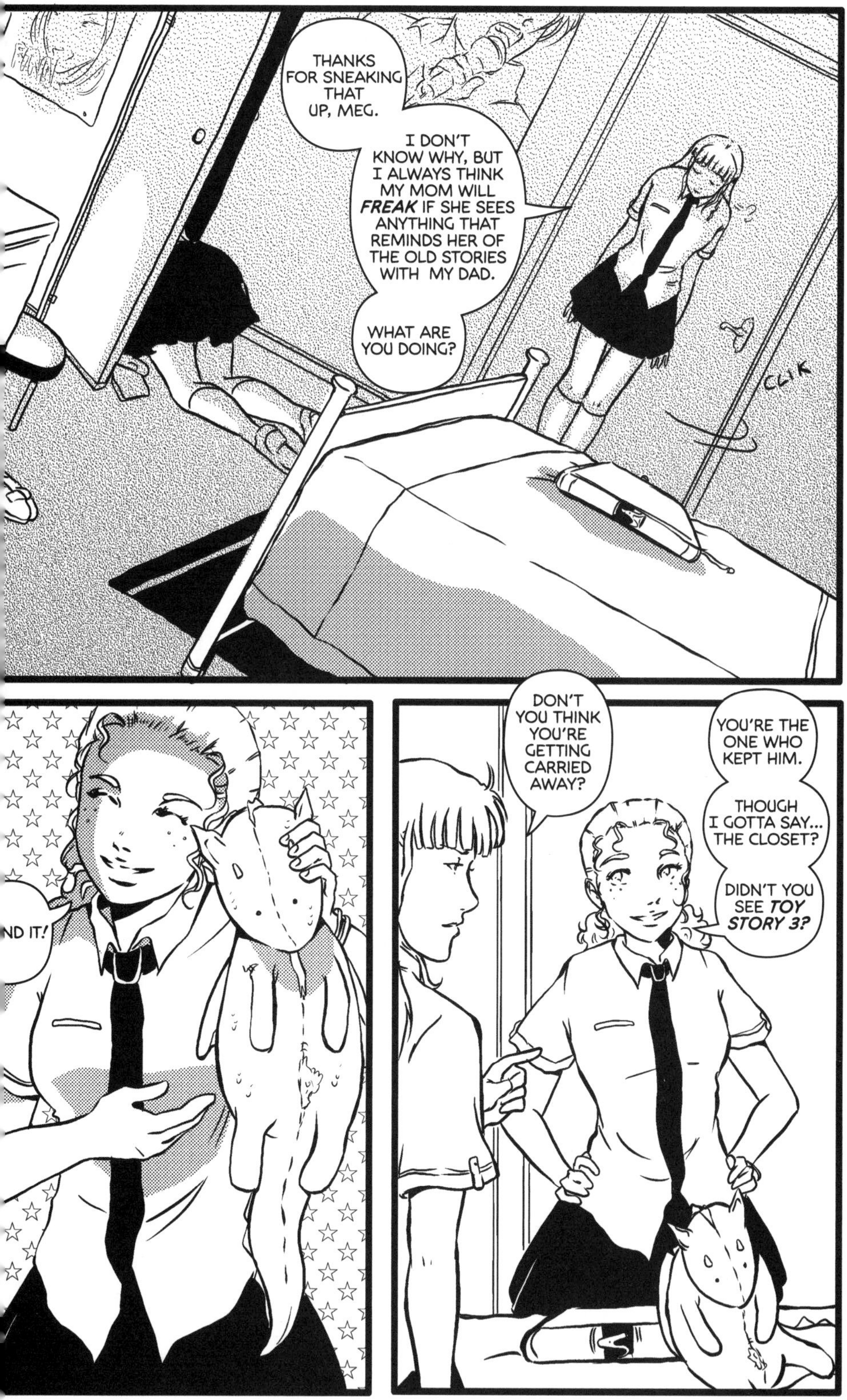
THANKS FOR SNEAKING THAT UP, MEG.
I DON'T KNOW WHY, BUT I ALWAYS THINK MY MOM WILL ***FREAK*** IF SHE SEES ANYTHING THAT REMINDS HER OF THE OLD STORIES WITH MY DAD.
WHAT ARE YOU DOING?
CLIK
ND IT!
DON'T YOU THINK YOU'RE GETTING CARRIED AWAY?
YOU'RE THE ONE WHO KEPT HIM.
THOUGH I GOTTA SAY... THE CLOSET?
DIDN'T YOU SEE ***TOY STORY 3?***

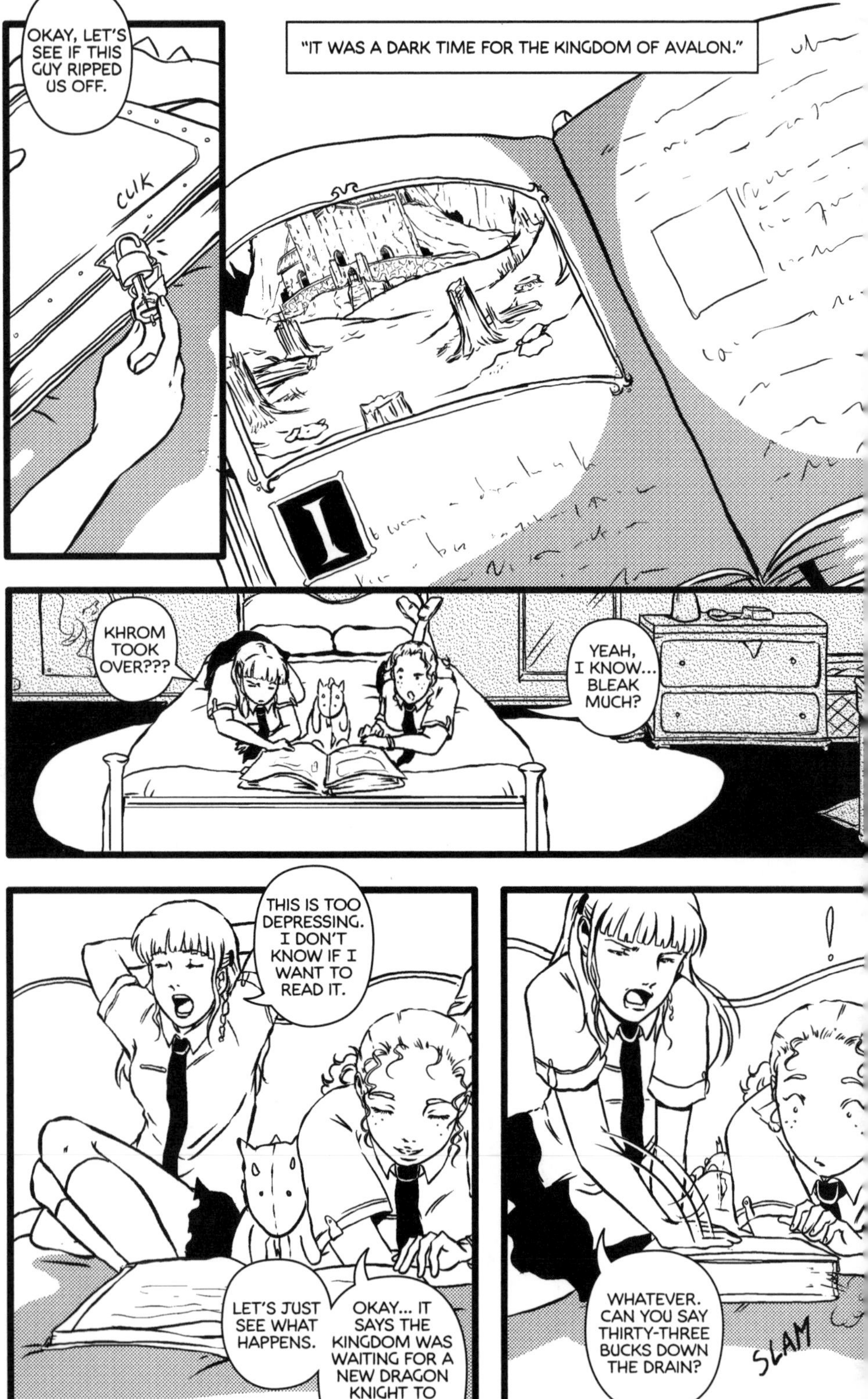
OKAY, LET'S SEE IF THIS GUY RIPPED US OFF.
CLIK
"IT WAS A DARK TIME FOR THE KINGDOM OF AVALON."
KHROM TOOK OVER???
YEAH, I KNOW... BLEAK MUCH?
THIS IS TOO DEPRESSING. I DON'T KNOW IF I WANT TO READ IT.
LET'S JUST SEE WHAT HAPPENS.
OKAY... IT SAYS THE KINGDOM WAS WAITING FOR A NEW DRAGON KNIGHT TO *AWAKEN* THE LAST DRAGON.
!
WHATEVER. CAN YOU SAY THIRTY-THREE BUCKS DOWN THE DRAIN?
SLAM

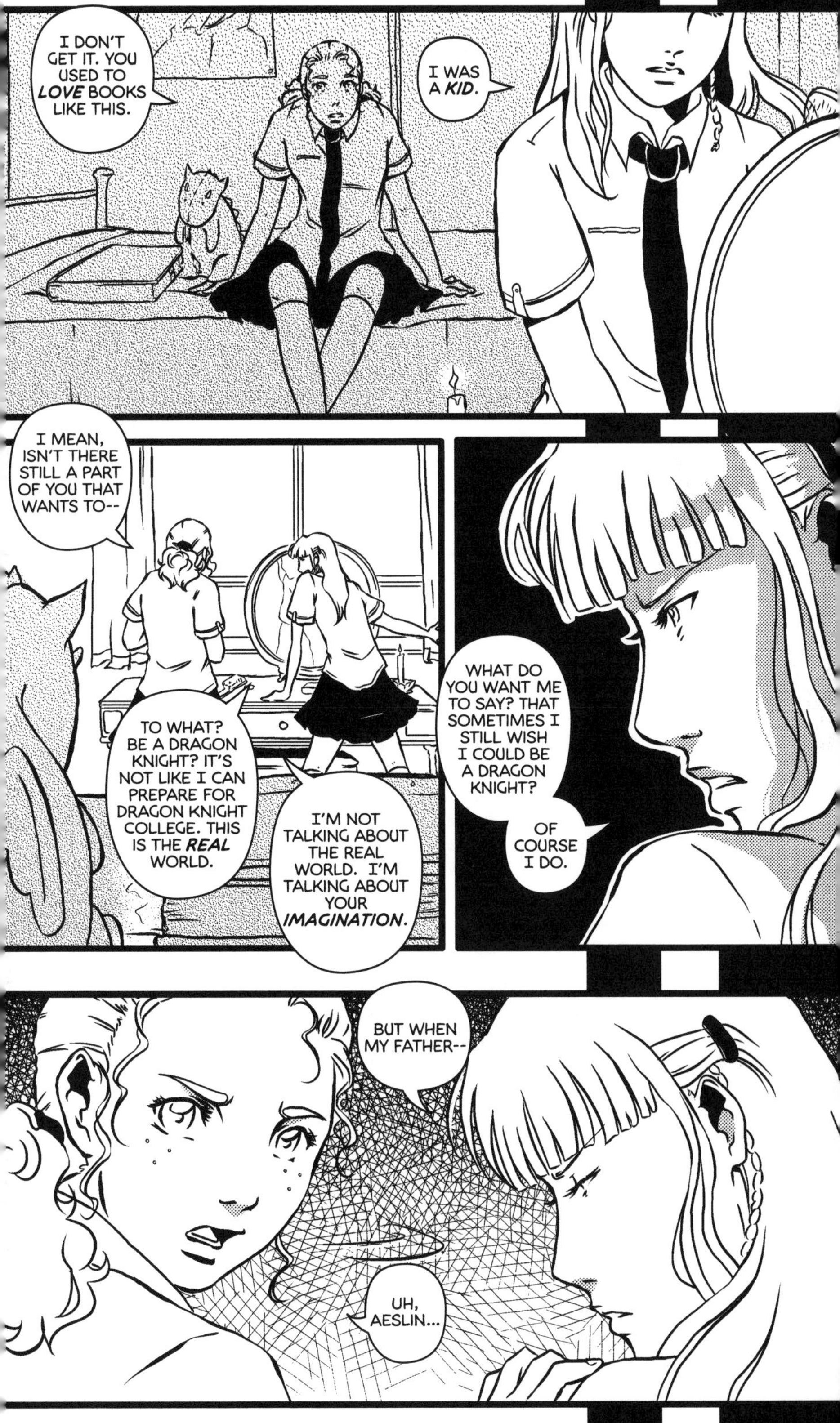
I DON'T GET IT. YOU USED TO *LOVE* BOOKS LIKE THIS.
I WAS A *KID*.
I MEAN, ISN'T THERE STILL A PART OF YOU THAT WANTS TO--
TO WHAT? BE A DRAGON KNIGHT? IT'S NOT LIKE I CAN PREPARE FOR DRAGON KNIGHT COLLEGE. THIS IS THE *REAL* WORLD.
I'M NOT TALKING ABOUT THE REAL WORLD. I'M TALKING ABOUT YOUR *IMAGINATION*.
WHAT DO YOU WANT ME TO SAY? THAT SOMETIMES I STILL WISH I COULD BE A DRAGON KNIGHT?
OF COURSE I DO.
BUT WHEN MY FATHER--
UH, AESLIN...

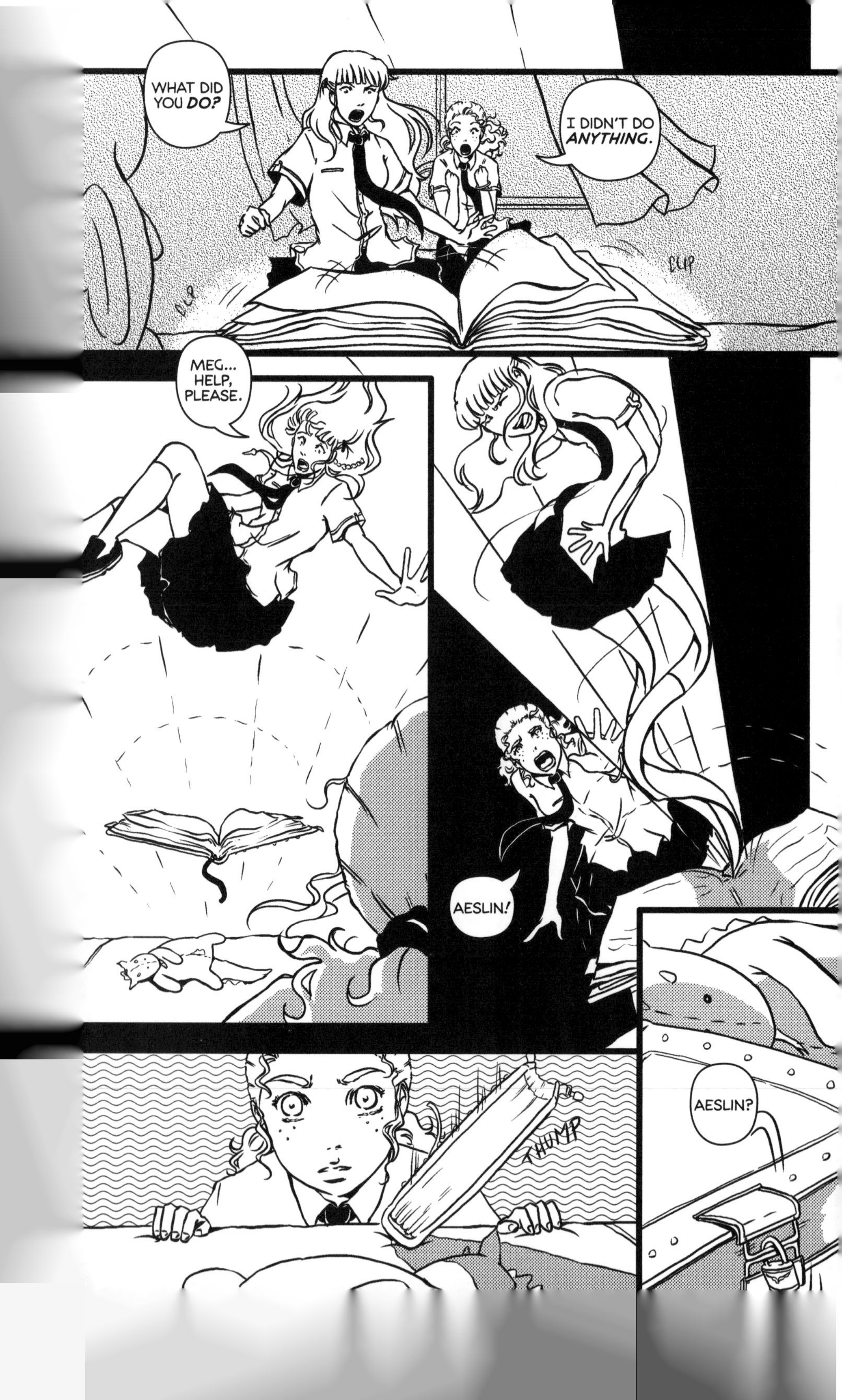
WHAT DID YOU DO?
I DIDN'T DO ANYTHING.
MEG... HELP, PLEASE.
AESLIN!
THUMP
AESLIN?

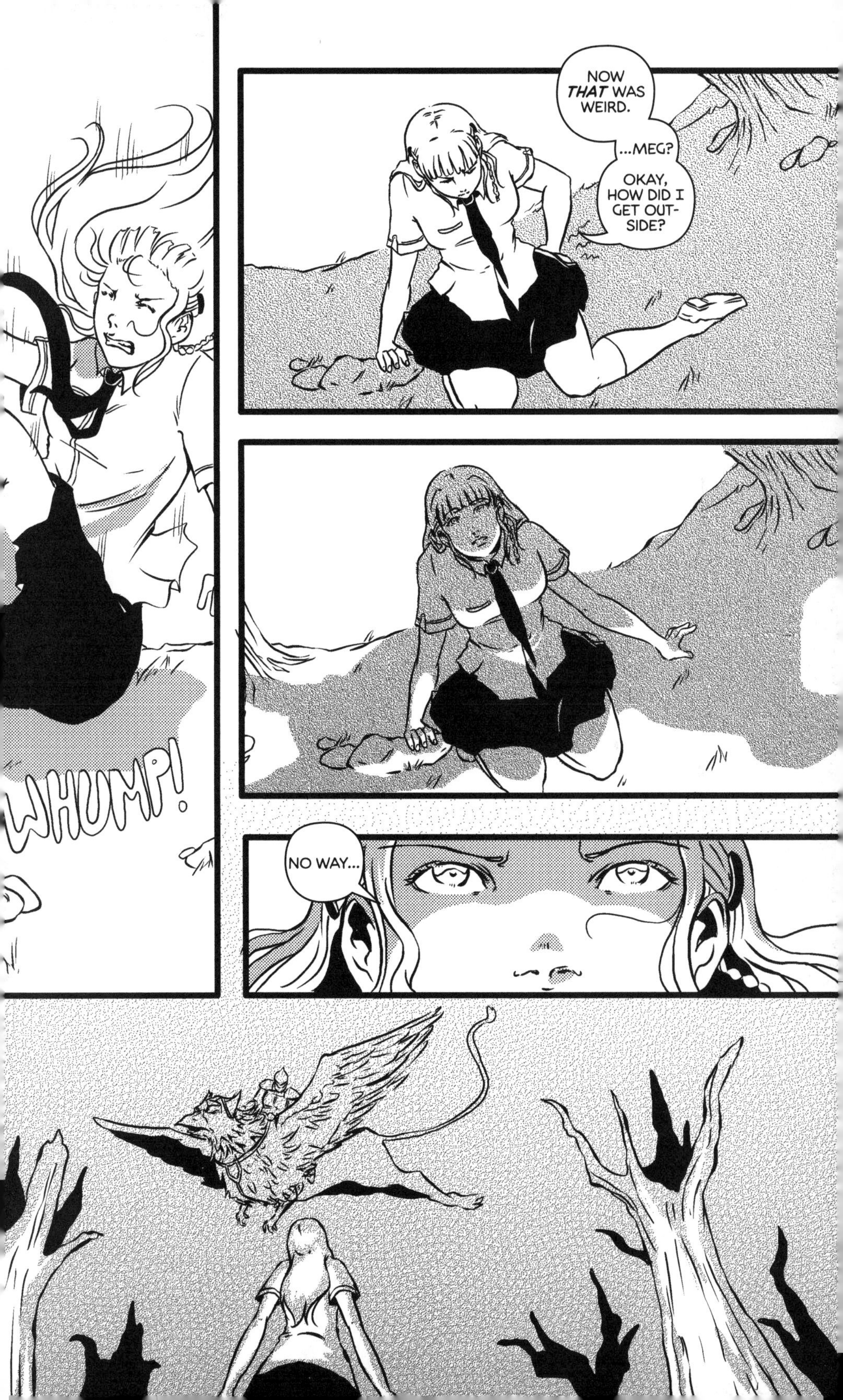
WHUMP!
NOW THAT WAS WEIRD.
...MEG?
OKAY, HOW DID I GET OUT-SIDE?
NO WAY...

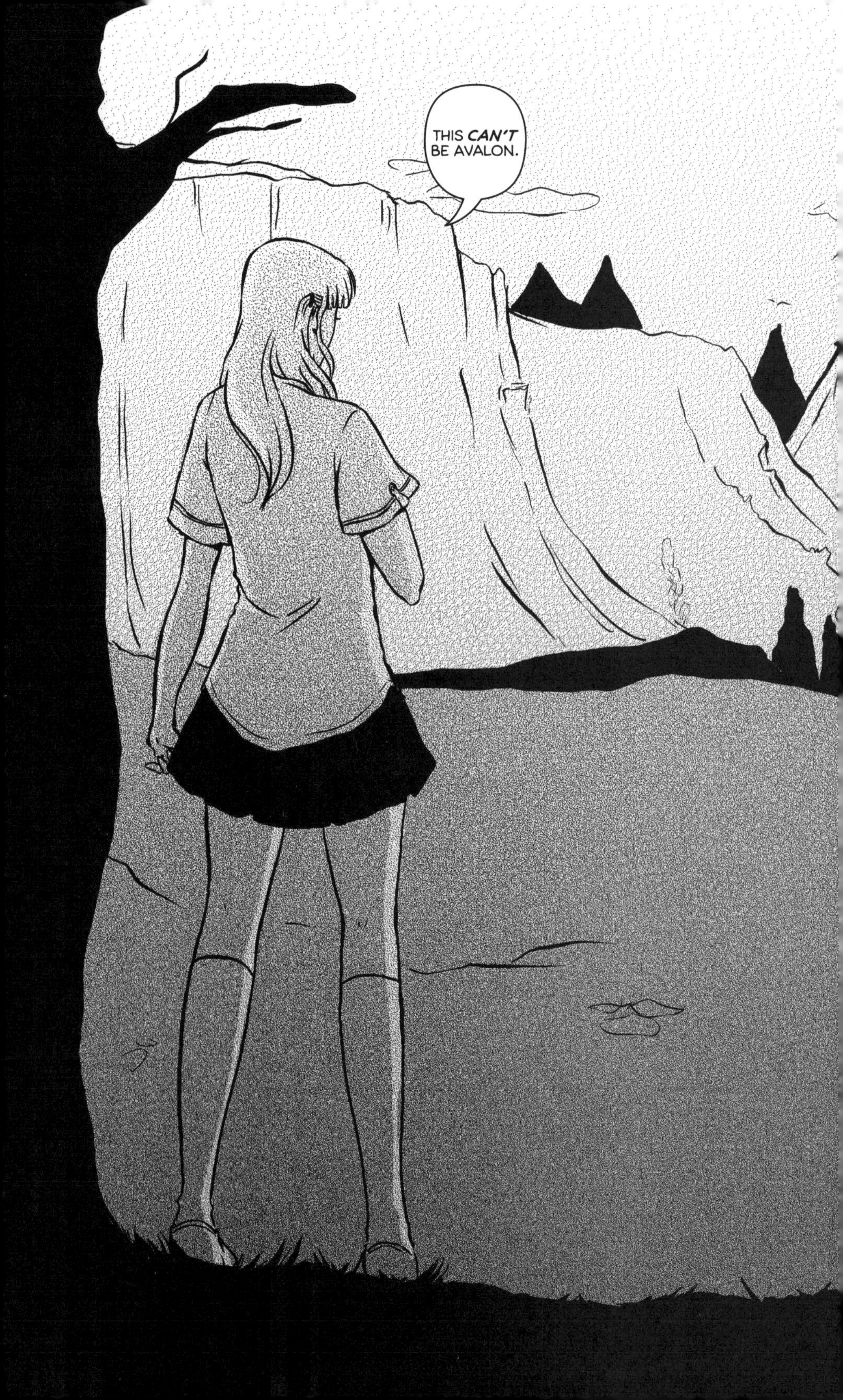
THIS CAN'T BE AVALON.

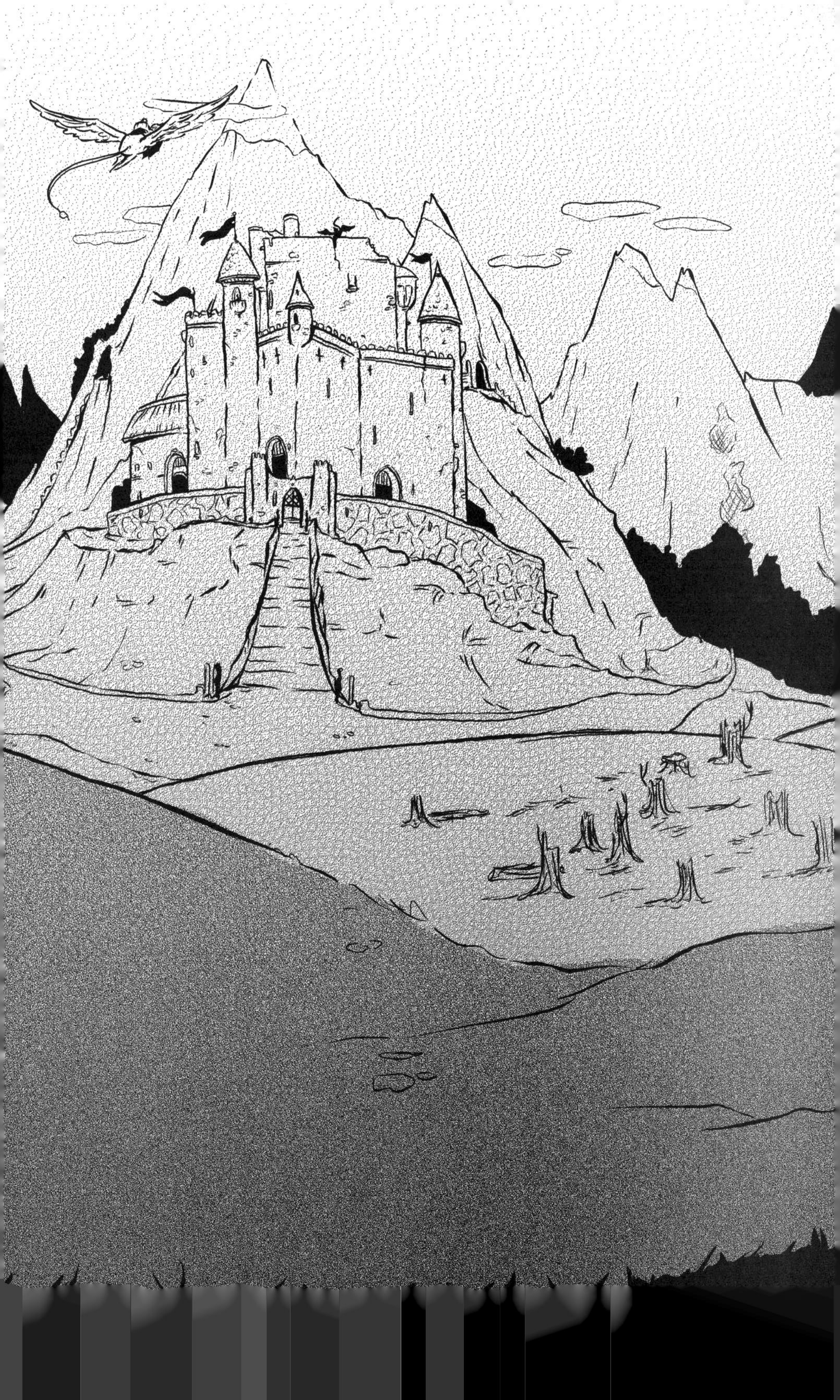

Chapter 2

Another World

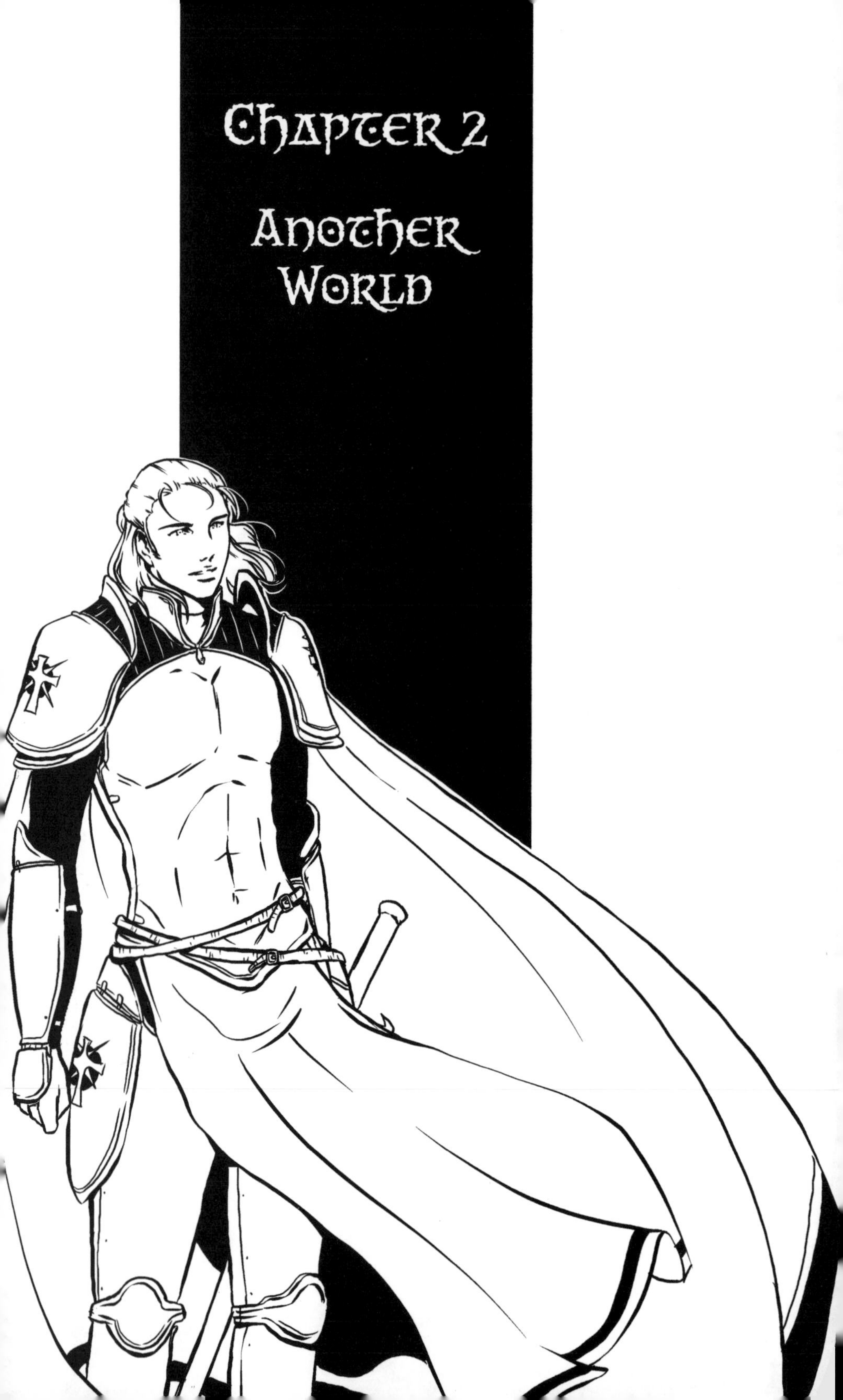

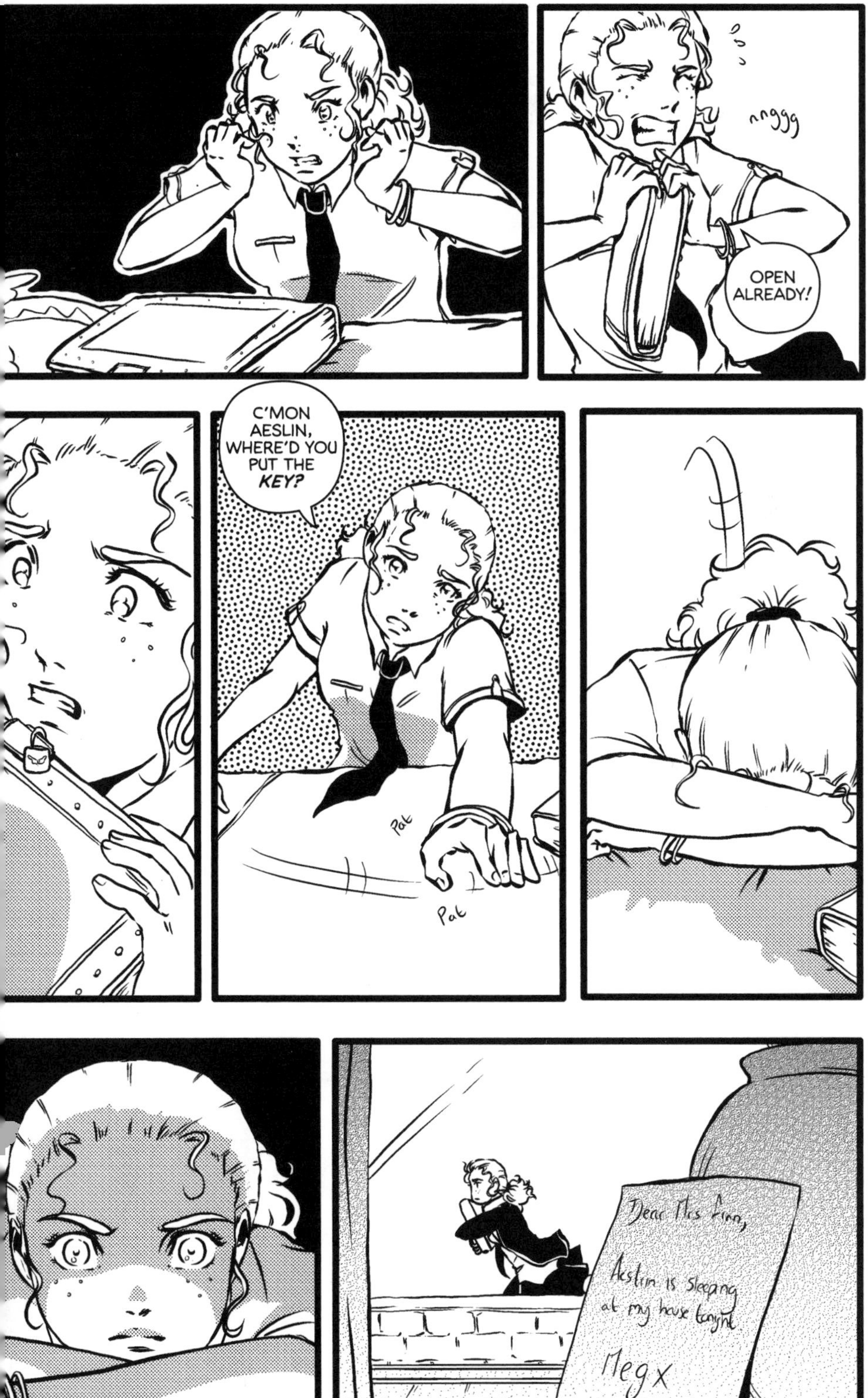
nnggg
OPEN ALREADY!
C'MON AESLIN, WHERE'D YOU PUT THE KEY?
Pat
Pat
Dear Mrs Finn,
Aeslin is sleeping at my house tonight
Meg x

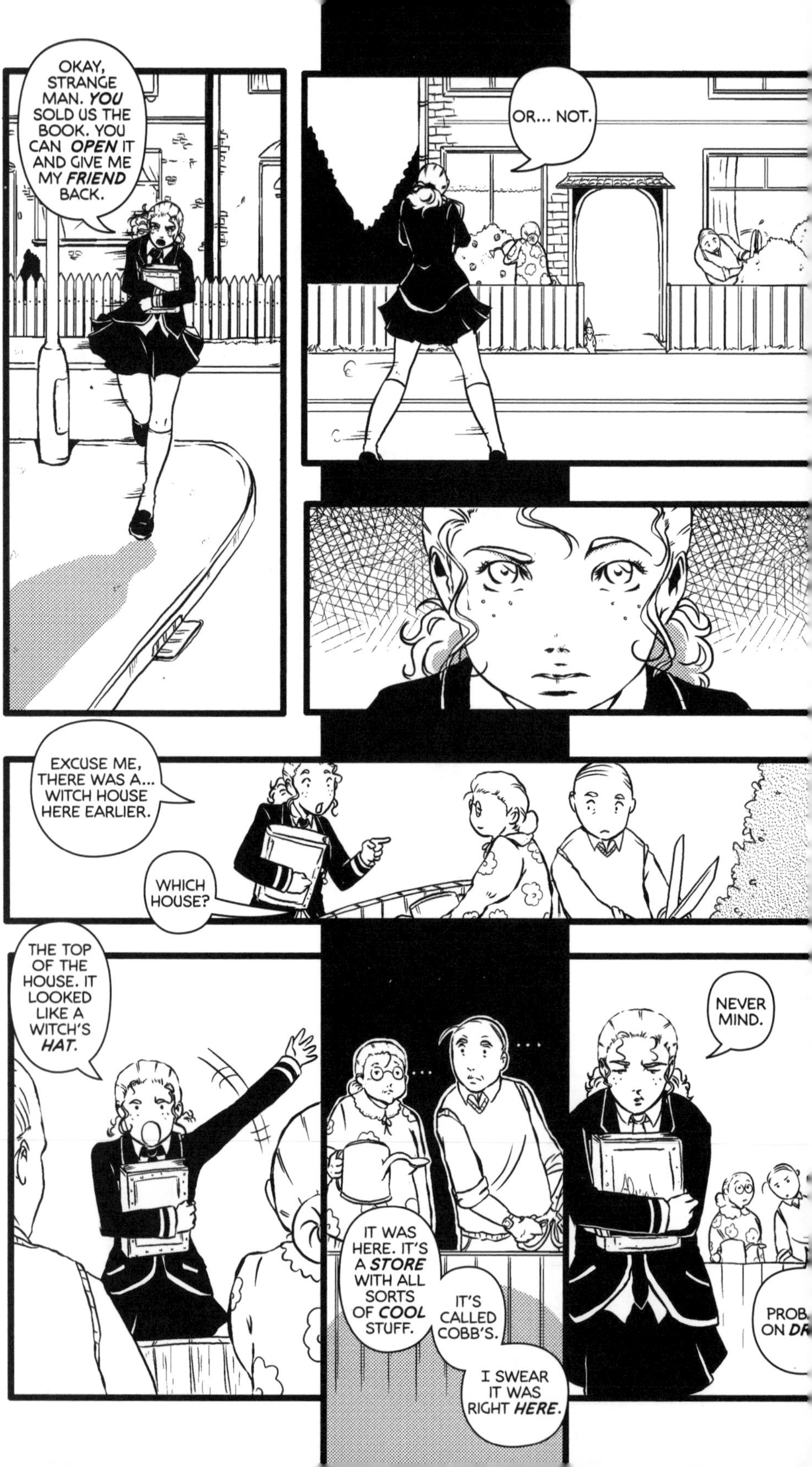
OKAY, STRANGE MAN. YOU SOLD US THE BOOK. YOU CAN OPEN IT AND GIVE ME MY FRIEND BACK.
OR... NOT.
EXCUSE ME, THERE WAS A... WITCH HOUSE HERE EARLIER.
WHICH HOUSE?
THE TOP OF THE HOUSE. IT LOOKED LIKE A WITCH'S HAT.
IT WAS HERE. IT'S A STORE WITH ALL SORTS OF COOL STUFF.
IT'S CALLED COBB'S.
I SWEAR IT WAS RIGHT HERE.
NEVER MIND.
PROB ON DR

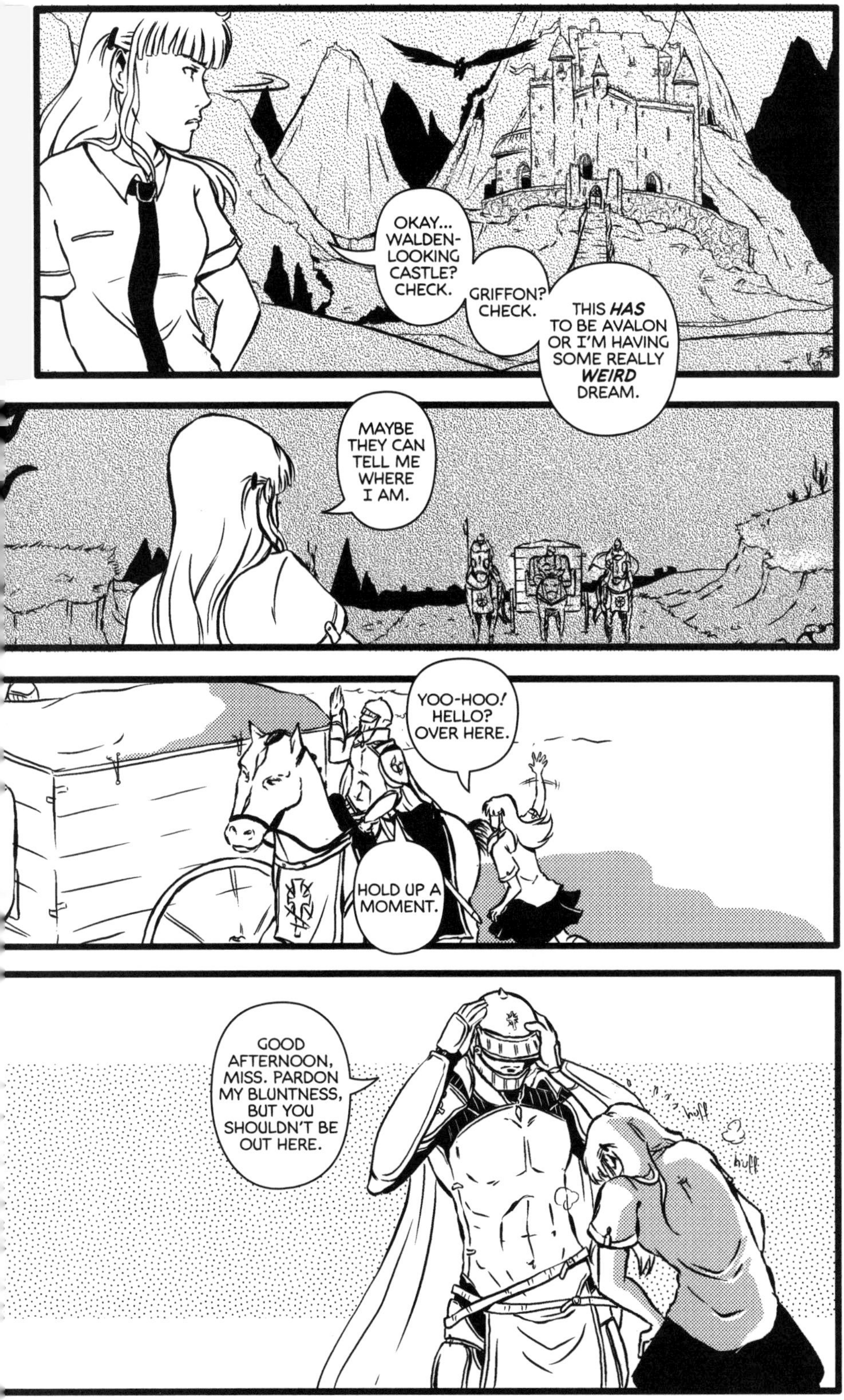
OKAY... WALDEN-LOOKING CASTLE? CHECK.
GRIFFON? CHECK.
THIS **HAS** TO BE AVALON OR I'M HAVING SOME REALLY **WEIRD** DREAM.
MAYBE THEY CAN TELL ME WHERE I AM.
YOO-HOO! HELLO? OVER HERE.
HOLD UP A MOMENT.
GOOD AFTERNOON, MISS. PARDON MY BLUNTNESS, BUT YOU SHOULDN'T BE OUT HERE.
huff
huff

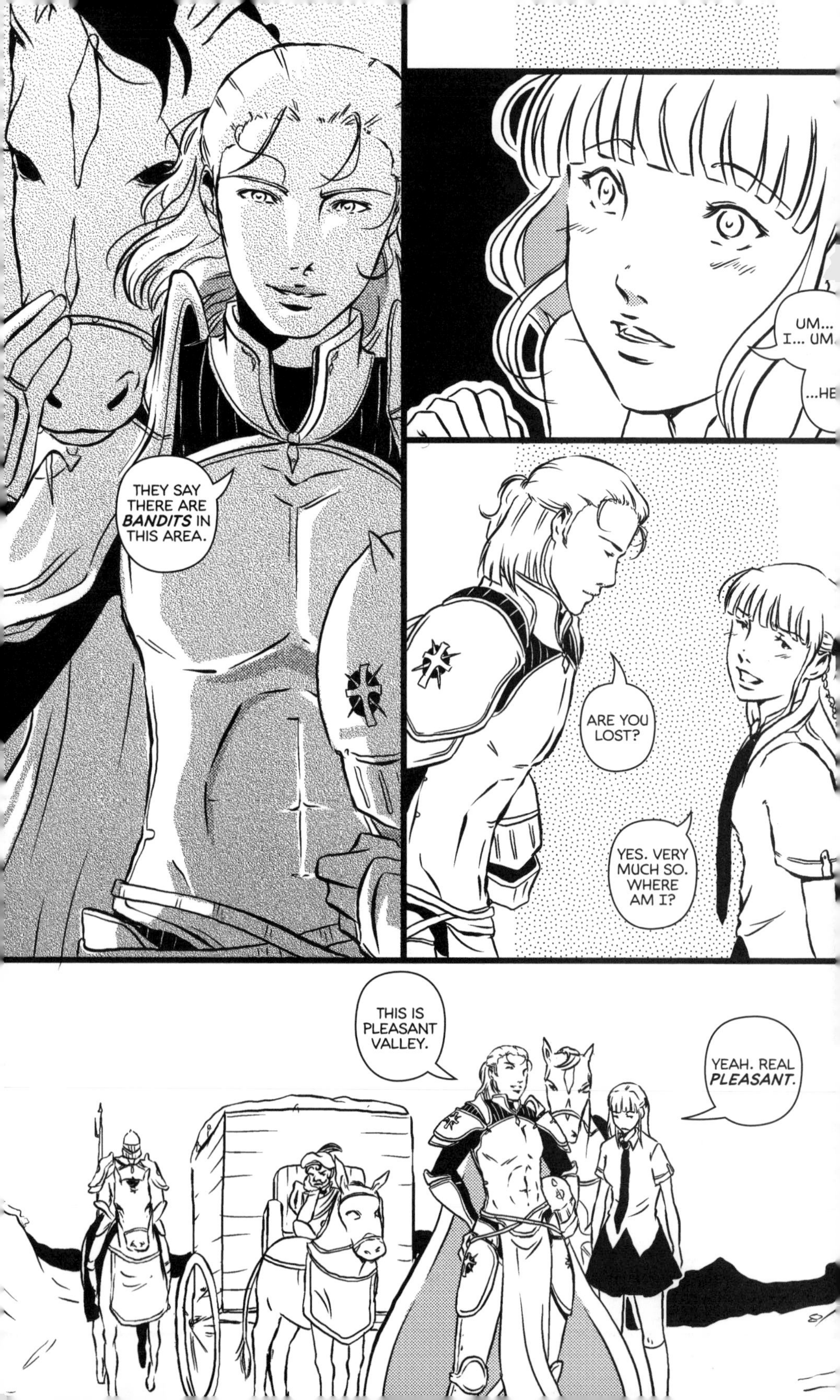
THEY SAY THERE ARE *BANDITS* IN THIS AREA.
UM... I... UM.
...HE
ARE YOU LOST?
YES. VERY MUCH SO. WHERE AM I?
THIS IS PLEASANT VALLEY.
YEAH. REAL *PLEASANT*.

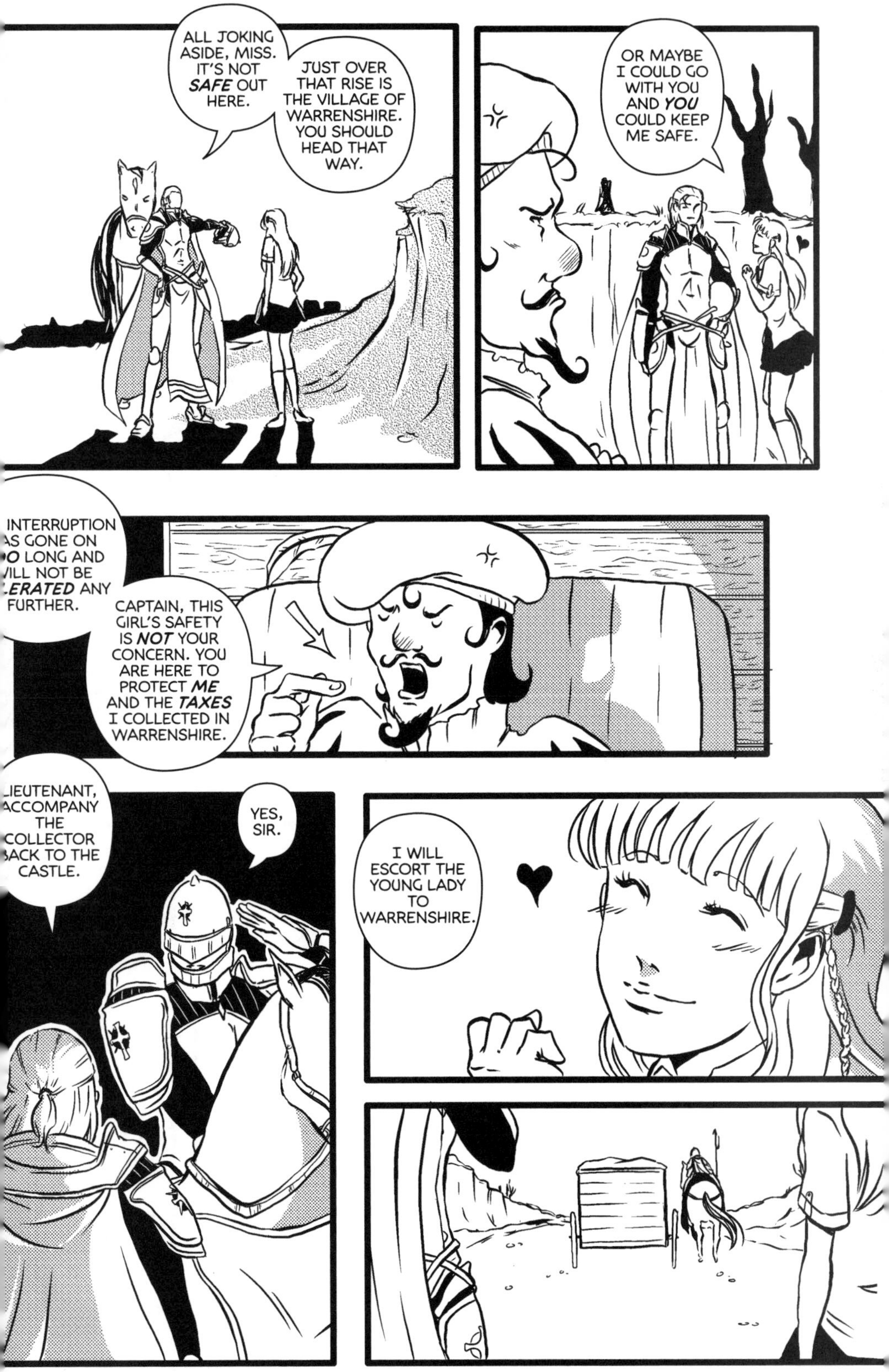

ALL JOKING ASIDE, MISS. IT'S NOT *SAFE* OUT HERE.
JUST OVER THAT RISE IS THE VILLAGE OF WARRENSHIRE. YOU SHOULD HEAD THAT WAY.
OR MAYBE I COULD GO WITH YOU AND *YOU* COULD KEEP ME SAFE.
INTERRUPTION AS GONE ON O LONG AND VILL NOT BE ERATED ANY FURTHER.
CAPTAIN, THIS GIRL'S SAFETY IS *NOT* YOUR CONCERN. YOU ARE HERE TO PROTECT *ME* AND THE *TAXES* I COLLECTED IN WARRENSHIRE.
LIEUTENANT, ACCOMPANY THE COLLECTOR BACK TO THE CASTLE.
YES, SIR.
I WILL ESCORT THE YOUNG LADY TO WARRENSHIRE.

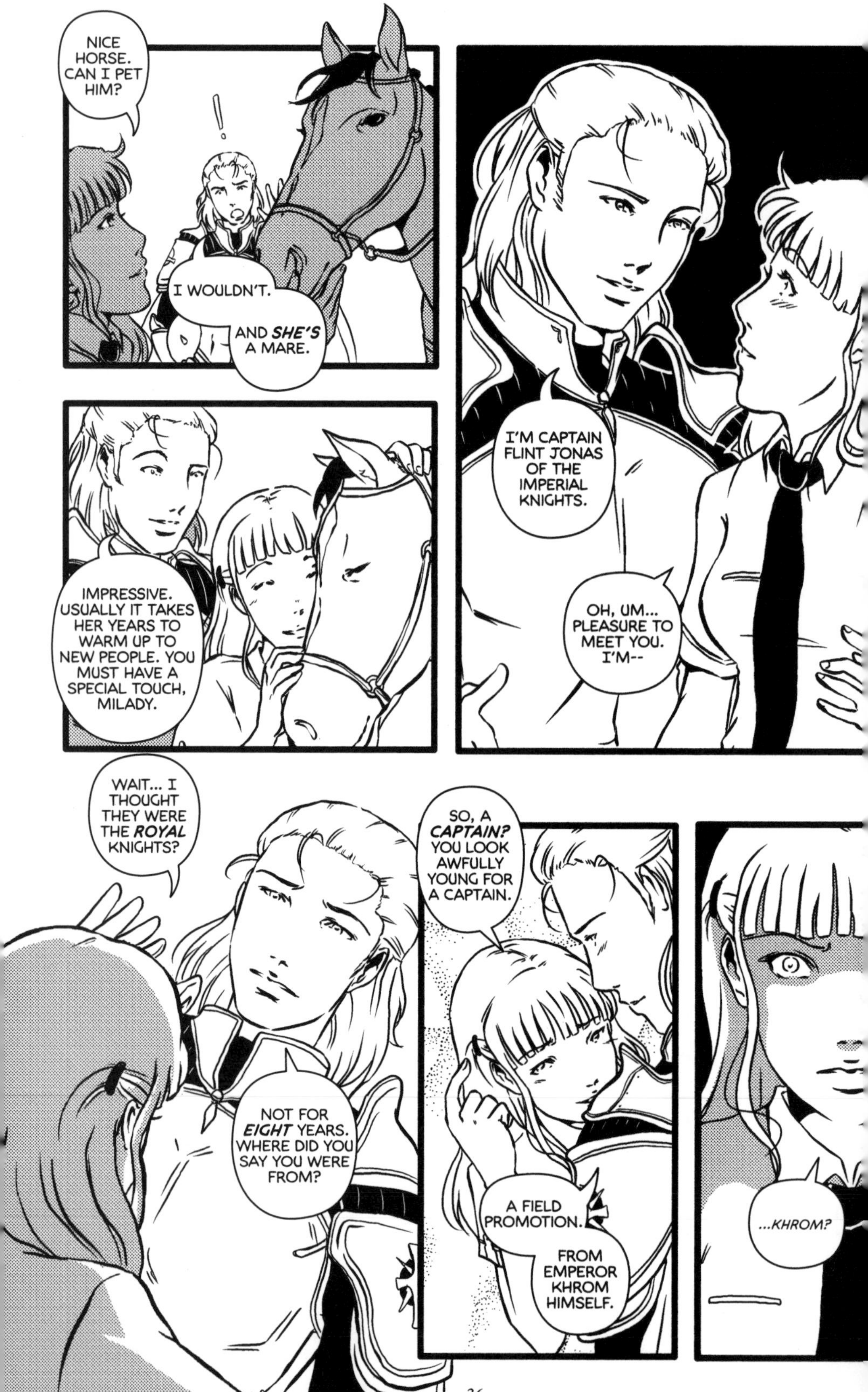
NICE HORSE. CAN I PET HIM?
!
I WOULDN'T.
AND *SHE'S* A MARE.
I'M CAPTAIN FLINT JONAS OF THE IMPERIAL KNIGHTS.
OH, UM... PLEASURE TO MEET YOU. I'M--
IMPRESSIVE. USUALLY IT TAKES HER YEARS TO WARM UP TO NEW PEOPLE. YOU MUST HAVE A SPECIAL TOUCH, MILADY.
WAIT... I THOUGHT THEY WERE THE *ROYAL* KNIGHTS?
NOT FOR *EIGHT* YEARS. WHERE DID YOU SAY YOU WERE FROM?
SO, A *CAPTAIN?* YOU LOOK AWFULLY YOUNG FOR A CAPTAIN.
A FIELD PROMOTION.
FROM EMPEROR KHROM HIMSELF.
...*KHROM?*

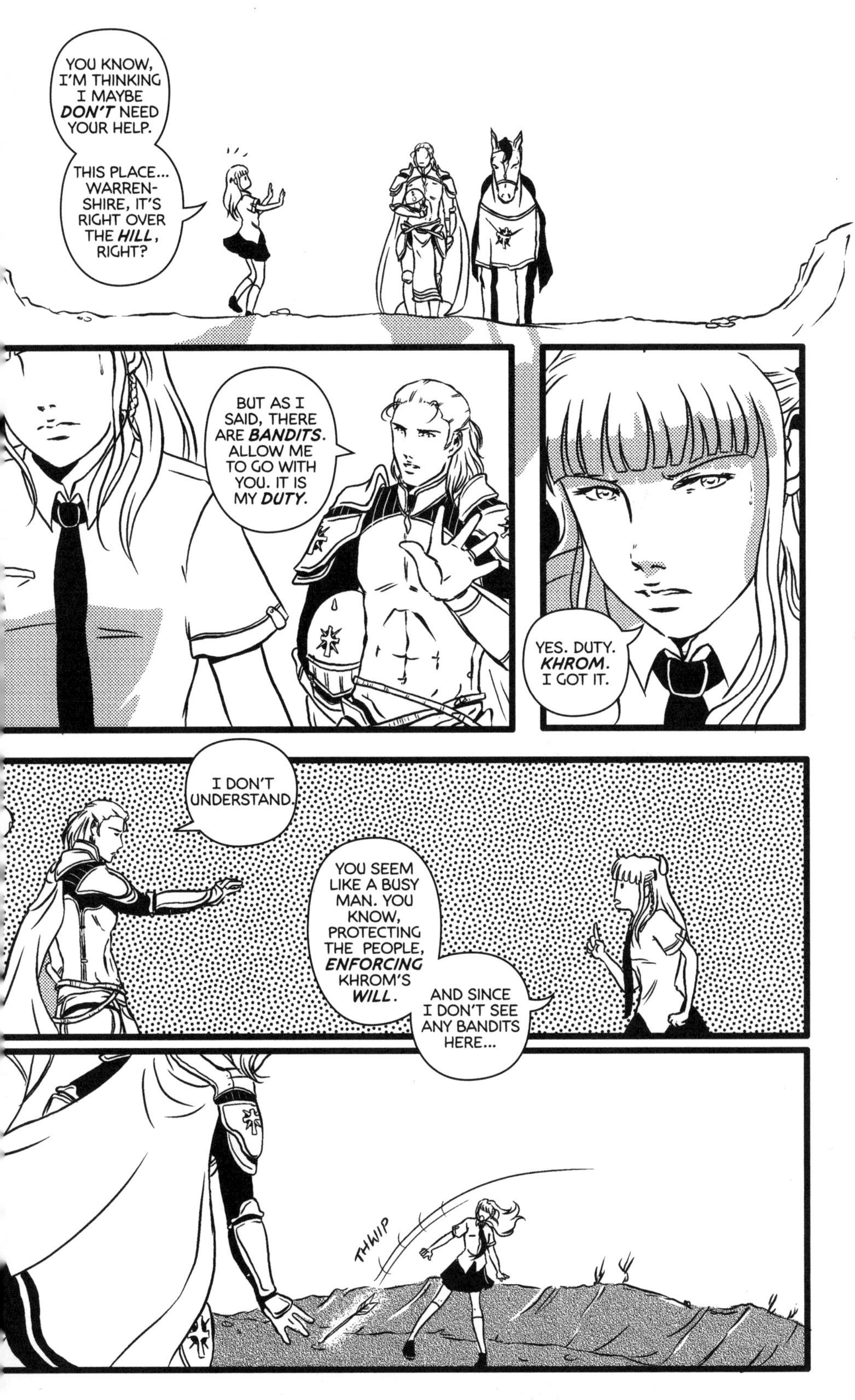
YOU KNOW, I'M THINKING I MAYBE ***DON'T*** NEED YOUR HELP.
THIS PLACE... WARREN-SHIRE, IT'S RIGHT OVER THE ***HILL***, RIGHT?
BUT AS I SAID, THERE ARE ***BANDITS***. ALLOW ME TO GO WITH YOU. IT IS MY ***DUTY***.
YES. DUTY. ***KHROM***. I GOT IT.
I DON'T UNDERSTAND.
YOU SEEM LIKE A BUSY MAN. YOU KNOW, PROTECTING THE PEOPLE, ***ENFORCING*** KHROM'S ***WILL***.
AND SINCE I DON'T SEE ANY BANDITS HERE...
THWIP

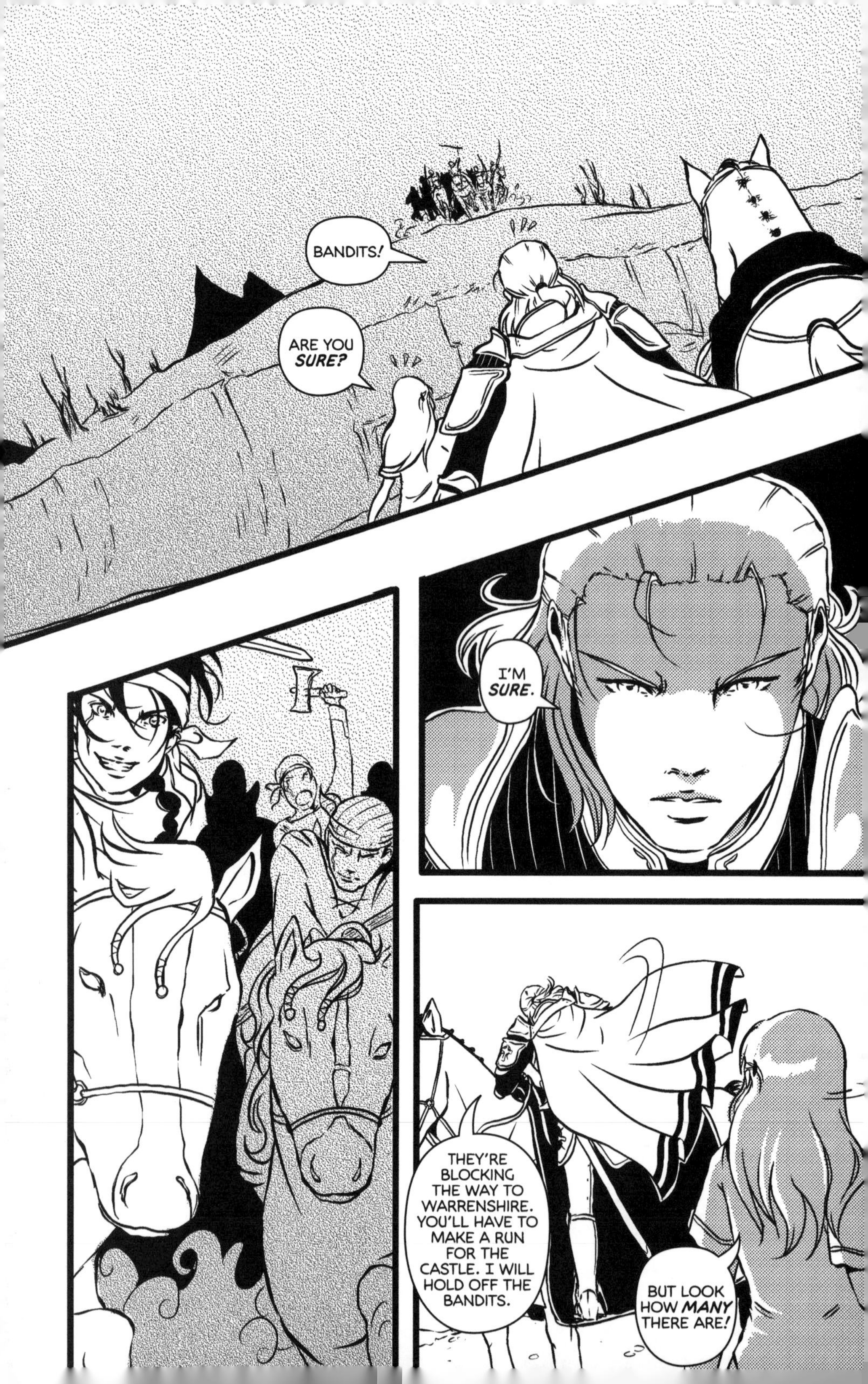
BANDITS!
ARE YOU SURE?
I'M SURE.
THEY'RE BLOCKING THE WAY TO WARRENSHIRE. YOU'LL HAVE TO MAKE A RUN FOR THE CASTLE. I WILL HOLD OFF THE BANDITS.
BUT LOOK HOW MANY THERE ARE!

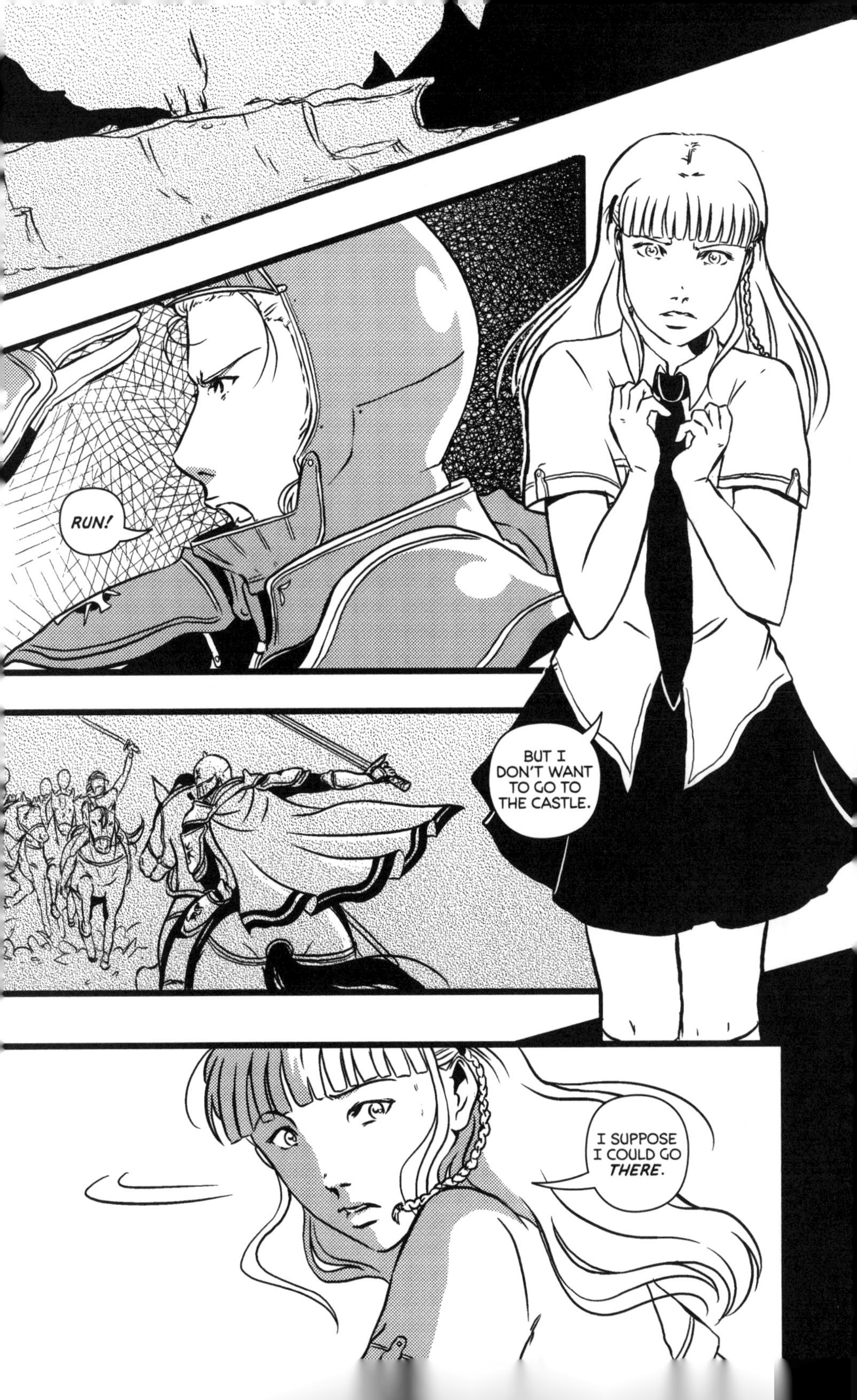
RUN!
BUT I DON'T WANT TO GO TO THE CASTLE.
I SUPPOSE I COULD GO *THERE*.

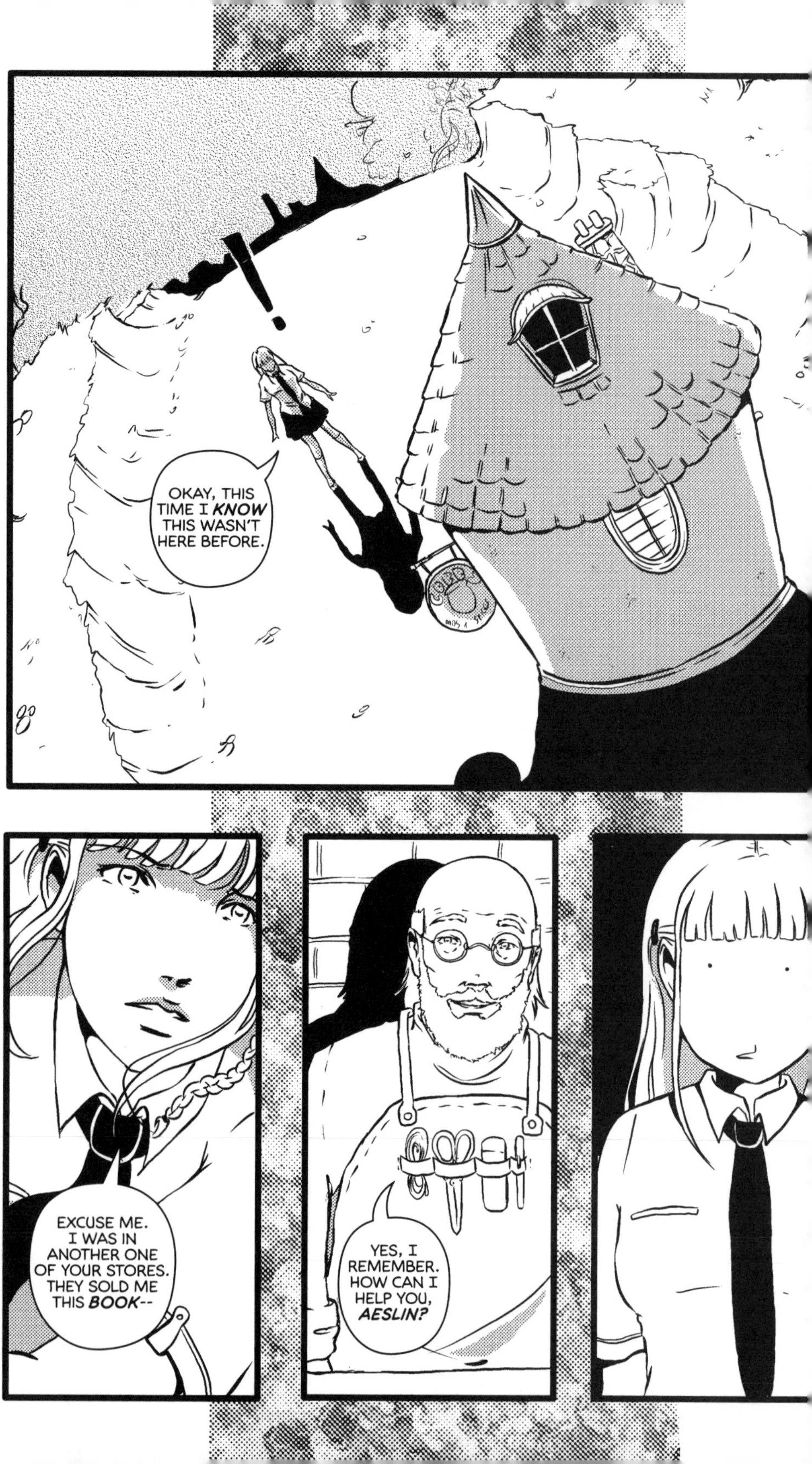
OKAY, THIS TIME I ***KNOW*** THIS WASN'T HERE BEFORE.
EXCUSE ME. I WAS IN ANOTHER ONE OF YOUR STORES. THEY SOLD ME THIS ***BOOK***--
YES, I REMEMBER. HOW CAN I HELP YOU, ***AESLIN?***

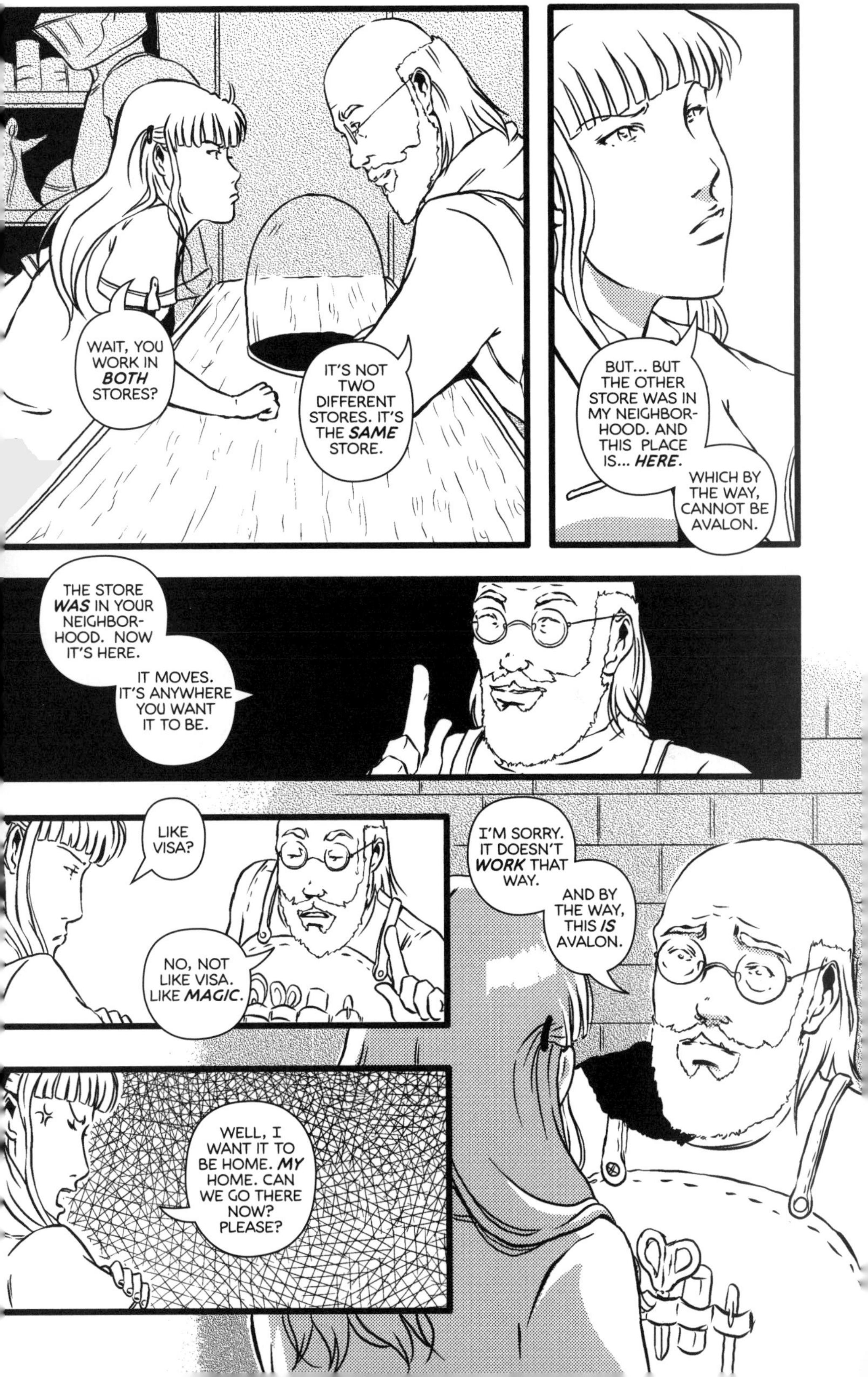
WAIT, YOU WORK IN ***BOTH*** STORES?
IT'S NOT TWO DIFFERENT STORES. IT'S THE ***SAME*** STORE.
BUT... BUT THE OTHER STORE WAS IN MY NEIGHBOR-HOOD. AND THIS PLACE IS... ***HERE***.
WHICH BY THE WAY, CANNOT BE AVALON.
THE STORE ***WAS*** IN YOUR NEIGHBOR-HOOD. NOW IT'S HERE.
IT MOVES. IT'S ANYWHERE YOU WANT IT TO BE.
LIKE VISA?
NO, NOT LIKE VISA. LIKE ***MAGIC***.
I'M SORRY. IT DOESN'T ***WORK*** THAT WAY.
AND BY THE WAY, THIS ***IS*** AVALON.
WELL, I WANT IT TO BE HOME. ***MY*** HOME. CAN WE GO THERE NOW? PLEASE?

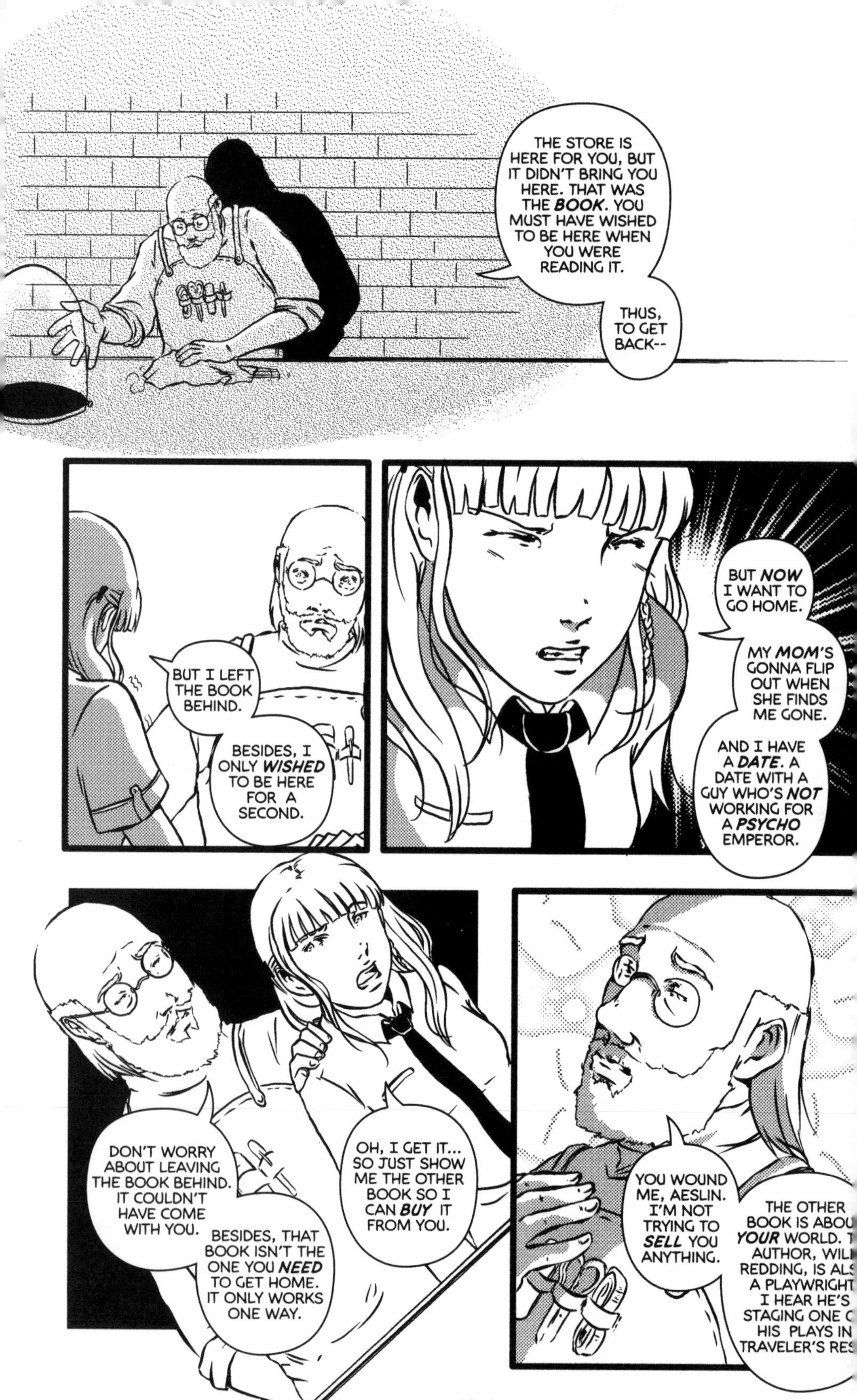
THE STORE IS HERE FOR YOU, BUT IT DIDN'T BRING YOU HERE. THAT WAS THE ***BOOK***. YOU MUST HAVE WISHED TO BE HERE WHEN YOU WERE READING IT.
THUS, TO GET BACK--
BUT I LEFT THE BOOK BEHIND.
BESIDES, I ONLY ***WISHED*** TO BE HERE FOR A SECOND.
BUT ***NOW*** I WANT TO GO HOME.
MY ***MOM***'S GONNA FLIP OUT WHEN SHE FINDS ME GONE.
AND I HAVE A ***DATE***. A DATE WITH A GUY WHO'S ***NOT*** WORKING FOR A ***PSYCHO*** EMPEROR.
DON'T WORRY ABOUT LEAVING THE BOOK BEHIND. IT COULDN'T HAVE COME WITH YOU.
BESIDES, THAT BOOK ISN'T THE ONE YOU ***NEED*** TO GET HOME. IT ONLY WORKS ONE WAY.
OH, I GET IT... SO JUST SHOW ME THE OTHER BOOK SO I CAN ***BUY*** IT FROM YOU.
YOU WOUND ME, AESLIN. I'M NOT TRYING TO ***SELL*** YOU ANYTHING.
THE OTHER BOOK IS ABOU ***YOUR*** WORLD. T AUTHOR, WIL REDDING, IS ALS A PLAYWRIGHT I HEAR HE'S STAGING ONE C HIS PLAYS IN TRAVELER'S RES

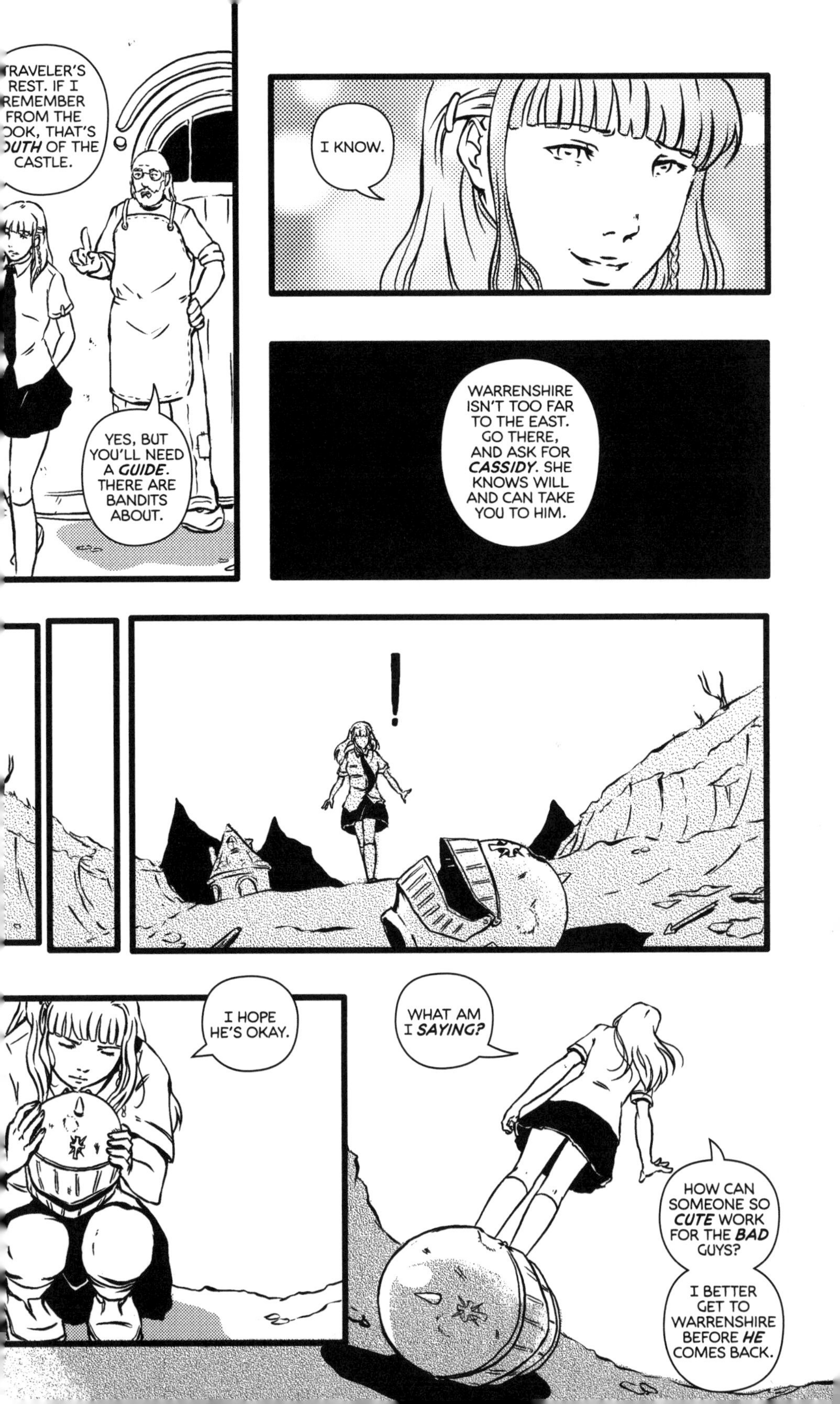

TRAVELER'S REST. IF I REMEMBER FROM THE BOOK, THAT'S SOUTH OF THE CASTLE.
YES, BUT YOU'LL NEED A ***GUIDE***. THERE ARE BANDITS ABOUT.
I KNOW.
WARRENSHIRE ISN'T TOO FAR TO THE EAST. GO THERE, AND ASK FOR ***CASSIDY***. SHE KNOWS WILL AND CAN TAKE YOU TO HIM.
!
I HOPE HE'S OKAY.
WHAT AM I ***SAYING?***
HOW CAN SOMEONE SO ***CUTE*** WORK FOR THE ***BAD*** GUYS?
I BETTER GET TO WARRENSHIRE BEFORE ***HE*** COMES BACK.

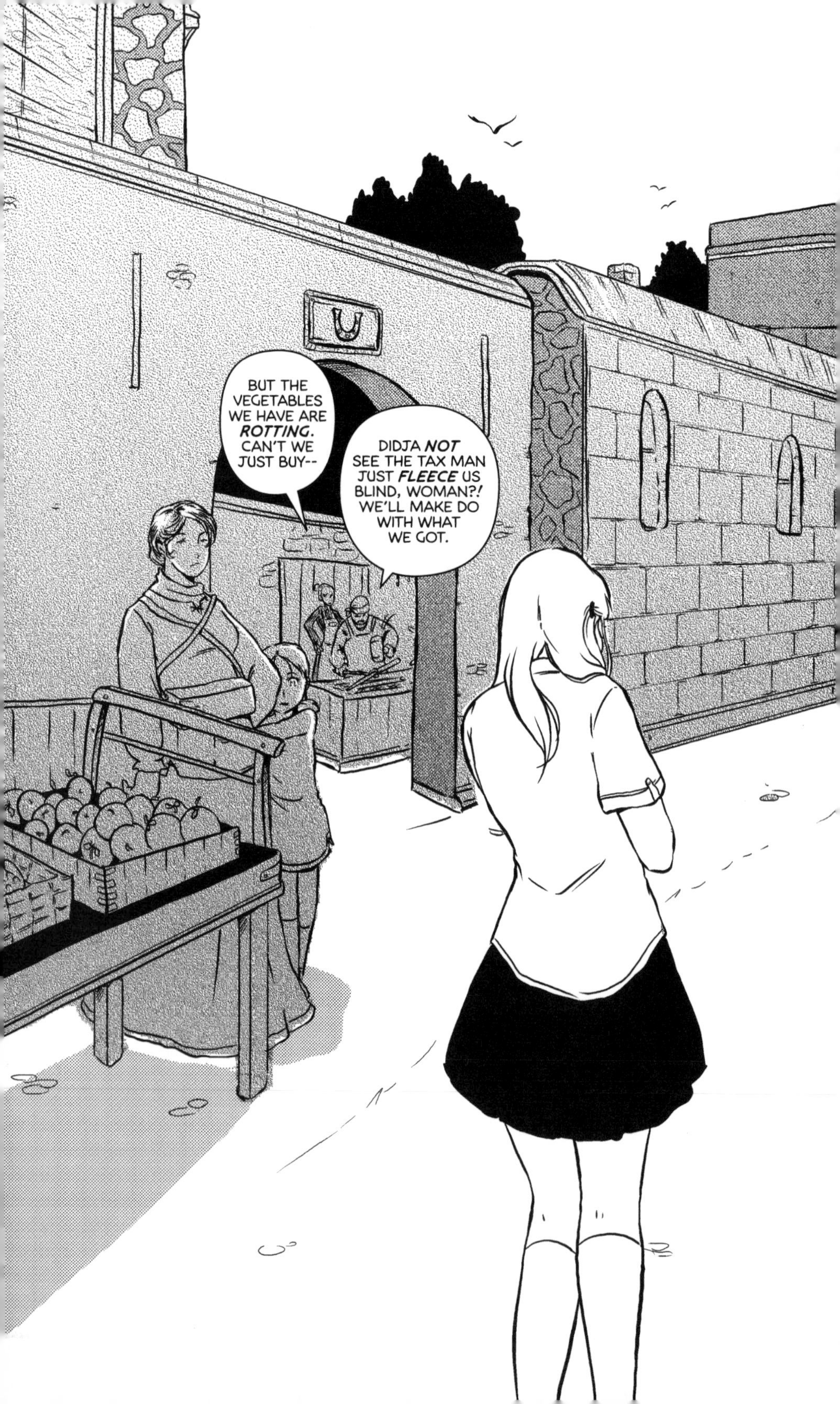
BUT THE VEGETABLES WE HAVE ARE ROTTING. CAN'T WE JUST BUY--
DIDJA NOT SEE THE TAX MAN JUST FLEECE US BLIND, WOMAN?! WE'LL MAKE DO WITH WHAT WE GOT.

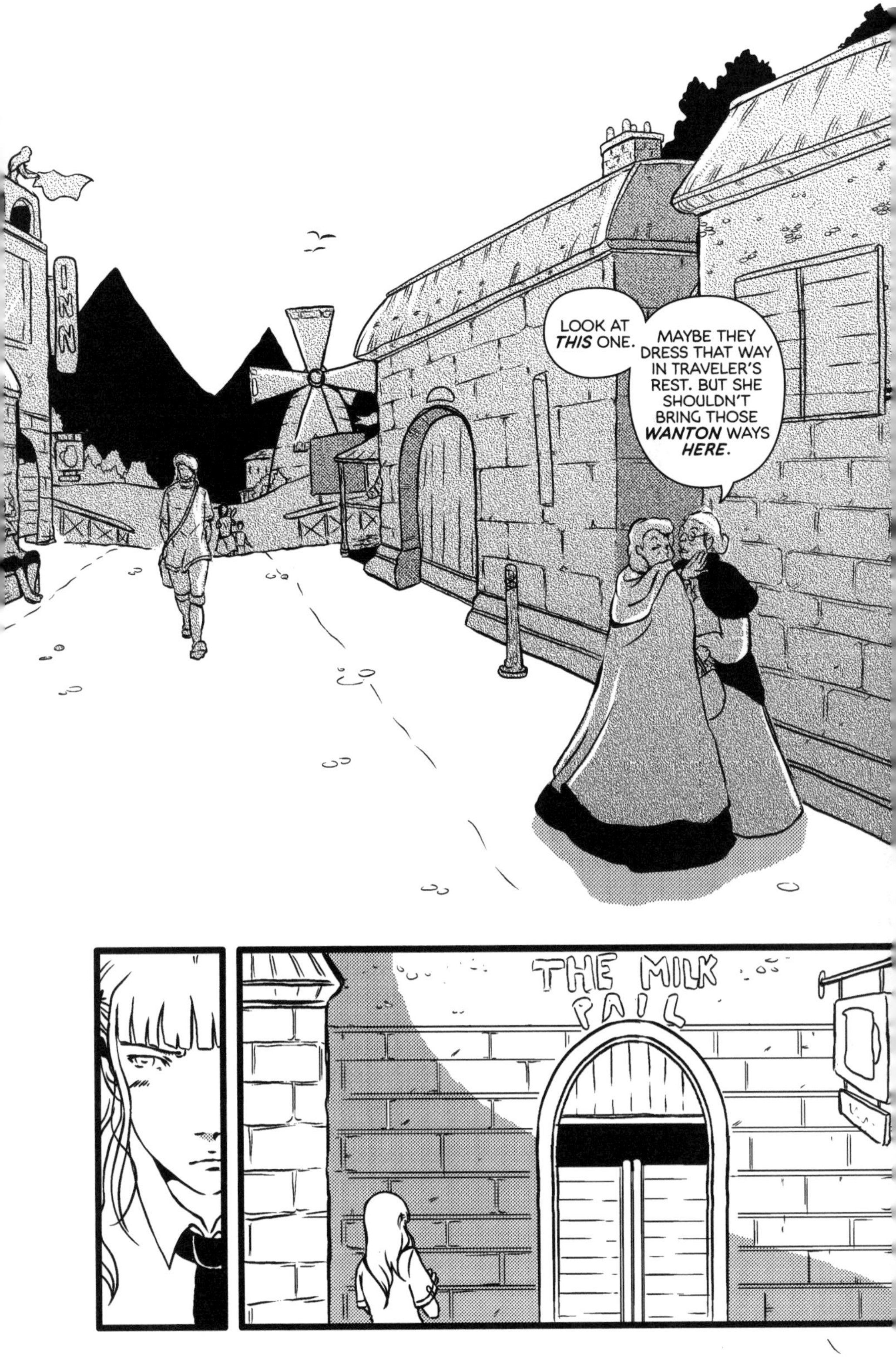
INN
LOOK AT *THIS* ONE.
MAYBE THEY DRESS THAT WAY IN TRAVELER'S REST. BUT SHE SHOULDN'T BRING THOSE *WANTON* WAYS *HERE*.
THE MILK PAIL

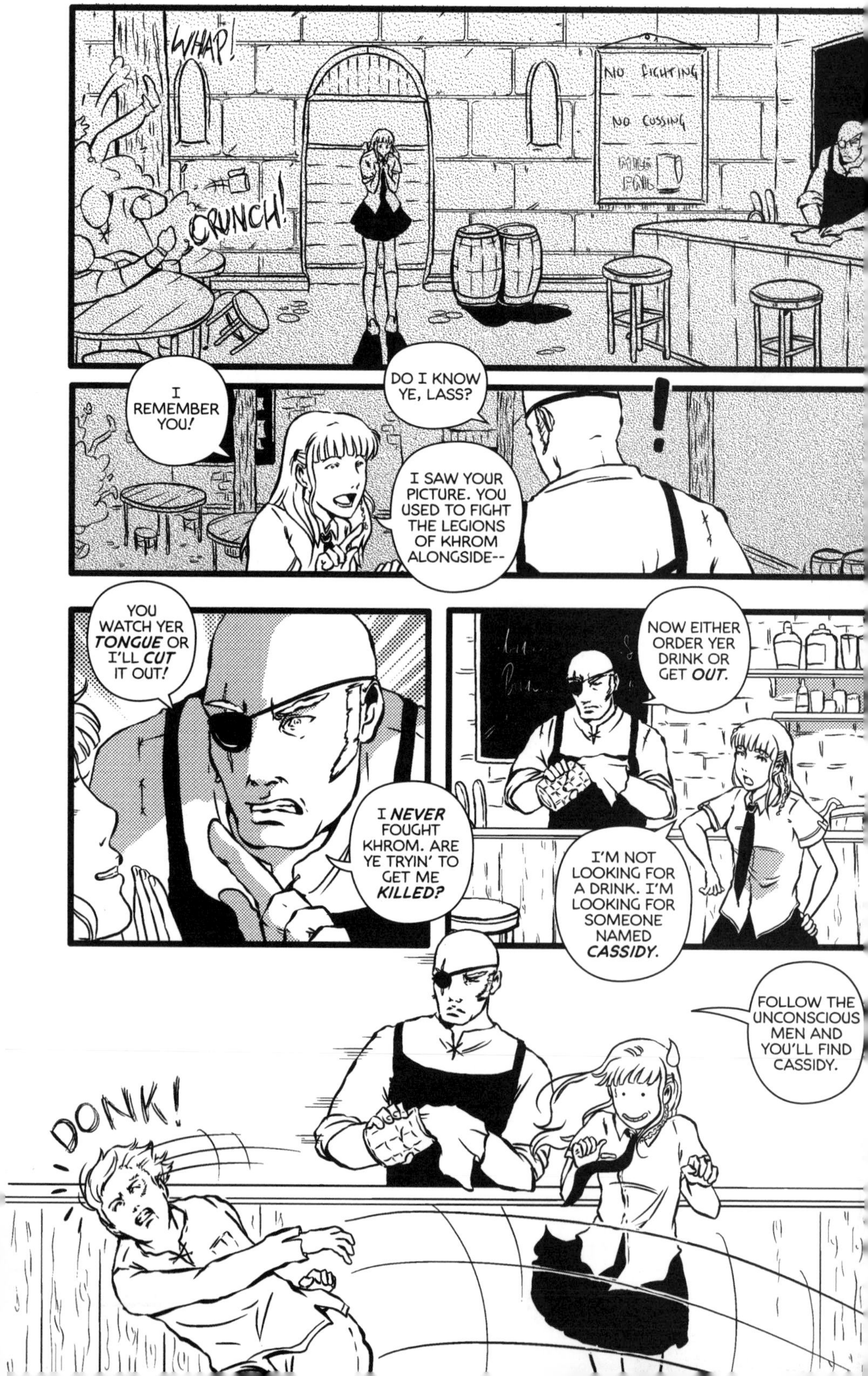
WHAP!
CRUNCH!
NO FIGHTING
NO CUSSING
I REMEMBER YOU!
DO I KNOW YE, LASS?
!
I SAW YOUR PICTURE. YOU USED TO FIGHT THE LEGIONS OF KHROM ALONGSIDE--
YOU WATCH YER *TONGUE* OR I'LL *CUT* IT OUT!
I *NEVER* FOUGHT KHROM. ARE YE TRYIN' TO GET ME *KILLED?*
NOW EITHER ORDER YER DRINK OR GET *OUT*.
I'M NOT LOOKING FOR A DRINK. I'M LOOKING FOR SOMEONE NAMED *CASSIDY*.
FOLLOW THE UNCONSCIOUS MEN AND YOU'LL FIND CASSIDY.
DONK!

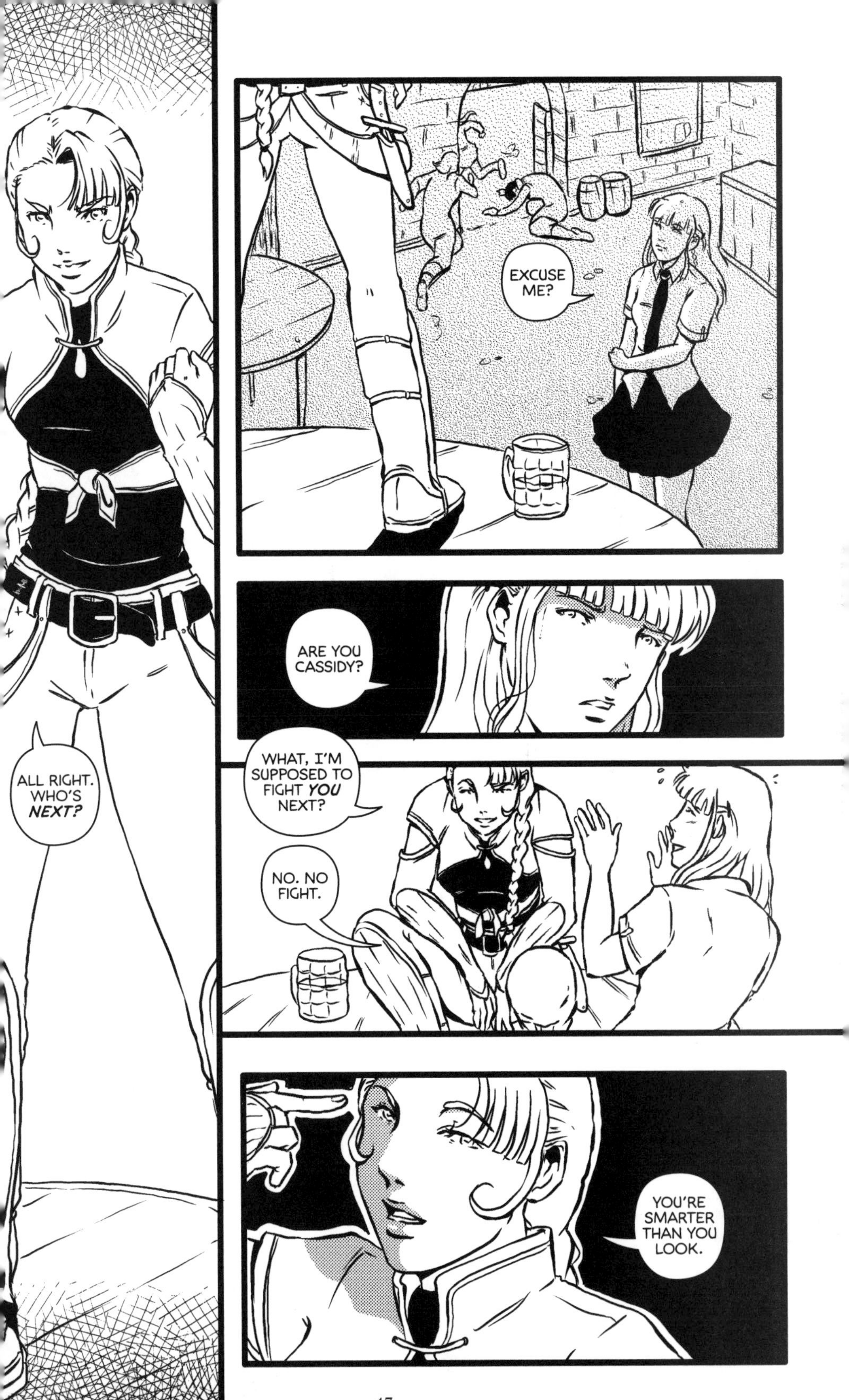
ALL RIGHT. WHO'S *NEXT?*
EXCUSE ME?
ARE YOU CASSIDY?
WHAT, I'M SUPPOSED TO FIGHT *YOU* NEXT?
NO. NO FIGHT.
YOU'RE SMARTER THAN YOU LOOK.

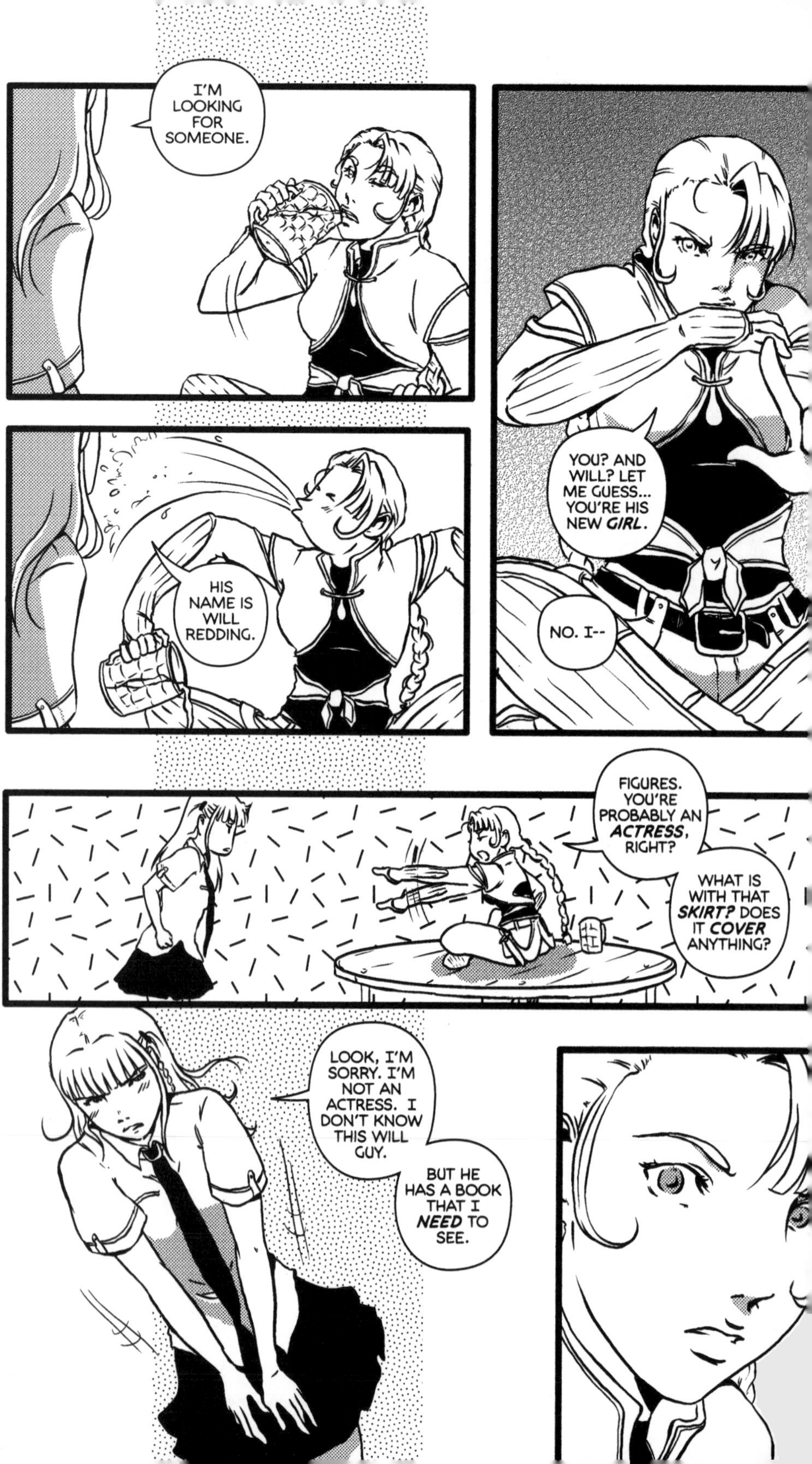
I'M LOOKING FOR SOMEONE.
HIS NAME IS WILL REDDING.
YOU? AND WILL? LET ME GUESS... YOU'RE HIS NEW *GIRL*.
NO. I--
FIGURES. YOU'RE PROBABLY AN *ACTRESS*, RIGHT?
WHAT IS WITH THAT *SKIRT?* DOES IT *COVER* ANYTHING?
LOOK, I'M SORRY. I'M NOT AN ACTRESS. I DON'T KNOW THIS WILL GUY.
BUT HE HAS A BOOK THAT I *NEED* TO SEE.

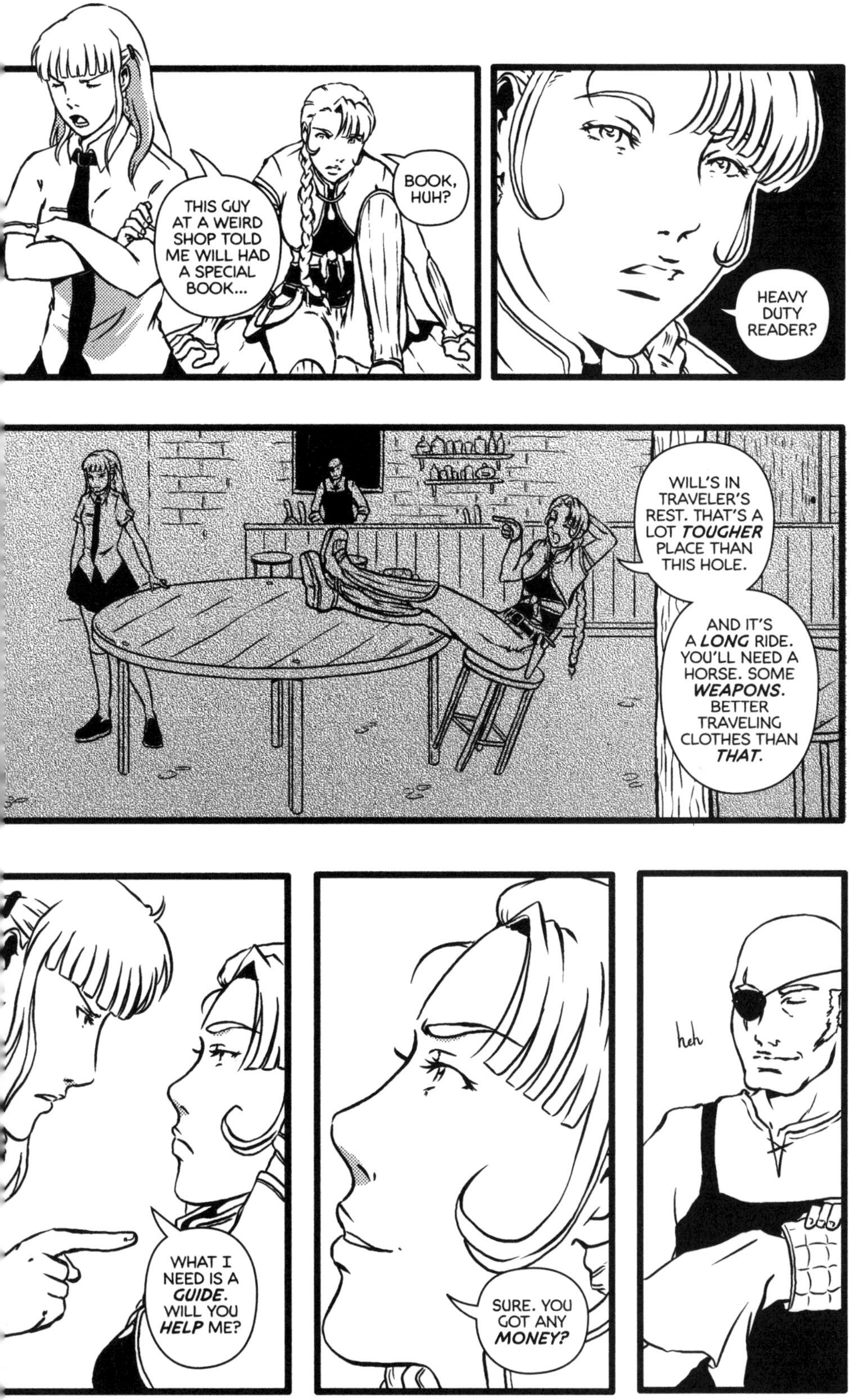

THIS GUY AT A WEIRD SHOP TOLD ME WILL HAD A SPECIAL BOOK...
BOOK, HUH?
HEAVY DUTY READER?
WILL'S IN TRAVELER'S REST. THAT'S A LOT TOUGHER PLACE THAN THIS HOLE.
AND IT'S A LONG RIDE. YOU'LL NEED A HORSE. SOME WEAPONS. BETTER TRAVELING CLOTHES THAN THAT.
WHAT I NEED IS A GUIDE. WILL YOU HELP ME?
SURE. YOU GOT ANY MONEY?
heh

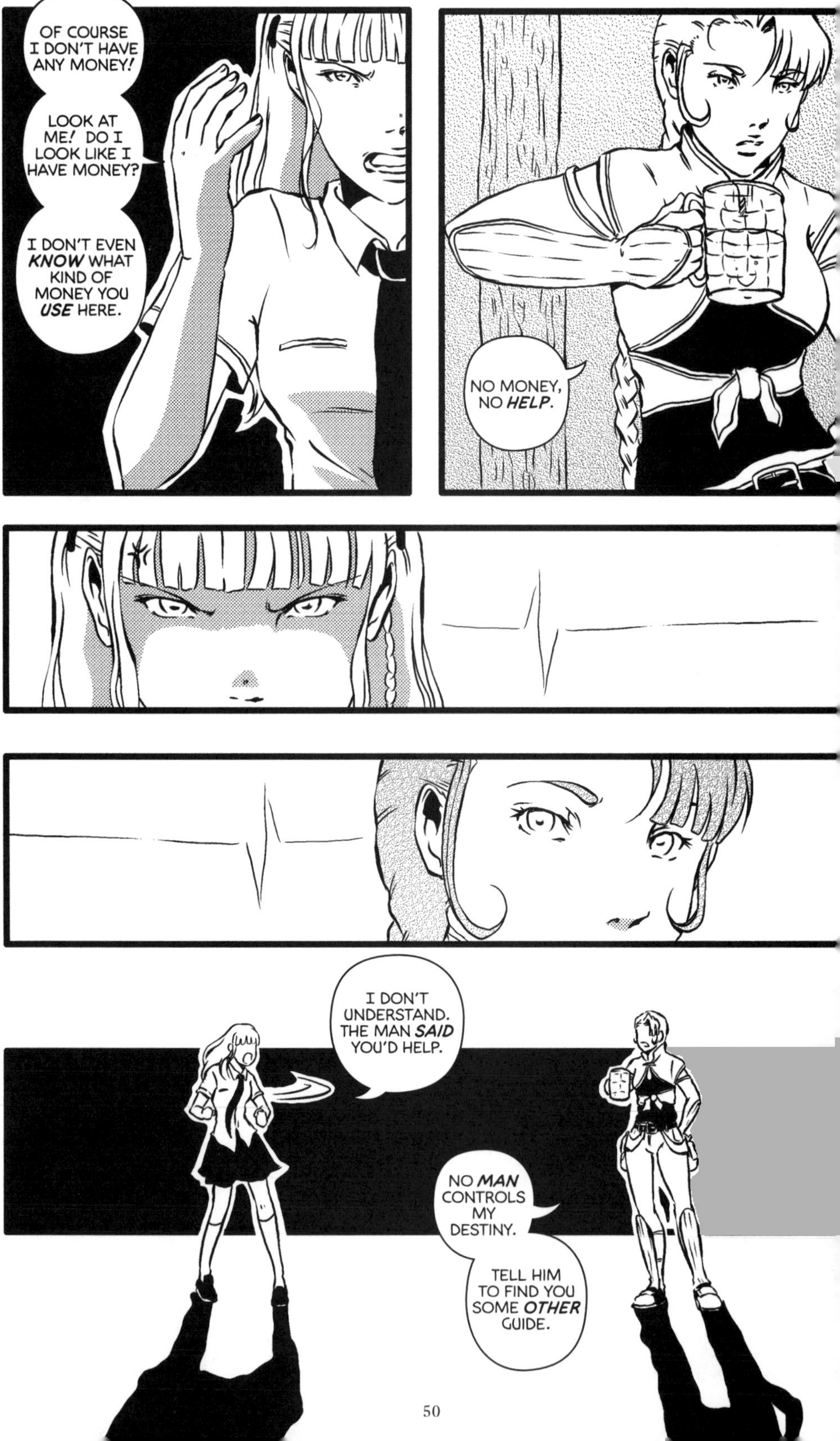
OF COURSE I DON'T HAVE ANY MONEY!
LOOK AT ME! DO I LOOK LIKE I HAVE MONEY?
I DON'T EVEN KNOW WHAT KIND OF MONEY YOU USE HERE.
NO MONEY, NO HELP.
I DON'T UNDERSTAND. THE MAN SAID YOU'D HELP.
NO MAN CONTROLS MY DESTINY.
TELL HIM TO FIND YOU SOME OTHER GUIDE.

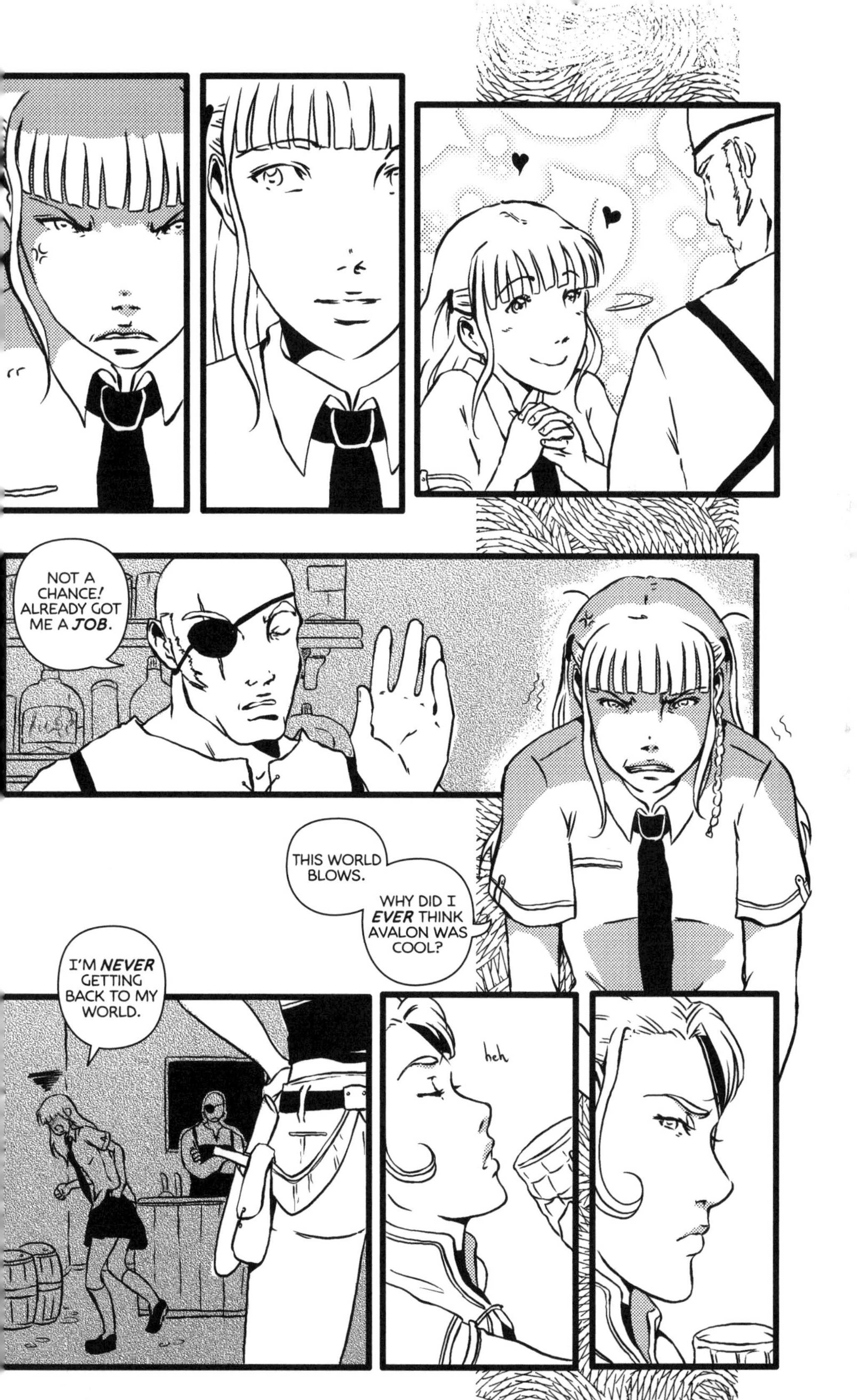

NOT A CHANCE! ALREADY GOT ME A *JOB*.
THIS WORLD BLOWS.
WHY DID I *EVER* THINK AVALON WAS COOL?
I'M *NEVER* GETTING BACK TO MY WORLD.
heh

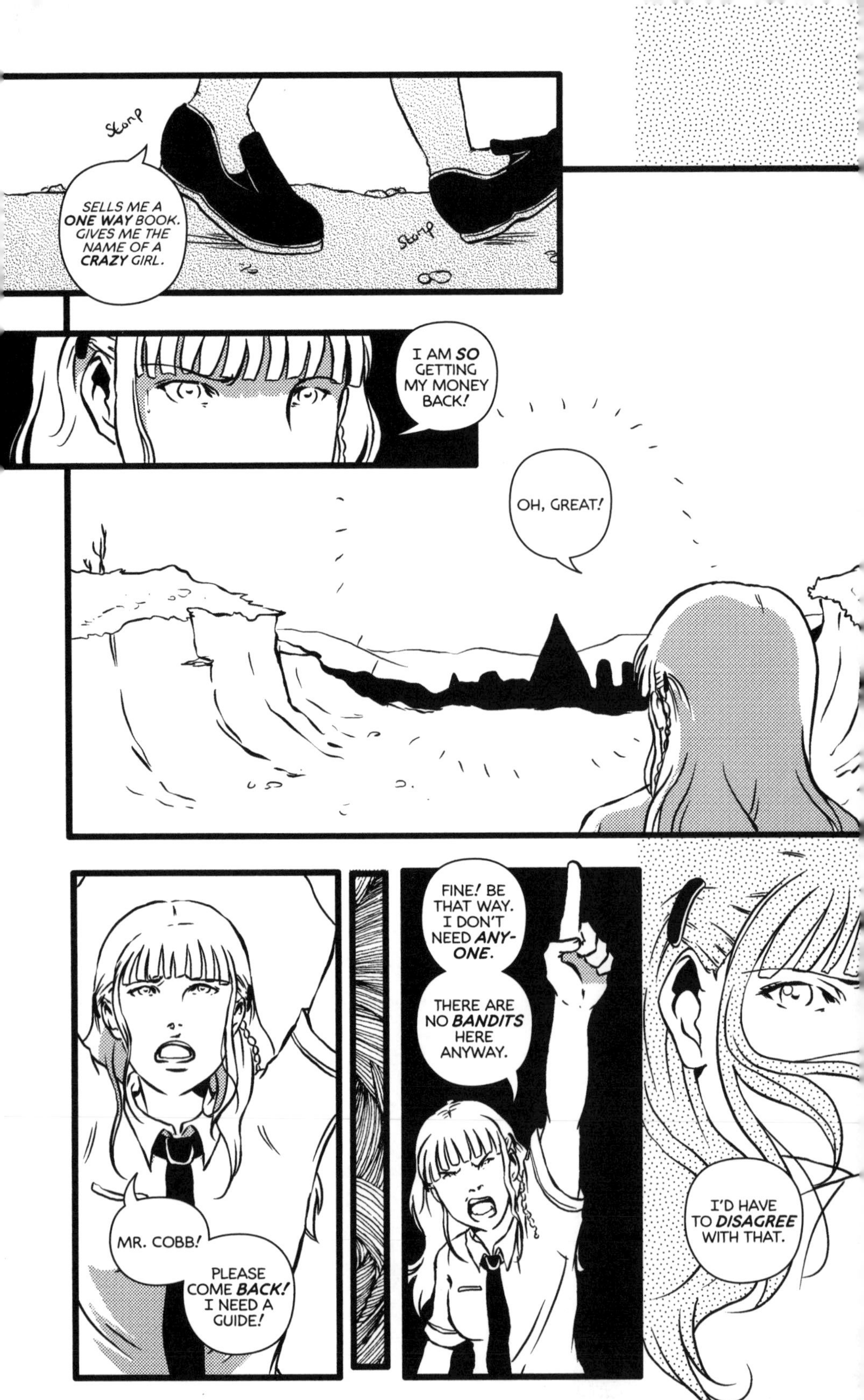
Stomp
SELLS ME A ONE WAY BOOK. GIVES ME THE NAME OF A CRAZY GIRL.
Stomp
I AM SO GETTING MY MONEY BACK!
OH, GREAT!
MR. COBB!
PLEASE COME BACK! I NEED A GUIDE!
FINE! BE THAT WAY. I DON'T NEED ANY-ONE.
THERE ARE NO BANDITS HERE ANYWAY.
I'D HAVE TO DISAGREE WITH THAT.

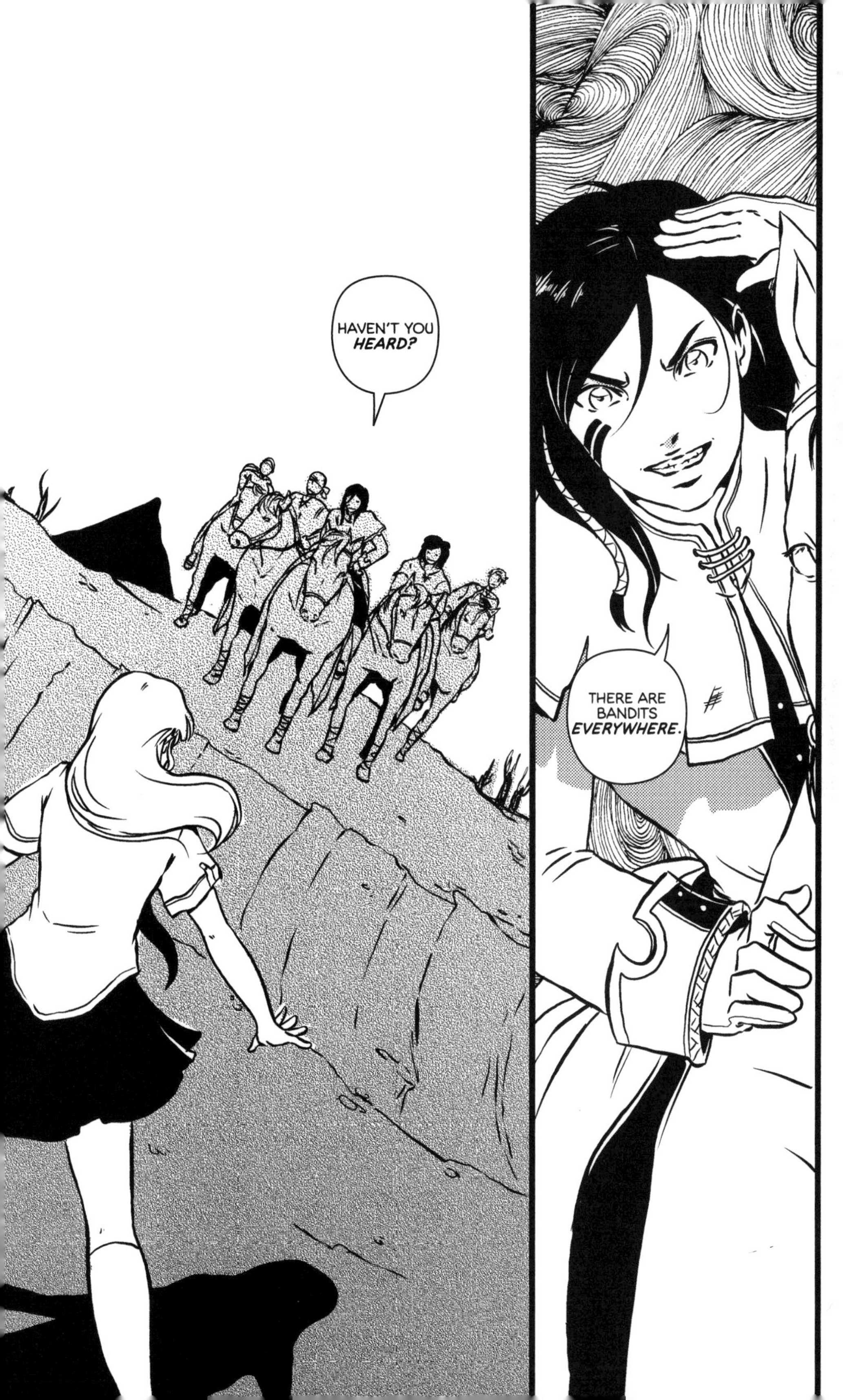
HAVEN'T YOU *HEARD?*
THERE ARE BANDITS *EVERYWHERE.*

Chapter 3

Destiny

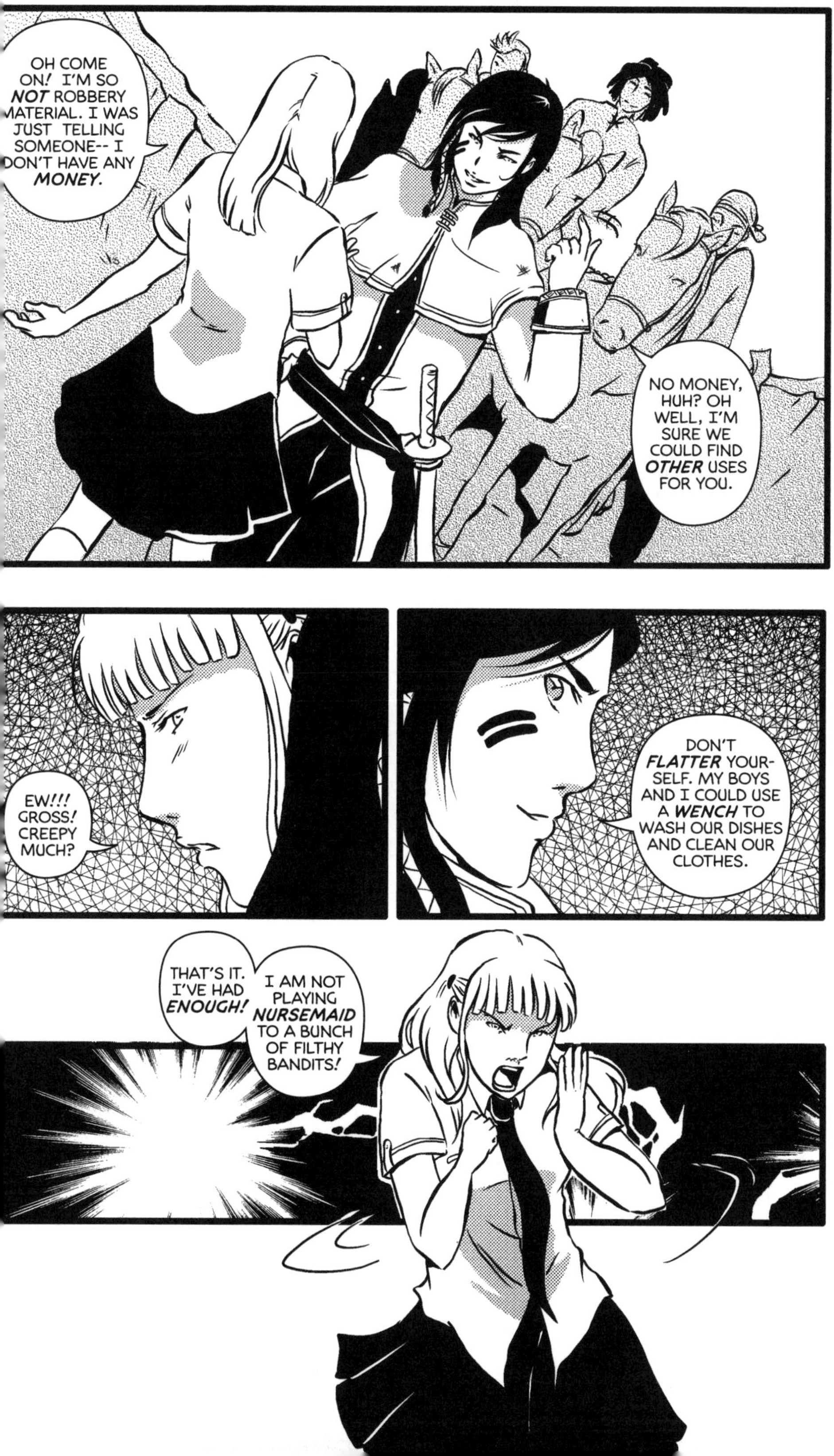
OH COME ON! I'M SO NOT ROBBERY MATERIAL. I WAS JUST TELLING SOMEONE-- I DON'T HAVE ANY MONEY.
NO MONEY, HUH? OH WELL, I'M SURE WE COULD FIND OTHER USES FOR YOU.
EW!!! GROSS! CREEPY MUCH?
DON'T FLATTER YOURSELF. MY BOYS AND I COULD USE A WENCH TO WASH OUR DISHES AND CLEAN OUR CLOTHES.
THAT'S IT. I'VE HAD ENOUGH!
I AM NOT PLAYING NURSEMAID TO A BUNCH OF FILTHY BANDITS!

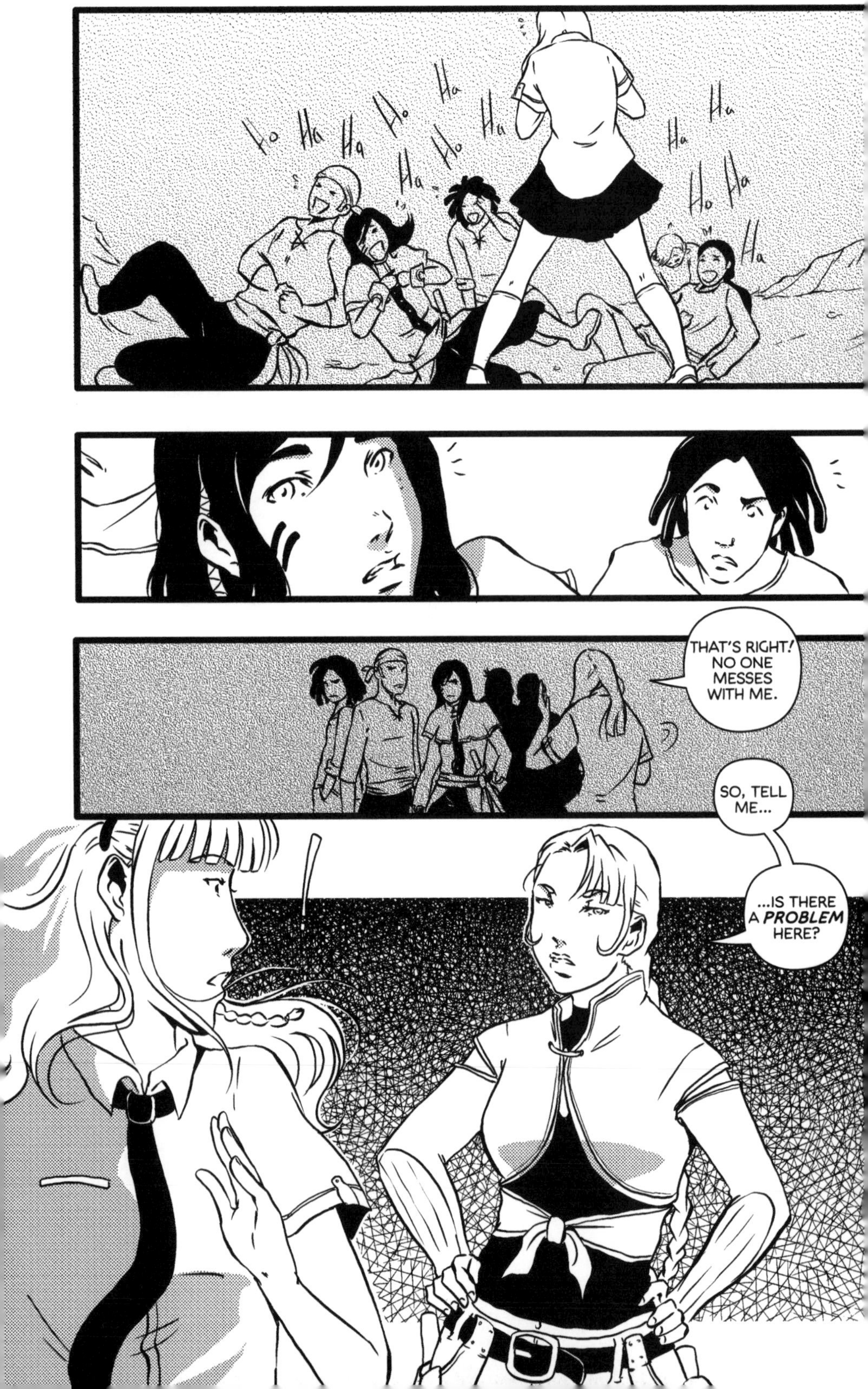
Ha Ha Ha Ha Ha Ha Ha Ha Ha
Ha Ha Ha Ha Ha
THAT'S RIGHT! NO ONE MESSES WITH ME.
SO, TELL ME...
...IS THERE A *PROBLEM* HERE?

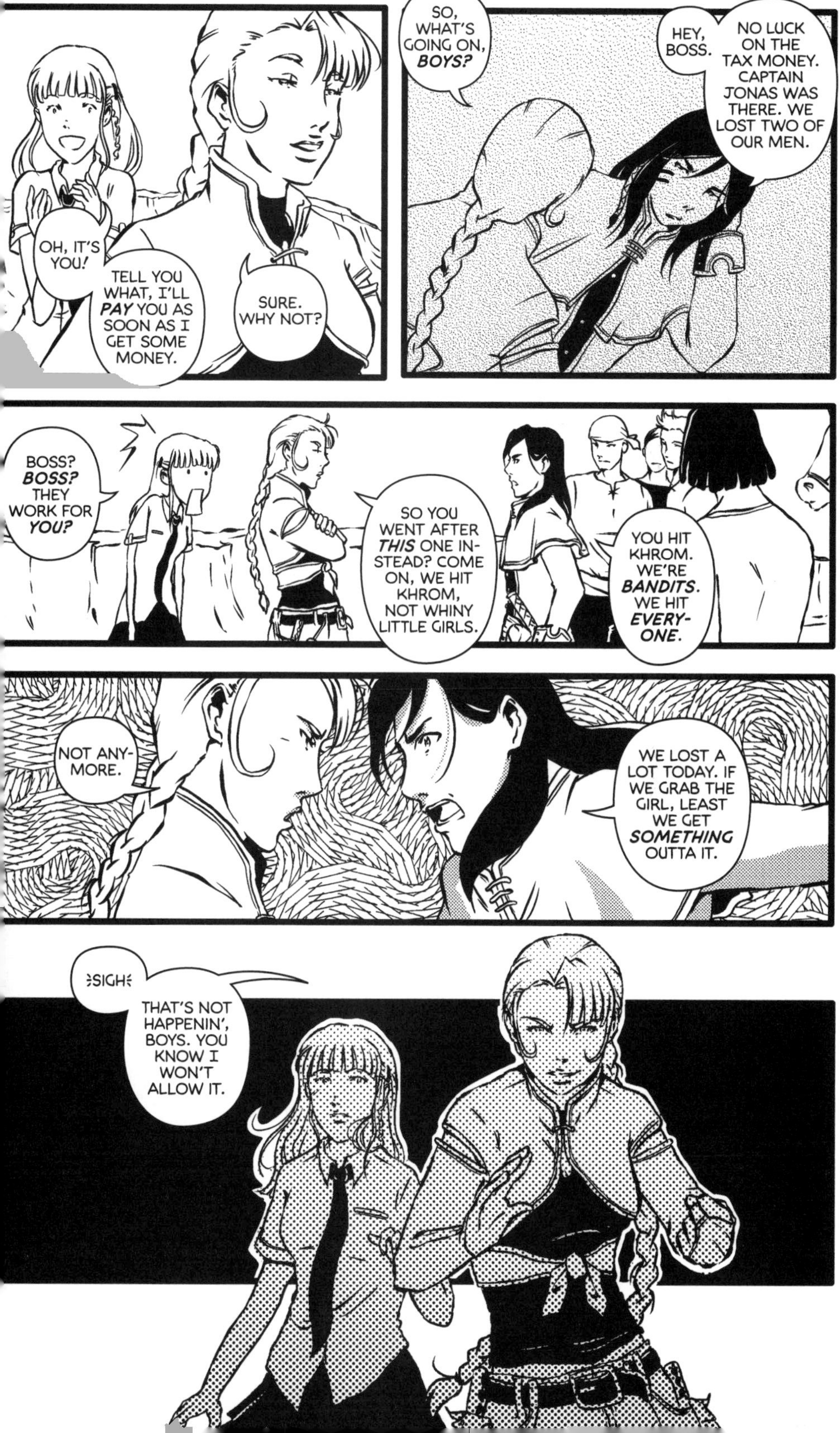
OH, IT'S YOU!
TELL YOU WHAT, I'LL PAY YOU AS SOON AS I GET SOME MONEY.
SURE. WHY NOT?
SO, WHAT'S GOING ON, BOYS?
HEY, BOSS.
NO LUCK ON THE TAX MONEY. CAPTAIN JONAS WAS THERE. WE LOST TWO OF OUR MEN.
BOSS? BOSS? THEY WORK FOR YOU?
SO YOU WENT AFTER THIS ONE INSTEAD? COME ON, WE HIT KHROM, NOT WHINY LITTLE GIRLS.
YOU HIT KHROM. WE'RE BANDITS. WE HIT EVERYONE.
NOT ANYMORE.
WE LOST A LOT TODAY. IF WE GRAB THE GIRL, LEAST WE GET SOMETHING OUTTA IT.
SIGH
THAT'S NOT HAPPENIN', BOYS. YOU KNOW I WON'T ALLOW IT.

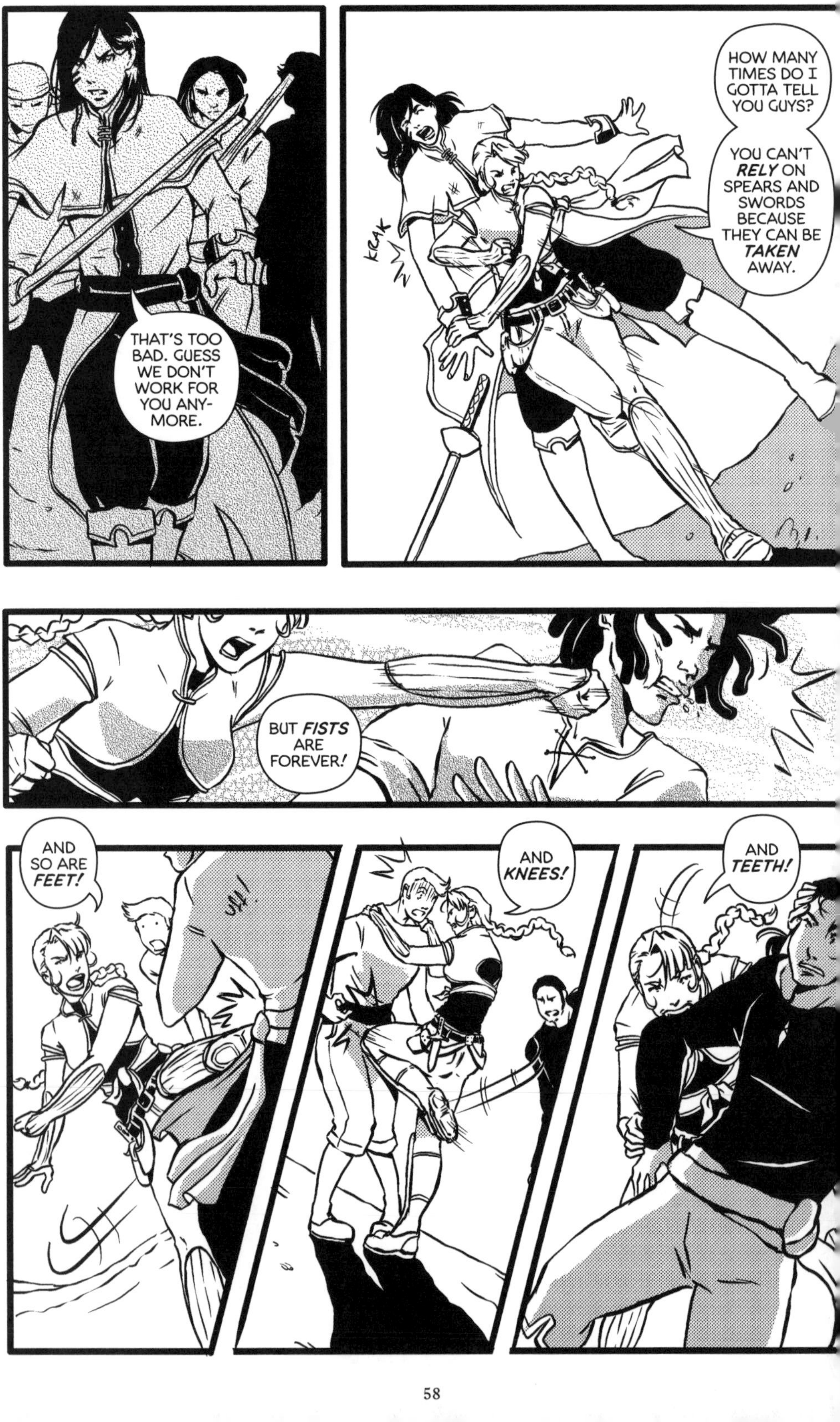
THAT'S TOO BAD. GUESS WE DON'T WORK FOR YOU ANY-MORE.
HOW MANY TIMES DO I GOTTA TELL YOU GUYS?
YOU CAN'T *RELY* ON SPEARS AND SWORDS BECAUSE THEY CAN BE *TAKEN* AWAY.
KRAK
BUT *FISTS* ARE FOREVER!
AND SO ARE *FEET!*
AND *KNEES!*
AND *TEETH!*

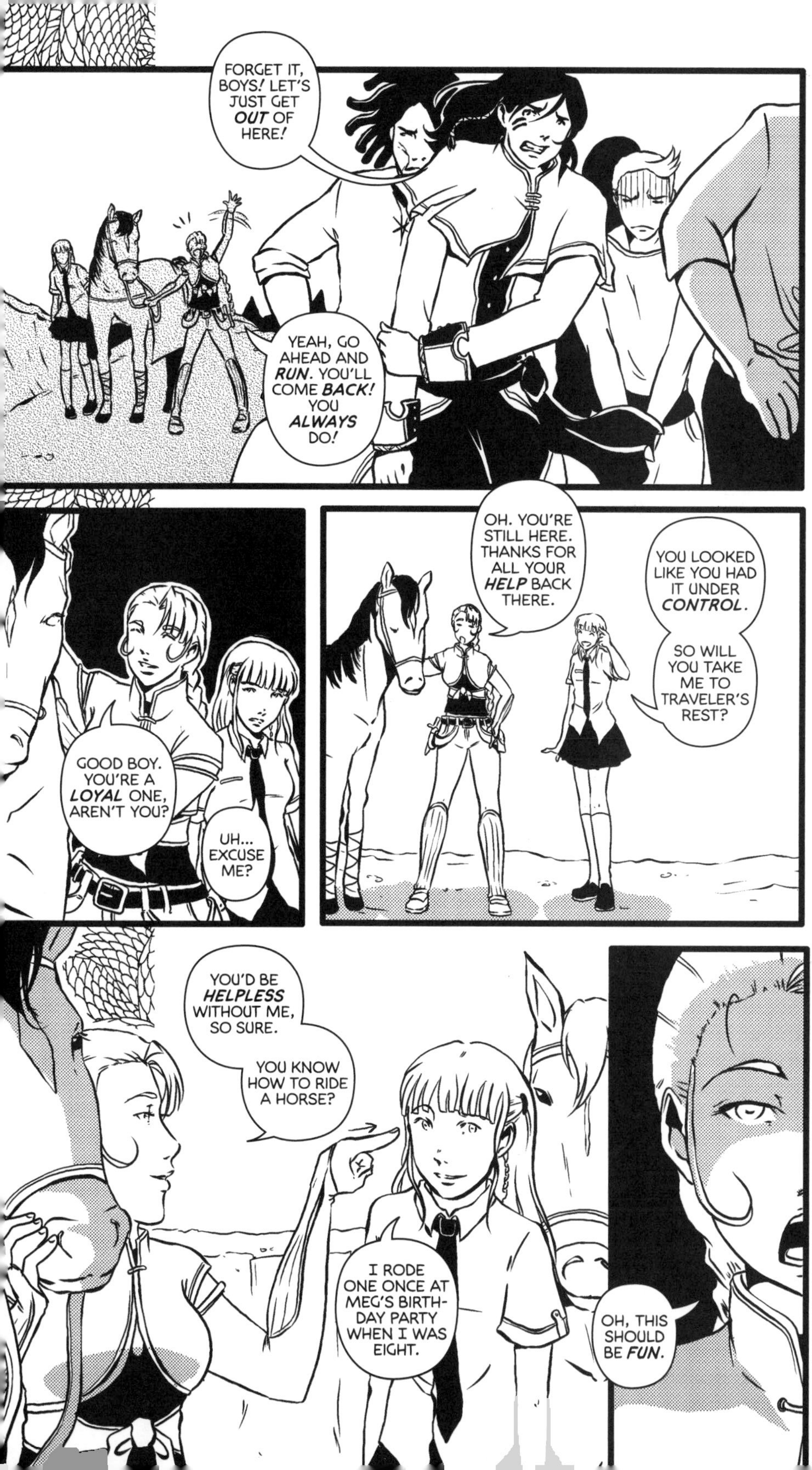
FORGET IT, BOYS! LET'S JUST GET OUT OF HERE!
YEAH, GO AHEAD AND RUN. YOU'LL COME BACK! YOU ALWAYS DO!
GOOD BOY. YOU'RE A LOYAL ONE, AREN'T YOU?
UH... EXCUSE ME?
OH. YOU'RE STILL HERE. THANKS FOR ALL YOUR HELP BACK THERE.
YOU LOOKED LIKE YOU HAD IT UNDER CONTROL.
SO WILL YOU TAKE ME TO TRAVELER'S REST?
YOU'D BE HELPLESS WITHOUT ME, SO SURE.
YOU KNOW HOW TO RIDE A HORSE?
I RODE ONE ONCE AT MEG'S BIRTH-DAY PARTY WHEN I WAS EIGHT.
OH, THIS SHOULD BE FUN.

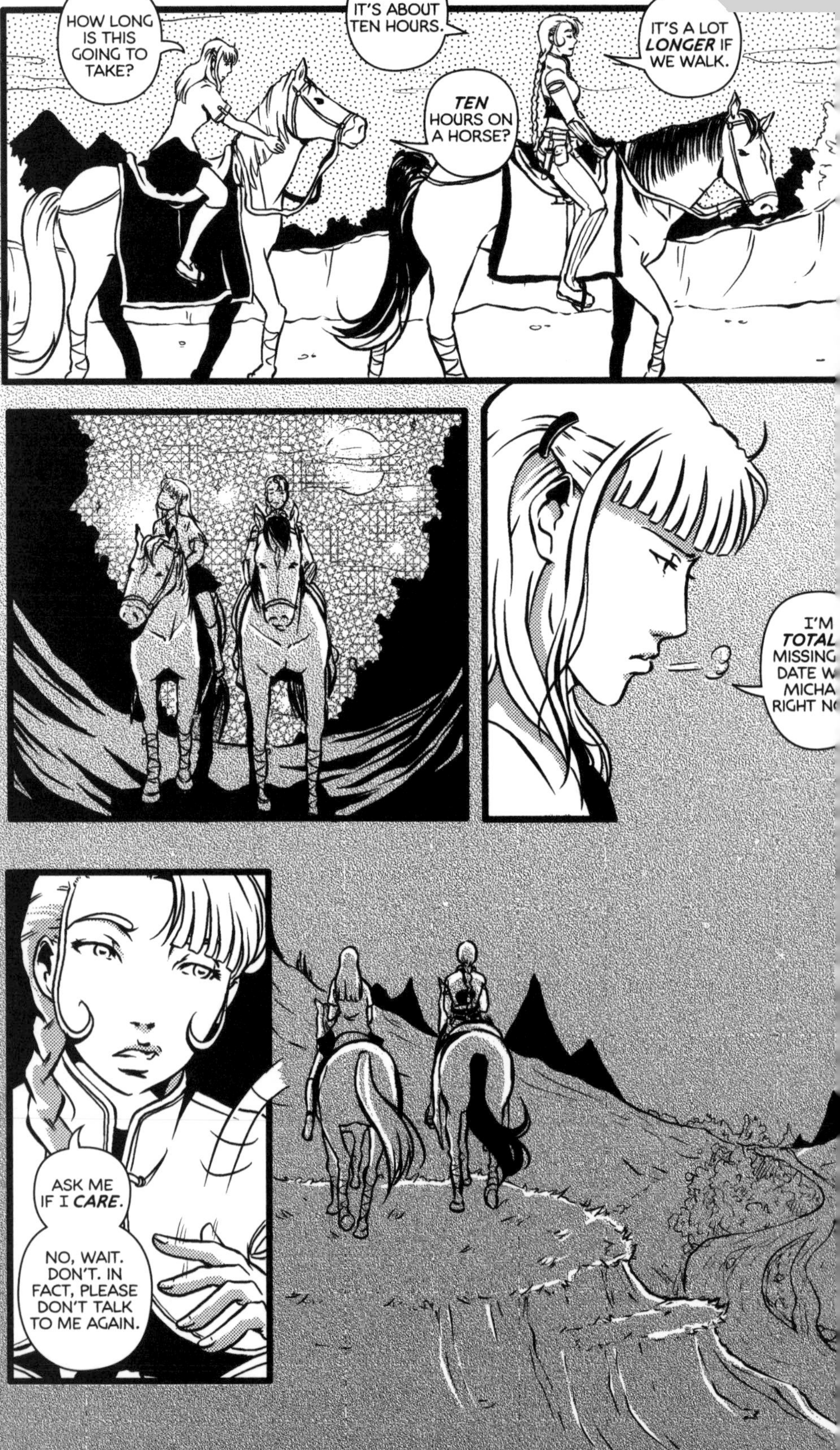
HOW LONG IS THIS GOING TO TAKE?
IT'S ABOUT TEN HOURS.
TEN HOURS ON A HORSE?
IT'S A LOT *LONGER* IF WE WALK.
I'M *TOTAL* MISSING DATE W MICHA RIGHT N
ASK ME IF I *CARE*.
NO, WAIT. DON'T. IN FACT, PLEASE DON'T TALK TO ME AGAIN.

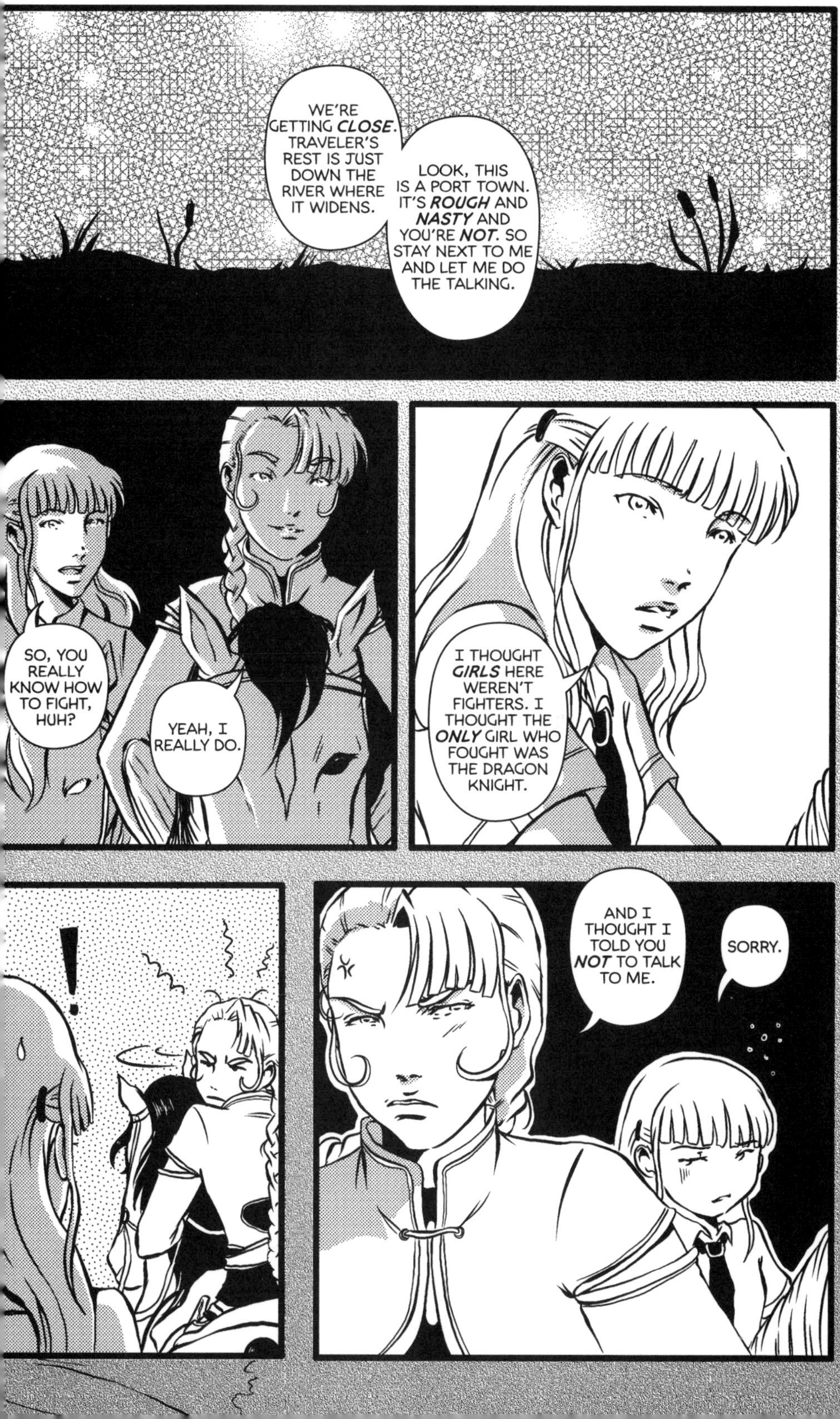
WE'RE GETTING *CLOSE*. TRAVELER'S REST IS JUST DOWN THE RIVER WHERE IT WIDENS.
LOOK, THIS IS A PORT TOWN. IT'S *ROUGH* AND *NASTY* AND YOU'RE *NOT*. SO STAY NEXT TO ME AND LET ME DO THE TALKING.
SO, YOU REALLY KNOW HOW TO FIGHT, HUH?
YEAH, I REALLY DO.
I THOUGHT *GIRLS* HERE WEREN'T FIGHTERS. I THOUGHT THE *ONLY* GIRL WHO FOUGHT WAS THE DRAGON KNIGHT.
!
AND I THOUGHT I TOLD YOU *NOT* TO TALK TO ME.
SORRY.

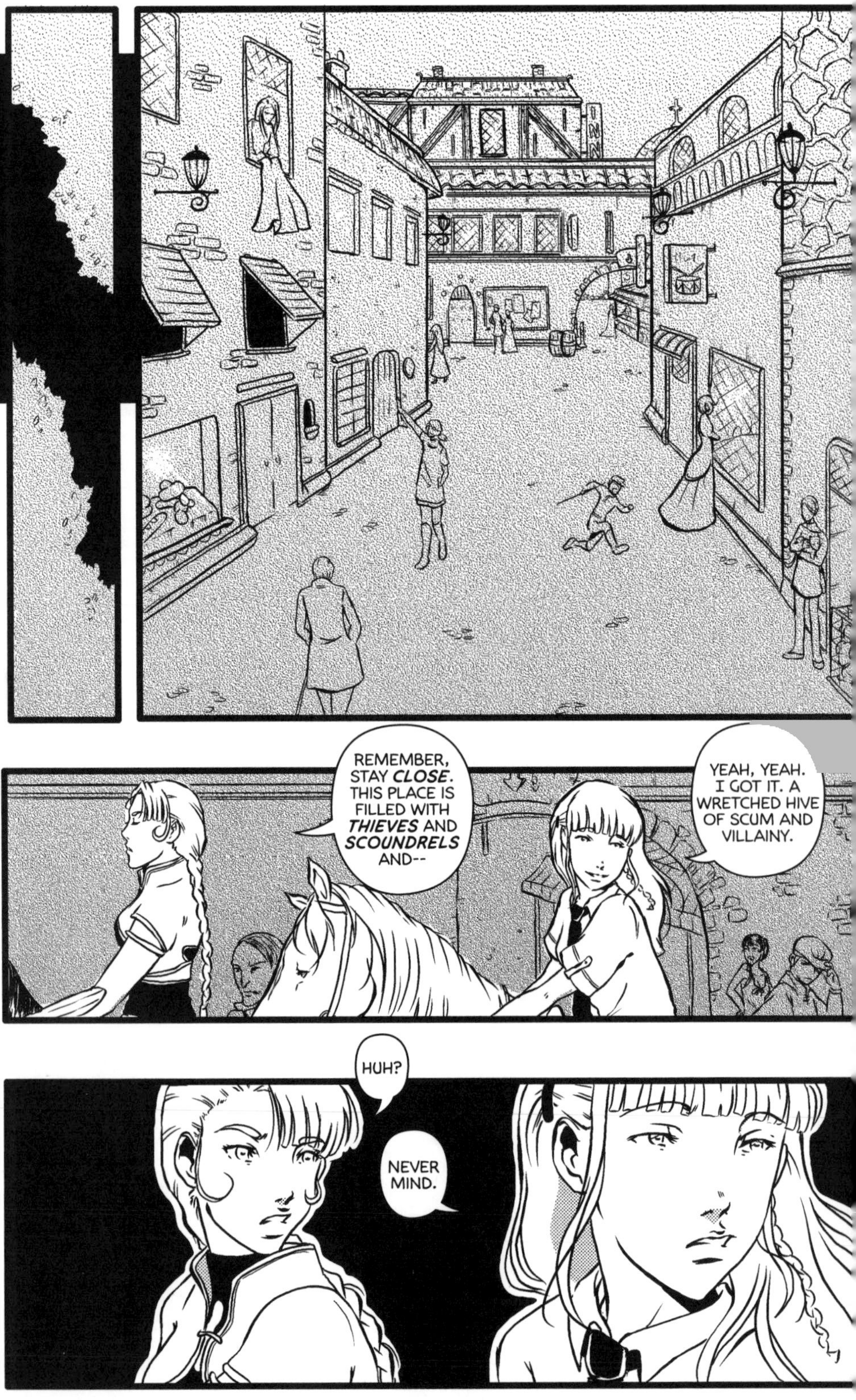
REMEMBER, STAY CLOSE. THIS PLACE IS FILLED WITH THIEVES AND SCOUNDRELS AND--
YEAH, YEAH. I GOT IT. A WRETCHED HIVE OF SCUM AND VILLAINY.
HUH?
NEVER MIND.

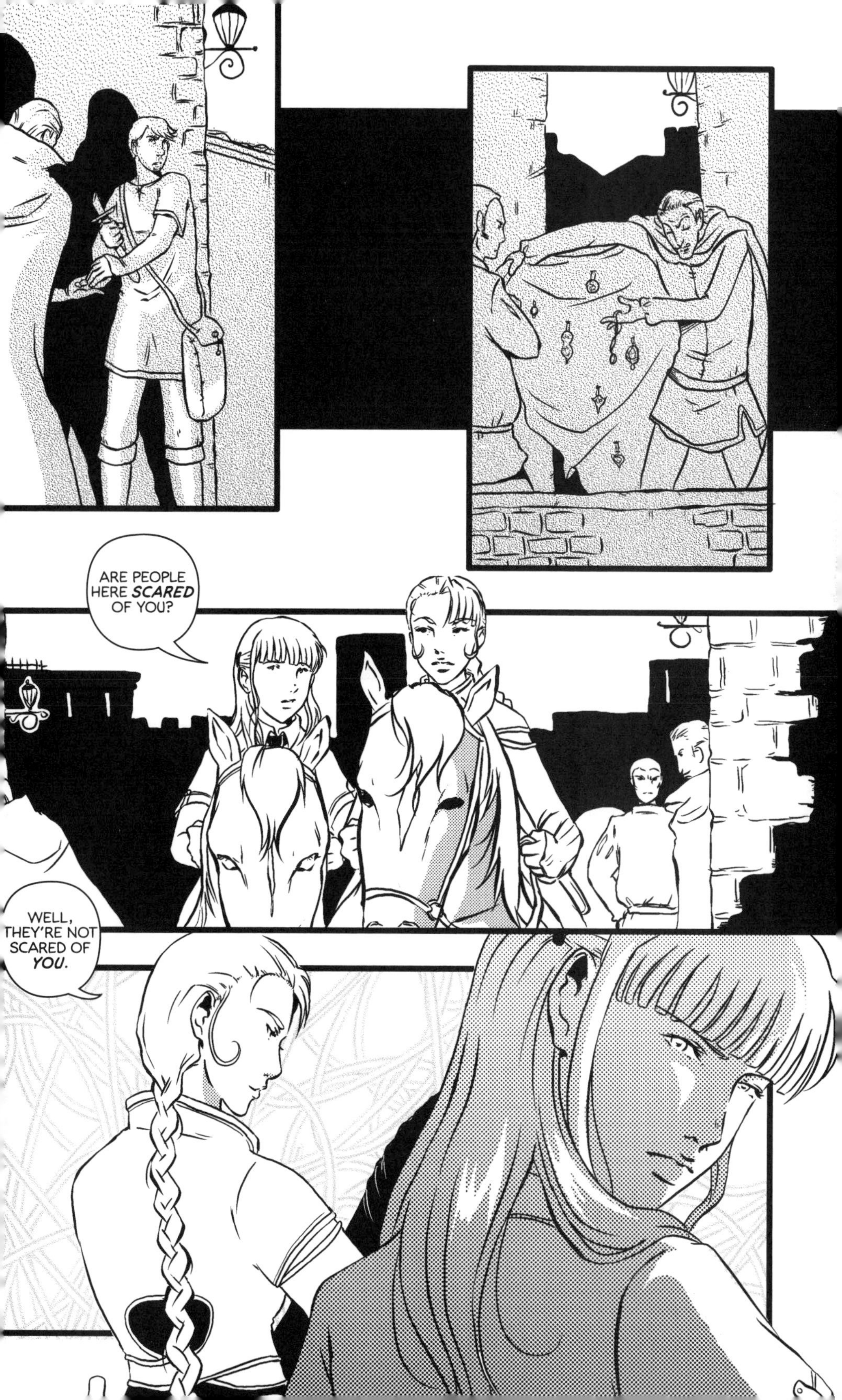
ARE PEOPLE HERE *SCARED* OF YOU?
WELL, THEY'RE NOT SCARED OF *YOU*.

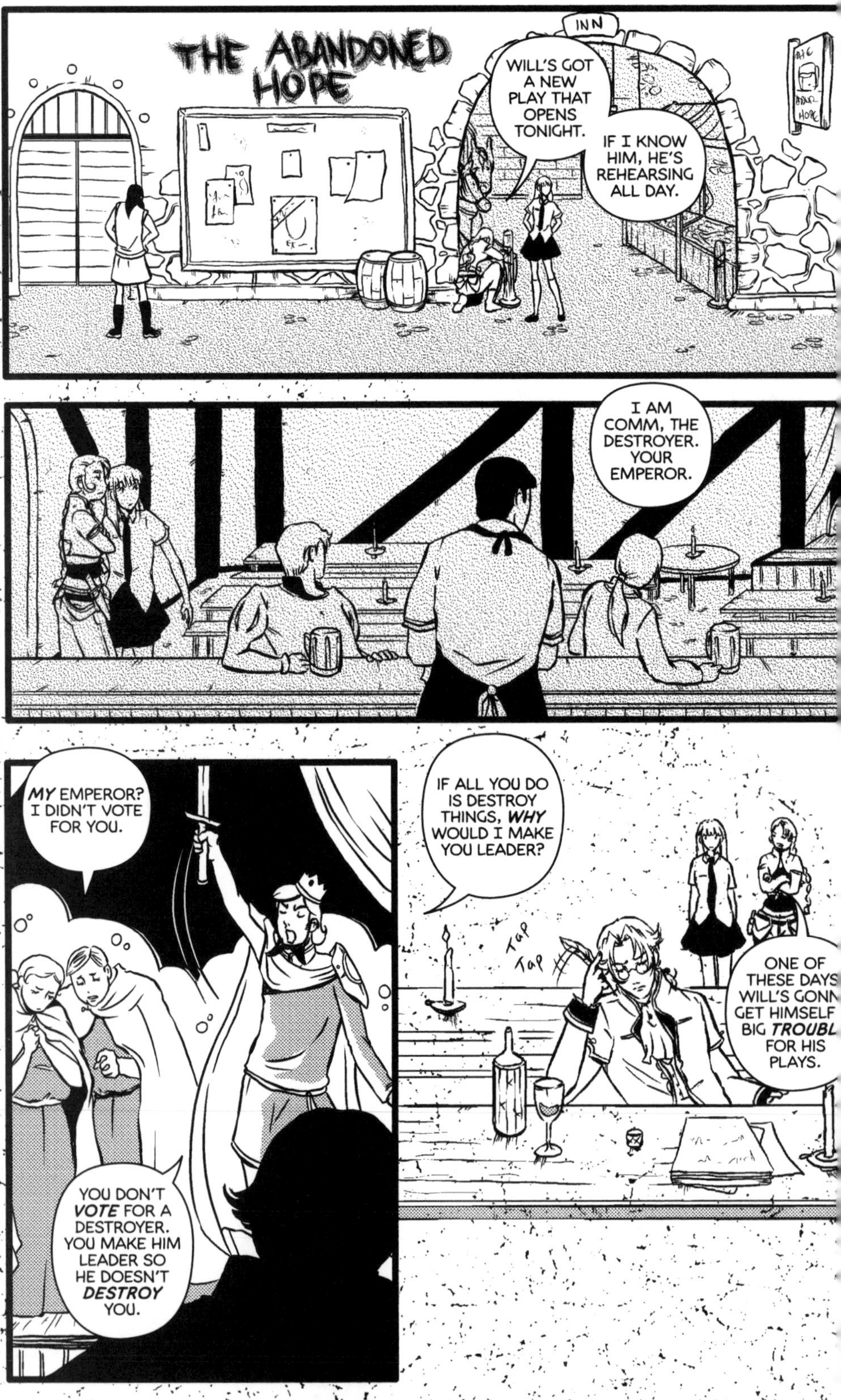
THE ABANDONED HOPE
INN
WILL'S GOT A NEW PLAY THAT OPENS TONIGHT.
IF I KNOW HIM, HE'S REHEARSING ALL DAY.
I AM COMM, THE DESTROYER. YOUR EMPEROR.
MY EMPEROR? I DIDN'T VOTE FOR YOU.
IF ALL YOU DO IS DESTROY THINGS, WHY WOULD I MAKE YOU LEADER?
TAP TAP
ONE OF THESE DAYS WILL'S GONN GET HIMSELF BIG TROUBL FOR HIS PLAYS.
YOU DON'T VOTE FOR A DESTROYER. YOU MAKE HIM LEADER SO HE DOESN'T DESTROY YOU.

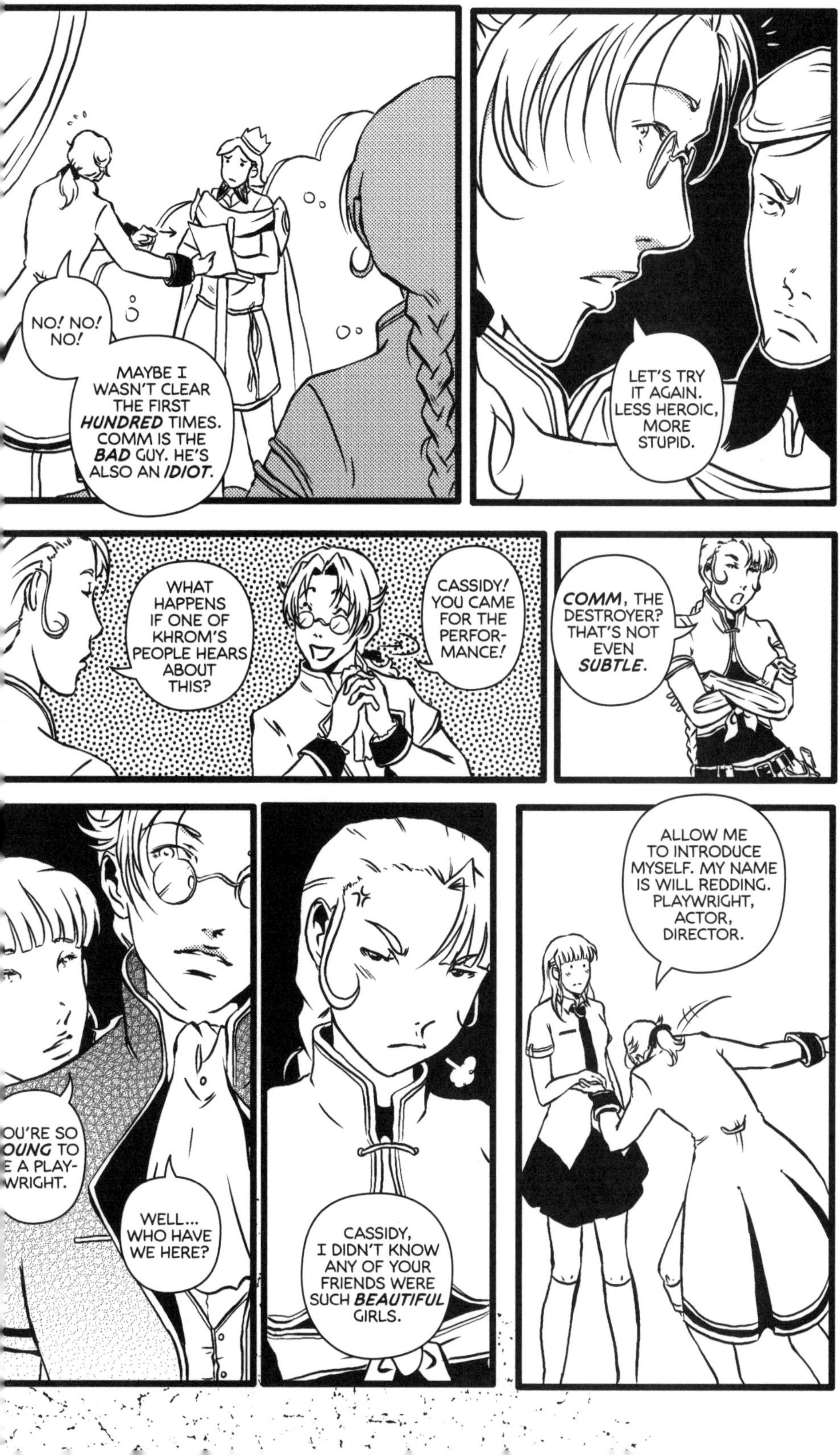

NO! NO! NO!
MAYBE I WASN'T CLEAR THE FIRST **HUNDRED** TIMES. COMM IS THE **BAD** GUY. HE'S ALSO AN ***IDIOT***.
LET'S TRY IT AGAIN. LESS HEROIC, MORE STUPID.
WHAT HAPPENS IF ONE OF KHROM'S PEOPLE HEARS ABOUT THIS?
CASSIDY! YOU CAME FOR THE PERFOR-MANCE!
COMM, THE DESTROYER? THAT'S NOT EVEN ***SUBTLE***.
OU'RE SO ***OUNG*** TO E A PLAY-WRIGHT.
WELL... WHO HAVE WE HERE?
CASSIDY, I DIDN'T KNOW ANY OF YOUR FRIENDS WERE SUCH ***BEAUTIFUL*** GIRLS.
ALLOW ME TO INTRODUCE MYSELF. MY NAME IS WILL REDDING. PLAYWRIGHT, ACTOR, DIRECTOR.

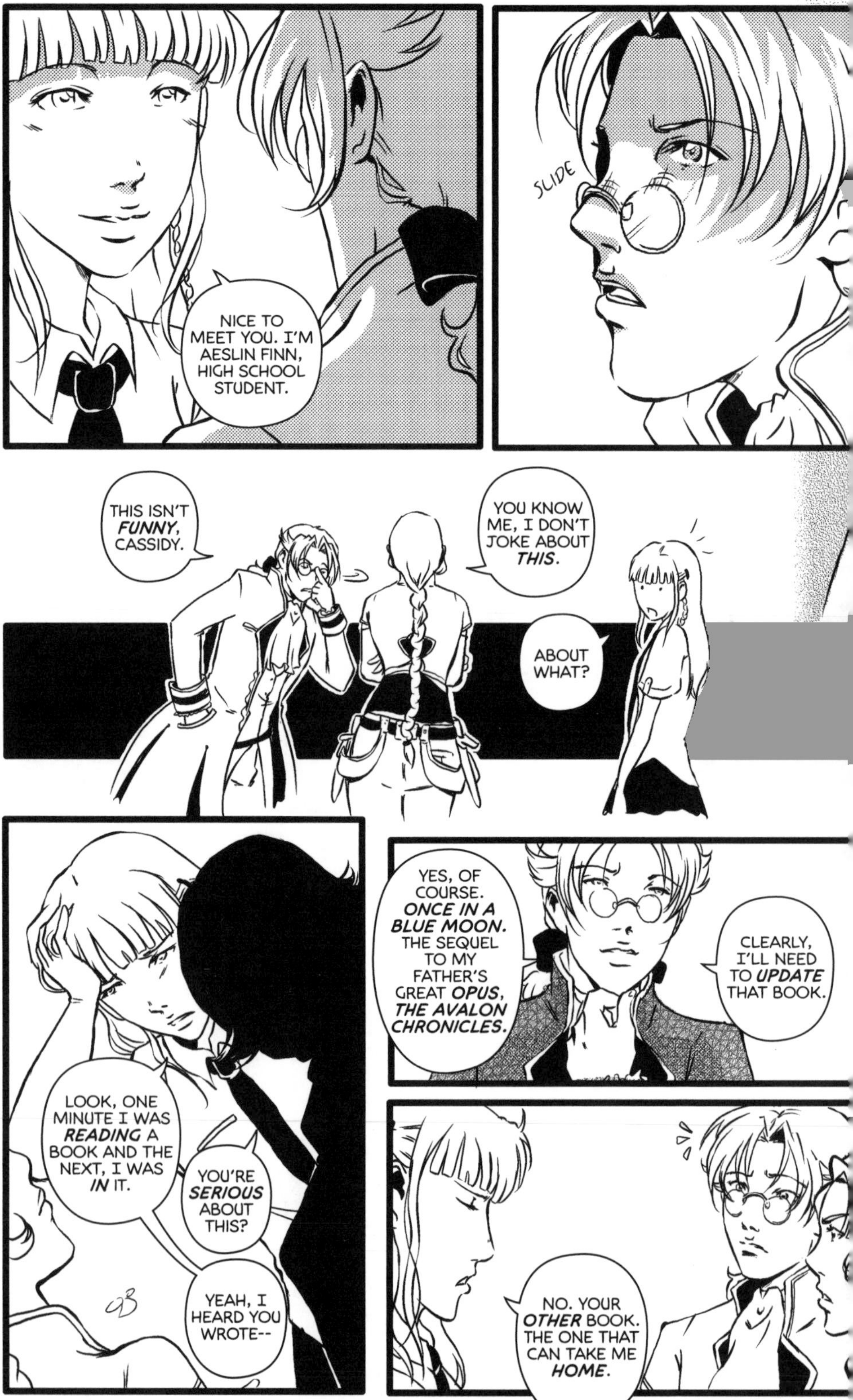

NICE TO MEET YOU. I'M AESLIN FINN, HIGH SCHOOL STUDENT.
SLIDE
THIS ISN'T *FUNNY*, CASSIDY.
YOU KNOW ME, I DON'T JOKE ABOUT *THIS*.
ABOUT WHAT?
LOOK, ONE MINUTE I WAS *READING* A BOOK AND THE NEXT, I WAS *IN* IT.
YOU'RE *SERIOUS* ABOUT THIS?
YEAH, I HEARD YOU WROTE--
YES, OF COURSE. ***ONCE IN A BLUE MOON.*** THE SEQUEL TO MY FATHER'S GREAT ***OPUS, THE AVALON CHRONICLES.***
CLEARLY, I'LL NEED TO *UPDATE* THAT BOOK.
NO. YOUR *OTHER* BOOK. THE ONE THAT CAN TAKE ME *HOME*.

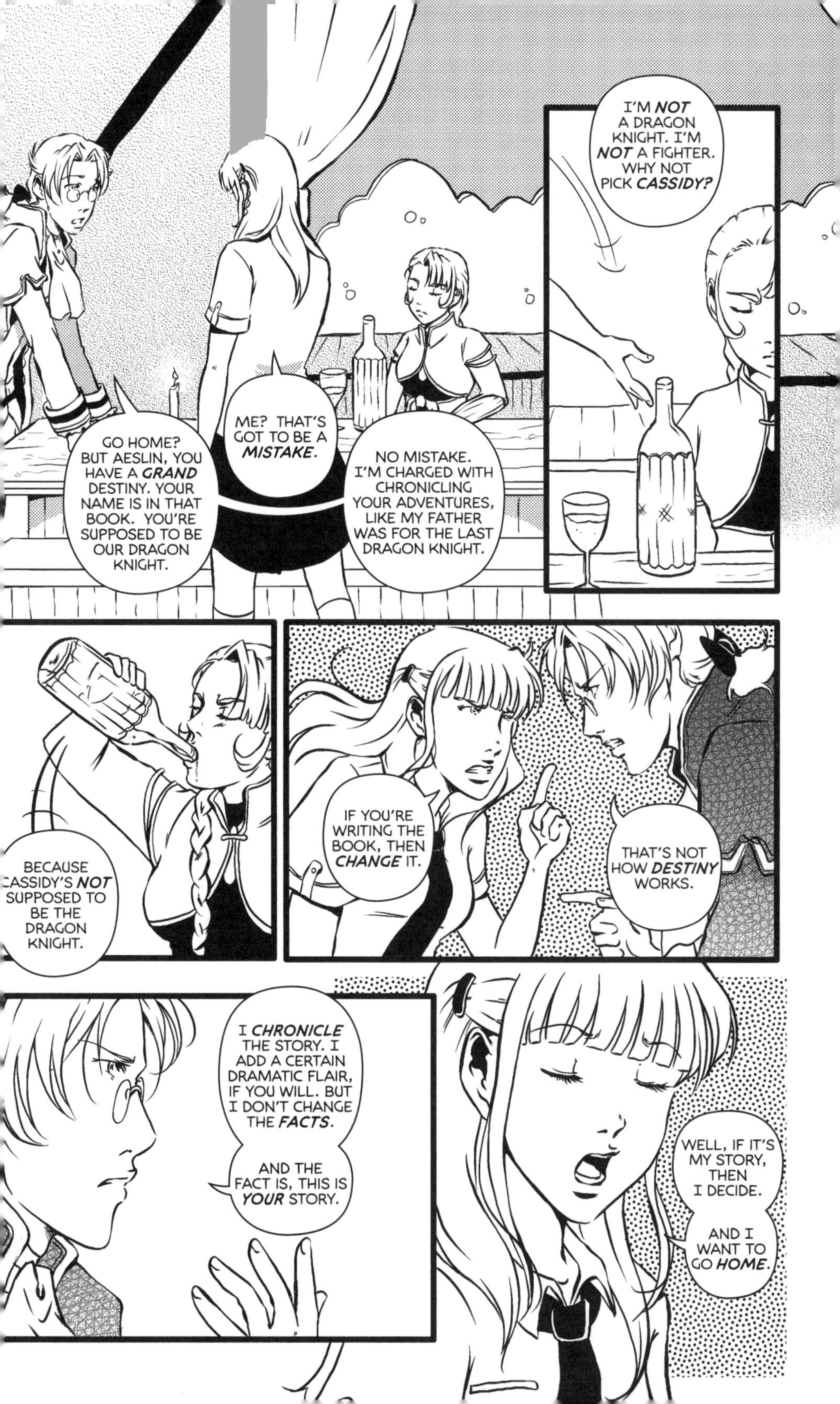
GO HOME? BUT AESLIN, YOU HAVE A *GRAND* DESTINY. YOUR NAME IS IN THAT BOOK. YOU'RE SUPPOSED TO BE OUR DRAGON KNIGHT.
ME? THAT'S GOT TO BE A *MISTAKE*.
NO MISTAKE. I'M CHARGED WITH CHRONICLING YOUR ADVENTURES, LIKE MY FATHER WAS FOR THE LAST DRAGON KNIGHT.
I'M *NOT* A DRAGON KNIGHT. I'M *NOT* A FIGHTER. WHY NOT PICK *CASSIDY?*
BECAUSE CASSIDY'S *NOT* SUPPOSED TO BE THE DRAGON KNIGHT.
IF YOU'RE WRITING THE BOOK, THEN *CHANGE* IT.
THAT'S NOT HOW *DESTINY* WORKS.
I *CHRONICLE* THE STORY. I ADD A CERTAIN DRAMATIC FLAIR, IF YOU WILL. BUT I DON'T CHANGE THE *FACTS*.
AND THE FACT IS, THIS IS *YOUR* STORY.
WELL, IF IT'S MY STORY, THEN I DECIDE.
AND I WANT TO GO *HOME*.

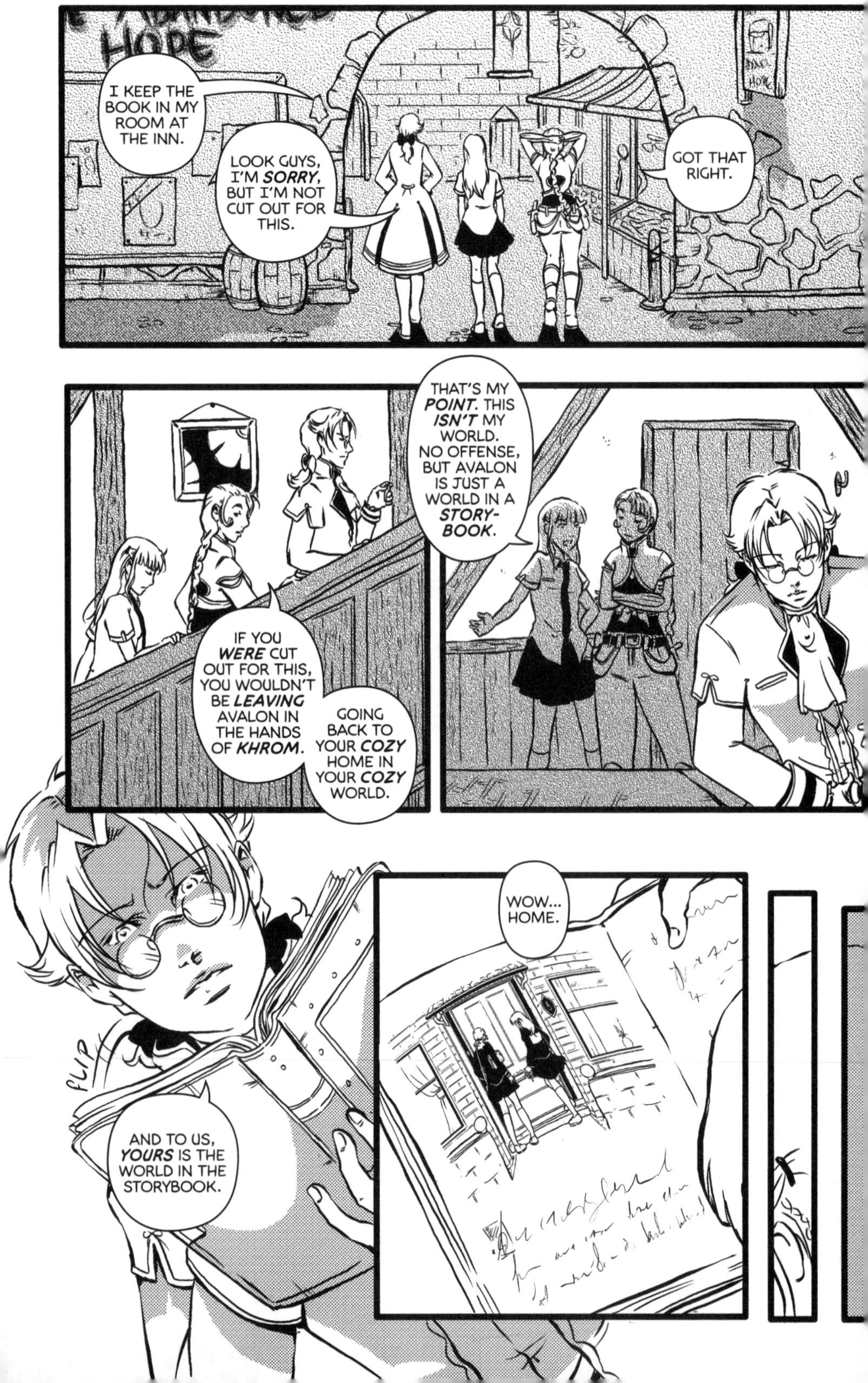
HOPE
I KEEP THE BOOK IN MY ROOM AT THE INN.
LOOK GUYS, I'M *SORRY*, BUT I'M NOT CUT OUT FOR THIS.
GOT THAT RIGHT.
THAT'S MY *POINT*. THIS *ISN'T* MY WORLD. NO OFFENSE, BUT AVALON IS JUST A WORLD IN A *STORY-BOOK*.
IF YOU *WERE* CUT OUT FOR THIS, YOU WOULDN'T BE *LEAVING* AVALON IN THE HANDS OF *KHROM*.
GOING BACK TO YOUR *COZY* HOME IN YOUR *COZY* WORLD.
FLIP
AND TO US, *YOURS* IS THE WORLD IN THE STORYBOOK.
WOW... HOME.

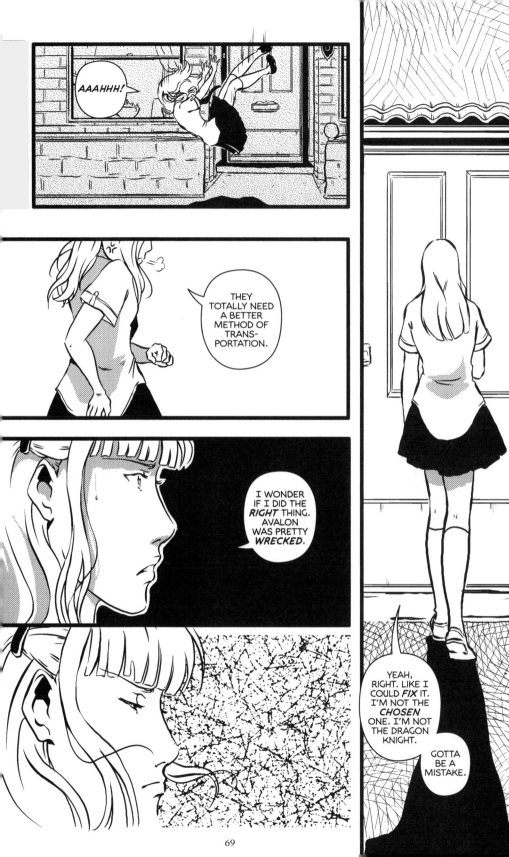

AAAHHH!

THEY TOTALLY NEED A BETTER METHOD OF TRANS-PORTATION.

I WONDER IF I DID THE *RIGHT* THING. AVALON WAS PRETTY *WRECKED*.

YEAH, RIGHT. LIKE I COULD *FIX* IT. I'M NOT THE *CHOSEN* ONE. I'M NOT THE DRAGON KNIGHT.

GOTTA BE A MISTAKE.

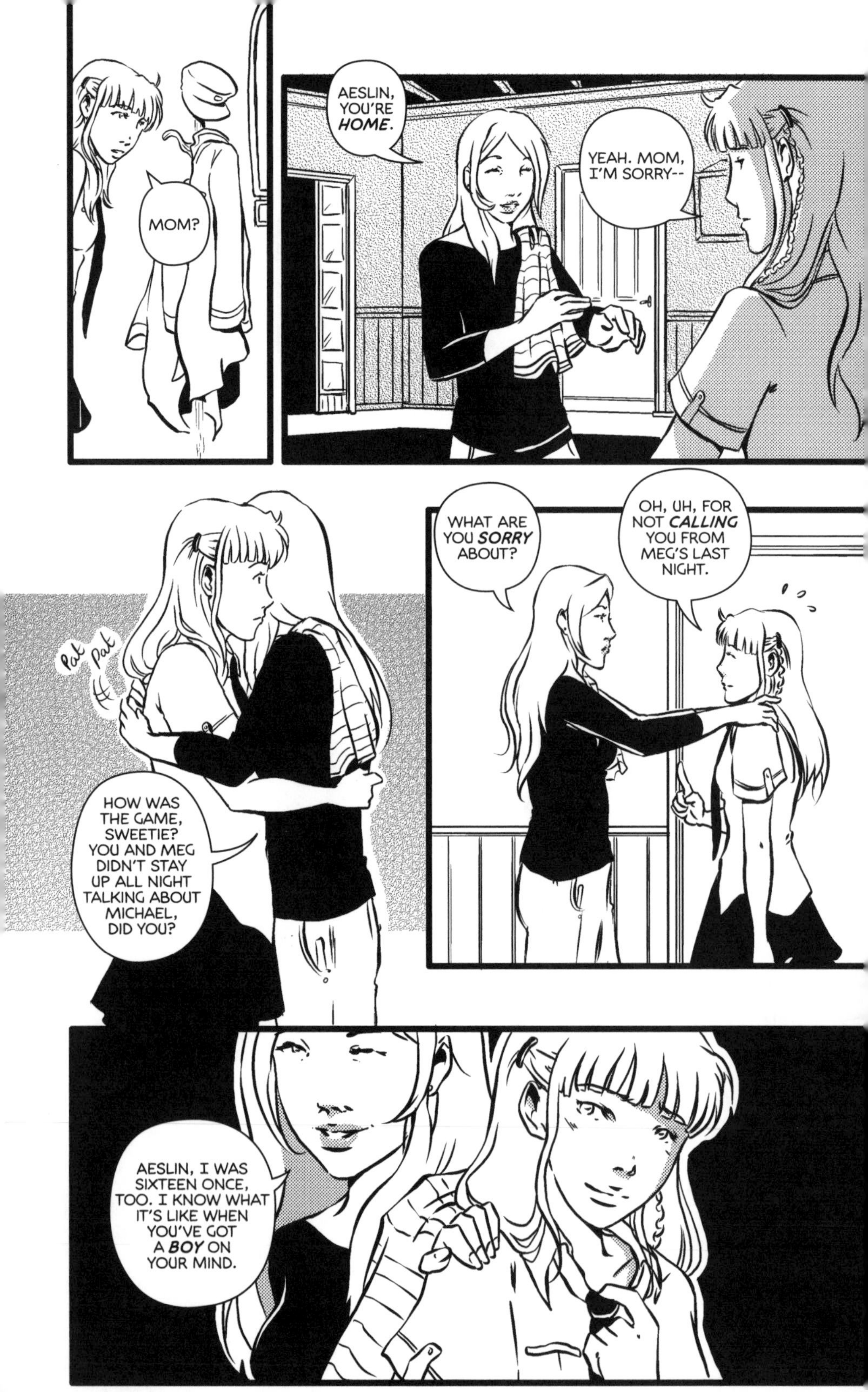
MOM?
AESLIN, YOU'RE HOME.
YEAH. MOM, I'M SORRY--
WHAT ARE YOU SORRY ABOUT?
OH, UH, FOR NOT CALLING YOU FROM MEG'S LAST NIGHT.
Pat Pat
HOW WAS THE GAME, SWEETIE? YOU AND MEG DIDN'T STAY UP ALL NIGHT TALKING ABOUT MICHAEL, DID YOU?
AESLIN, I WAS SIXTEEN ONCE, TOO. I KNOW WHAT IT'S LIKE WHEN YOU'VE GOT A BOY ON YOUR MIND.

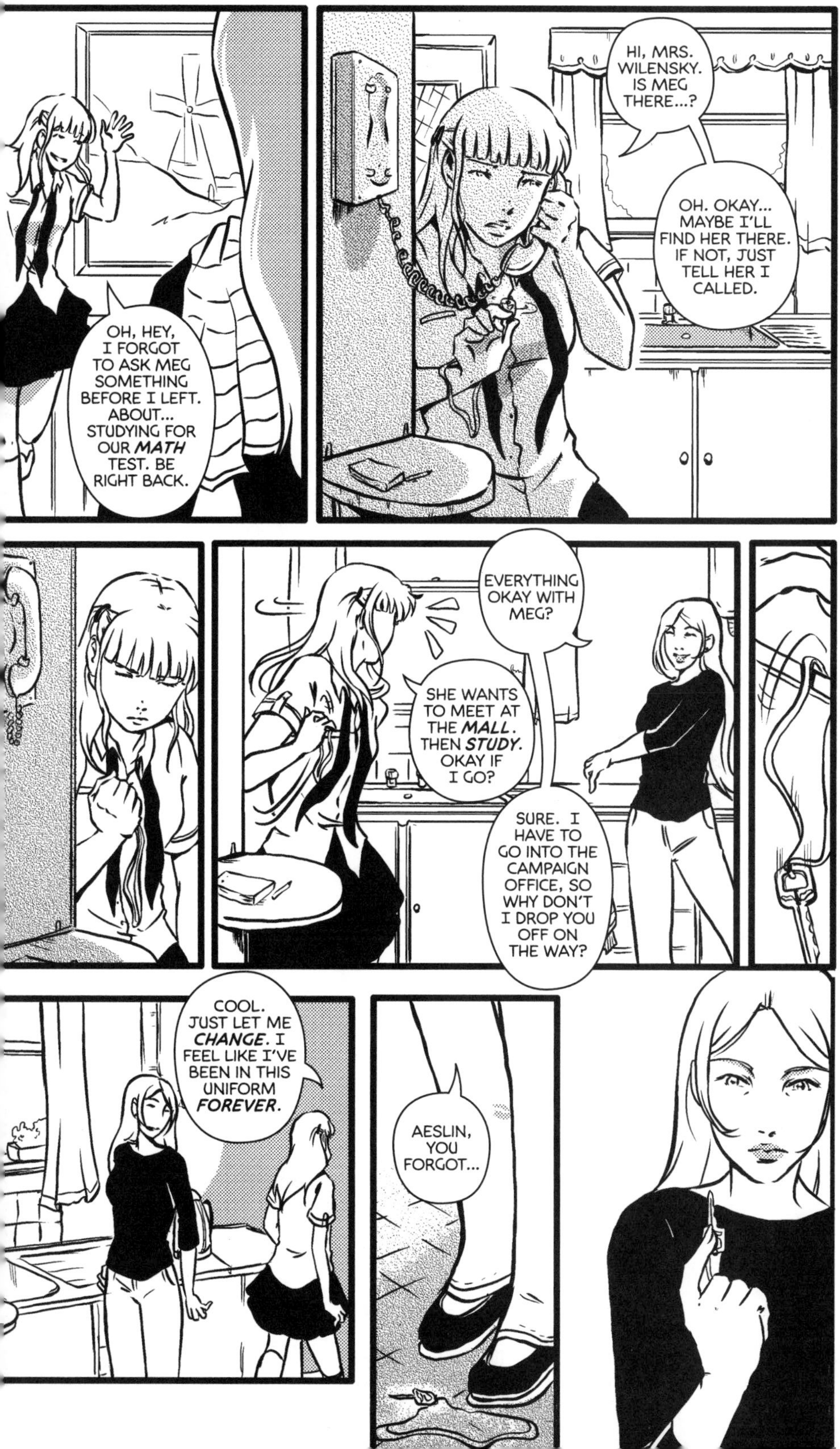
OH, HEY, I FORGOT TO ASK MEG SOMETHING BEFORE I LEFT. ABOUT... STUDYING FOR OUR MATH TEST. BE RIGHT BACK.
HI, MRS. WILENSKY. IS MEG THERE...?
OH. OKAY... MAYBE I'LL FIND HER THERE. IF NOT, JUST TELL HER I CALLED.
EVERYTHING OKAY WITH MEG?
SHE WANTS TO MEET AT THE MALL. THEN STUDY. OKAY IF I GO?
SURE. I HAVE TO GO INTO THE CAMPAIGN OFFICE, SO WHY DON'T I DROP YOU OFF ON THE WAY?
COOL. JUST LET ME CHANGE. I FEEL LIKE I'VE BEEN IN THIS UNIFORM FOREVER.
AESLIN, YOU FORGOT...

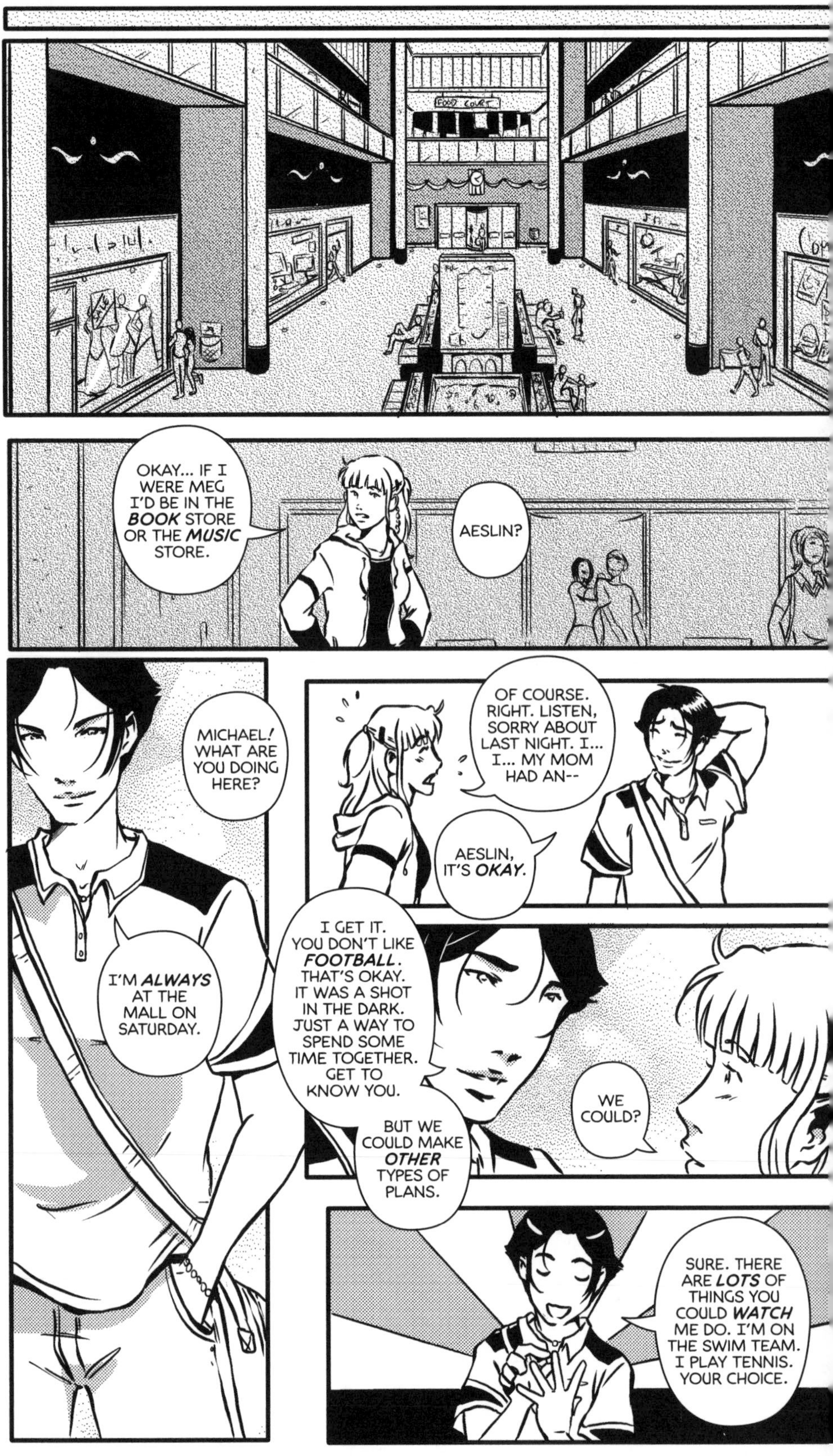
FOOD COURT
OKAY... IF I WERE MEG I'D BE IN THE BOOK STORE OR THE MUSIC STORE.
AESLIN?
MICHAEL! WHAT ARE YOU DOING HERE?
I'M ALWAYS AT THE MALL ON SATURDAY.
OF COURSE. RIGHT. LISTEN, SORRY ABOUT LAST NIGHT. I... I... MY MOM HAD AN--
AESLIN, IT'S OKAY.
I GET IT. YOU DON'T LIKE FOOTBALL. THAT'S OKAY. IT WAS A SHOT IN THE DARK. JUST A WAY TO SPEND SOME TIME TOGETHER. GET TO KNOW YOU.
BUT WE COULD MAKE OTHER TYPES OF PLANS.
WE COULD?
SURE. THERE ARE LOTS OF THINGS YOU COULD WATCH ME DO. I'M ON THE SWIM TEAM. I PLAY TENNIS. YOUR CHOICE.

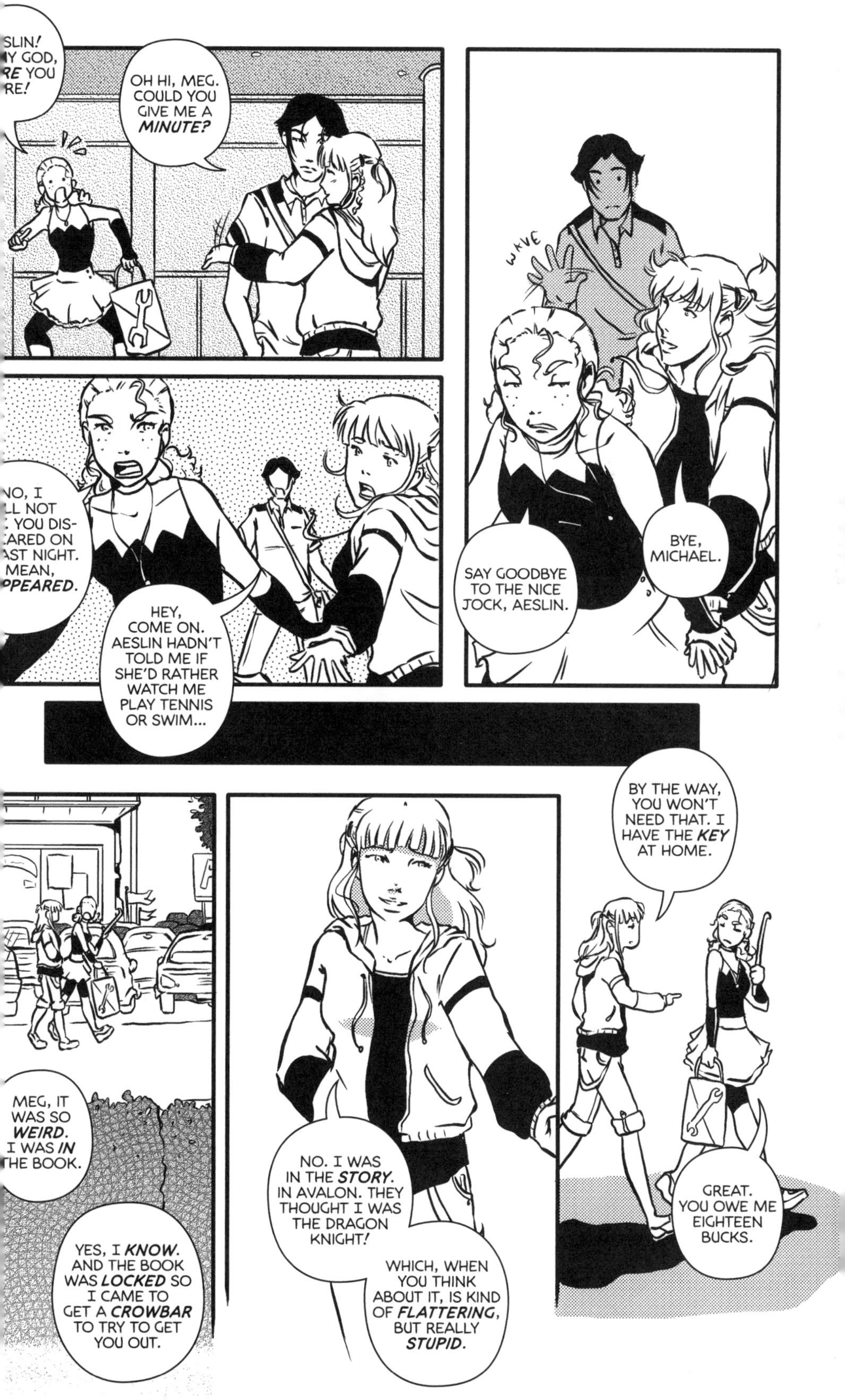
SLIN! Y GOD, RE YOU RE!
OH HI, MEG. COULD YOU GIVE ME A ***MINUTE?***
WAVE
NO, I LL NOT YOU DIS- ARED ON AST NIGHT. MEAN, PPEARED.
HEY, COME ON. AESLIN HADN'T TOLD ME IF SHE'D RATHER WATCH ME PLAY TENNIS OR SWIM...
SAY GOODBYE TO THE NICE JOCK, AESLIN.
BYE, MICHAEL.
MEG, IT WAS SO ***WEIRD.*** I WAS ***IN*** THE BOOK.
YES, I ***KNOW.*** AND THE BOOK WAS ***LOCKED*** SO I CAME TO GET A ***CROWBAR*** TO TRY TO GET YOU OUT.
NO. I WAS IN THE ***STORY.*** IN AVALON. THEY THOUGHT I WAS THE DRAGON KNIGHT!
WHICH, WHEN YOU THINK ABOUT IT, IS KIND OF ***FLATTERING,*** BUT REALLY ***STUPID.***
BY THE WAY, YOU WON'T NEED THAT. I HAVE THE ***KEY*** AT HOME.
GREAT. YOU OWE ME EIGHTEEN BUCKS.

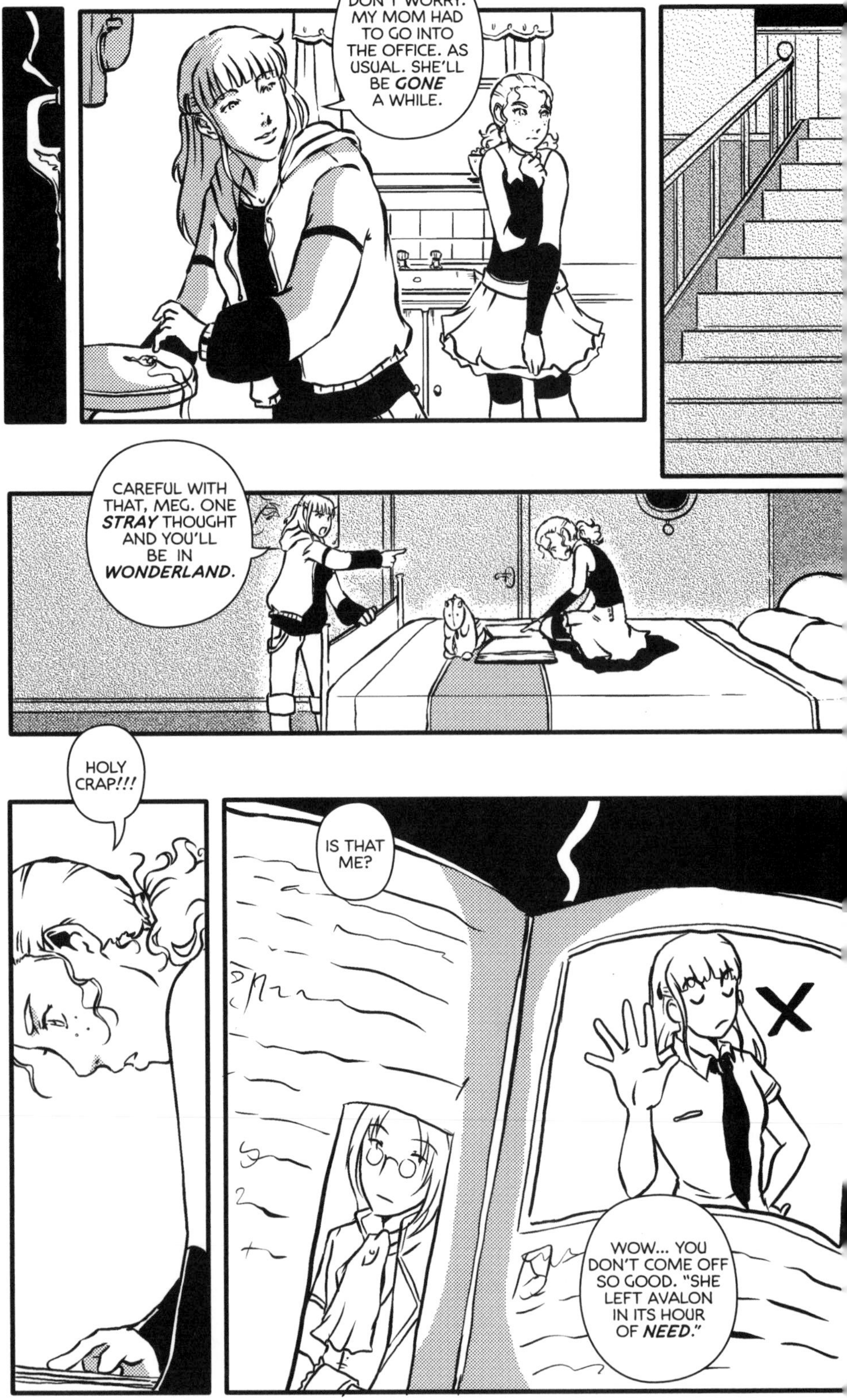
DON'T WORRY. MY MOM HAD TO GO INTO THE OFFICE. AS USUAL. SHE'LL BE GONE A WHILE.
CAREFUL WITH THAT, MEG. ONE STRAY THOUGHT AND YOU'LL BE IN WONDERLAND.
HOLY CRAP!!!
IS THAT ME?
WOW... YOU DON'T COME OFF SO GOOD. "SHE LEFT AVALON IN ITS HOUR OF NEED."

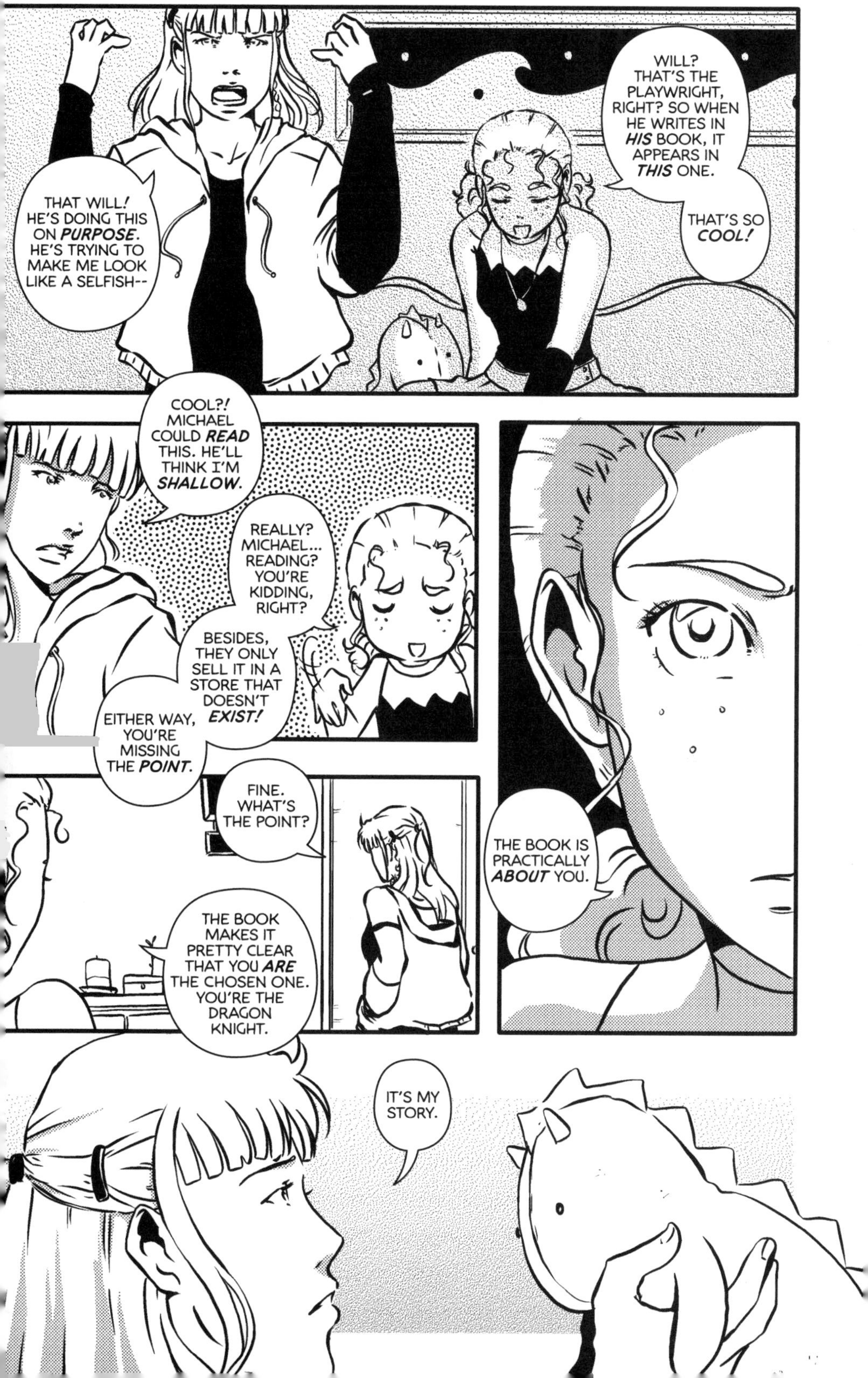
THAT WILL! HE'S DOING THIS ON PURPOSE. HE'S TRYING TO MAKE ME LOOK LIKE A SELFISH--
WILL? THAT'S THE PLAYWRIGHT, RIGHT? SO WHEN HE WRITES IN HIS BOOK, IT APPEARS IN THIS ONE.
THAT'S SO COOL!
COOL?! MICHAEL COULD READ THIS. HE'LL THINK I'M SHALLOW.
REALLY? MICHAEL... READING? YOU'RE KIDDING, RIGHT?
BESIDES, THEY ONLY SELL IT IN A STORE THAT DOESN'T EXIST!
EITHER WAY, YOU'RE MISSING THE POINT.
THE BOOK IS PRACTICALLY ABOUT YOU.
FINE. WHAT'S THE POINT?
THE BOOK MAKES IT PRETTY CLEAR THAT YOU ARE THE CHOSEN ONE. YOU'RE THE DRAGON KNIGHT.
IT'S MY STORY.

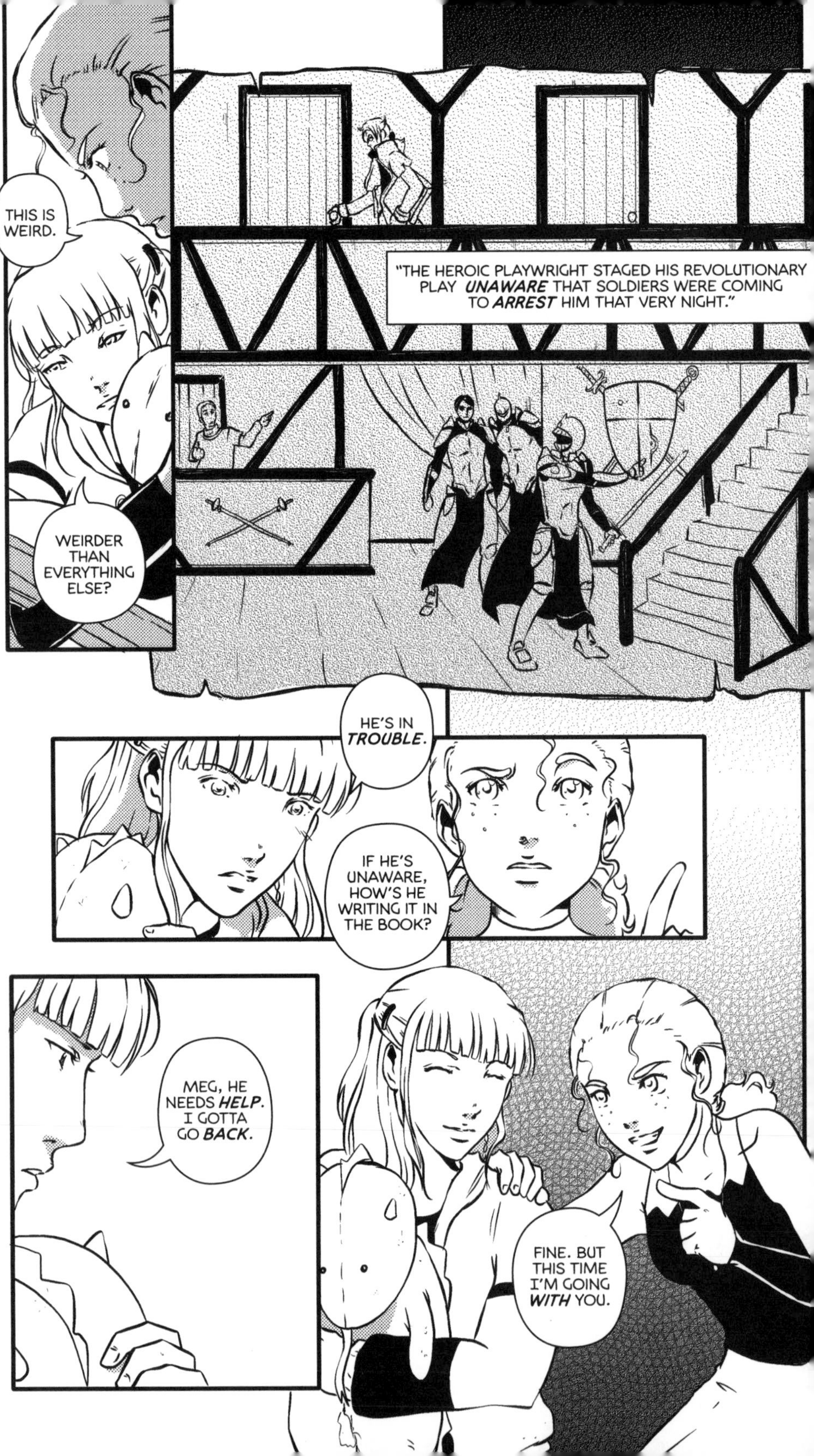
THIS IS WEIRD.
WEIRDER THAN EVERYTHING ELSE?
"THE HEROIC PLAYWRIGHT STAGED HIS REVOLUTIONARY PLAY UNAWARE THAT SOLDIERS WERE COMING TO ARREST HIM THAT VERY NIGHT."
HE'S IN TROUBLE.
IF HE'S UNAWARE, HOW'S HE WRITING IT IN THE BOOK?
MEG, HE NEEDS HELP. I GOTTA GO BACK.
FINE. BUT THIS TIME I'M GOING WITH YOU.

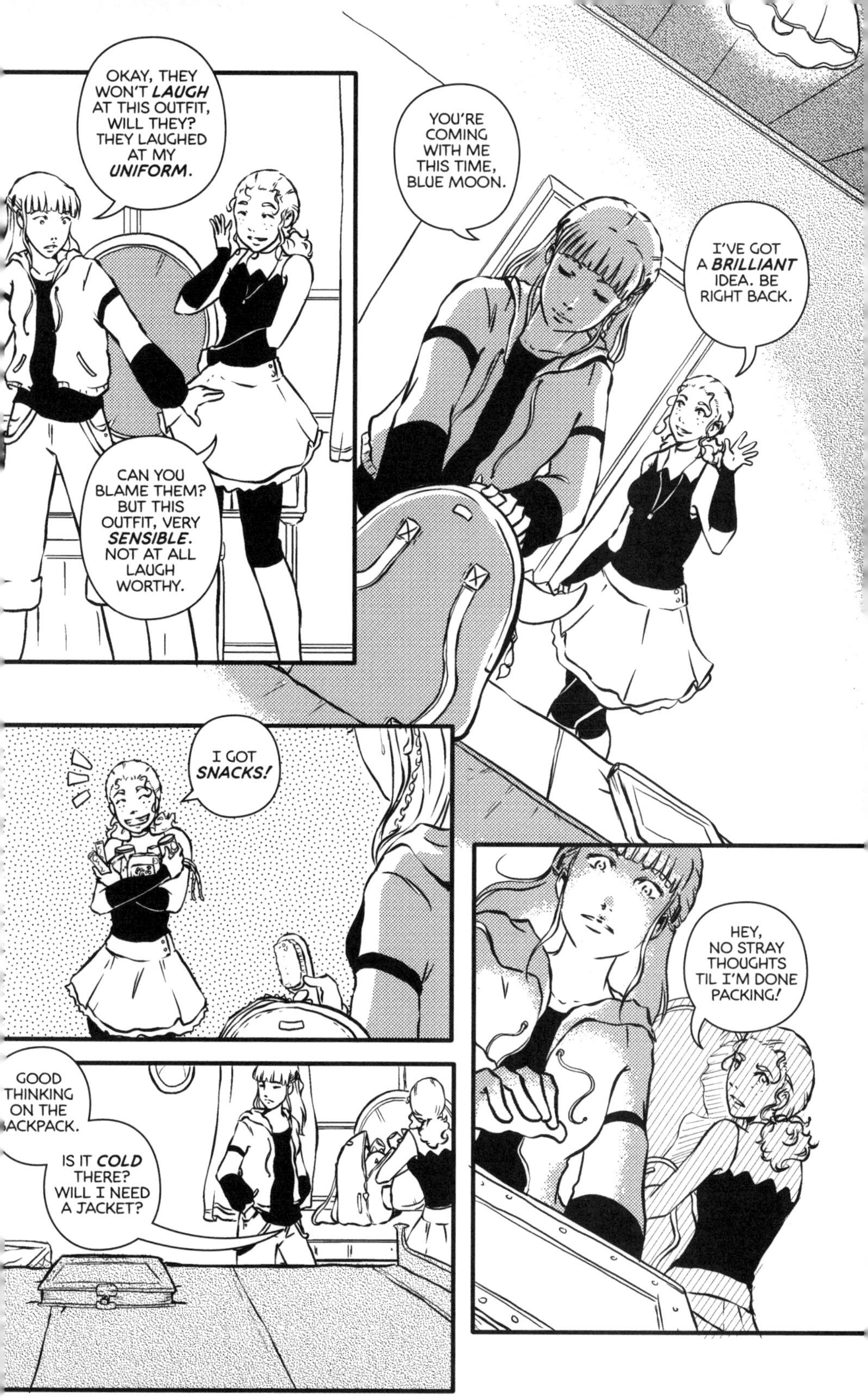
OKAY, THEY WON'T LAUGH AT THIS OUTFIT, WILL THEY? THEY LAUGHED AT MY UNIFORM.
CAN YOU BLAME THEM? BUT THIS OUTFIT, VERY SENSIBLE. NOT AT ALL LAUGH WORTHY.
YOU'RE COMING WITH ME THIS TIME, BLUE MOON.
I'VE GOT A BRILLIANT IDEA. BE RIGHT BACK.
I GOT SNACKS!
GOOD THINKING ON THE BACKPACK.
IS IT COLD THERE? WILL I NEED A JACKET?
HEY, NO STRAY THOUGHTS TIL I'M DONE PACKING!

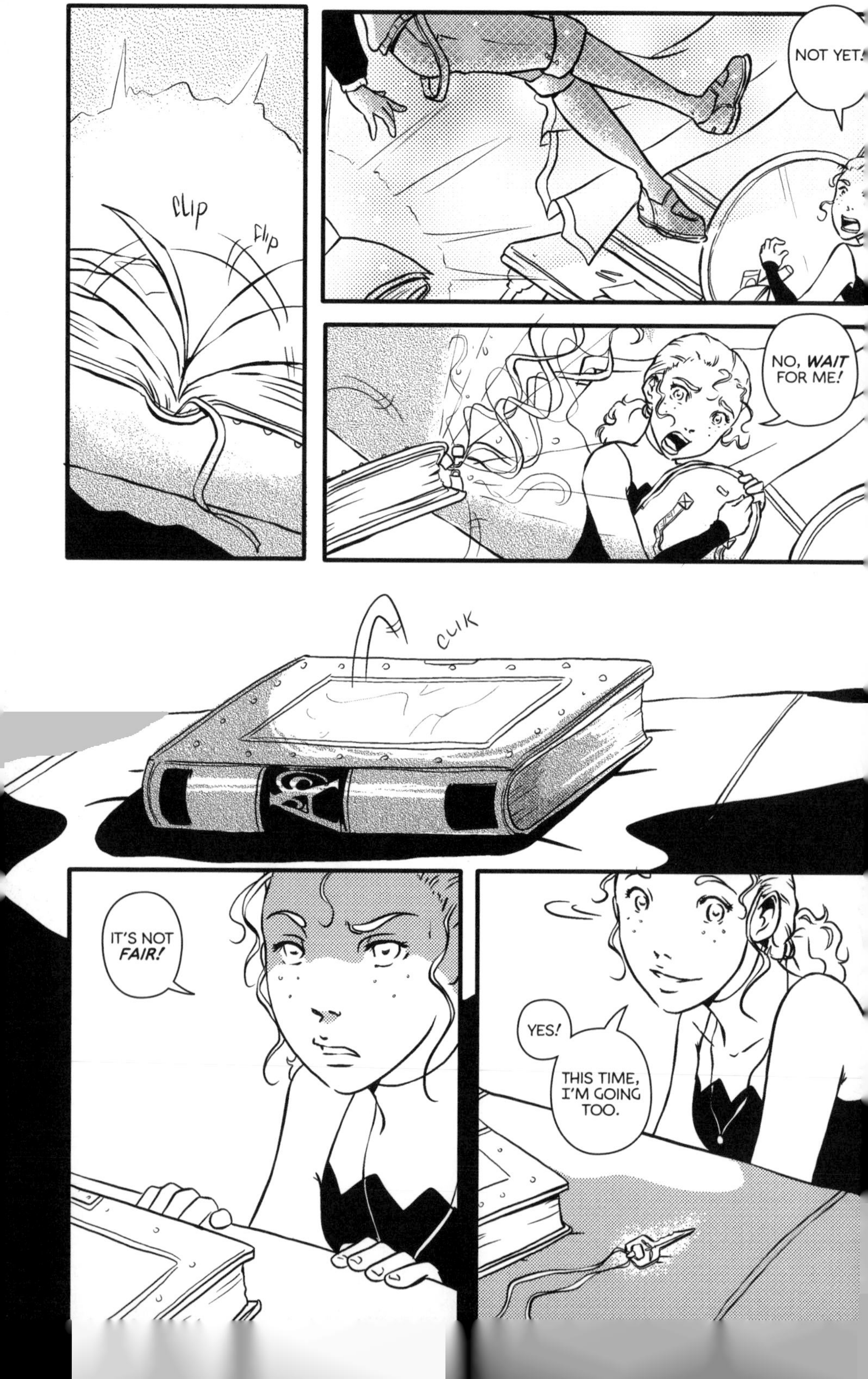

CLIP
CLIP
NOT YET!
NO, WAIT FOR ME!
CLIK
IT'S NOT FAIR!
YES!
THIS TIME, I'M GOING TOO.

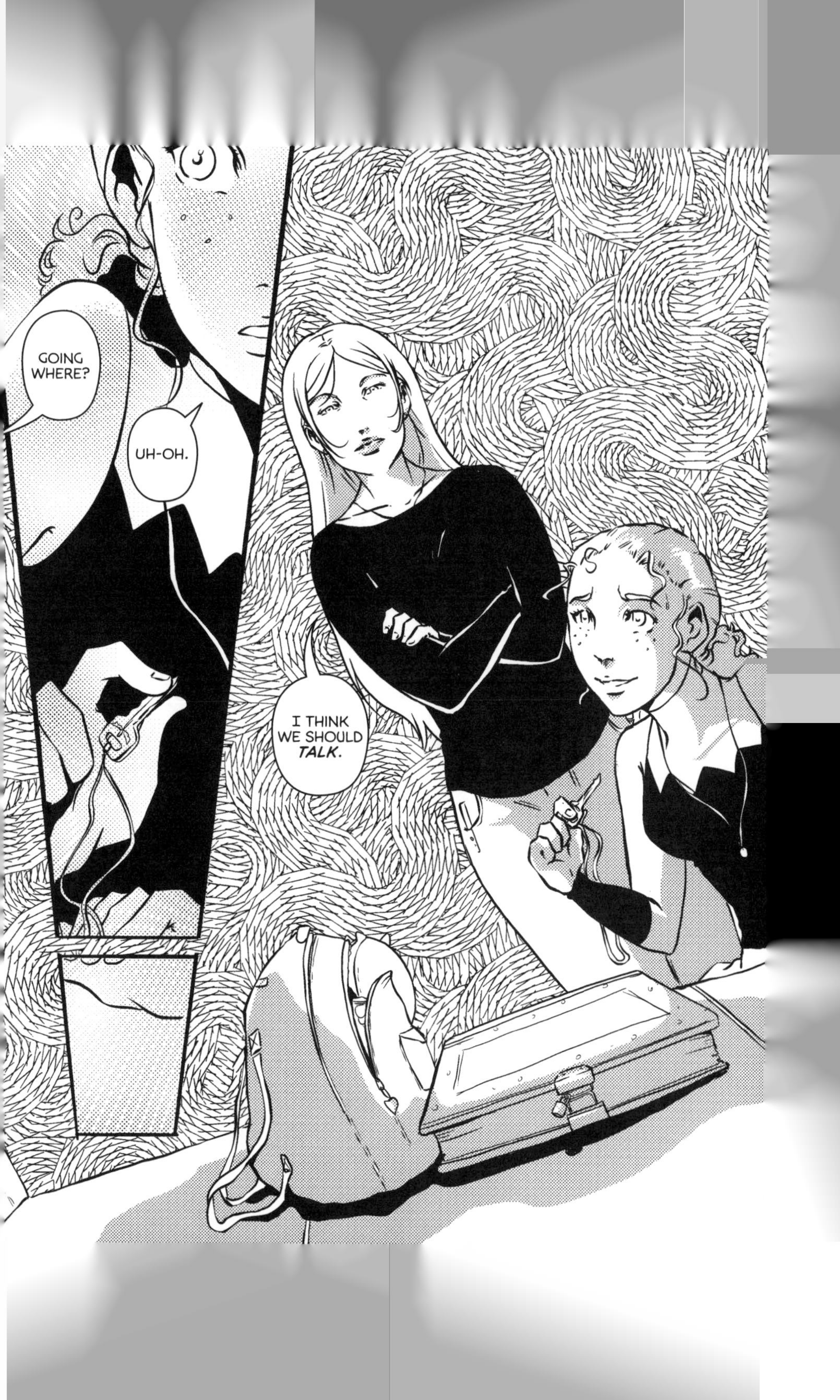
GOING WHERE?
UH-OH.
I THINK WE SHOULD *TALK*.

Chapter 4

The Chosen One

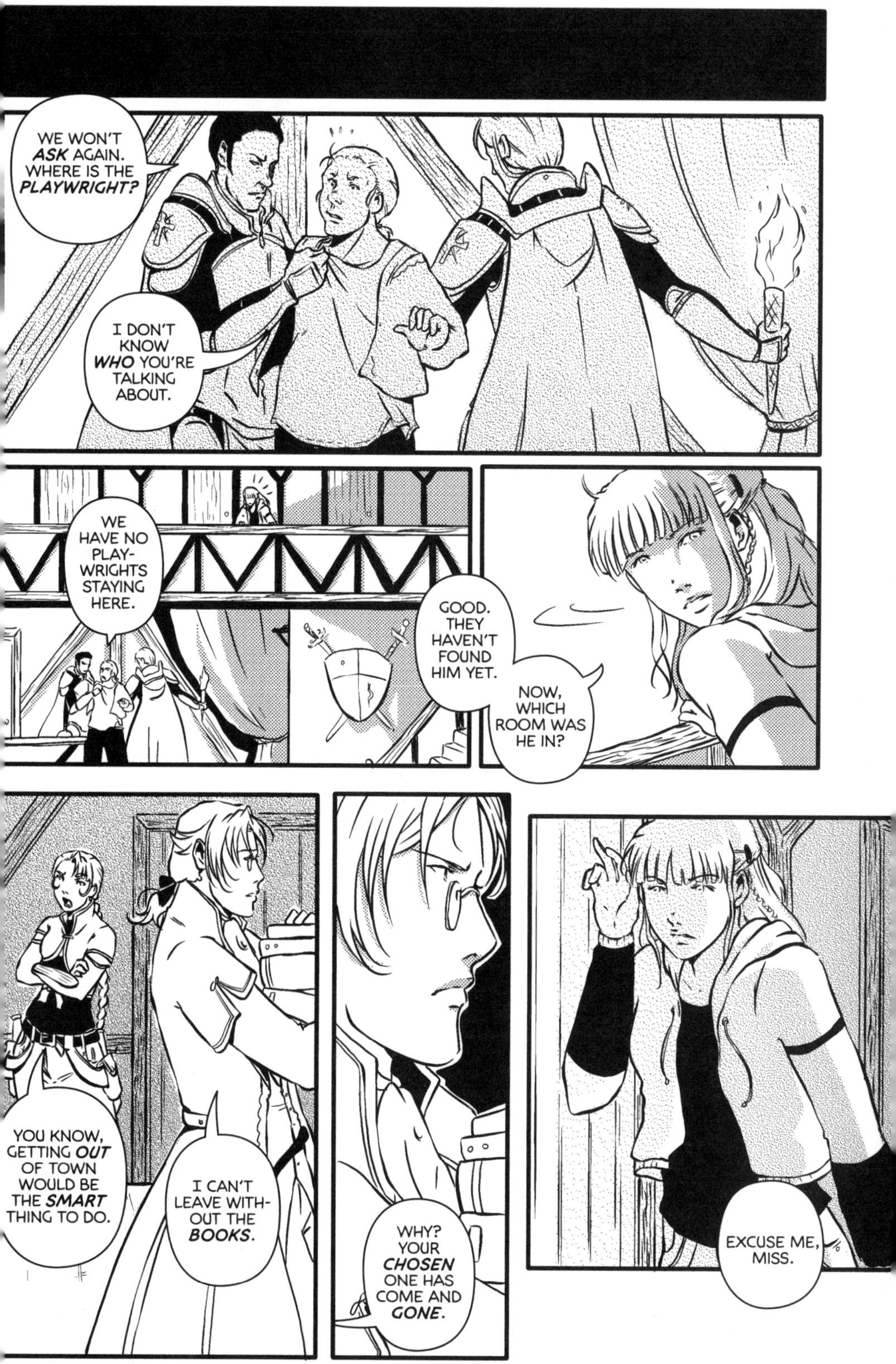

WE WON'T ASK AGAIN. WHERE IS THE PLAYWRIGHT?
I DON'T KNOW WHO YOU'RE TALKING ABOUT.
WE HAVE NO PLAY-WRIGHTS STAYING HERE.
GOOD. THEY HAVEN'T FOUND HIM YET.
NOW, WHICH ROOM WAS HE IN?
YOU KNOW, GETTING OUT OF TOWN WOULD BE THE SMART THING TO DO.
I CAN'T LEAVE WITH-OUT THE BOOKS.
WHY? YOUR CHOSEN ONE HAS COME AND GONE.
EXCUSE ME, MISS.

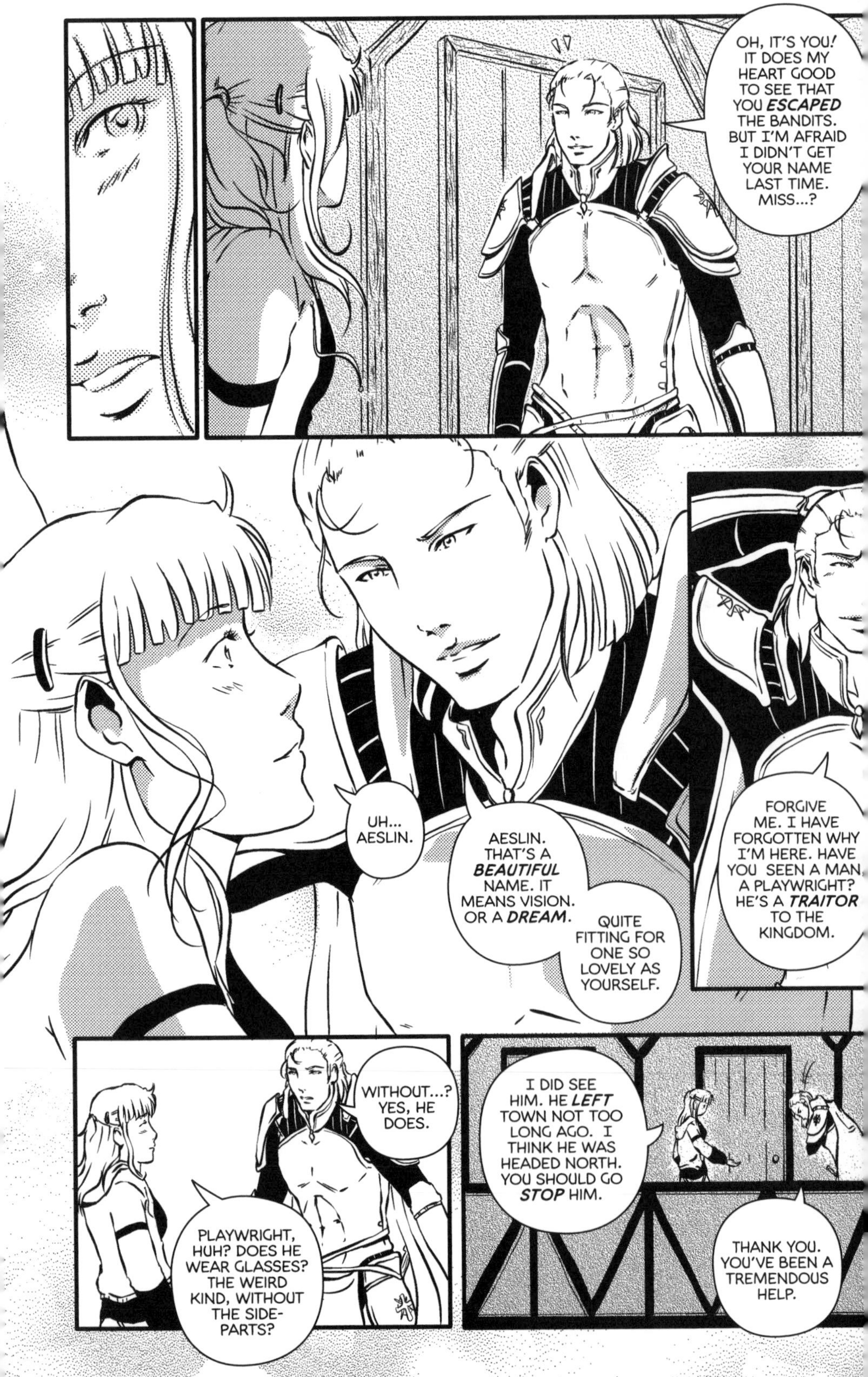
OH, IT'S YOU! IT DOES MY HEART GOOD TO SEE THAT YOU ESCAPED THE BANDITS. BUT I'M AFRAID I DIDN'T GET YOUR NAME LAST TIME. MISS...?
UH... AESLIN.
AESLIN. THAT'S A BEAUTIFUL NAME. IT MEANS VISION. OR A DREAM.
QUITE FITTING FOR ONE SO LOVELY AS YOURSELF.
FORGIVE ME. I HAVE FORGOTTEN WHY I'M HERE. HAVE YOU SEEN A MAN A PLAYWRIGHT? HE'S A TRAITOR TO THE KINGDOM.
PLAYWRIGHT, HUH? DOES HE WEAR GLASSES? THE WEIRD KIND, WITHOUT THE SIDE-PARTS?
WITHOUT...? YES, HE DOES.
I DID SEE HIM. HE LEFT TOWN NOT TOO LONG AGO. I THINK HE WAS HEADED NORTH. YOU SHOULD GO STOP HIM.
THANK YOU. YOU'VE BEEN A TREMENDOUS HELP.

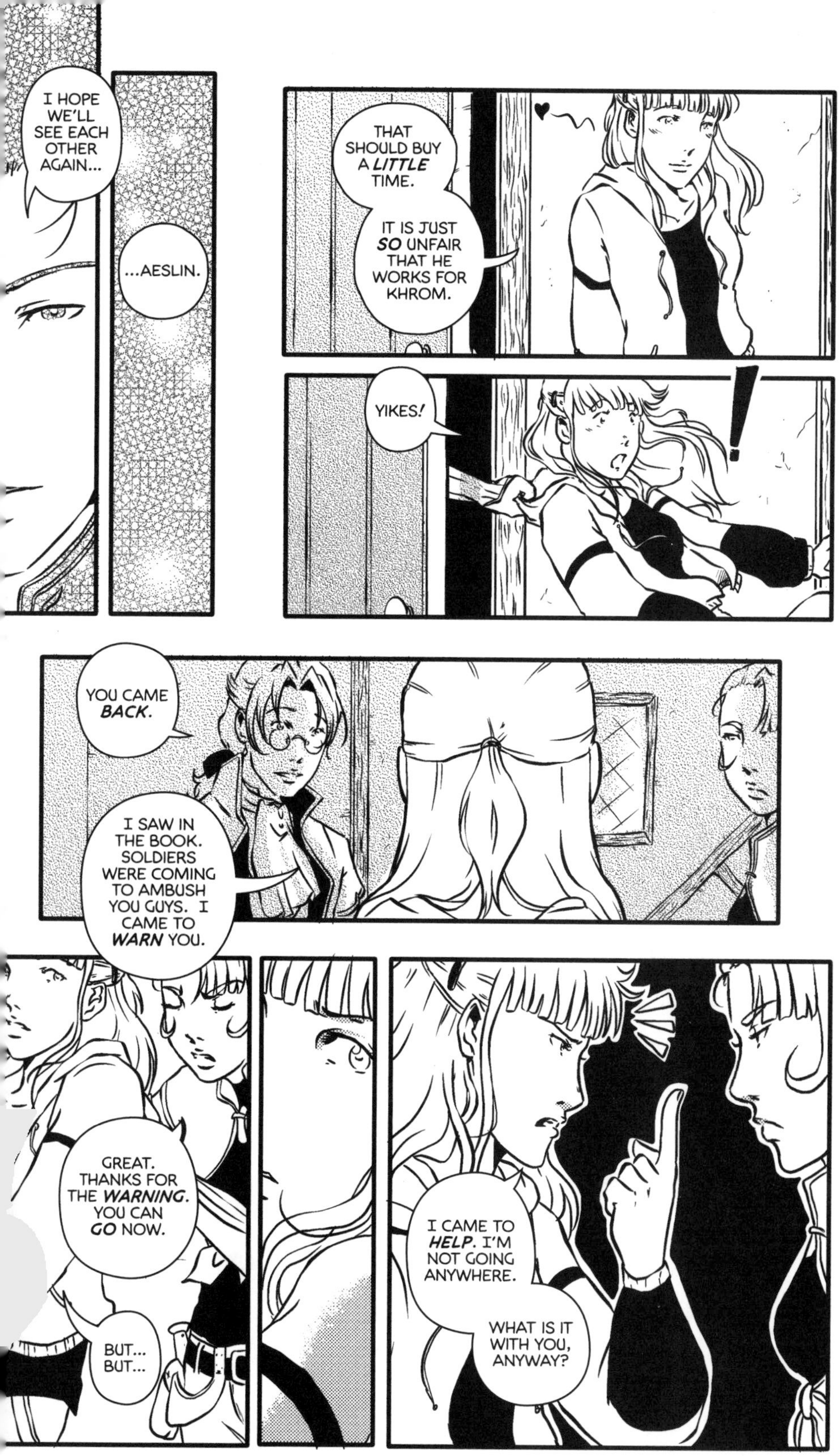
I HOPE WE'LL SEE EACH OTHER AGAIN...
...AESLIN.
THAT SHOULD BUY A LITTLE TIME.
IT IS JUST SO UNFAIR THAT HE WORKS FOR KHROM.
YIKES!
!
YOU CAME BACK.
I SAW IN THE BOOK. SOLDIERS WERE COMING TO AMBUSH YOU GUYS. I CAME TO WARN YOU.
GREAT. THANKS FOR THE WARNING. YOU CAN GO NOW.
BUT... BUT...
I CAME TO HELP. I'M NOT GOING ANYWHERE.
WHAT IS IT WITH YOU, ANYWAY?

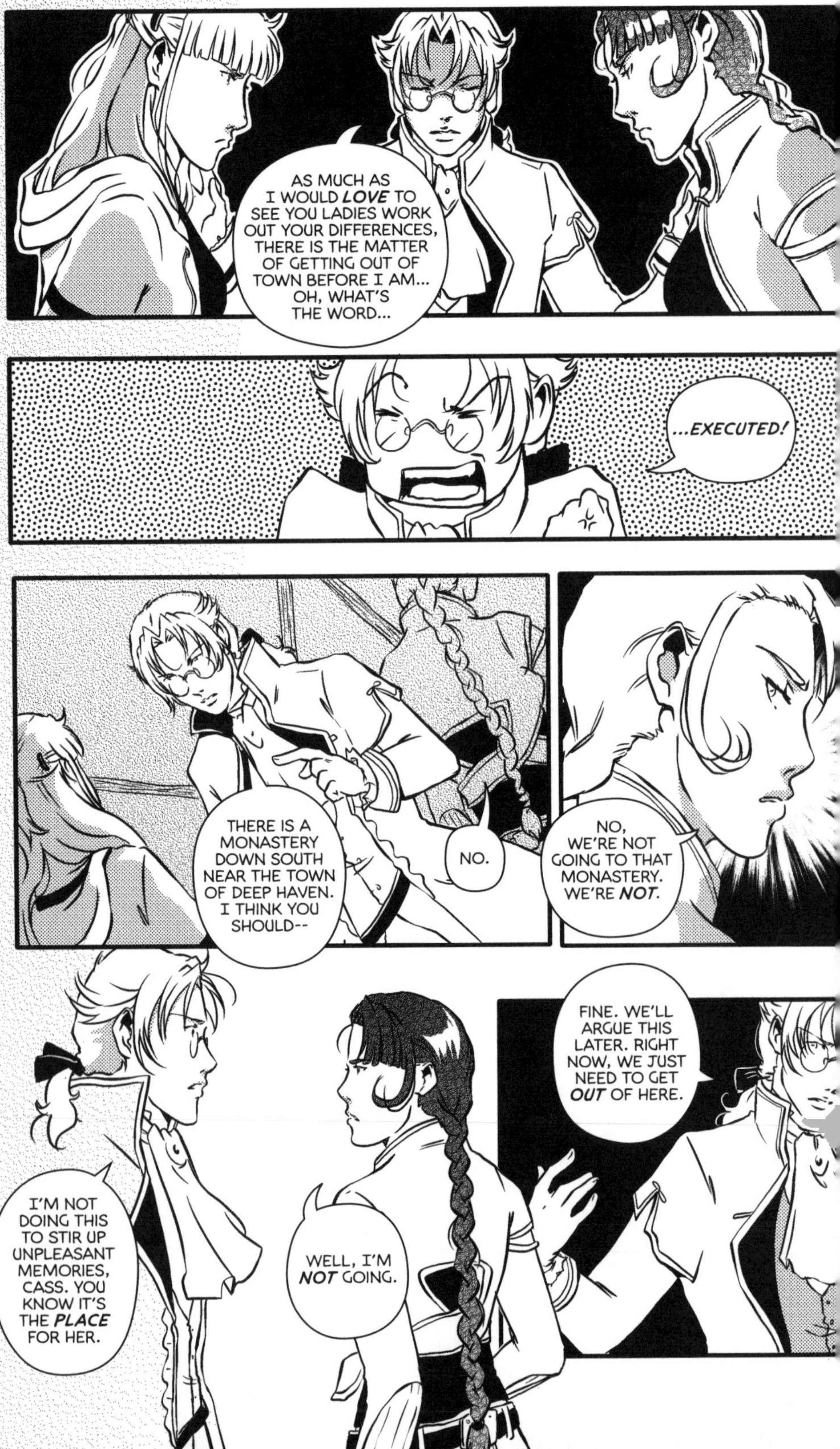

AS MUCH AS I WOULD *LOVE* TO SEE YOU LADIES WORK OUT YOUR DIFFERENCES, THERE IS THE MATTER OF GETTING OUT OF TOWN BEFORE I AM... OH, WHAT'S THE WORD...
...EXECUTED!
THERE IS A MONASTERY DOWN SOUTH NEAR THE TOWN OF DEEP HAVEN. I THINK YOU SHOULD--
NO.
NO, WE'RE NOT GOING TO THAT MONASTERY. WE'RE *NOT*.
I'M NOT DOING THIS TO STIR UP UNPLEASANT MEMORIES, CASS. YOU KNOW IT'S THE *PLACE* FOR HER.
WELL, I'M *NOT* GOING.
FINE. WE'LL ARGUE THIS LATER. RIGHT NOW, WE JUST NEED TO GET *OUT* OF HERE.

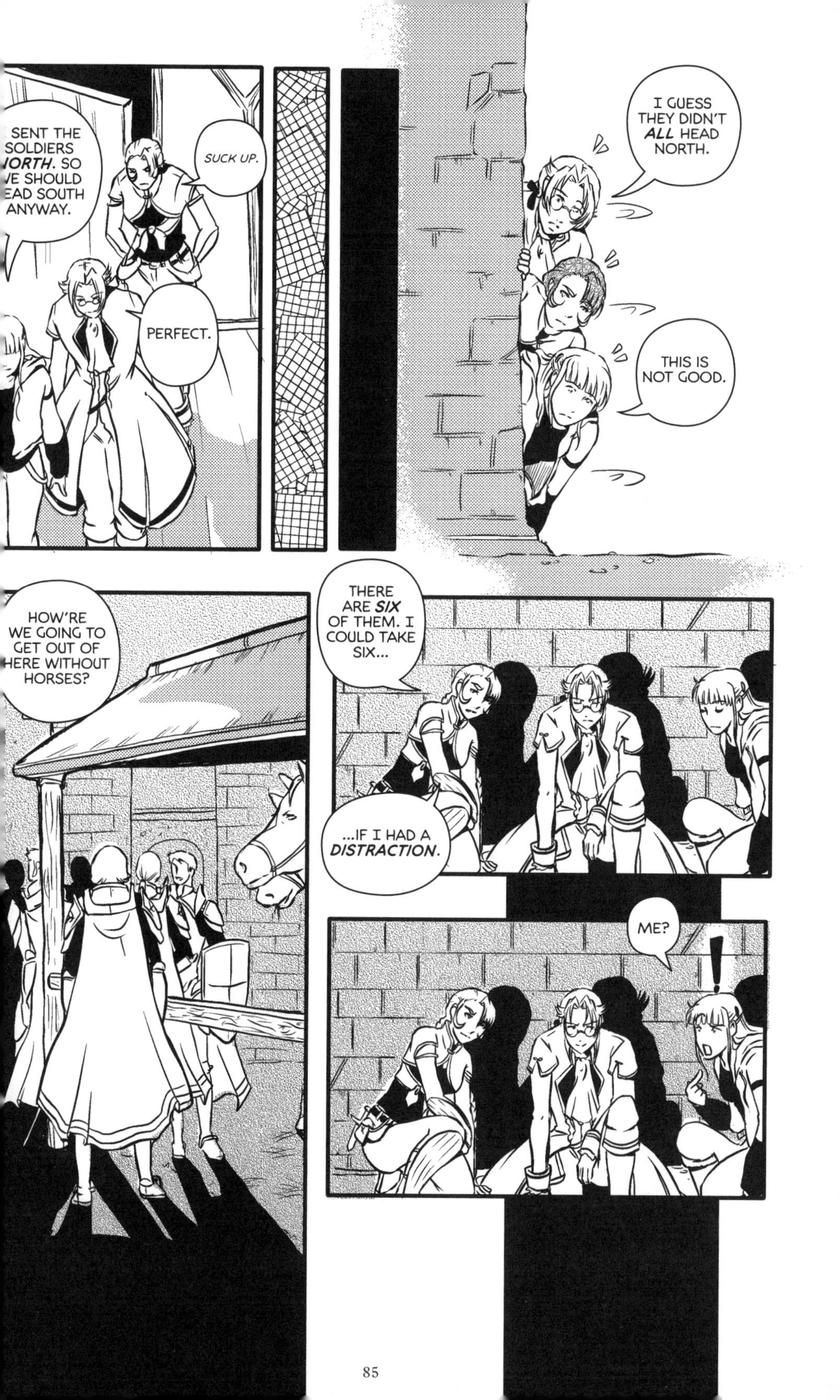

SENT THE SOLDIERS NORTH. SO WE SHOULD HEAD SOUTH ANYWAY.
SUCK UP.
PERFECT.
I GUESS THEY DIDN'T ALL HEAD NORTH.
THIS IS NOT GOOD.
HOW'RE WE GOING TO GET OUT OF HERE WITHOUT HORSES?
THERE ARE SIX OF THEM. I COULD TAKE SIX...
...IF I HAD A DISTRACTION.
ME?
!

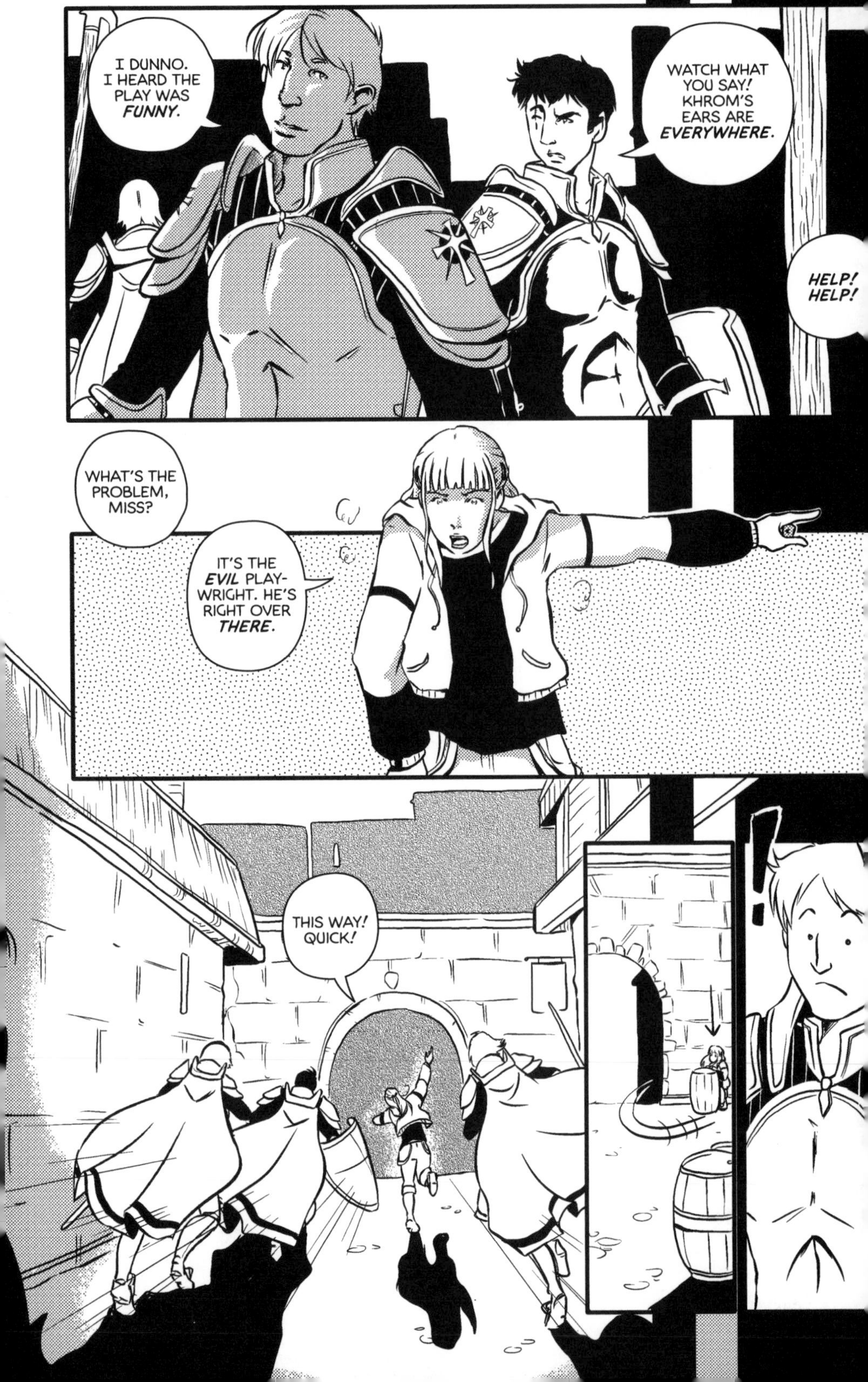
I DUNNO. I HEARD THE PLAY WAS *FUNNY*.
WATCH WHAT YOU SAY! KHROM'S EARS ARE *EVERYWHERE*.
HELP! HELP!
WHAT'S THE PROBLEM, MISS?
IT'S THE *EVIL* PLAY-WRIGHT. HE'S RIGHT OVER *THERE*.
THIS WAY! QUICK!
!

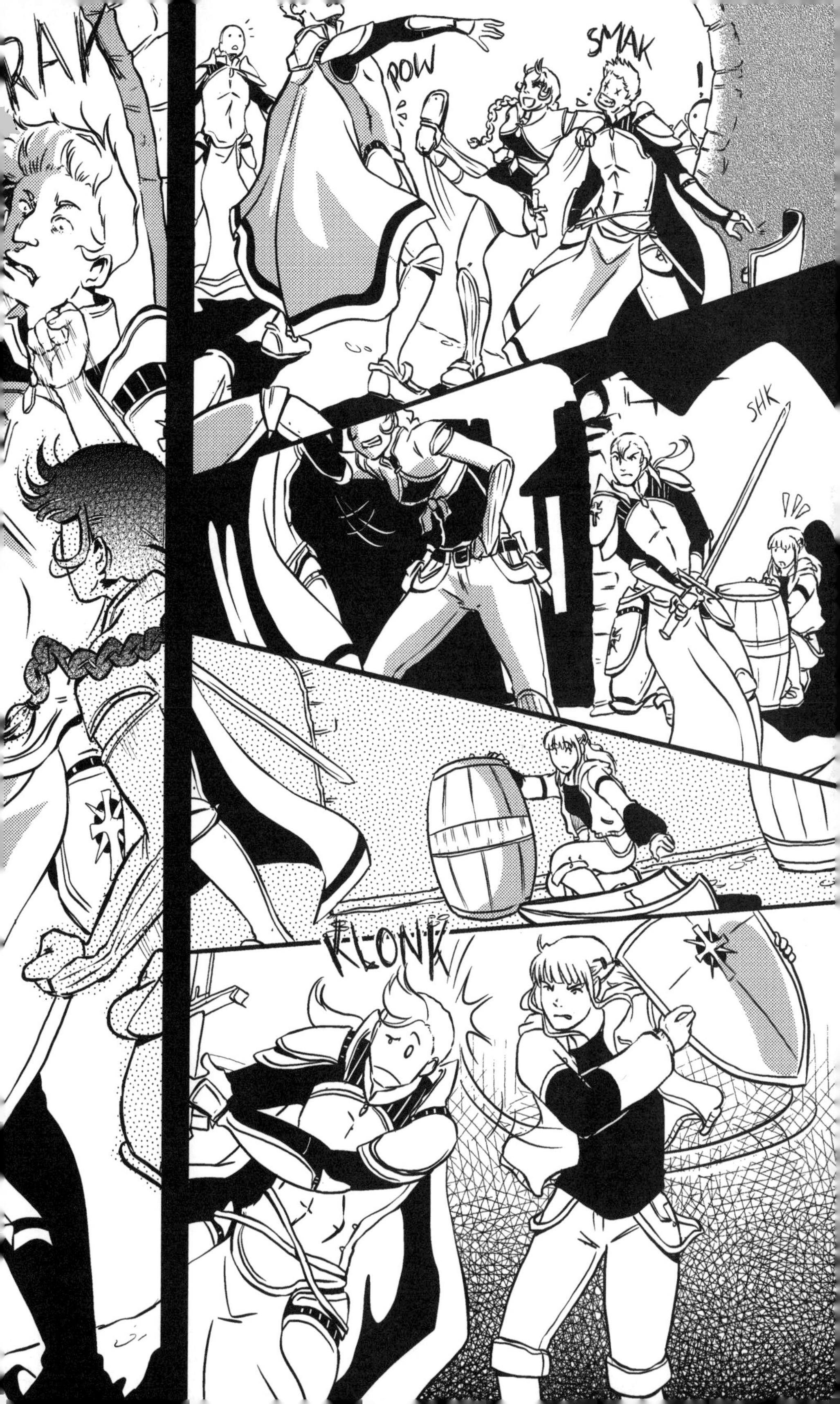
RAK
POW
SMAK
!
SHK
!!!
KLONK

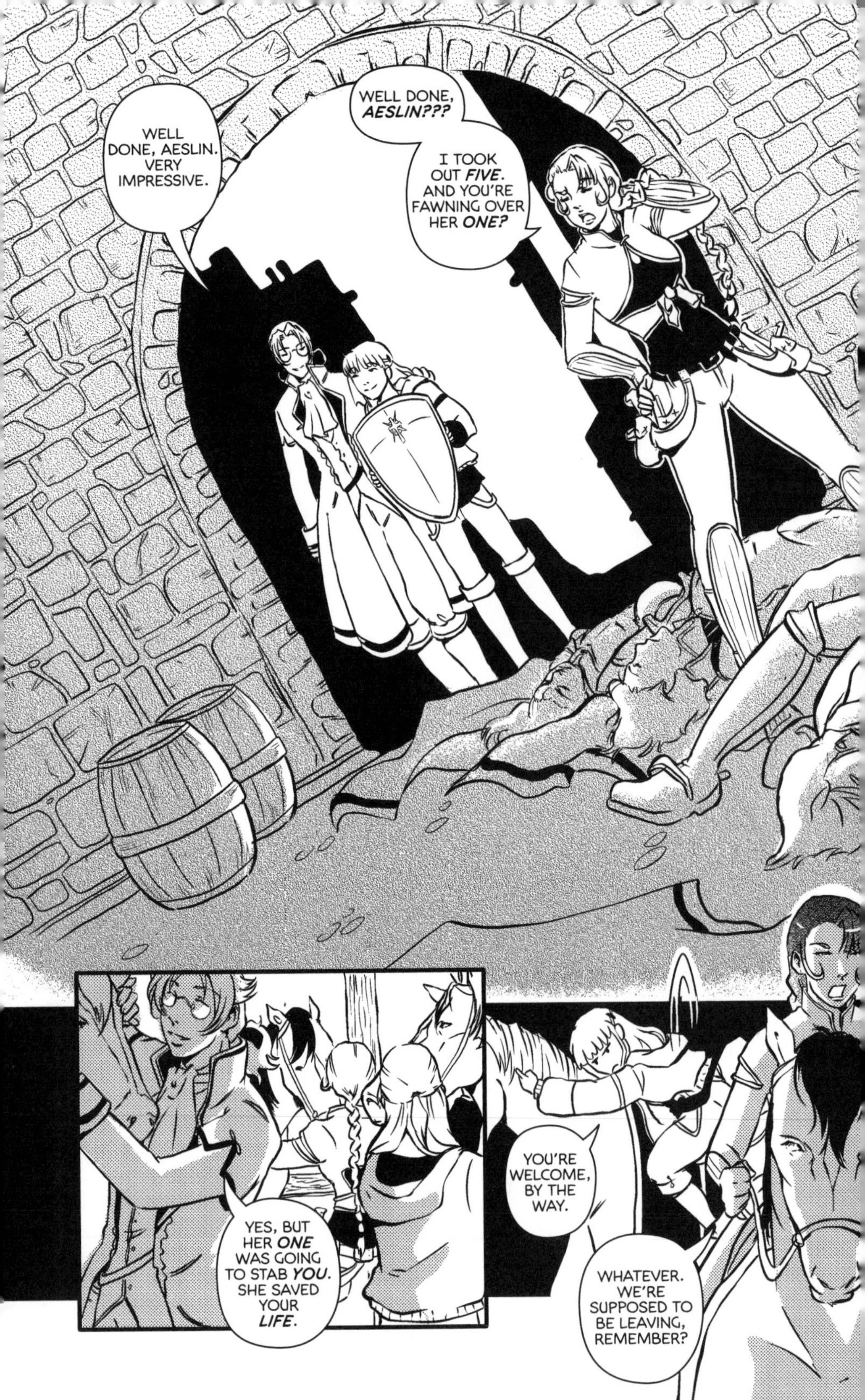
WELL DONE, AESLIN. VERY IMPRESSIVE.
WELL DONE, *AESLIN???*
I TOOK OUT *FIVE*. AND YOU'RE FAWNING OVER HER *ONE?*
YES, BUT HER *ONE* WAS GOING TO STAB *YOU*. SHE SAVED YOUR *LIFE*.
YOU'RE WELCOME, BY THE WAY.
WHATEVER. WE'RE SUPPOSED TO BE LEAVING, REMEMBER?

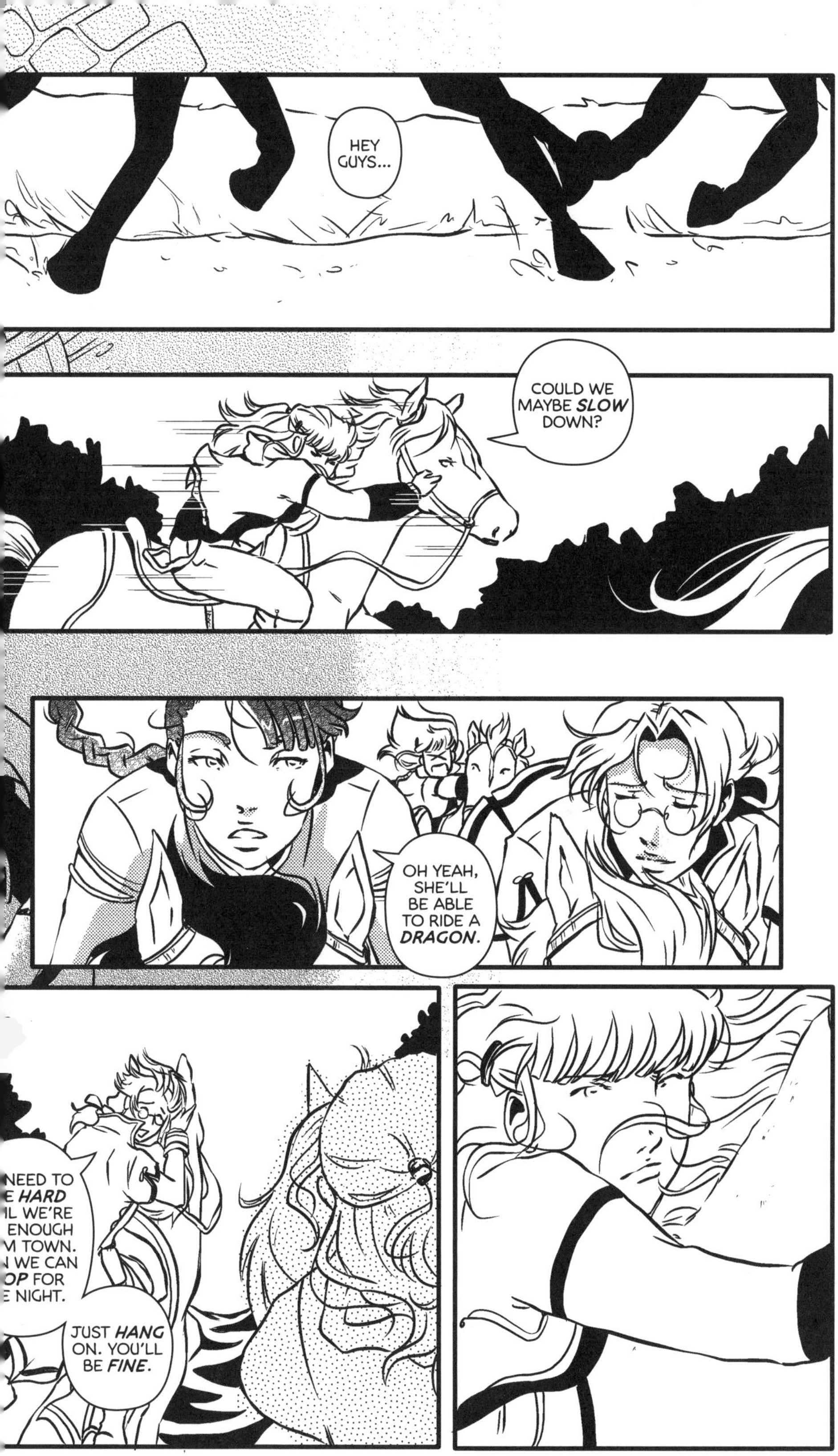
HEY GUYS...
COULD WE MAYBE SLOW DOWN?
OH YEAH, SHE'LL BE ABLE TO RIDE A DRAGON.
NEED TO
E HARD
IL WE'RE
ENOUGH
M TOWN.
N WE CAN
OP FOR
E NIGHT.
JUST HANG ON. YOU'LL BE FINE.

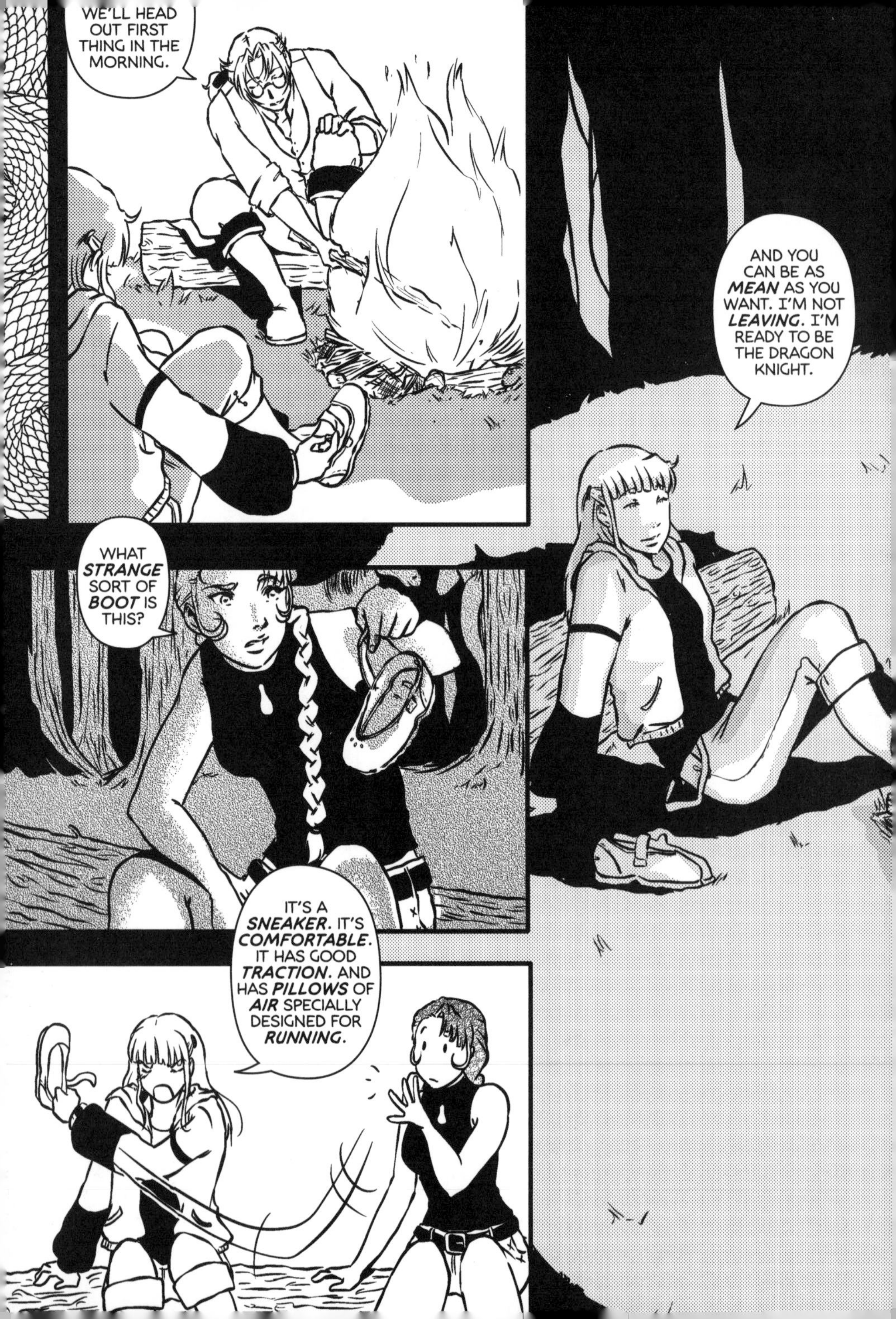
WE'LL HEAD OUT FIRST THING IN THE MORNING.
AND YOU CAN BE AS *MEAN* AS YOU WANT. I'M NOT *LEAVING*. I'M READY TO BE THE DRAGON KNIGHT.
WHAT *STRANGE* SORT OF *BOOT* IS THIS?
IT'S A *SNEAKER*. IT'S *COMFORTABLE*. IT HAS GOOD *TRACTION*. AND HAS *PILLOWS* OF *AIR* SPECIALLY DESIGNED FOR *RUNNING*.

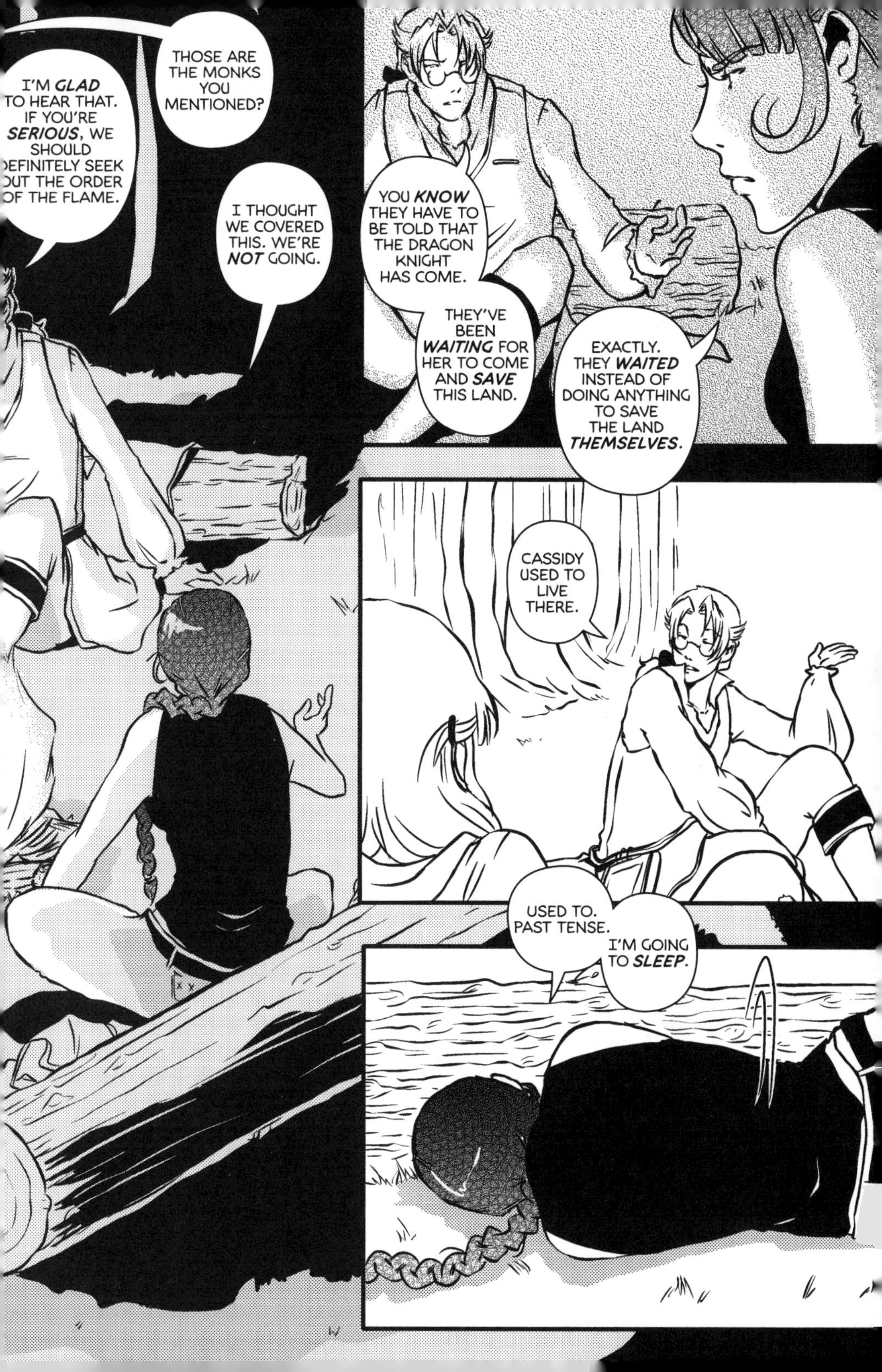
I'M GLAD TO HEAR THAT. IF YOU'RE SERIOUS, WE SHOULD DEFINITELY SEEK OUT THE ORDER OF THE FLAME.
THOSE ARE THE MONKS YOU MENTIONED?
I THOUGHT WE COVERED THIS. WE'RE NOT GOING.
YOU KNOW THEY HAVE TO BE TOLD THAT THE DRAGON KNIGHT HAS COME.
THEY'VE BEEN WAITING FOR HER TO COME AND SAVE THIS LAND.
EXACTLY. THEY WAITED INSTEAD OF DOING ANYTHING TO SAVE THE LAND THEMSELVES.
CASSIDY USED TO LIVE THERE.
USED TO. PAST TENSE.
I'M GOING TO SLEEP.

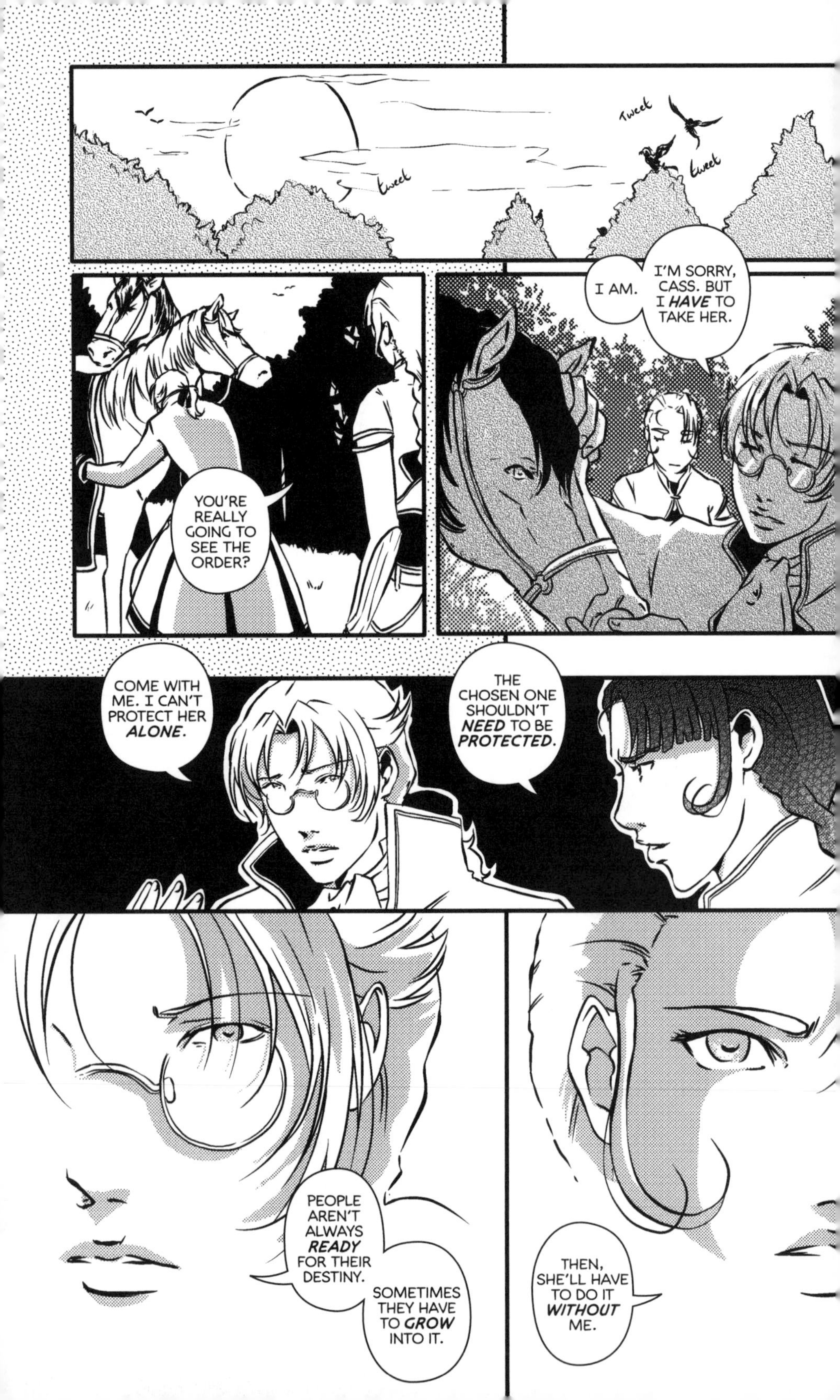
Tweet
Tweet
Tweet
YOU'RE REALLY GOING TO SEE THE ORDER?
I AM.
I'M SORRY, CASS. BUT I HAVE TO TAKE HER.
COME WITH ME. I CAN'T PROTECT HER ALONE.
THE CHOSEN ONE SHOULDN'T NEED TO BE PROTECTED.
PEOPLE AREN'T ALWAYS READY FOR THEIR DESTINY.
SOMETIMES THEY HAVE TO GROW INTO IT.
THEN, SHE'LL HAVE TO DO IT WITHOUT ME.

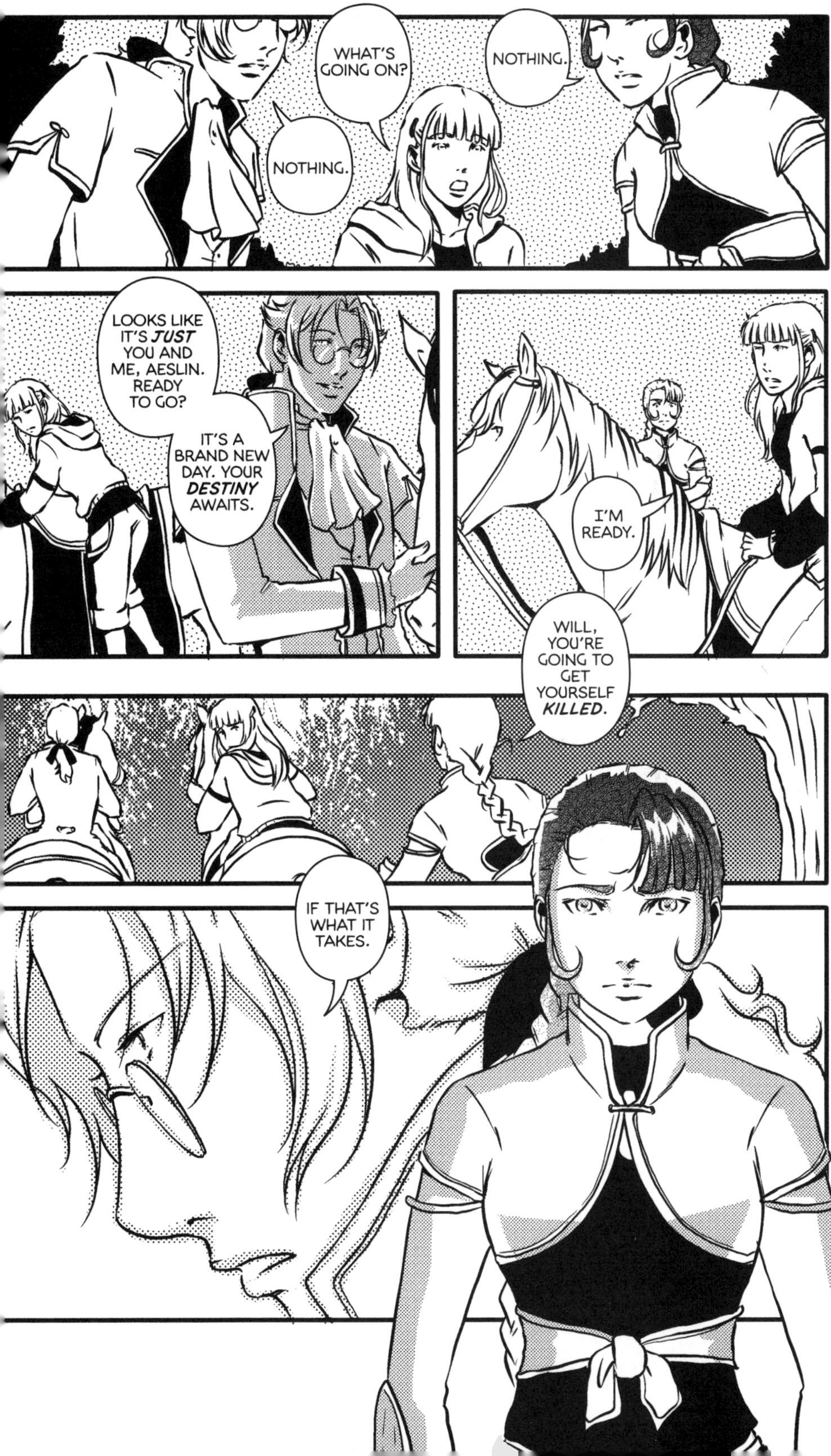
WHAT'S GOING ON?
NOTHING.
NOTHING.
LOOKS LIKE IT'S *JUST* YOU AND ME, AESLIN. READY TO GO?
IT'S A BRAND NEW DAY. YOUR ***DESTINY*** AWAITS.
I'M READY.
WILL, YOU'RE GOING TO GET YOURSELF ***KILLED***.
IF THAT'S WHAT IT TAKES.

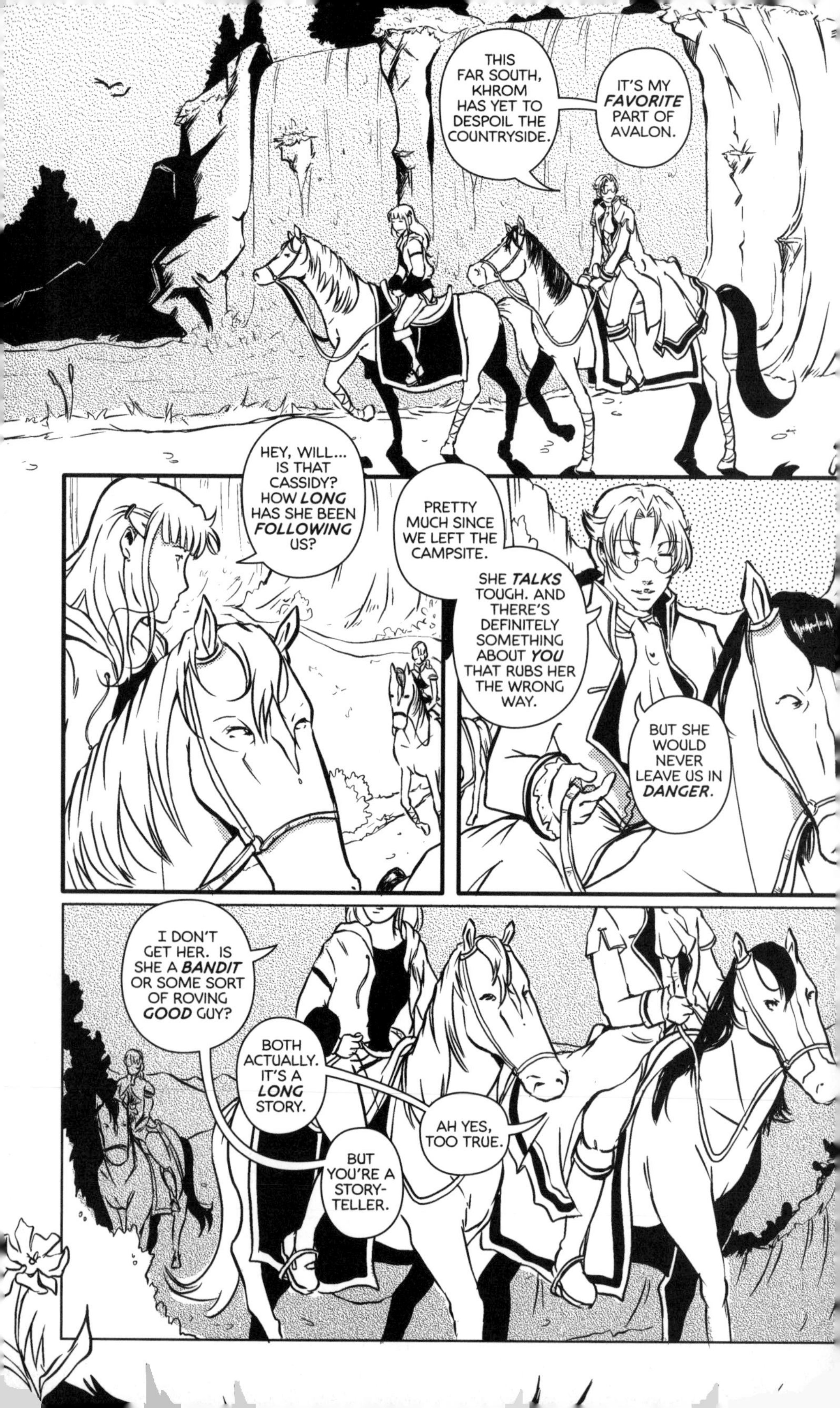
THIS FAR SOUTH, KHROM HAS YET TO DESPOIL THE COUNTRYSIDE.
IT'S MY *FAVORITE* PART OF AVALON.
HEY, WILL... IS THAT CASSIDY? HOW *LONG* HAS SHE BEEN *FOLLOWING* US?
PRETTY MUCH SINCE WE LEFT THE CAMPSITE.
SHE *TALKS* TOUGH. AND THERE'S DEFINITELY SOMETHING ABOUT *YOU* THAT RUBS HER THE WRONG WAY.
BUT SHE WOULD NEVER LEAVE US IN *DANGER*.
I DON'T GET HER. IS SHE A *BANDIT* OR SOME SORT OF ROVING *GOOD* GUY?
BOTH ACTUALLY. IT'S A *LONG* STORY.
BUT YOU'RE A STORY-TELLER.
AH YES, TOO TRUE.

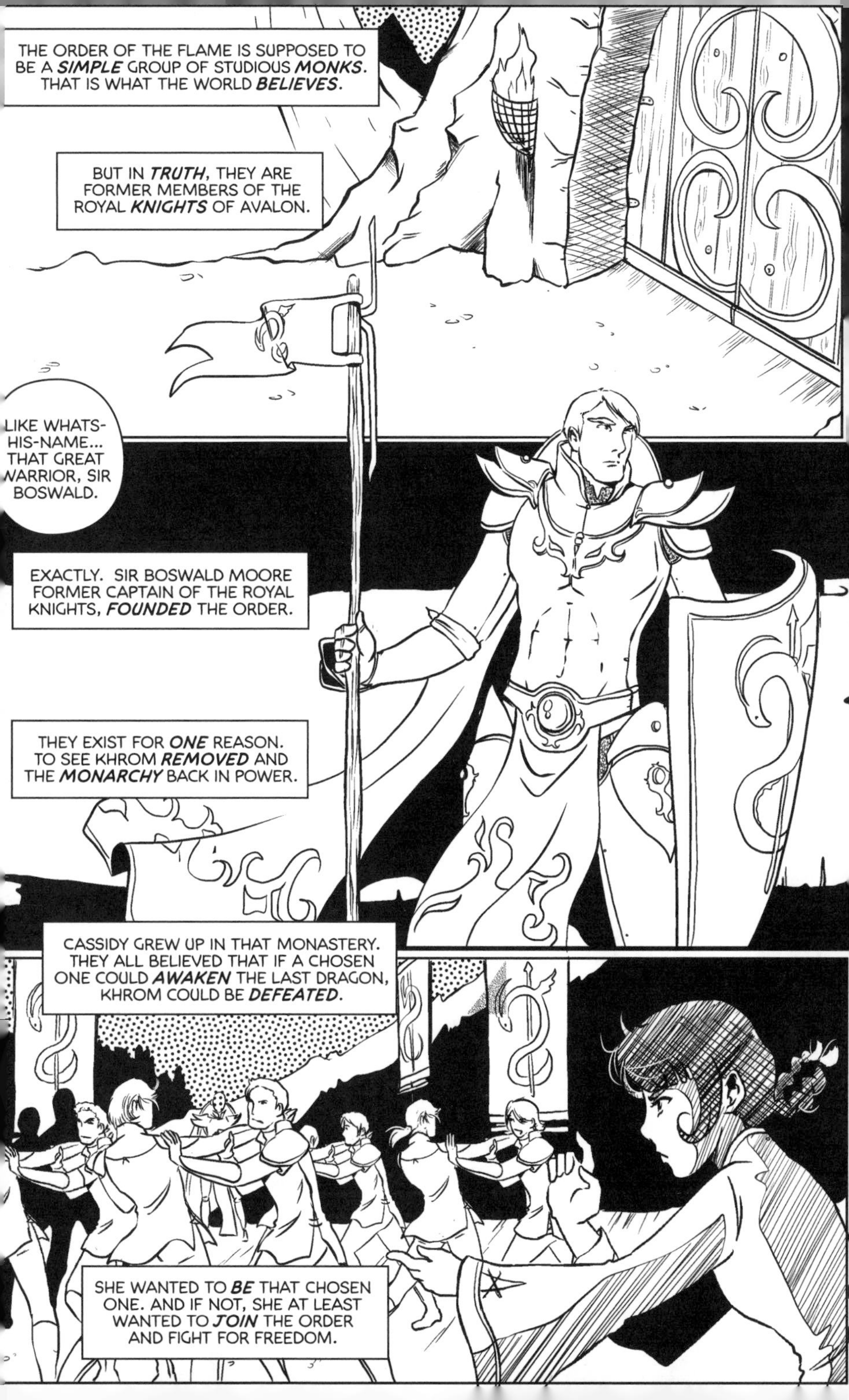
THE ORDER OF THE FLAME IS SUPPOSED TO BE A *SIMPLE* GROUP OF STUDIOUS *MONKS*. THAT IS WHAT THE WORLD *BELIEVES*.
BUT IN *TRUTH*, THEY ARE FORMER MEMBERS OF THE ROYAL *KNIGHTS* OF AVALON.
LIKE WHATS-HIS-NAME... THAT GREAT WARRIOR, SIR BOSWALD.
EXACTLY. SIR BOSWALD MOORE FORMER CAPTAIN OF THE ROYAL KNIGHTS, *FOUNDED* THE ORDER.
THEY EXIST FOR *ONE* REASON. TO SEE KHROM *REMOVED* AND THE *MONARCHY* BACK IN POWER.
CASSIDY GREW UP IN THAT MONASTERY. THEY ALL BELIEVED THAT IF A CHOSEN ONE COULD *AWAKEN* THE LAST DRAGON, KHROM COULD BE *DEFEATED*.
SHE WANTED TO *BE* THAT CHOSEN ONE. AND IF NOT, SHE AT LEAST WANTED TO *JOIN* THE ORDER AND FIGHT FOR FREEDOM.

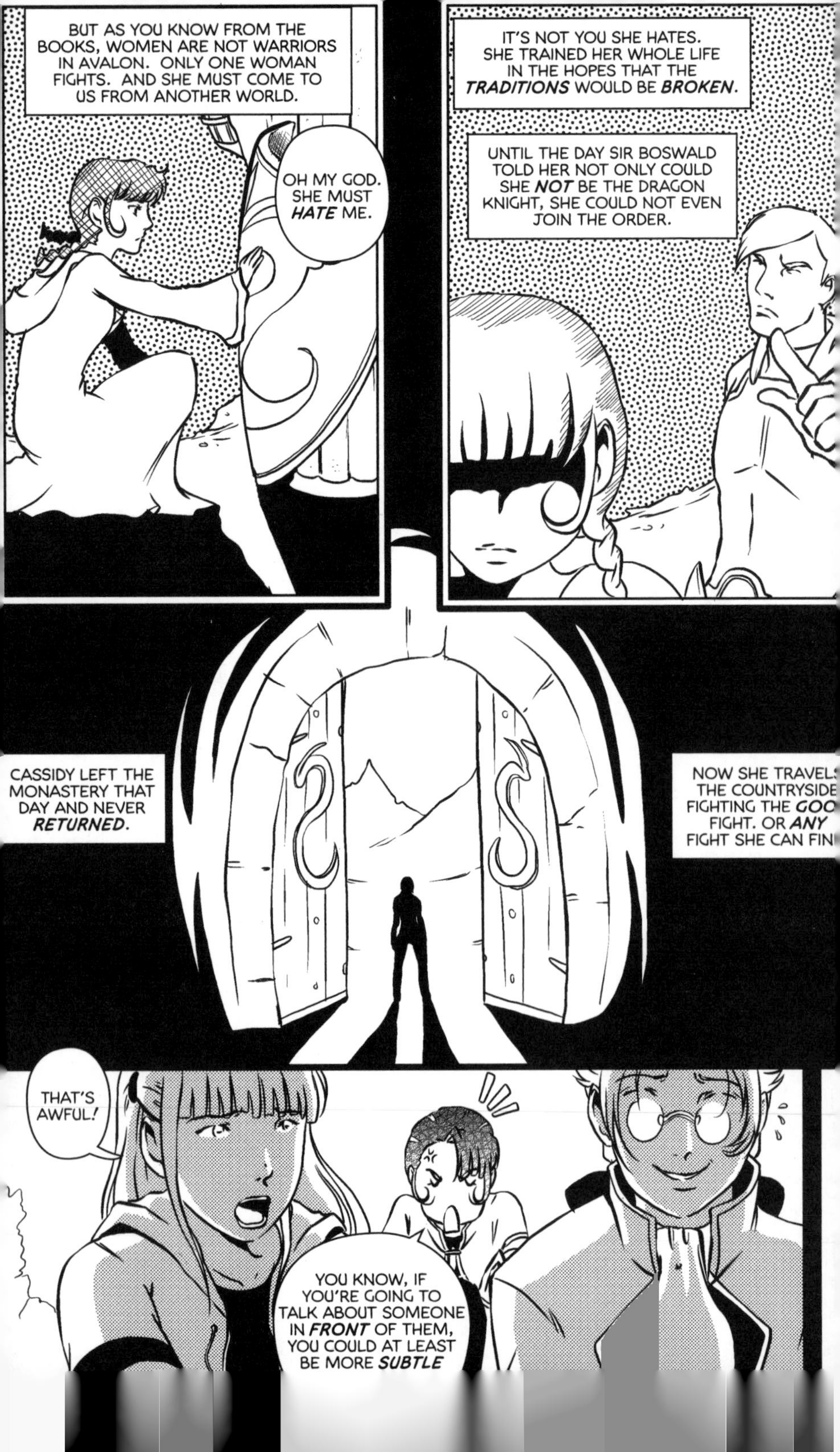
BUT AS YOU KNOW FROM THE BOOKS, WOMEN ARE NOT WARRIORS IN AVALON. ONLY ONE WOMAN FIGHTS. AND SHE MUST COME TO US FROM ANOTHER WORLD.
OH MY GOD. SHE MUST *HATE* ME.
IT'S NOT YOU SHE HATES. SHE TRAINED HER WHOLE LIFE IN THE HOPES THAT THE ***TRADITIONS*** WOULD BE ***BROKEN***.
UNTIL THE DAY SIR BOSWALD TOLD HER NOT ONLY COULD SHE ***NOT*** BE THE DRAGON KNIGHT, SHE COULD NOT EVEN JOIN THE ORDER.
CASSIDY LEFT THE MONASTERY THAT DAY AND NEVER ***RETURNED***.
NOW SHE TRAVEL THE COUNTRYSIDE FIGHTING THE ***GOO*** FIGHT. OR ***ANY*** FIGHT SHE CAN FIN
THAT'S AWFUL!
YOU KNOW, IF YOU'RE GOING TO TALK ABOUT SOMEONE IN ***FRONT*** OF THEM, YOU COULD AT LEAST BE MORE ***SUBTLE***

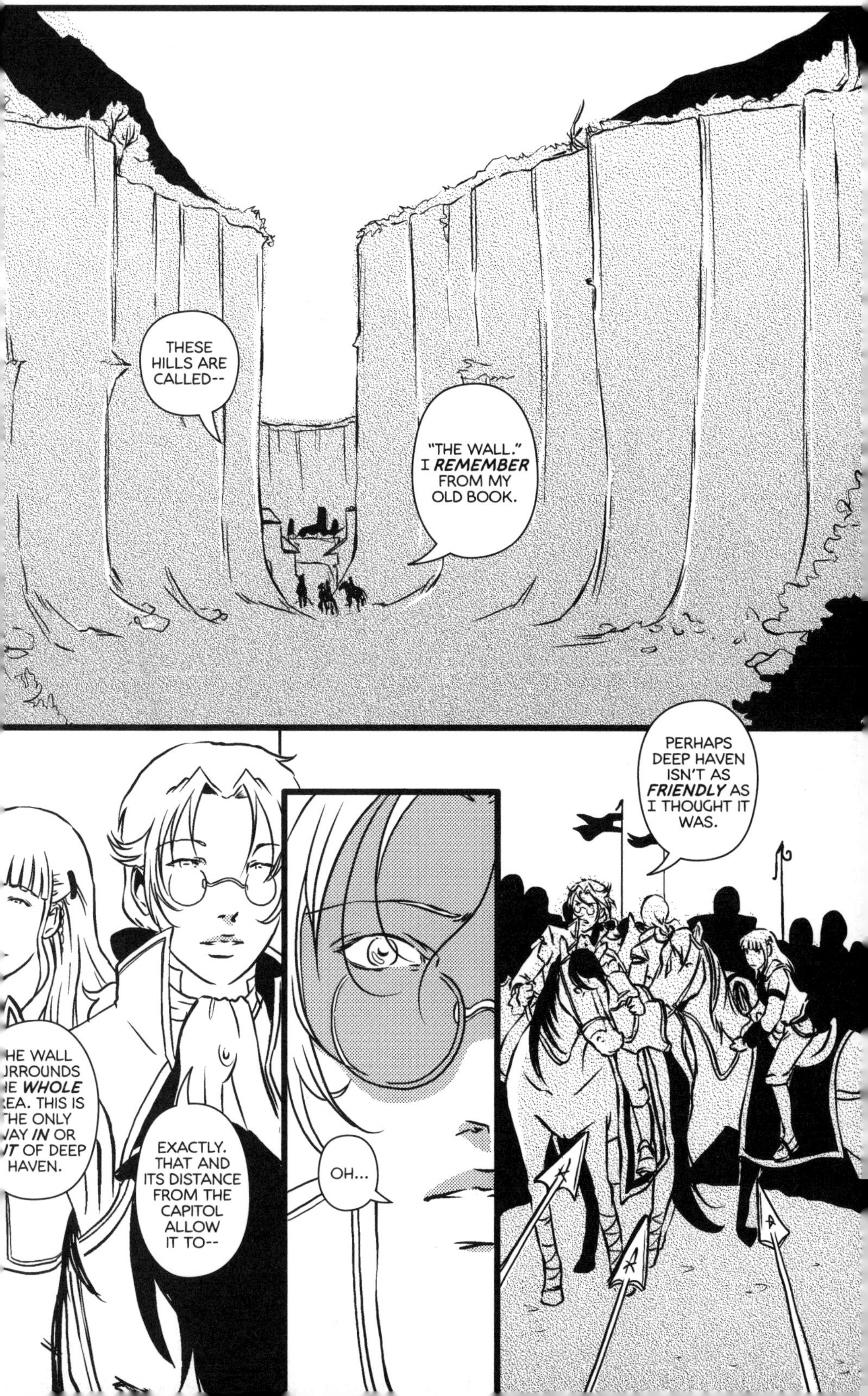
THESE HILLS ARE CALLED--
"THE WALL." I REMEMBER FROM MY OLD BOOK.
HE WALL URROUNDS HE WHOLE REA. THIS IS THE ONLY AY IN OR T OF DEEP HAVEN.
EXACTLY. THAT AND ITS DISTANCE FROM THE CAPITOL ALLOW IT TO--
OH...
PERHAPS DEEP HAVEN ISN'T AS FRIENDLY AS I THOUGHT IT WAS.

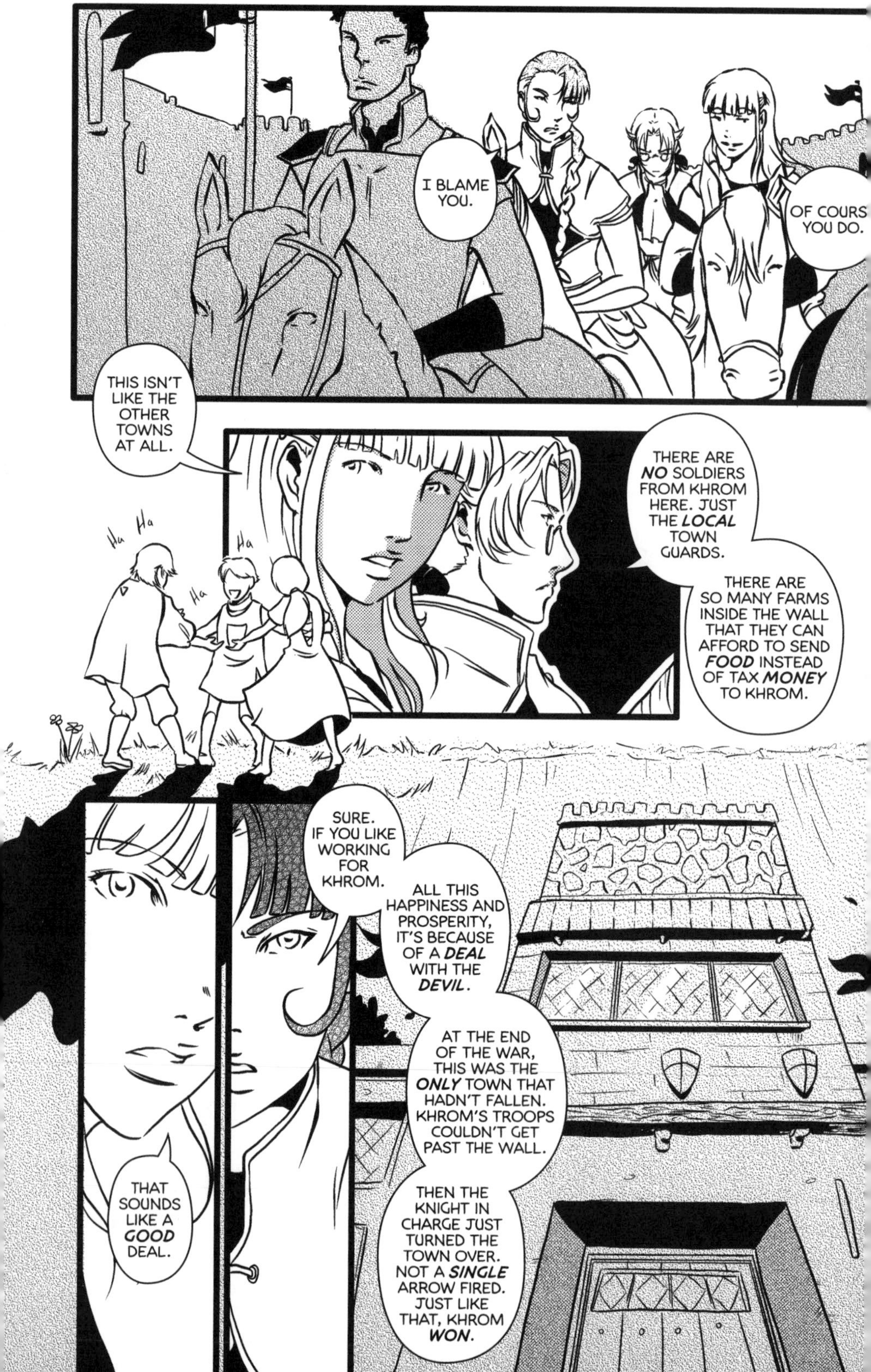
I BLAME YOU.
OF COURS YOU DO.
THIS ISN'T LIKE THE OTHER TOWNS AT ALL.
THERE ARE *NO* SOLDIERS FROM KHROM HERE. JUST THE *LOCAL* TOWN GUARDS.
THERE ARE SO MANY FARMS INSIDE THE WALL THAT THEY CAN AFFORD TO SEND *FOOD* INSTEAD OF TAX *MONEY* TO KHROM.
Ha Ha
Ha
Ha
SURE. IF YOU LIKE WORKING FOR KHROM.
ALL THIS HAPPINESS AND PROSPERITY, IT'S BECAUSE OF A *DEAL* WITH THE *DEVIL*.
AT THE END OF THE WAR, THIS WAS THE *ONLY* TOWN THAT HADN'T FALLEN. KHROM'S TROOPS COULDN'T GET PAST THE WALL.
THEN THE KNIGHT IN CHARGE JUST TURNED THE TOWN OVER. NOT A *SINGLE* ARROW FIRED. JUST LIKE THAT, KHROM *WON*.
THAT SOUNDS LIKE A *GOOD* DEAL.

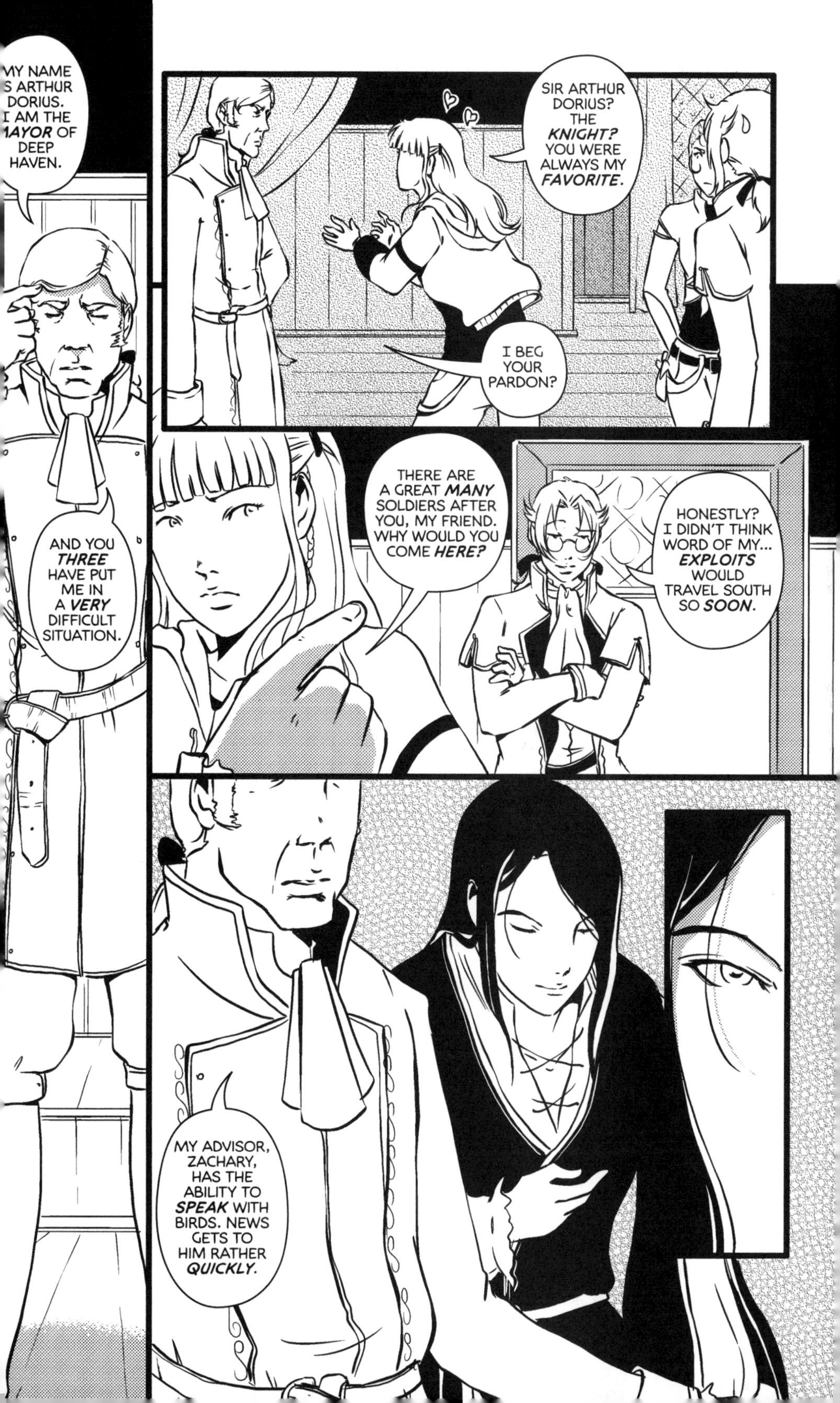
MY NAME IS ARTHUR DORIUS. I AM THE MAYOR OF DEEP HAVEN.
SIR ARTHUR DORIUS? THE KNIGHT? YOU WERE ALWAYS MY FAVORITE.
I BEG YOUR PARDON?
AND YOU THREE HAVE PUT ME IN A VERY DIFFICULT SITUATION.
THERE ARE A GREAT MANY SOLDIERS AFTER YOU, MY FRIEND. WHY WOULD YOU COME HERE?
HONESTLY? I DIDN'T THINK WORD OF MY... EXPLOITS WOULD TRAVEL SOUTH SO SOON.
MY ADVISOR, ZACHARY, HAS THE ABILITY TO SPEAK WITH BIRDS. NEWS GETS TO HIM RATHER QUICKLY.

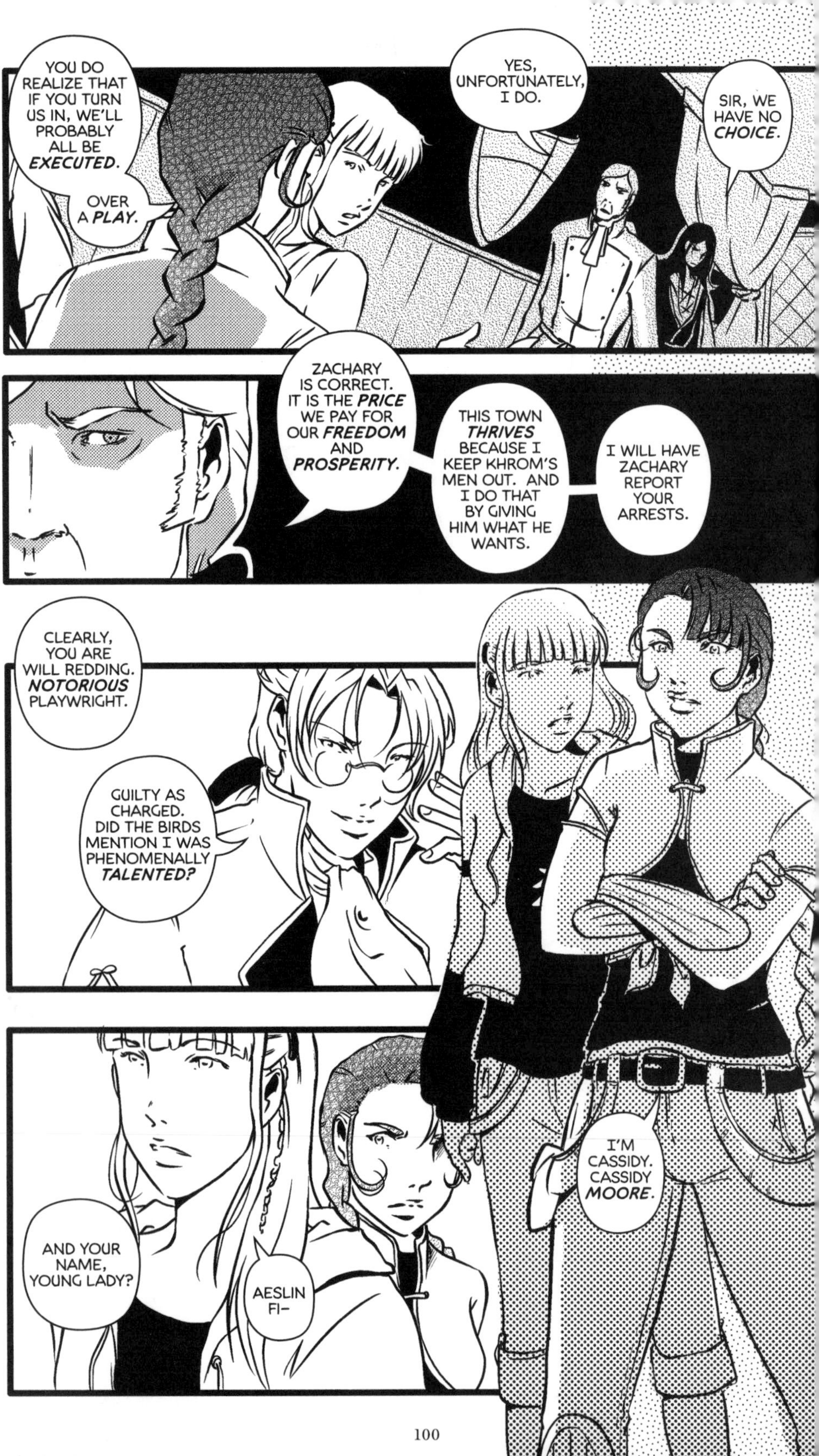
YOU DO REALIZE THAT IF YOU TURN US IN, WE'LL PROBABLY ALL BE *EXECUTED*.
OVER A *PLAY*.
YES, UNFORTUNATELY, I DO.
SIR, WE HAVE NO *CHOICE*.
ZACHARY IS CORRECT. IT IS THE *PRICE* WE PAY FOR OUR *FREEDOM* AND *PROSPERITY*.
THIS TOWN *THRIVES* BECAUSE I KEEP KHROM'S MEN OUT. AND I DO THAT BY GIVING HIM WHAT HE WANTS.
I WILL HAVE ZACHARY REPORT YOUR ARRESTS.
CLEARLY, YOU ARE WILL REDDING. *NOTORIOUS* PLAYWRIGHT.
GUILTY AS CHARGED. DID THE BIRDS MENTION I WAS PHENOMENALLY *TALENTED?*
I'M CASSIDY. CASSIDY *MOORE*.
AND YOUR NAME, YOUNG LADY?
AESLIN FI-

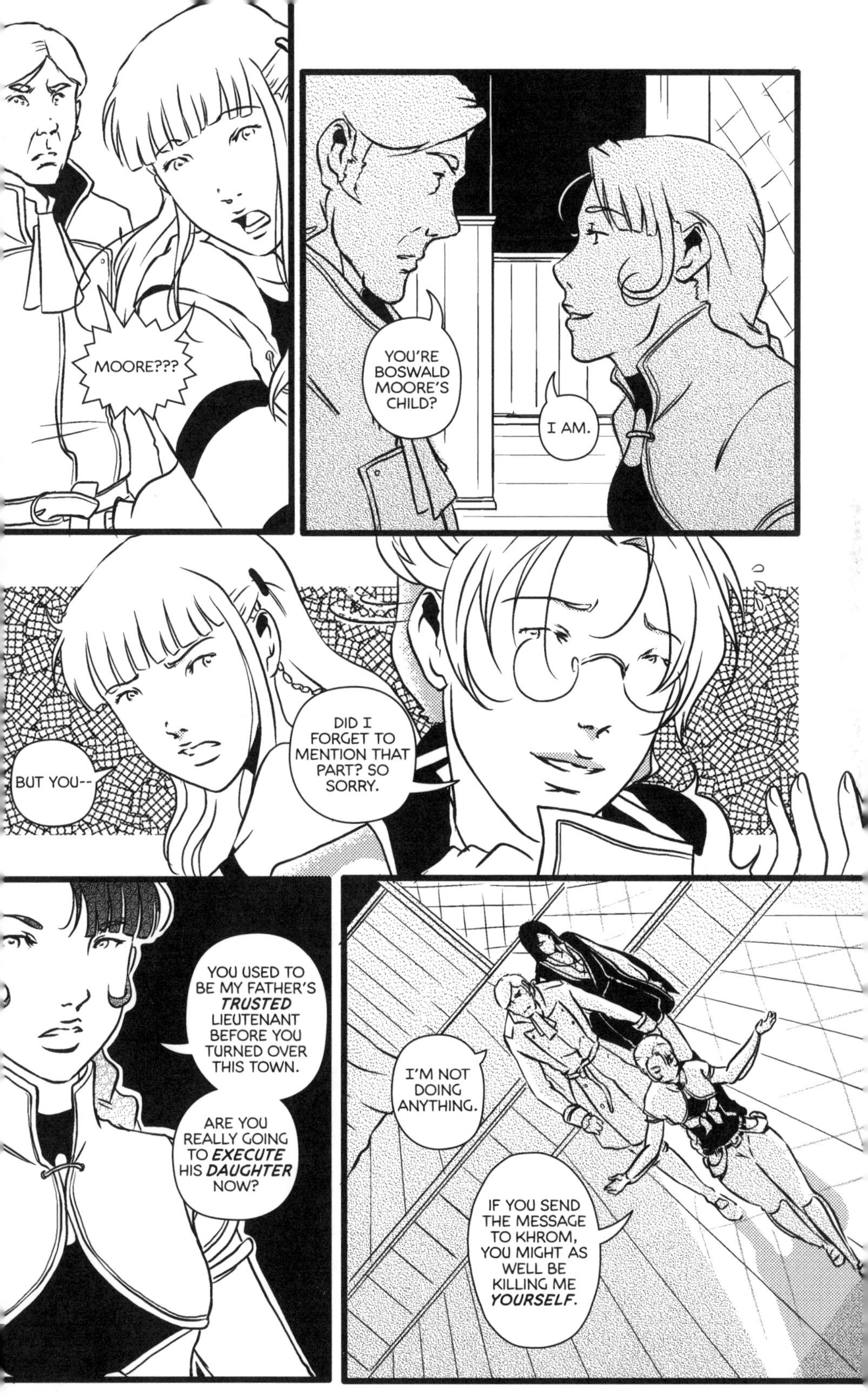
MOORE???
YOU'RE BOSWALD MOORE'S CHILD?
I AM.
BUT YOU--
DID I FORGET TO MENTION THAT PART? SO SORRY.
YOU USED TO BE MY FATHER'S ***TRUSTED*** LIEUTENANT BEFORE YOU TURNED OVER THIS TOWN.
ARE YOU REALLY GOING TO ***EXECUTE*** HIS ***DAUGHTER*** NOW?
I'M NOT DOING ANYTHING.
IF YOU SEND THE MESSAGE TO KHROM, YOU MIGHT AS WELL BE KILLING ME ***YOURSELF***.

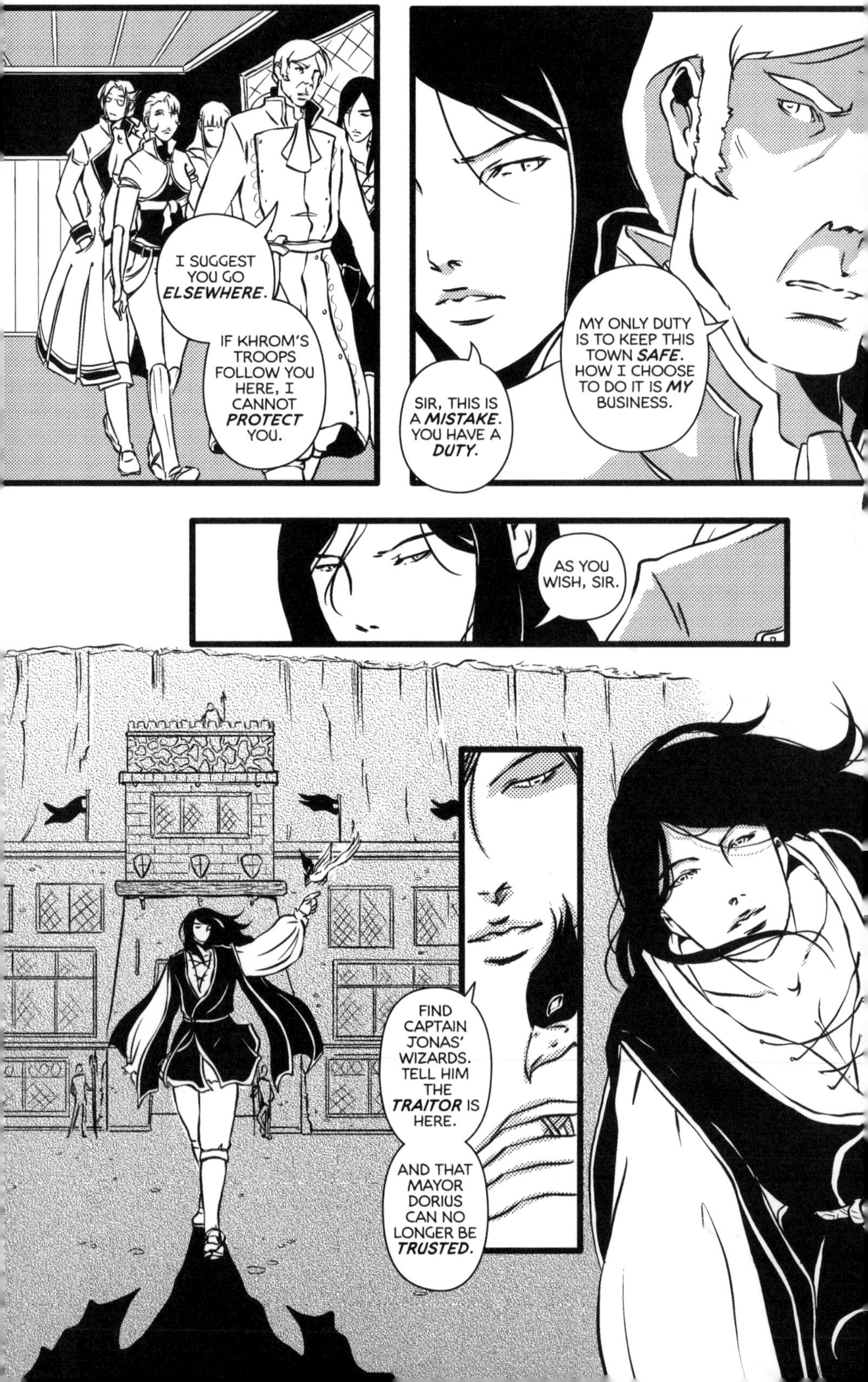
I SUGGEST YOU GO ELSEWHERE.
IF KHROM'S TROOPS FOLLOW YOU HERE, I CANNOT PROTECT YOU.
SIR, THIS IS A MISTAKE. YOU HAVE A DUTY.
MY ONLY DUTY IS TO KEEP THIS TOWN SAFE. HOW I CHOOSE TO DO IT IS MY BUSINESS.
AS YOU WISH, SIR.
FIND CAPTAIN JONAS' WIZARDS. TELL HIM THE TRAITOR IS HERE.
AND THAT MAYOR DORIUS CAN NO LONGER BE TRUSTED.

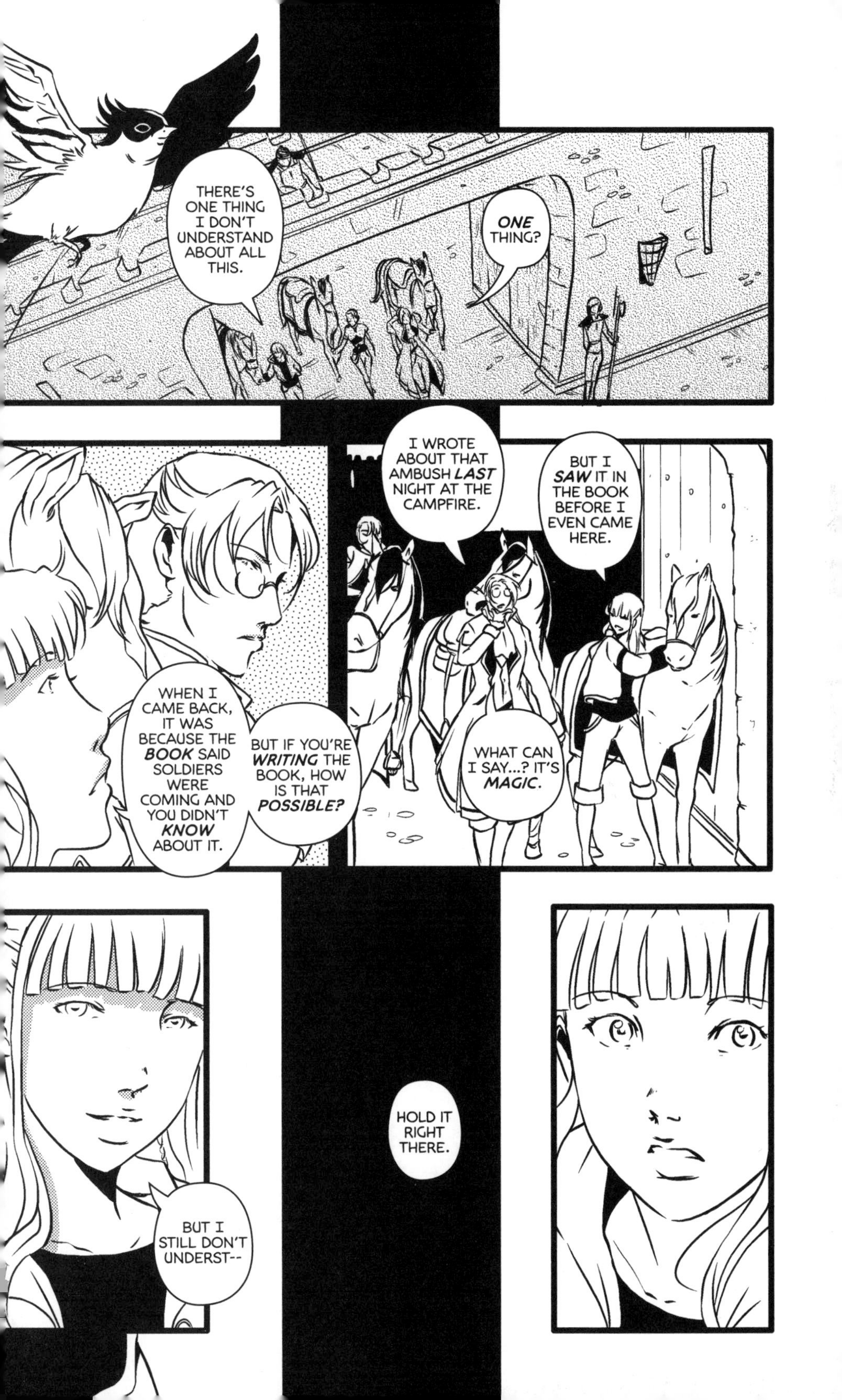
THERE'S ONE THING I DON'T UNDERSTAND ABOUT ALL THIS.
ONE THING?
I WROTE ABOUT THAT AMBUSH LAST NIGHT AT THE CAMPFIRE.
BUT I SAW IT IN THE BOOK BEFORE I EVEN CAME HERE.
WHEN I CAME BACK, IT WAS BECAUSE THE BOOK SAID SOLDIERS WERE COMING AND YOU DIDN'T KNOW ABOUT IT.
BUT IF YOU'RE WRITING THE BOOK, HOW IS THAT POSSIBLE?
WHAT CAN I SAY...? IT'S MAGIC.
BUT I STILL DON'T UNDERST--
HOLD IT RIGHT THERE.

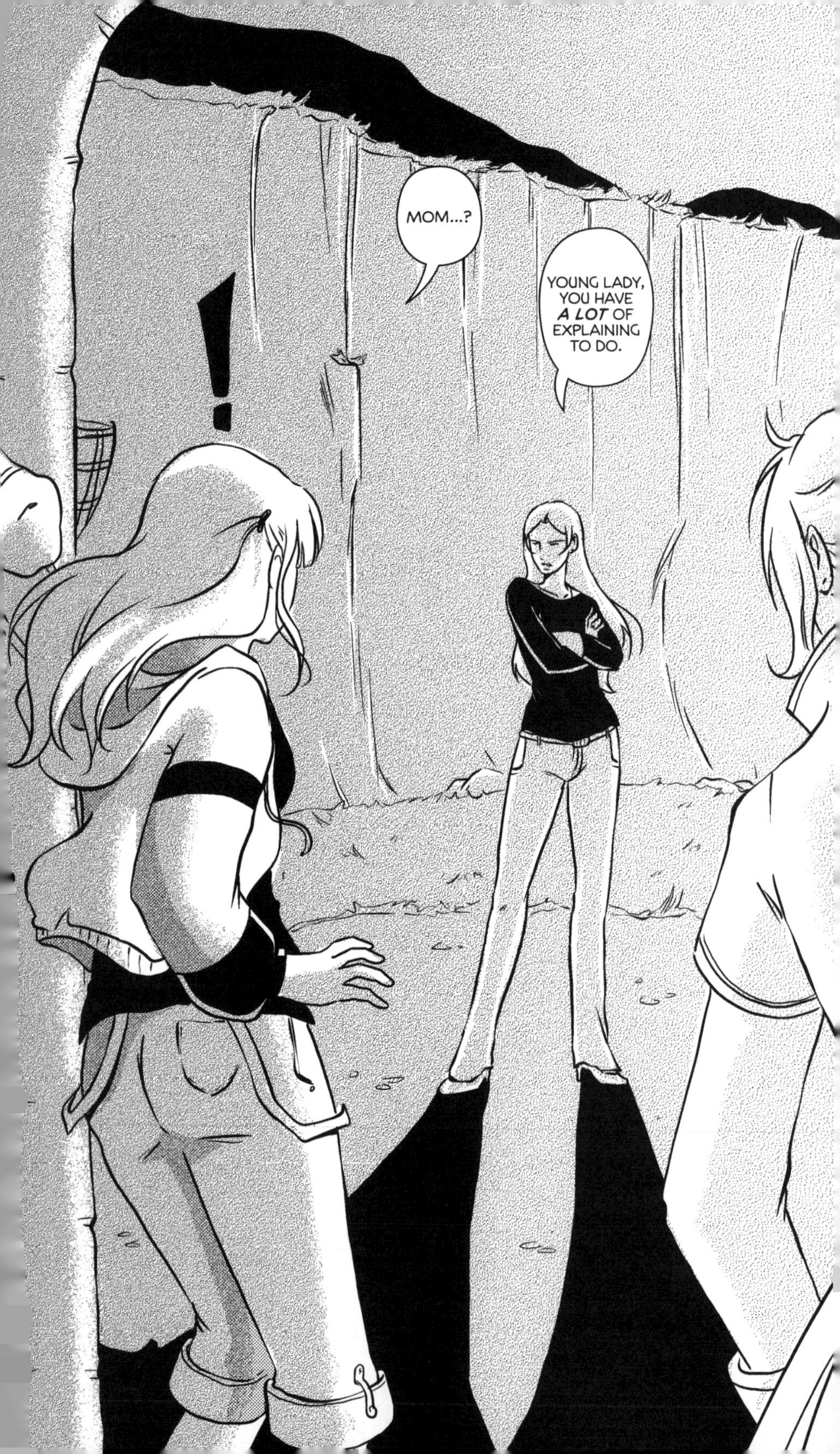
!
MOM...?
YOUNG LADY, YOU HAVE *A LOT* OF EXPLAINING TO DO.

Chapter 5

Parental Guidance

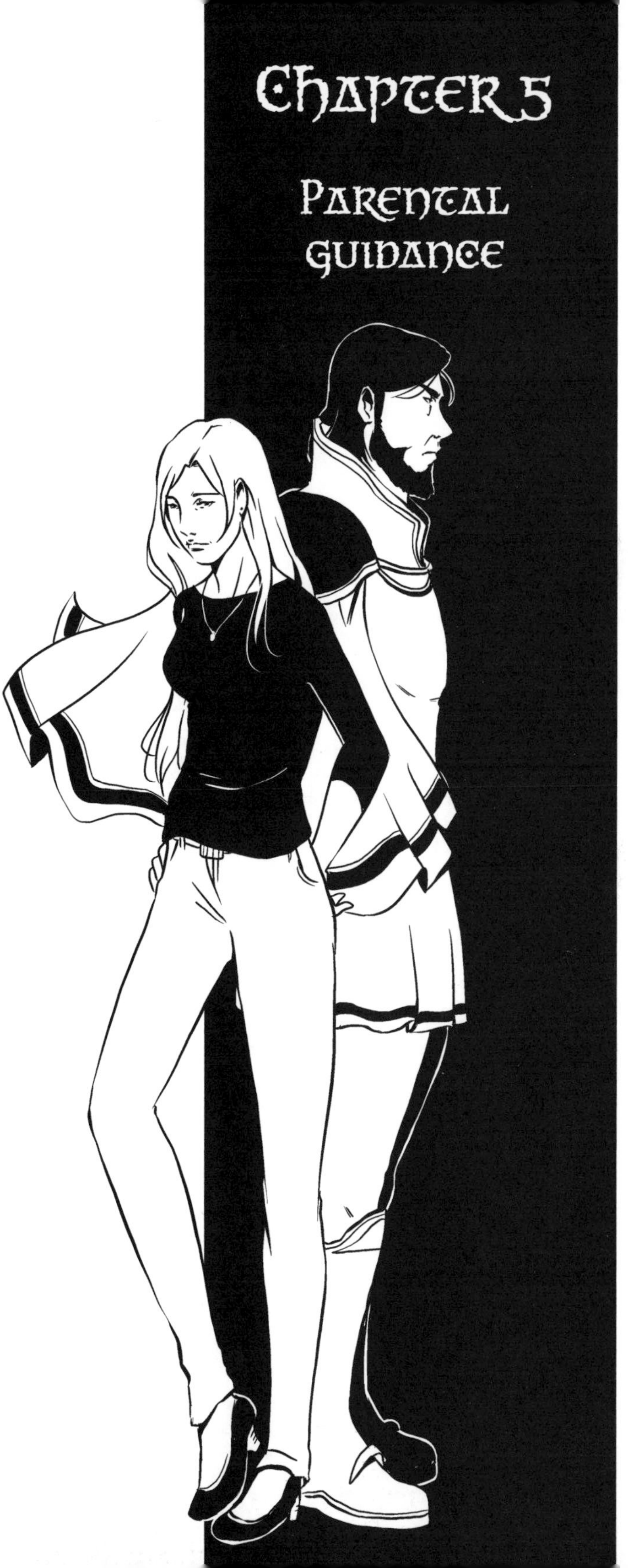

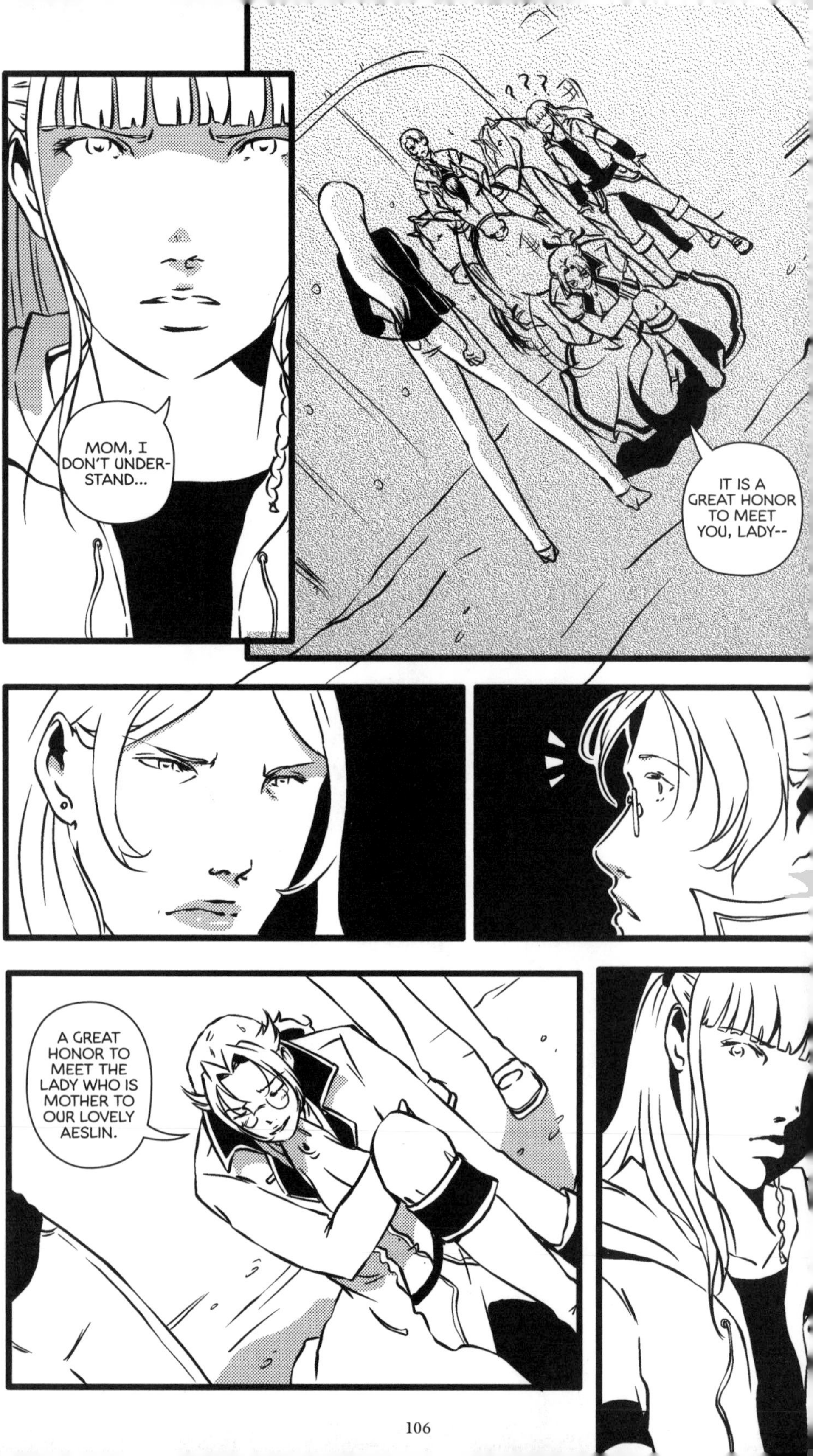

MOM, I DON'T UNDER-STAND...
IT IS A GREAT HONOR TO MEET YOU, LADY--
A GREAT HONOR TO MEET THE LADY WHO IS MOTHER TO OUR LOVELY AESLIN.

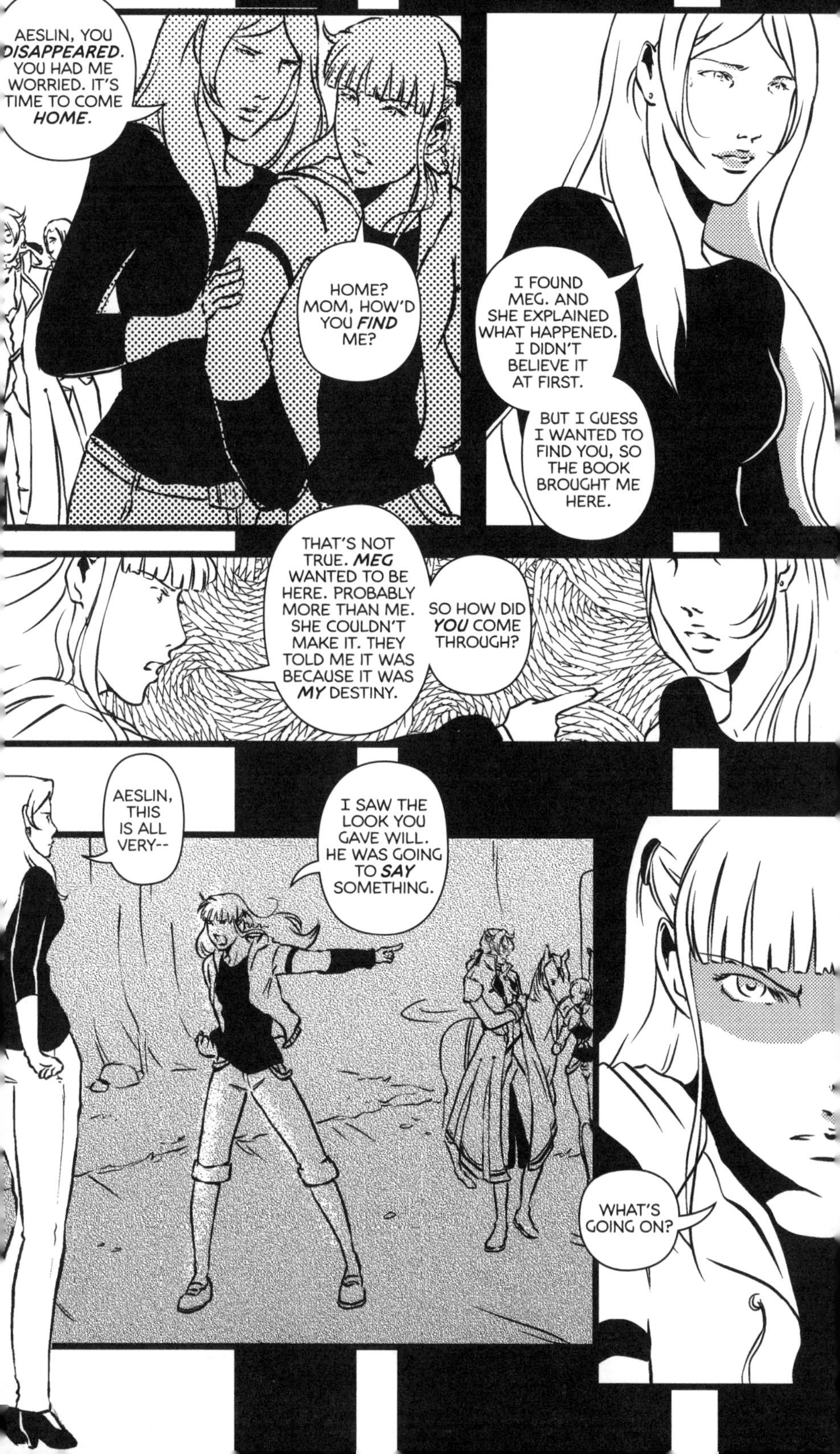
AESLIN, YOU *DISAPPEARED*. YOU HAD ME WORRIED. IT'S TIME TO COME *HOME*.
HOME? MOM, HOW'D YOU *FIND* ME?
I FOUND MEG. AND SHE EXPLAINED WHAT HAPPENED. I DIDN'T BELIEVE IT AT FIRST.
BUT I GUESS I WANTED TO FIND YOU, SO THE BOOK BROUGHT ME HERE.
THAT'S NOT TRUE. *MEG* WANTED TO BE HERE. PROBABLY MORE THAN ME. SHE COULDN'T MAKE IT. THEY TOLD ME IT WAS BECAUSE IT WAS *MY* DESTINY.
SO HOW DID *YOU* COME THROUGH?
AESLIN, THIS IS ALL VERY--
I SAW THE LOOK YOU GAVE WILL. HE WAS GOING TO *SAY* SOMETHING.
WHAT'S GOING ON?

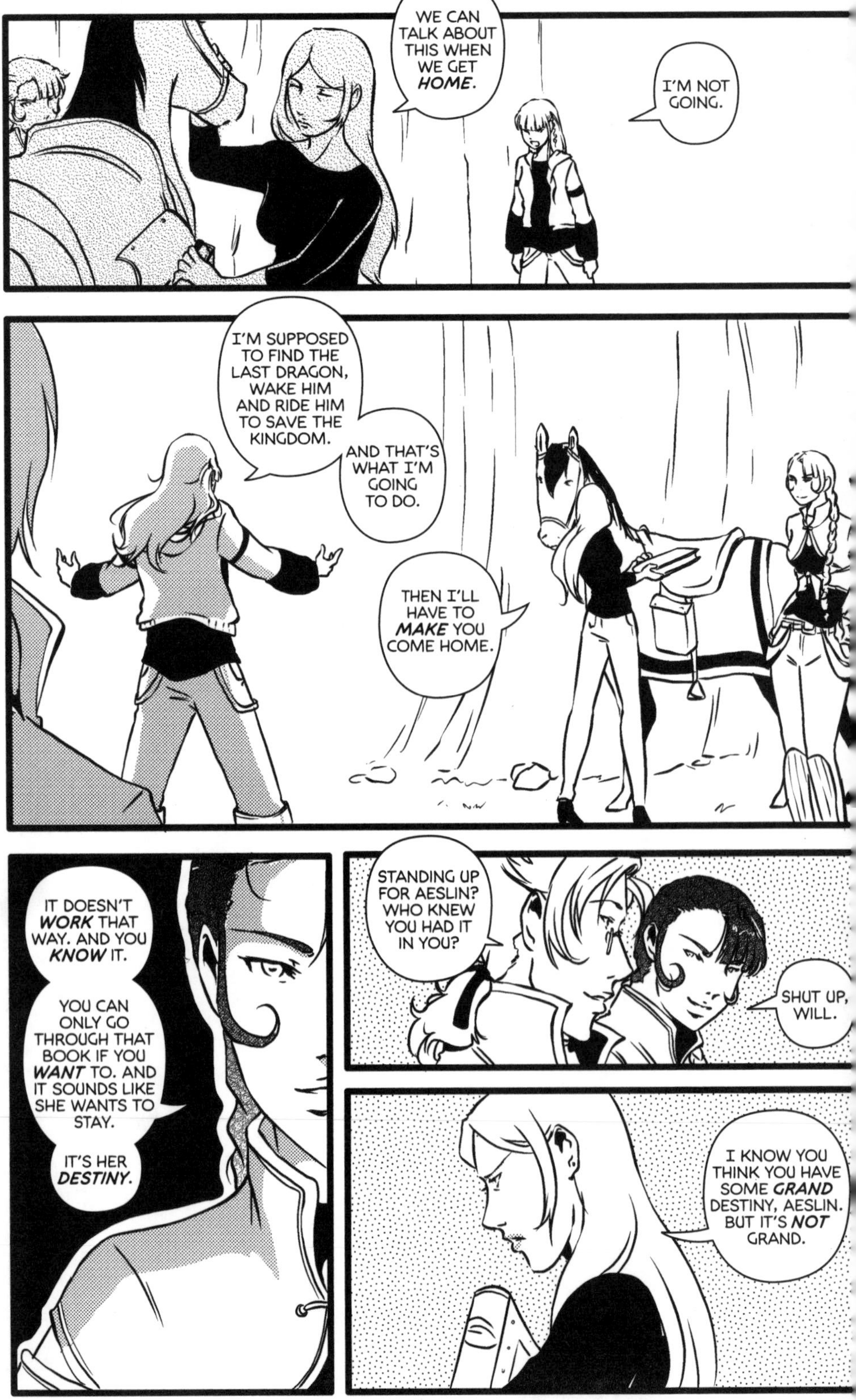
WE CAN TALK ABOUT THIS WHEN WE GET HOME.
I'M NOT GOING.
I'M SUPPOSED TO FIND THE LAST DRAGON, WAKE HIM AND RIDE HIM TO SAVE THE KINGDOM.
AND THAT'S WHAT I'M GOING TO DO.
THEN I'LL HAVE TO MAKE YOU COME HOME.
IT DOESN'T WORK THAT WAY. AND YOU KNOW IT.
YOU CAN ONLY GO THROUGH THAT BOOK IF YOU WANT TO. AND IT SOUNDS LIKE SHE WANTS TO STAY.
IT'S HER DESTINY.
STANDING UP FOR AESLIN? WHO KNEW YOU HAD IT IN YOU?
SHUT UP, WILL.
I KNOW YOU THINK YOU HAVE SOME GRAND DESTINY, AESLIN. BUT IT'S NOT GRAND.

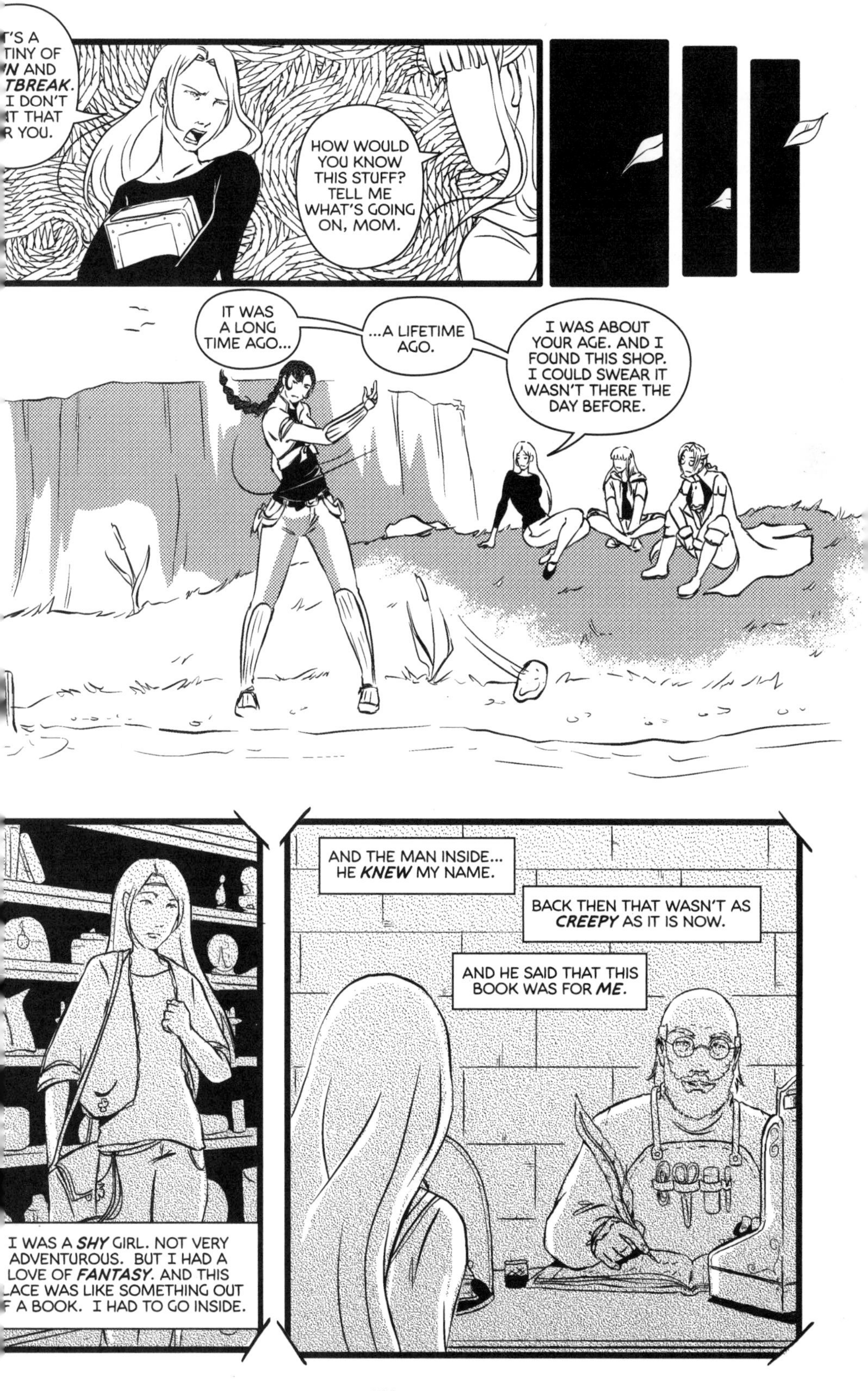
'S A
TINY OF
N AND
TBREAK.
I DON'T
T THAT
R YOU.
HOW WOULD YOU KNOW THIS STUFF? TELL ME WHAT'S GOING ON, MOM.
IT WAS A LONG TIME AGO...
...A LIFETIME AGO.
I WAS ABOUT YOUR AGE. AND I FOUND THIS SHOP. I COULD SWEAR IT WASN'T THERE THE DAY BEFORE.
I WAS A *SHY* GIRL. NOT VERY ADVENTUROUS. BUT I HAD A LOVE OF *FANTASY*. AND THIS
LACE WAS LIKE SOMETHING OUT
F A BOOK. I HAD TO GO INSIDE.
AND THE MAN INSIDE... HE *KNEW* MY NAME.
BACK THEN THAT WASN'T AS *CREEPY* AS IT IS NOW.
AND HE SAID THAT THIS BOOK WAS FOR *ME*.

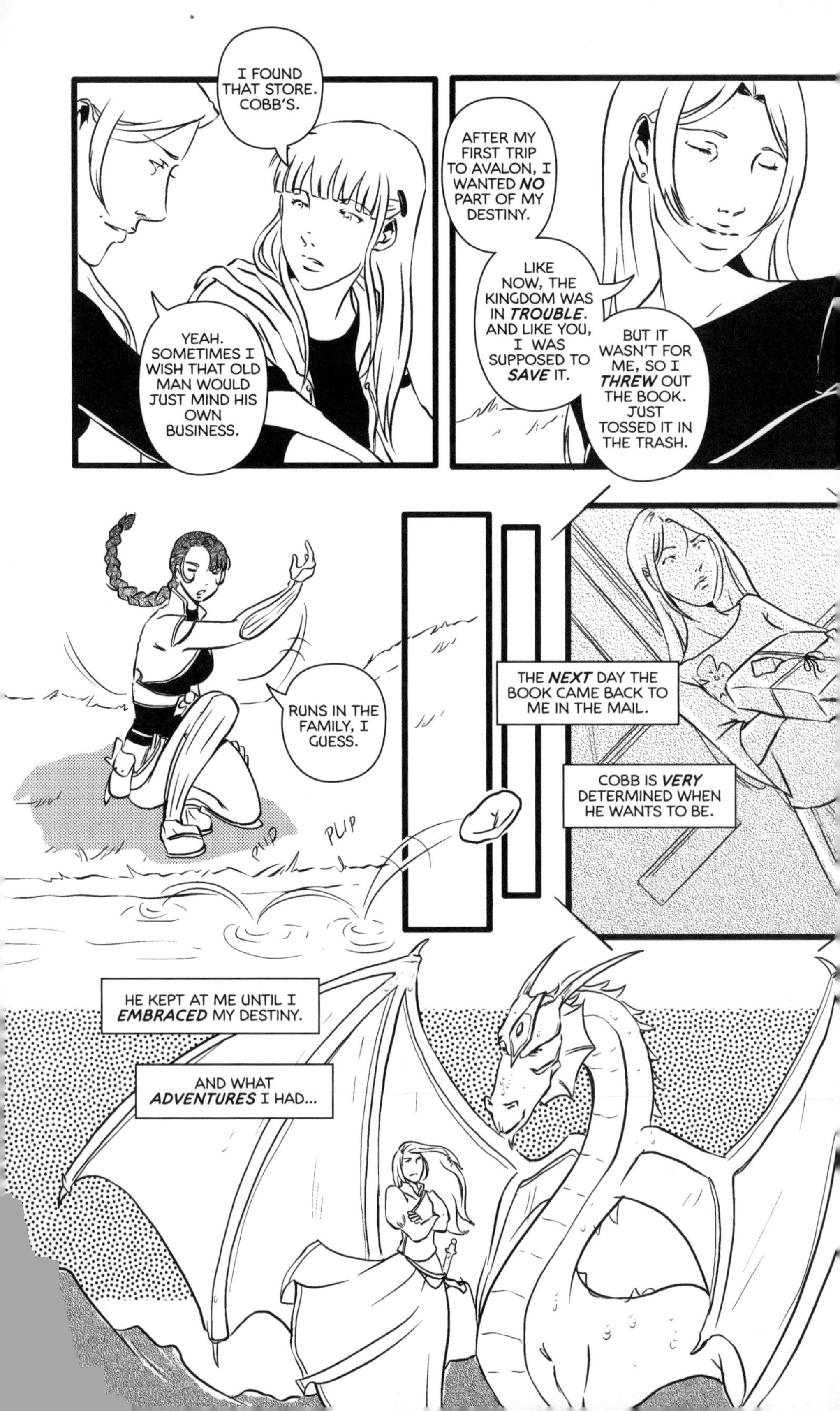
I FOUND THAT STORE. COBB'S.
YEAH. SOMETIMES I WISH THAT OLD MAN WOULD JUST MIND HIS OWN BUSINESS.
AFTER MY FIRST TRIP TO AVALON, I WANTED **NO** PART OF MY DESTINY.
LIKE NOW, THE KINGDOM WAS IN **TROUBLE**. AND LIKE YOU, I WAS SUPPOSED TO **SAVE** IT.
BUT IT WASN'T FOR ME, SO I **THREW** OUT THE BOOK. JUST TOSSED IT IN THE TRASH.
RUNS IN THE FAMILY, I GUESS.
PLIP
PLIP
THE **NEXT** DAY THE BOOK CAME BACK TO ME IN THE MAIL.
COBB IS **VERY** DETERMINED WHEN HE WANTS TO BE.
HE KEPT AT ME UNTIL I **EMBRACED** MY DESTINY.
AND WHAT **ADVENTURES** I HAD...

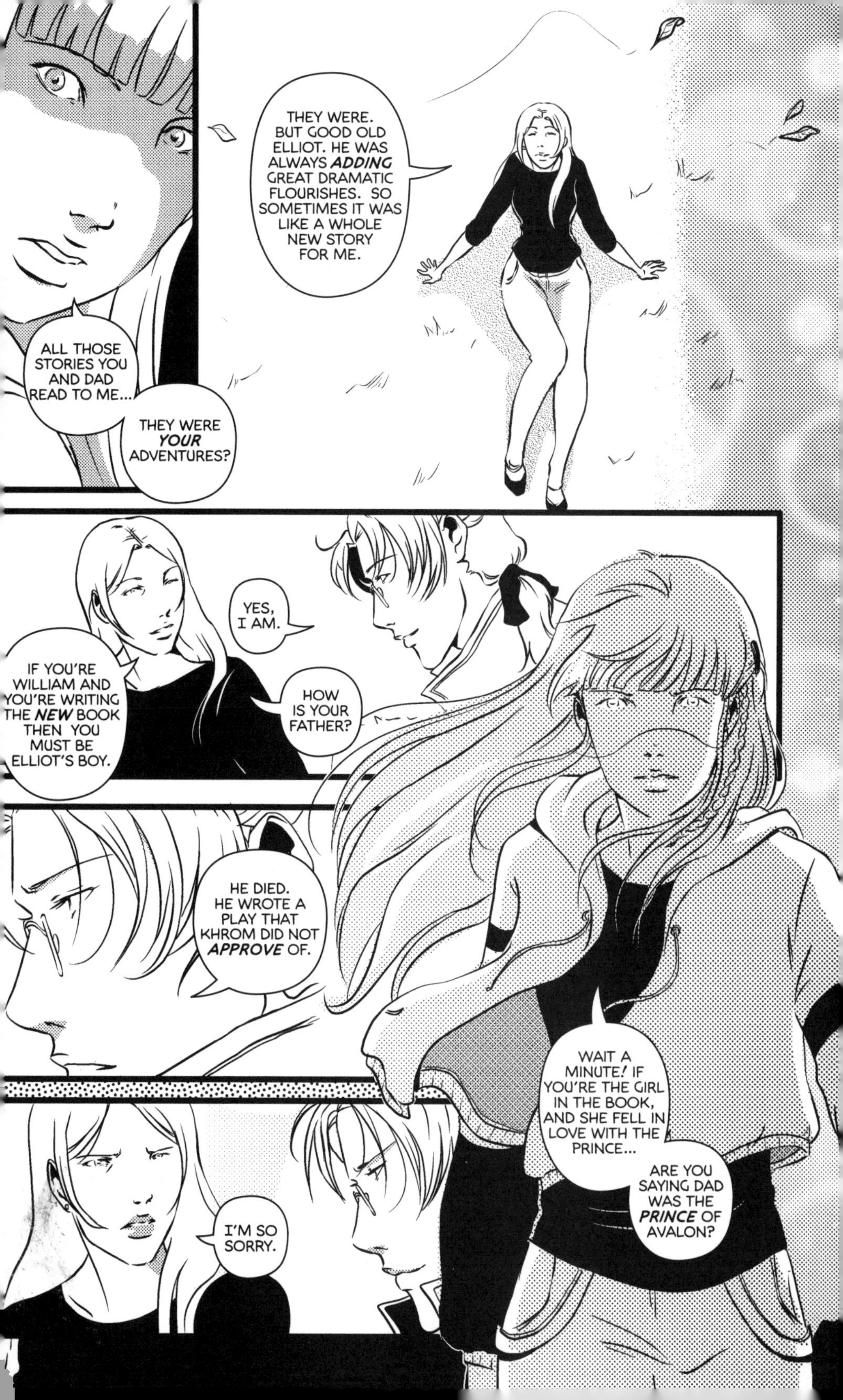

ALL THOSE STORIES YOU AND DAD READ TO ME...
THEY WERE *YOUR* ADVENTURES?
THEY WERE. BUT GOOD OLD ELLIOT. HE WAS ALWAYS *ADDING* GREAT DRAMATIC FLOURISHES. SO SOMETIMES IT WAS LIKE A WHOLE NEW STORY FOR ME.
IF YOU'RE WILLIAM AND YOU'RE WRITING THE *NEW* BOOK THEN YOU MUST BE ELLIOT'S BOY.
YES, I AM.
HOW IS YOUR FATHER?
HE DIED. HE WROTE A PLAY THAT KHROM DID NOT *APPROVE* OF.
I'M SO SORRY.
WAIT A MINUTE! IF YOU'RE THE GIRL IN THE BOOK, AND SHE FELL IN LOVE WITH THE PRINCE...
ARE YOU SAYING DAD WAS THE *PRINCE* OF AVALON?

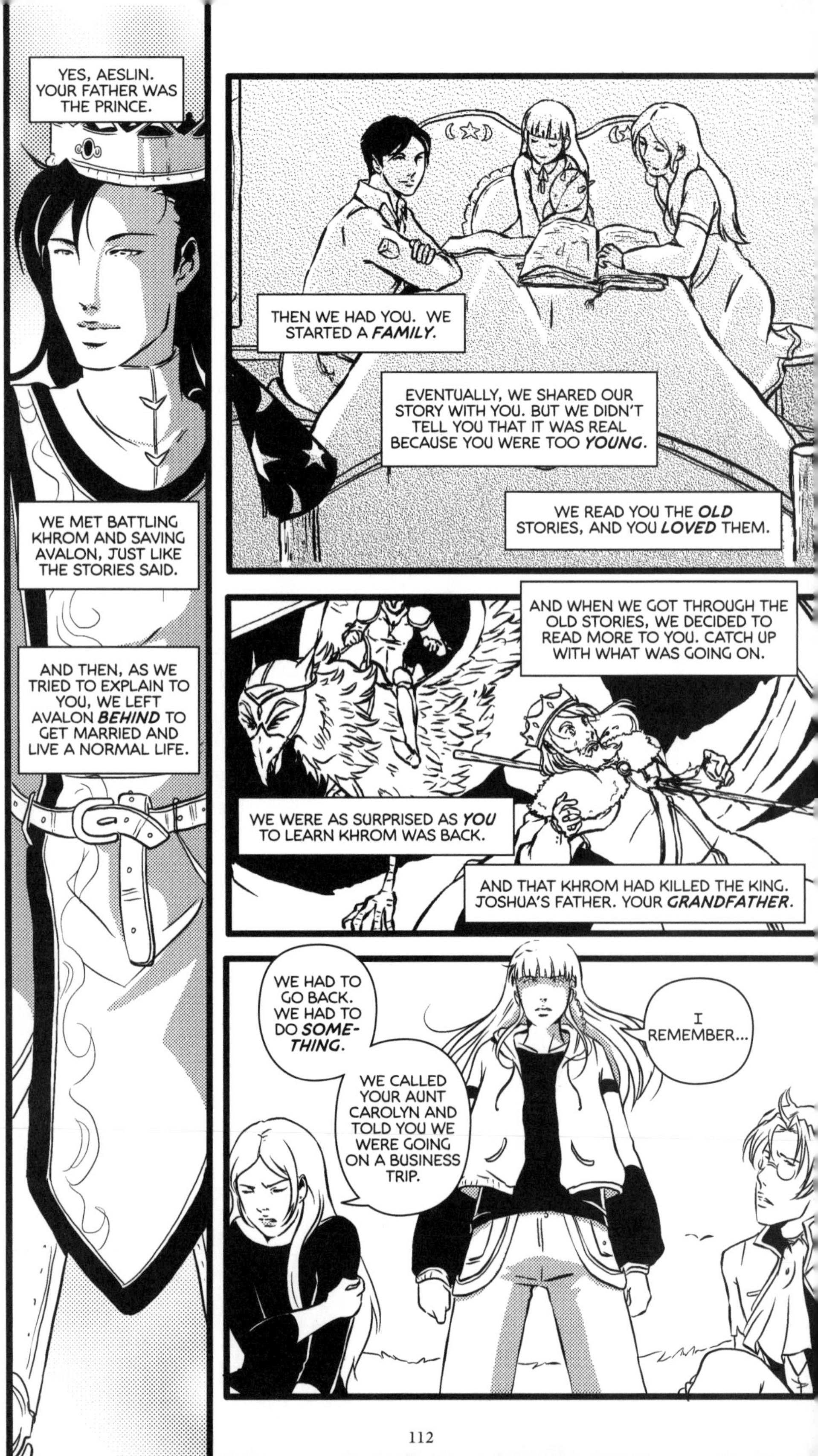
YES, AESLIN. YOUR FATHER WAS THE PRINCE.
WE MET BATTLING KHROM AND SAVING AVALON, JUST LIKE THE STORIES SAID.
AND THEN, AS WE TRIED TO EXPLAIN TO YOU, WE LEFT AVALON *BEHIND* TO GET MARRIED AND LIVE A NORMAL LIFE.
THEN WE HAD YOU. WE STARTED A *FAMILY*.
EVENTUALLY, WE SHARED OUR STORY WITH YOU. BUT WE DIDN'T TELL YOU THAT IT WAS REAL BECAUSE YOU WERE TOO *YOUNG*.
WE READ YOU THE *OLD* STORIES, AND YOU *LOVED* THEM.
AND WHEN WE GOT THROUGH THE OLD STORIES, WE DECIDED TO READ MORE TO YOU. CATCH UP WITH WHAT WAS GOING ON.
WE WERE AS SURPRISED AS *YOU* TO LEARN KHROM WAS BACK.
AND THAT KHROM HAD KILLED THE KING. JOSHUA'S FATHER. YOUR *GRANDFATHER*.
WE HAD TO GO BACK. WE HAD TO DO *SOME-THING*.
WE CALLED YOUR AUNT CAROLYN AND TOLD YOU WE WERE GOING ON A BUSINESS TRIP.
I REMEMBER...

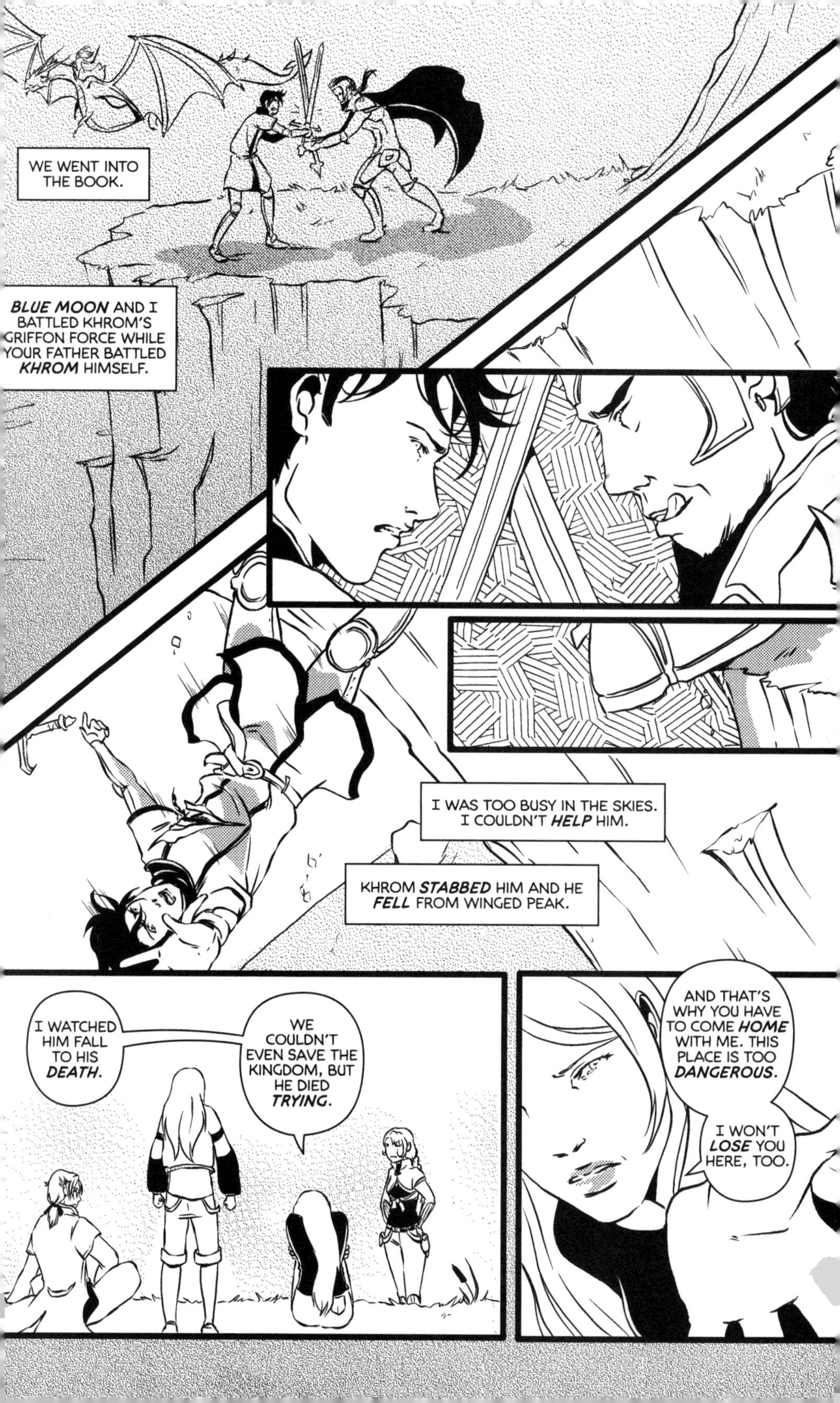
WE WENT INTO THE BOOK.
BLUE MOON AND I BATTLED KHROM'S GRIFFON FORCE WHILE YOUR FATHER BATTLED KHROM HIMSELF.
I WAS TOO BUSY IN THE SKIES. I COULDN'T HELP HIM.
KHROM STABBED HIM AND HE FELL FROM WINGED PEAK.
I WATCHED HIM FALL TO HIS DEATH.
WE COULDN'T EVEN SAVE THE KINGDOM, BUT HE DIED TRYING.
AND THAT'S WHY YOU HAVE TO COME HOME WITH ME. THIS PLACE IS TOO DANGEROUS.
I WON'T LOSE YOU HERE, TOO.

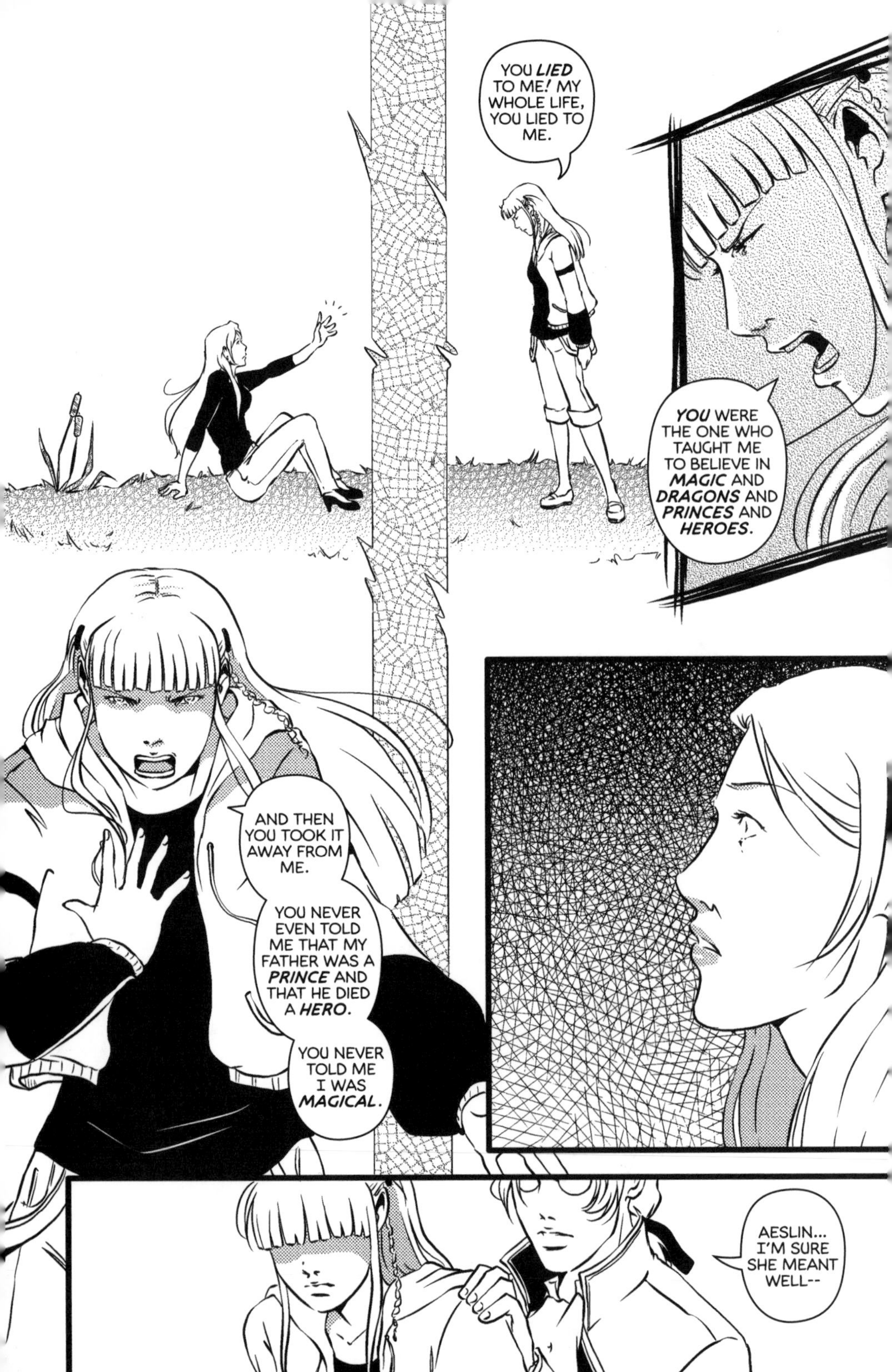
YOU LIED TO ME! MY WHOLE LIFE, YOU LIED TO ME.
YOU WERE THE ONE WHO TAUGHT ME TO BELIEVE IN MAGIC AND DRAGONS AND PRINCES AND HEROES.
AND THEN YOU TOOK IT AWAY FROM ME.
YOU NEVER EVEN TOLD ME THAT MY FATHER WAS A PRINCE AND THAT HE DIED A HERO.
YOU NEVER TOLD ME I WAS MAGICAL.
AESLIN... I'M SURE SHE MEANT WELL--

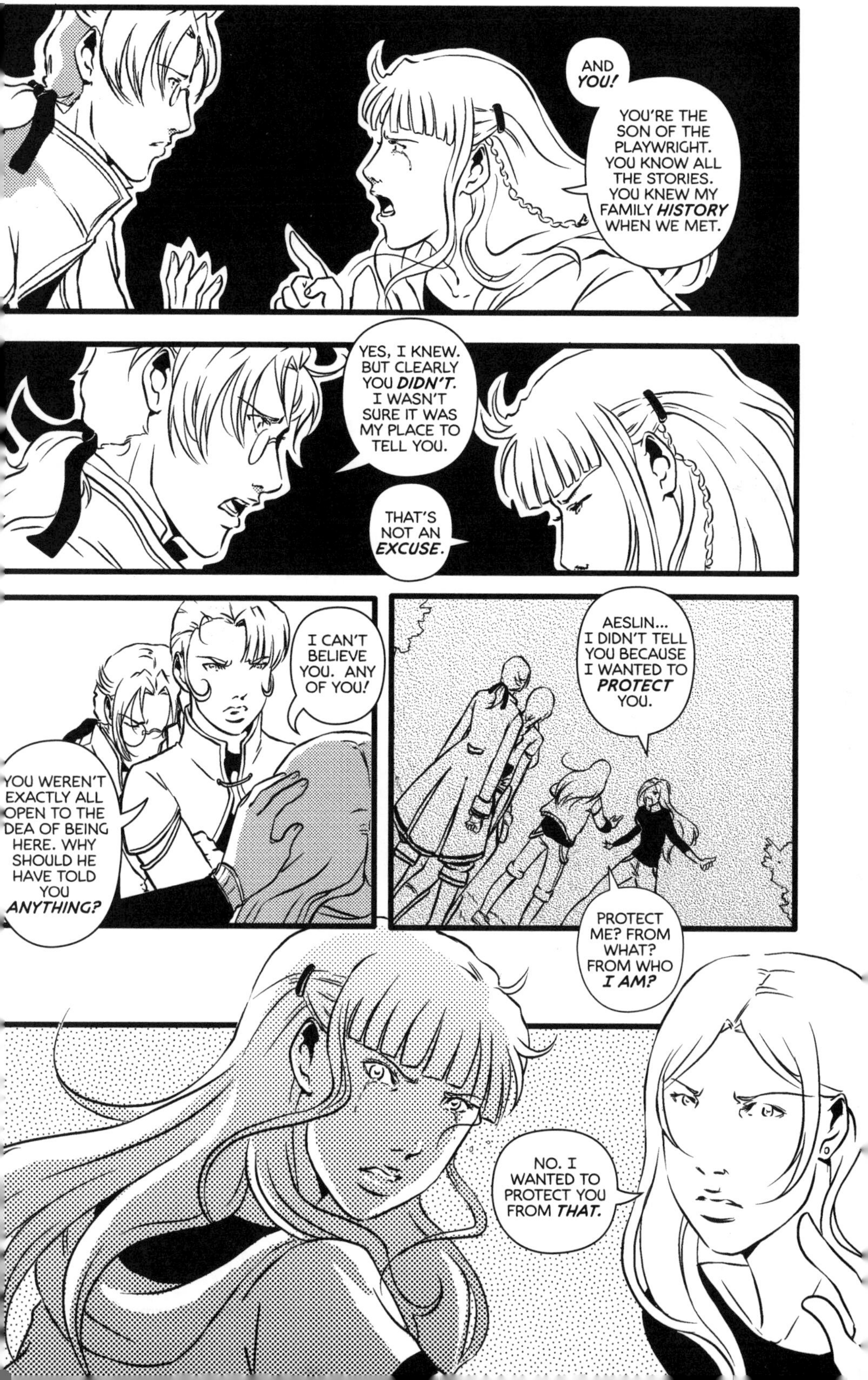
AND *YOU!*
YOU'RE THE SON OF THE PLAYWRIGHT. YOU KNOW ALL THE STORIES. YOU KNEW MY FAMILY *HISTORY* WHEN WE MET.
YES, I KNEW. BUT CLEARLY YOU *DIDN'T*. I WASN'T SURE IT WAS MY PLACE TO TELL YOU.
THAT'S NOT AN *EXCUSE*.
I CAN'T BELIEVE YOU. ANY OF YOU!
YOU WEREN'T EXACTLY ALL OPEN TO THE DEA OF BEING HERE. WHY SHOULD HE HAVE TOLD YOU *ANYTHING?*
AESLIN... I DIDN'T TELL YOU BECAUSE I WANTED TO *PROTECT* YOU.
PROTECT ME? FROM WHAT? FROM WHO *I AM?*
NO. I WANTED TO PROTECT YOU FROM *THAT.*

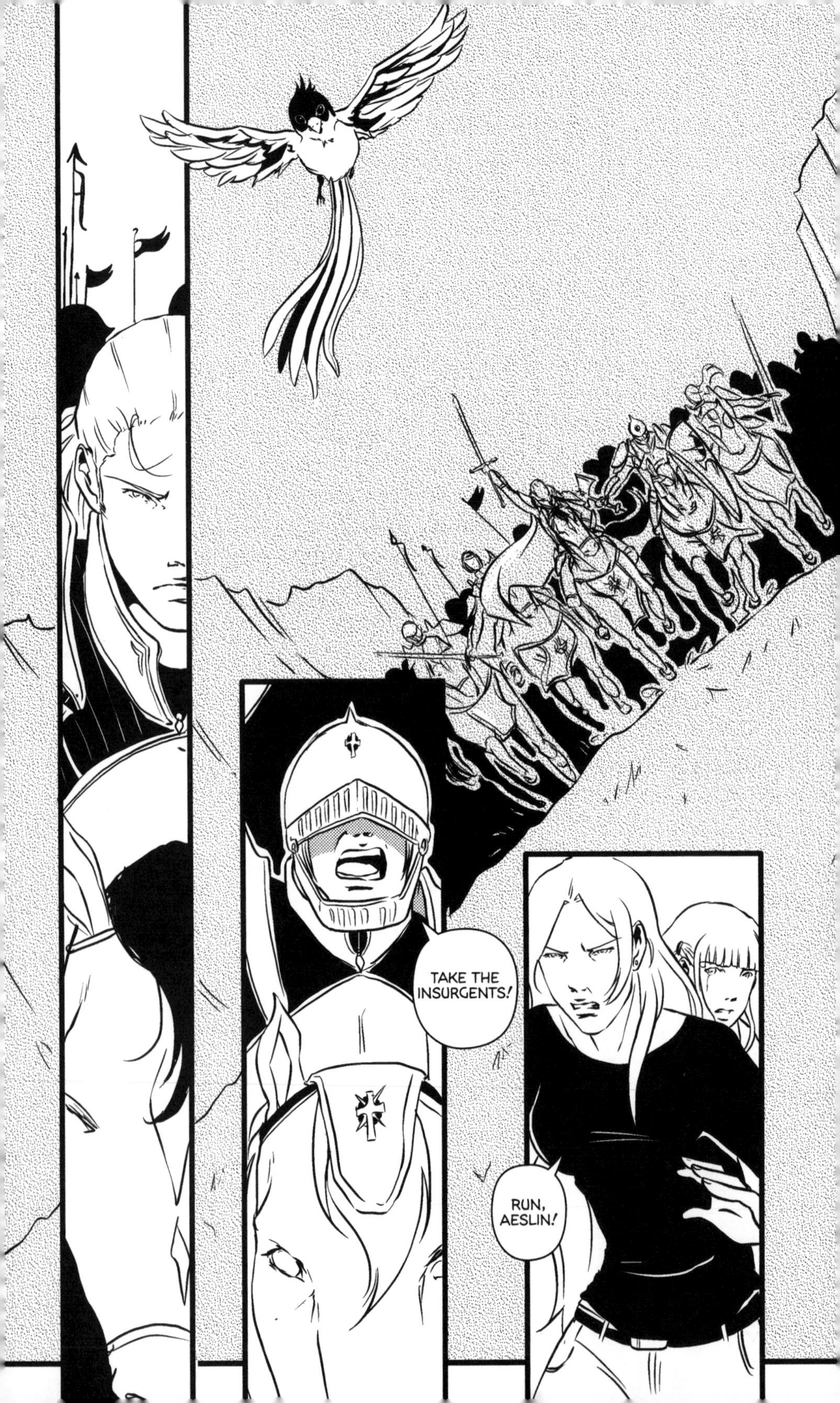
TAKE THE INSURGENTS!
RUN, AESLIN!

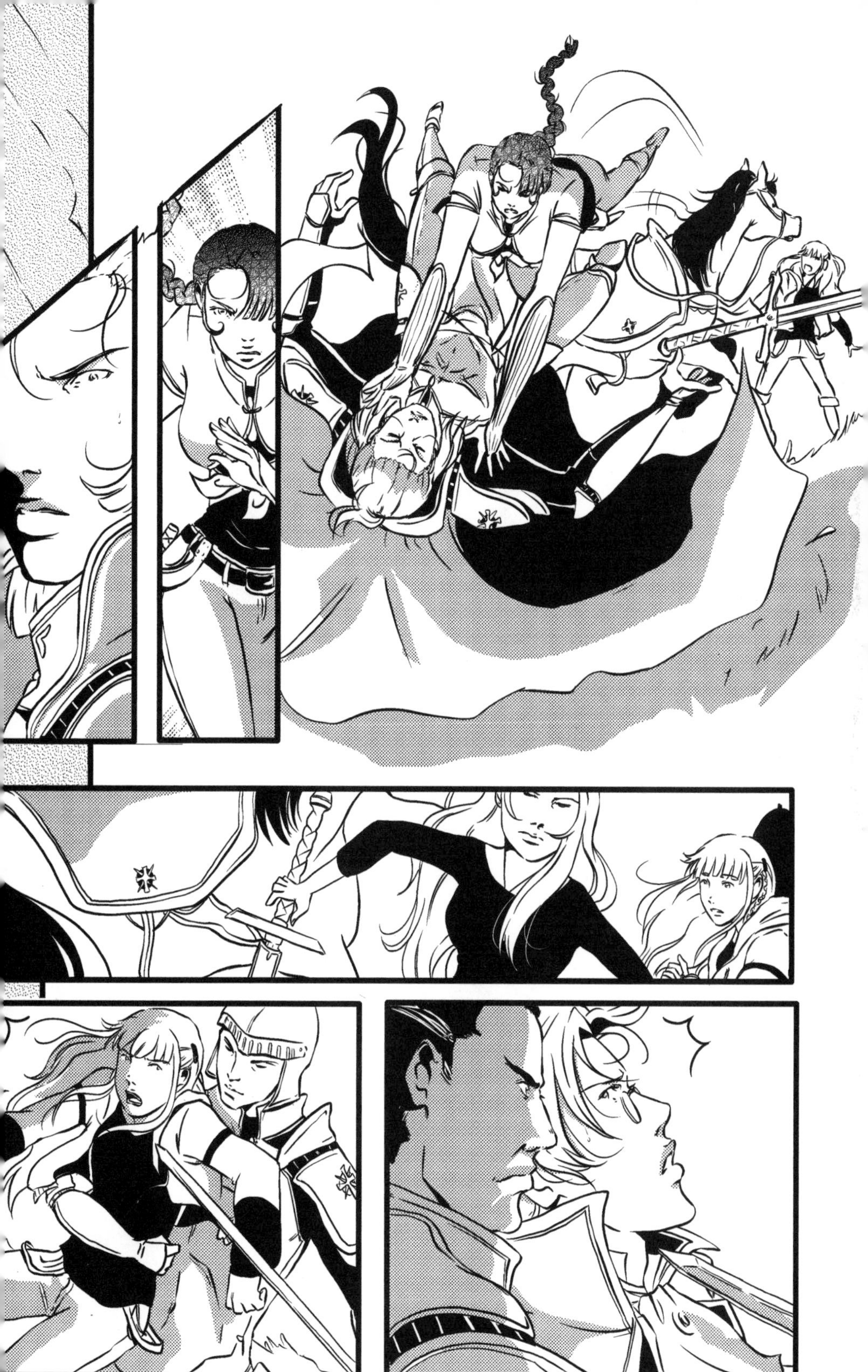

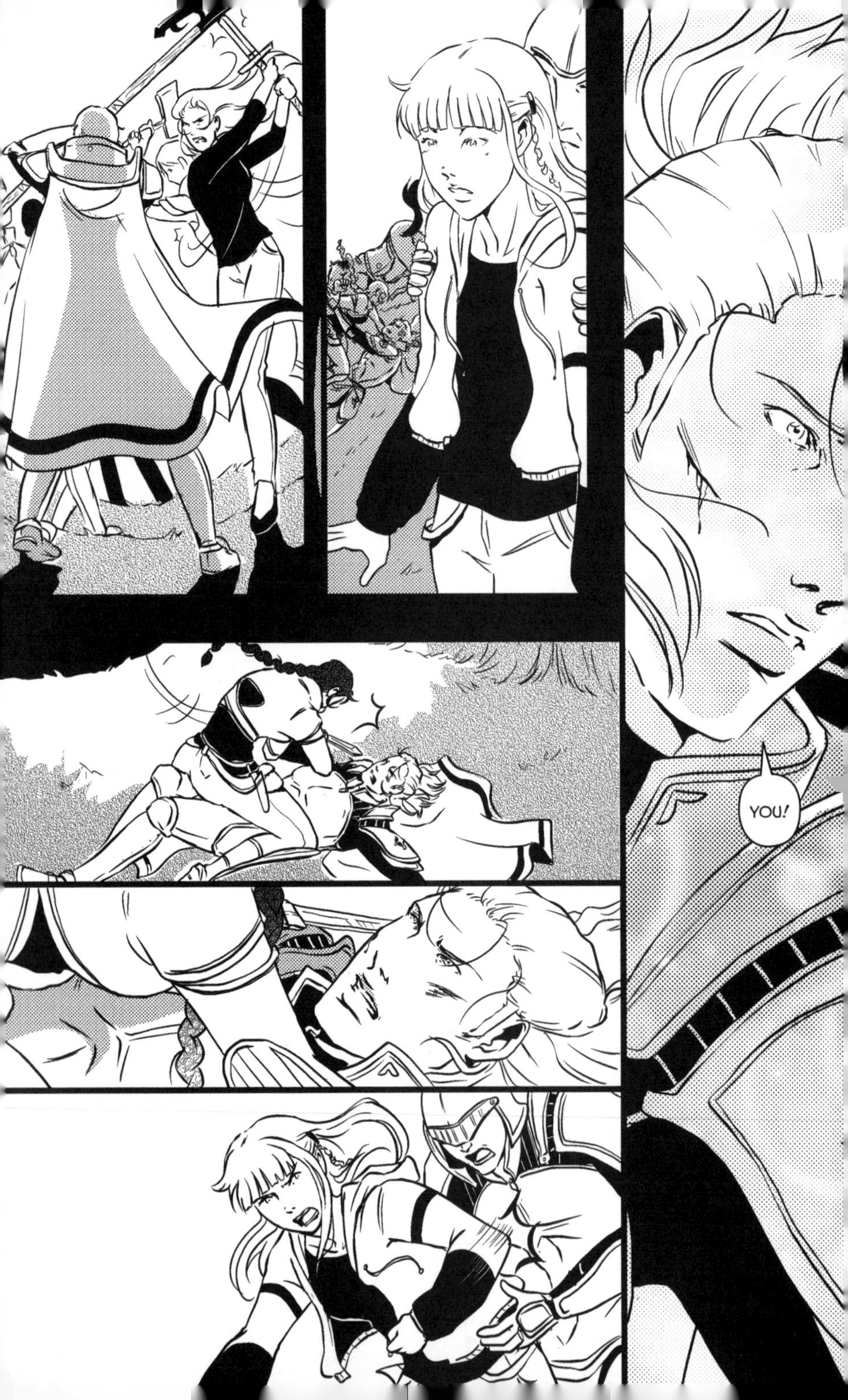
YOU!

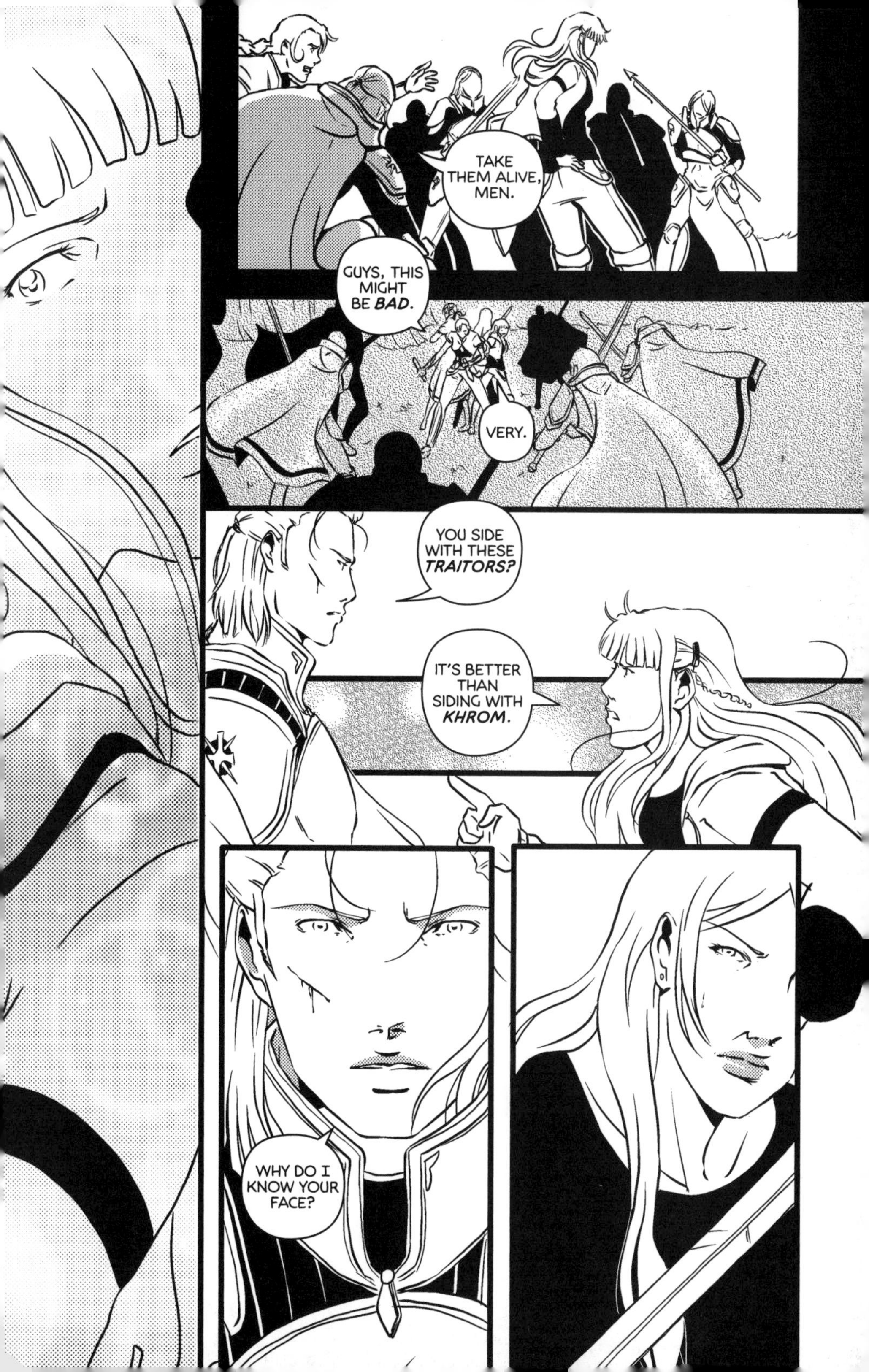
TAKE THEM ALIVE, MEN.
GUYS, THIS MIGHT BE *BAD*.
VERY.
YOU SIDE WITH THESE *TRAITORS?*
IT'S BETTER THAN SIDING WITH *KHROM*.
WHY DO I KNOW YOUR FACE?

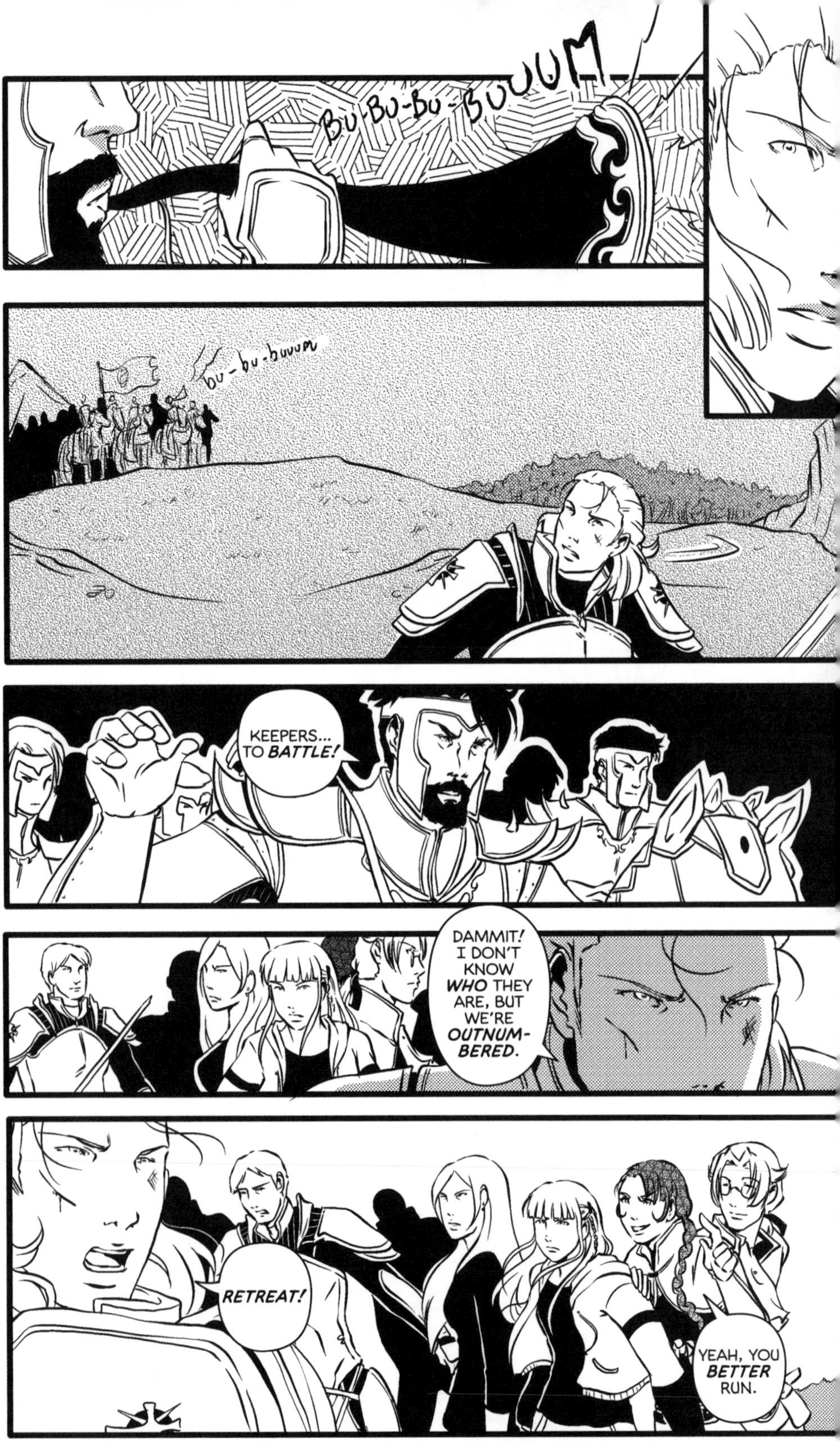
BU-BU-BU-BUUUM
bu-bu-buuum
KEEPERS... TO BATTLE!
DAMMIT! I DON'T KNOW WHO THEY ARE, BUT WE'RE OUTNUMBERED.
RETREAT!
YEAH, YOU BETTER RUN.

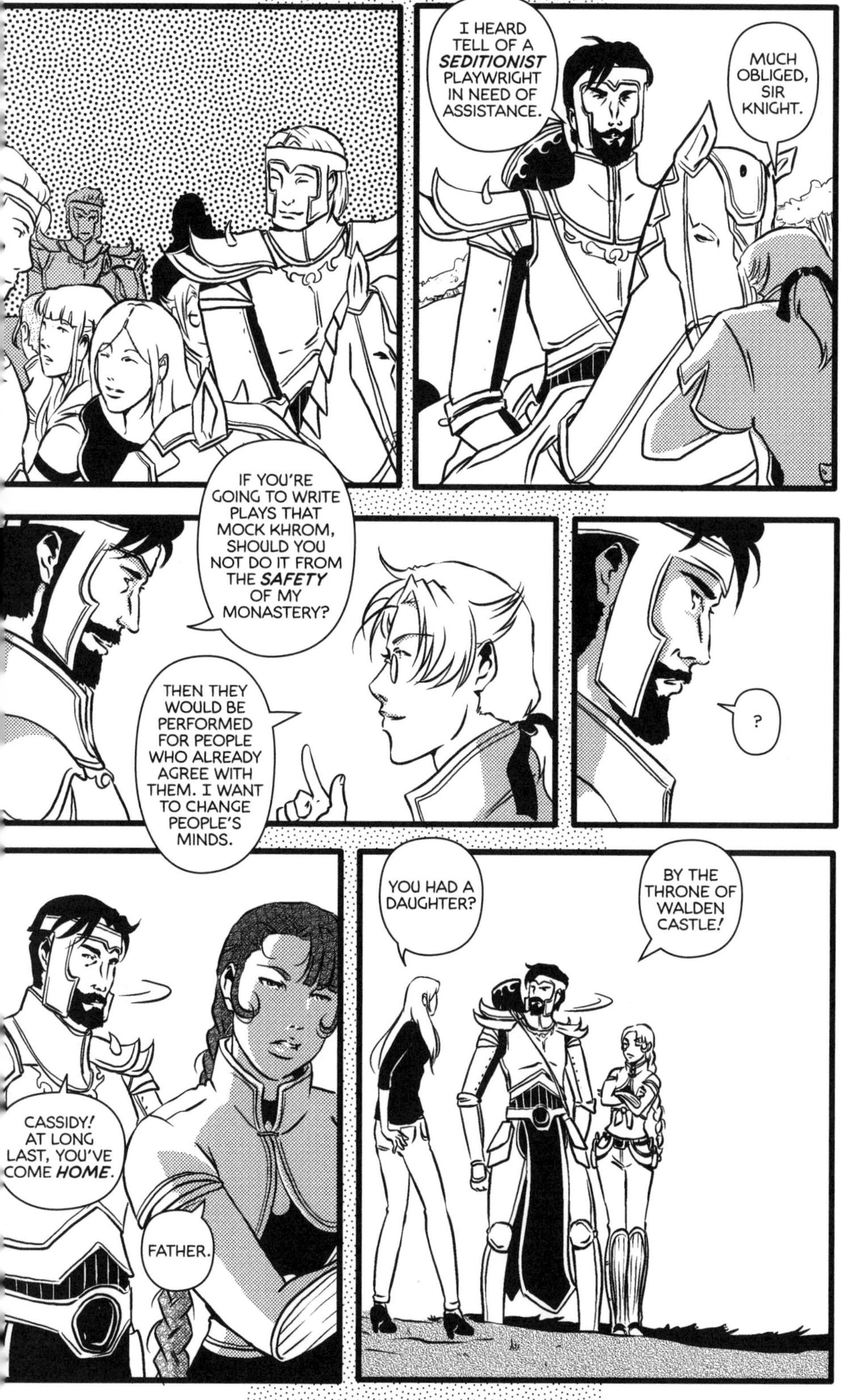
I HEARD TELL OF A *SEDITIONIST* PLAYWRIGHT IN NEED OF ASSISTANCE.
MUCH OBLIGED, SIR KNIGHT.
IF YOU'RE GOING TO WRITE PLAYS THAT MOCK KHROM, SHOULD YOU NOT DO IT FROM THE *SAFETY* OF MY MONASTERY?
THEN THEY WOULD BE PERFORMED FOR PEOPLE WHO ALREADY AGREE WITH THEM. I WANT TO CHANGE PEOPLE'S MINDS.
?
CASSIDY*!* AT LONG LAST, YOU'VE COME *HOME*.
FATHER.
YOU HAD A DAUGHTER?
BY THE THRONE OF WALDEN CASTLE*!*

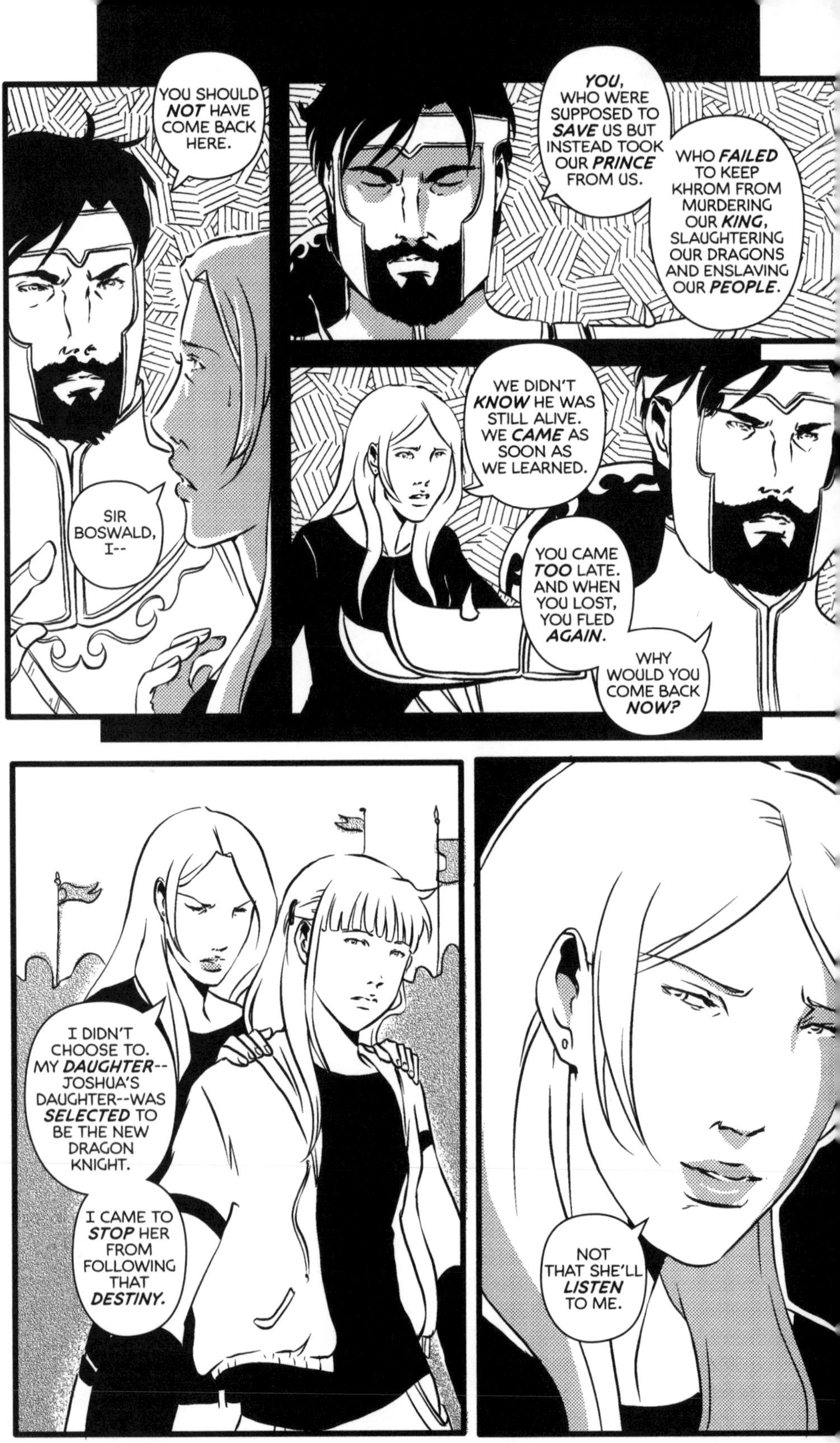

YOU SHOULD NOT HAVE COME BACK HERE.
SIR BOSWALD, I--
YOU, WHO WERE SUPPOSED TO SAVE US BUT INSTEAD TOOK OUR PRINCE FROM US.
WHO FAILED TO KEEP KHROM FROM MURDERING OUR KING, SLAUGHTERING OUR DRAGONS AND ENSLAVING OUR PEOPLE.
WE DIDN'T KNOW HE WAS STILL ALIVE. WE CAME AS SOON AS WE LEARNED.
YOU CAME TOO LATE. AND WHEN YOU LOST, YOU FLED AGAIN.
WHY WOULD YOU COME BACK NOW?
I DIDN'T CHOOSE TO. MY DAUGHTER-- JOSHUA'S DAUGHTER--WAS SELECTED TO BE THE NEW DRAGON KNIGHT.
I CAME TO STOP HER FROM FOLLOWING THAT DESTINY.
NOT THAT SHE'LL LISTEN TO ME.

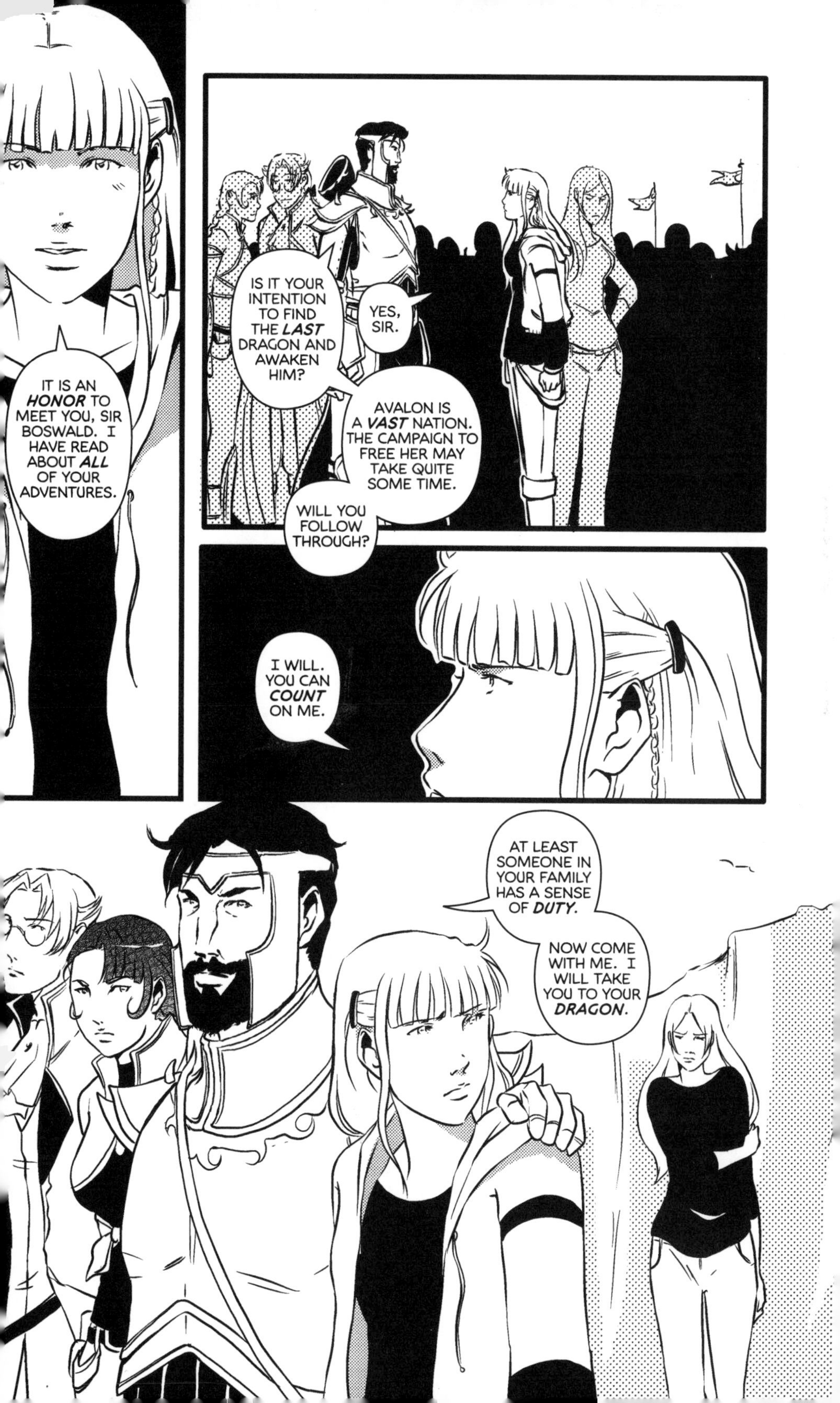
IT IS AN HONOR TO MEET YOU, SIR BOSWALD. I HAVE READ ABOUT ALL OF YOUR ADVENTURES.
IS IT YOUR INTENTION TO FIND THE LAST DRAGON AND AWAKEN HIM?
YES, SIR.
AVALON IS A VAST NATION. THE CAMPAIGN TO FREE HER MAY TAKE QUITE SOME TIME.
WILL YOU FOLLOW THROUGH?
I WILL. YOU CAN COUNT ON ME.
AT LEAST SOMEONE IN YOUR FAMILY HAS A SENSE OF DUTY.
NOW COME WITH ME. I WILL TAKE YOU TO YOUR DRAGON.

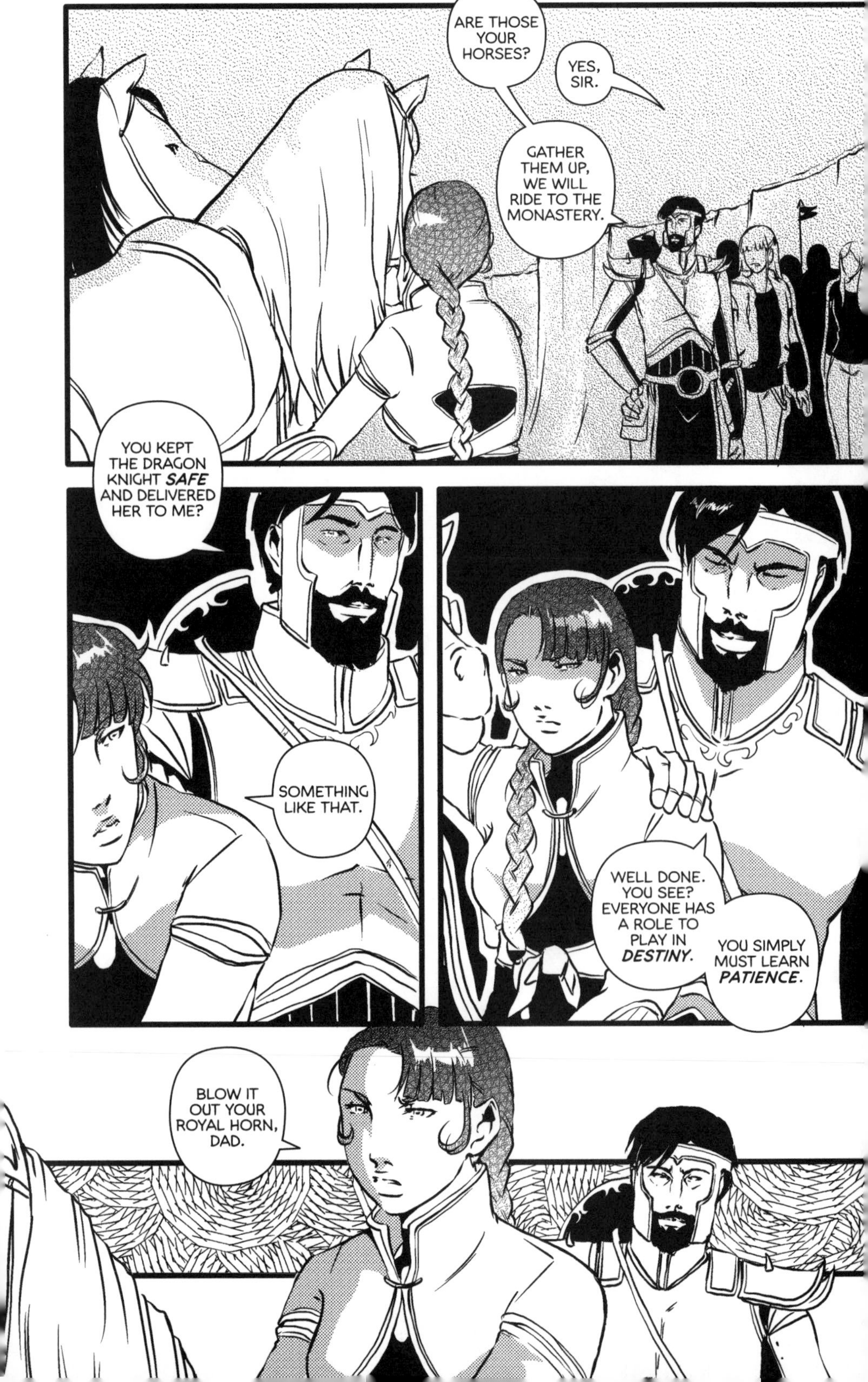
ARE THOSE YOUR HORSES?
YES, SIR.
GATHER THEM UP, WE WILL RIDE TO THE MONASTERY.
YOU KEPT THE DRAGON KNIGHT *SAFE* AND DELIVERED HER TO ME?
SOMETHING LIKE THAT.
WELL DONE. YOU SEE? EVERYONE HAS A ROLE TO PLAY IN *DESTINY*.
YOU SIMPLY MUST LEARN *PATIENCE*.
BLOW IT OUT YOUR ROYAL HORN, DAD.

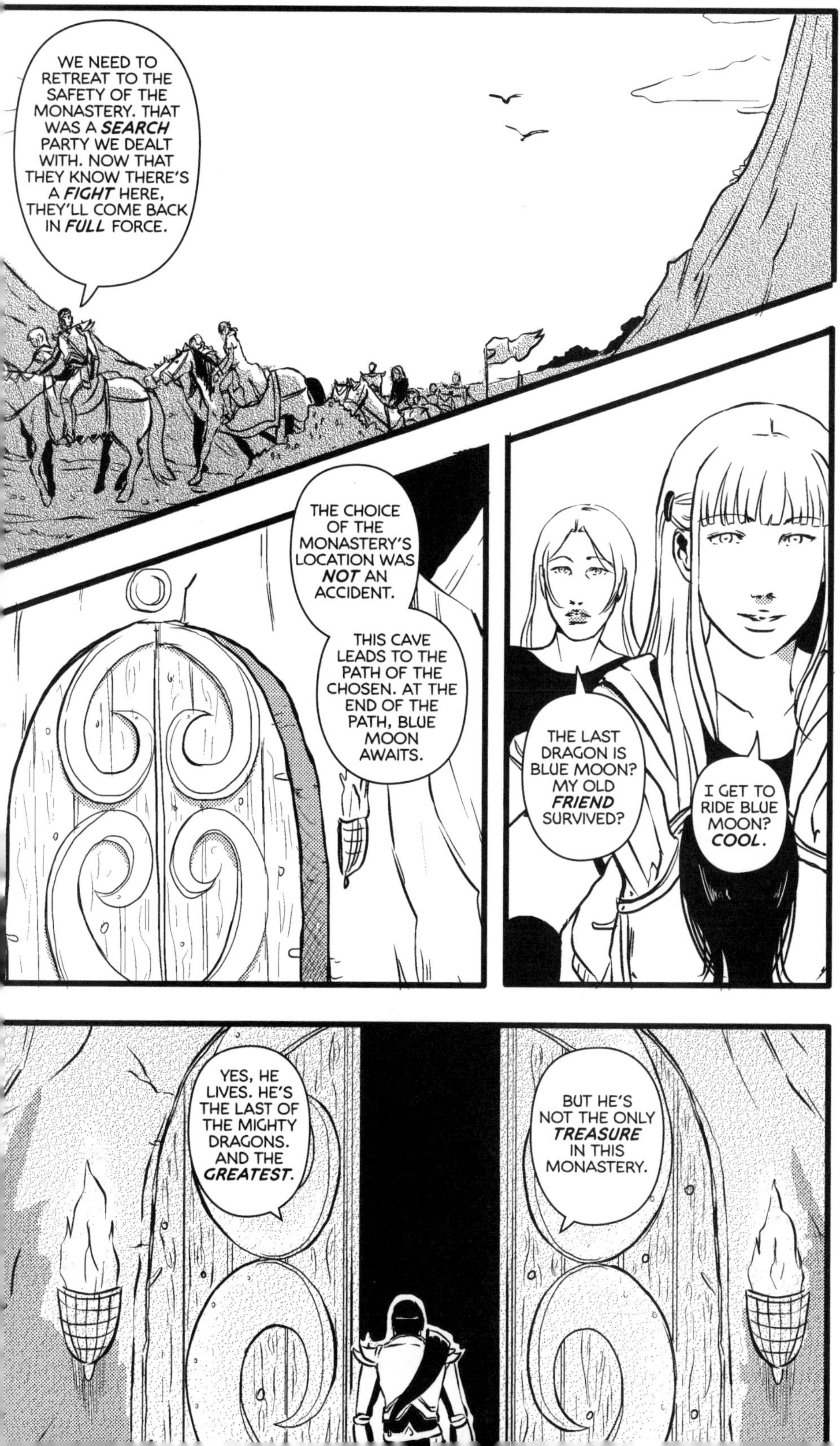
WE NEED TO RETREAT TO THE SAFETY OF THE MONASTERY. THAT WAS A *SEARCH* PARTY WE DEALT WITH. NOW THAT THEY KNOW THERE'S A *FIGHT* HERE, THEY'LL COME BACK IN *FULL* FORCE.
THE CHOICE OF THE MONASTERY'S LOCATION WAS *NOT* AN ACCIDENT.
THIS CAVE LEADS TO THE PATH OF THE CHOSEN. AT THE END OF THE PATH, BLUE MOON AWAITS.
THE LAST DRAGON IS BLUE MOON? MY OLD *FRIEND* SURVIVED?
I GET TO RIDE BLUE MOON? *COOL*.
YES, HE LIVES. HE'S THE LAST OF THE MIGHTY DRAGONS. AND THE *GREATEST*.
BUT HE'S NOT THE ONLY *TREASURE* IN THIS MONASTERY.

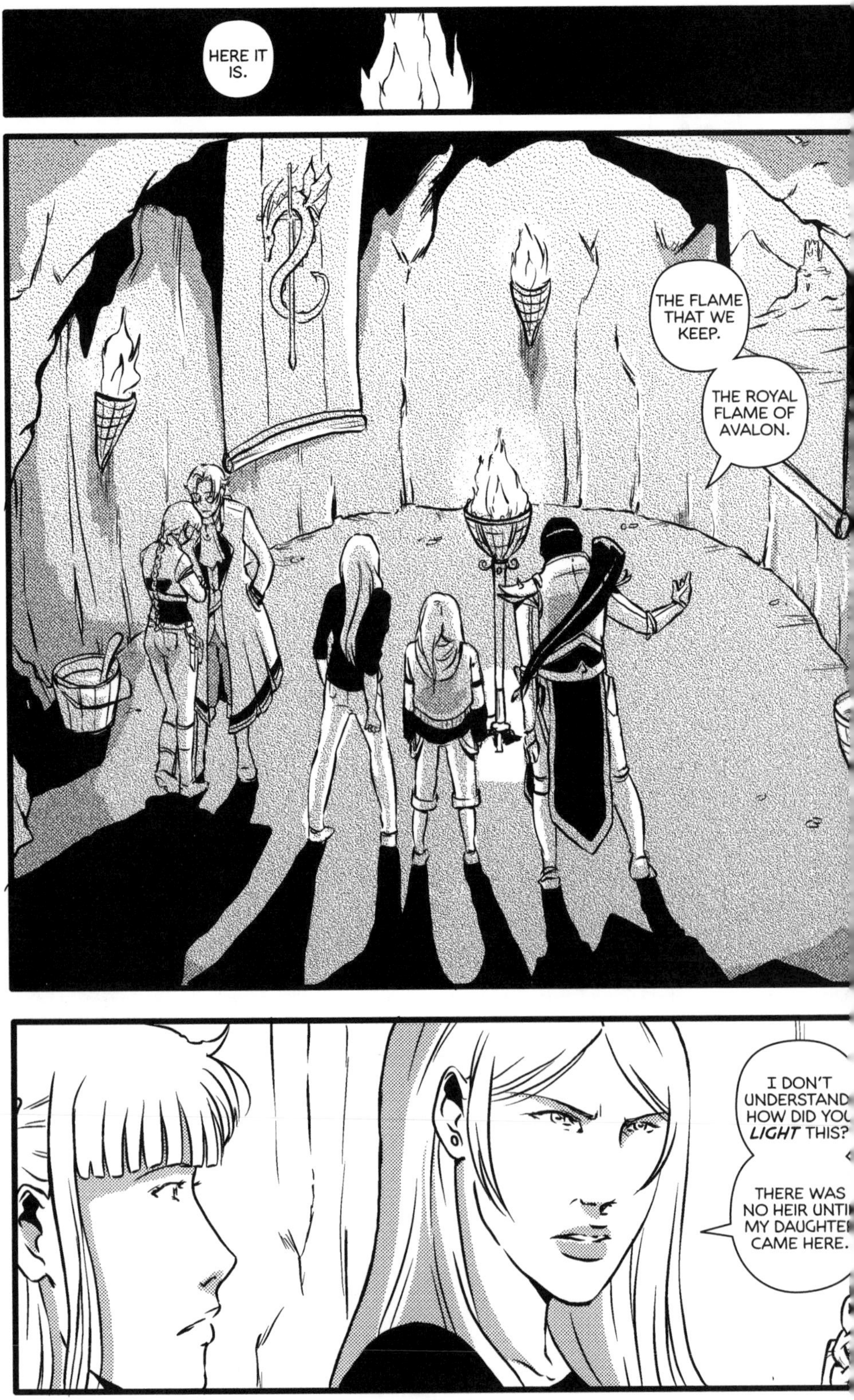
HERE IT IS.
THE FLAME THAT WE KEEP.
THE ROYAL FLAME OF AVALON.
I DON'T UNDERSTAND HOW DID YOU *LIGHT* THIS?
THERE WAS NO HEIR UNTI MY DAUGHTE CAME HERE.

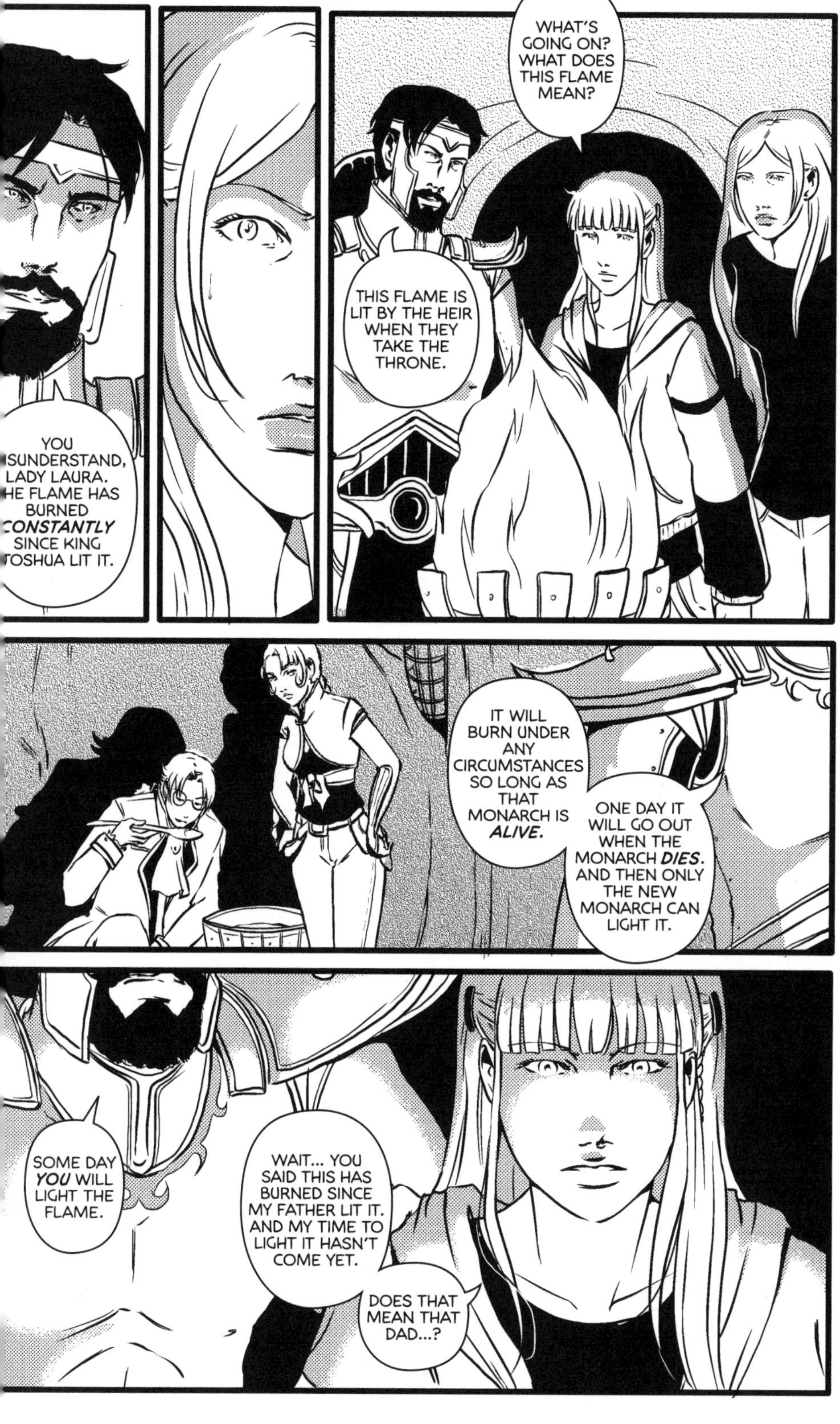
YOU
SUNDERSTAND, LADY LAURA. HE FLAME HAS BURNED *CONSTANTLY* SINCE KING OSHUA LIT IT.
WHAT'S GOING ON? WHAT DOES THIS FLAME MEAN?
THIS FLAME IS LIT BY THE HEIR WHEN THEY TAKE THE THRONE.
IT WILL BURN UNDER ANY CIRCUMSTANCES SO LONG AS THAT MONARCH IS *ALIVE.*
ONE DAY IT WILL GO OUT WHEN THE MONARCH *DIES.* AND THEN ONLY THE NEW MONARCH CAN LIGHT IT.
SOME DAY *YOU* WILL LIGHT THE FLAME.
WAIT... YOU SAID THIS HAS BURNED SINCE MY FATHER LIT IT. AND MY TIME TO LIGHT IT HASN'T COME YET.
DOES THAT MEAN THAT DAD...?

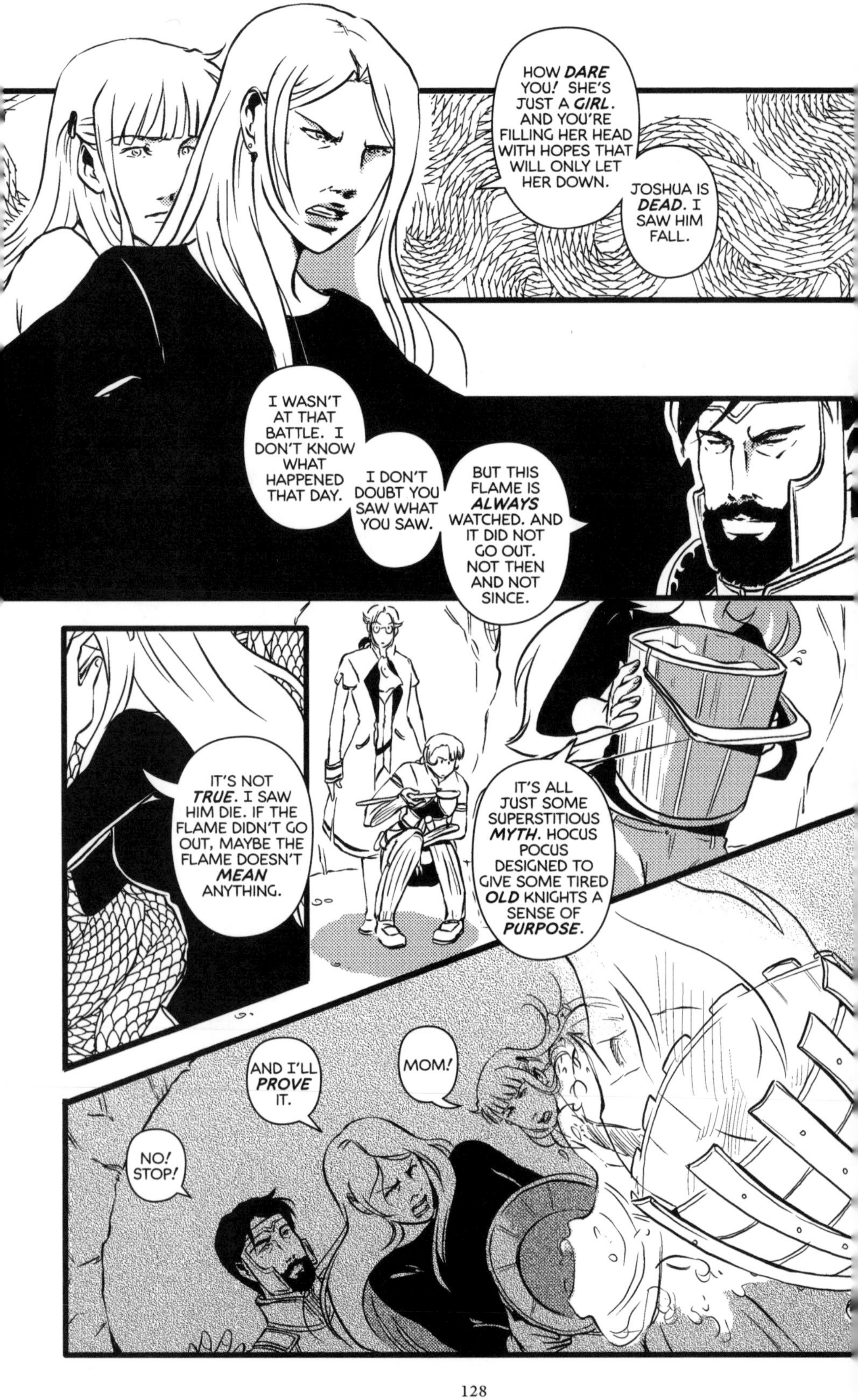

HOW DARE YOU! SHE'S JUST A GIRL. AND YOU'RE FILLING HER HEAD WITH HOPES THAT WILL ONLY LET HER DOWN.
JOSHUA IS DEAD. I SAW HIM FALL.
I WASN'T AT THAT BATTLE. I DON'T KNOW WHAT HAPPENED THAT DAY.
I DON'T DOUBT YOU SAW WHAT YOU SAW.
BUT THIS FLAME IS ALWAYS WATCHED. AND IT DID NOT GO OUT. NOT THEN AND NOT SINCE.
IT'S NOT TRUE. I SAW HIM DIE. IF THE FLAME DIDN'T GO OUT, MAYBE THE FLAME DOESN'T MEAN ANYTHING.
IT'S ALL JUST SOME SUPERSTITIOUS MYTH. HOCUS POCUS DESIGNED TO GIVE SOME TIRED OLD KNIGHTS A SENSE OF PURPOSE.
AND I'LL PROVE IT.
MOM!
NO! STOP!

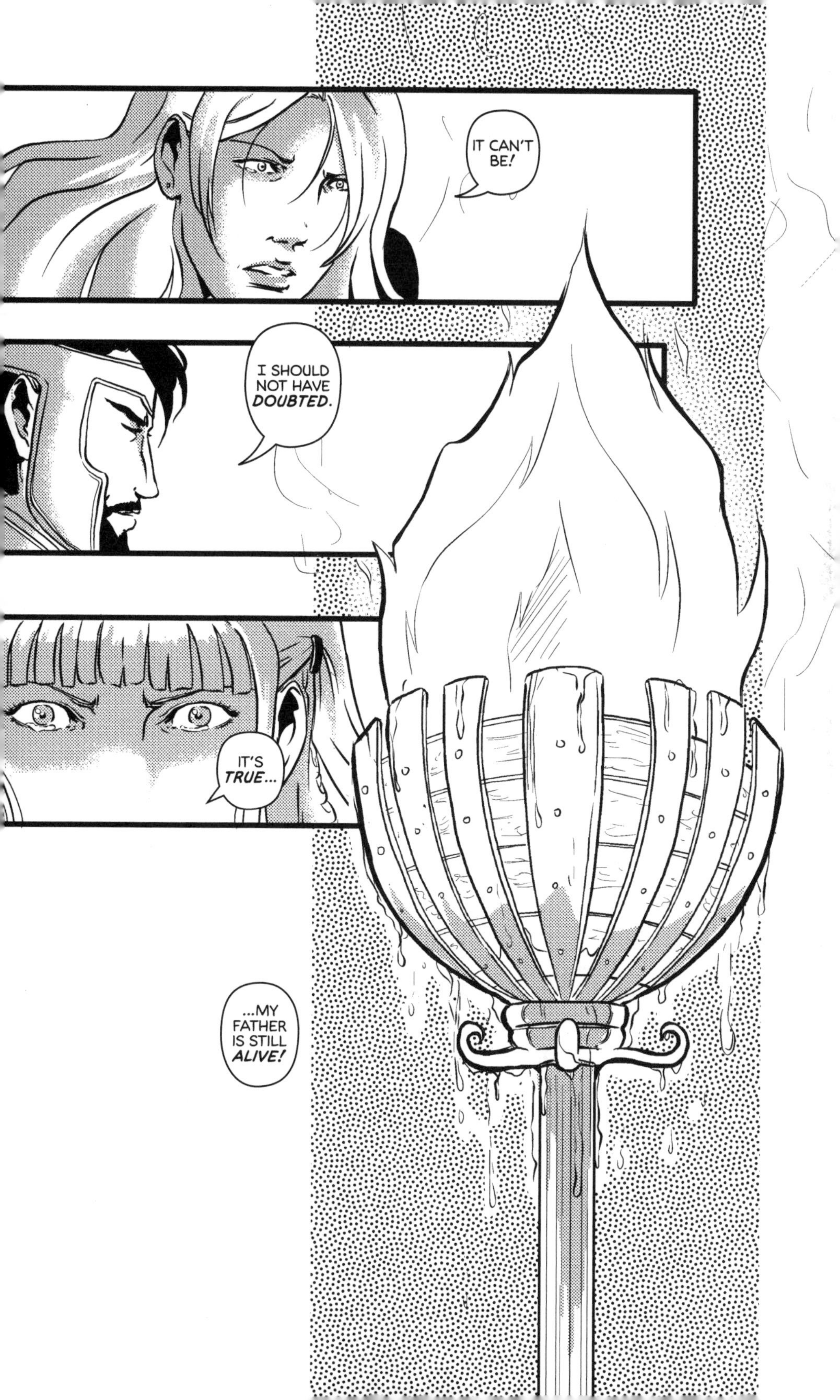
IT CAN'T BE!
I SHOULD NOT HAVE DOUBTED.
IT'S TRUE...
...MY FATHER IS STILL ALIVE!

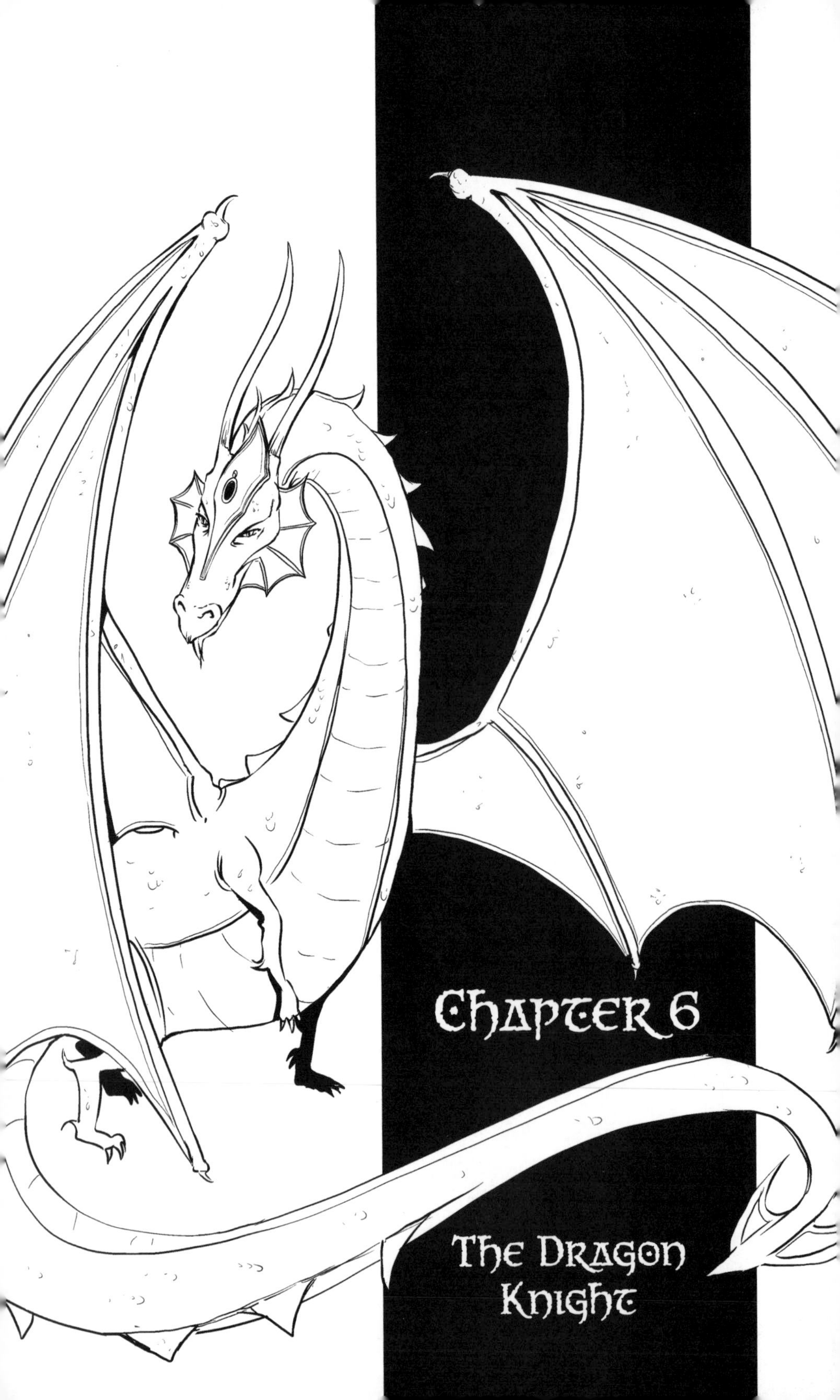

Chapter 6

The Dragon Knight

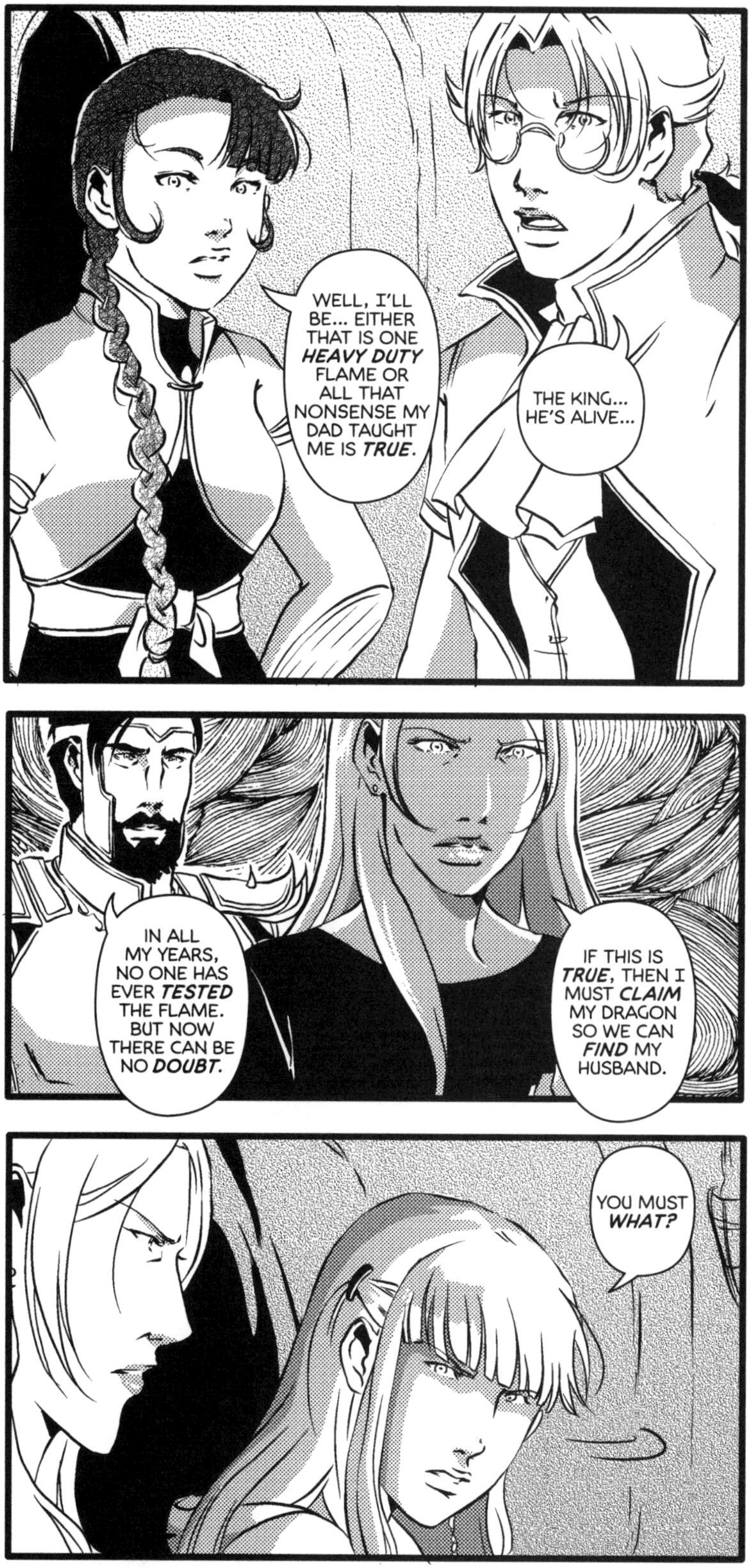
WELL, I'LL BE... EITHER THAT IS ONE ***HEAVY DUTY*** FLAME OR ALL THAT NONSENSE MY DAD TAUGHT ME IS ***TRUE***.
THE KING... HE'S ALIVE...
IF THIS IS ***TRUE***, THEN I MUST ***CLAIM*** MY DRAGON SO WE CAN ***FIND*** MY HUSBAND.
IN ALL MY YEARS, NO ONE HAS EVER ***TESTED*** THE FLAME. BUT NOW THERE CAN BE NO ***DOUBT***.
YOU MUST ***WHAT?***

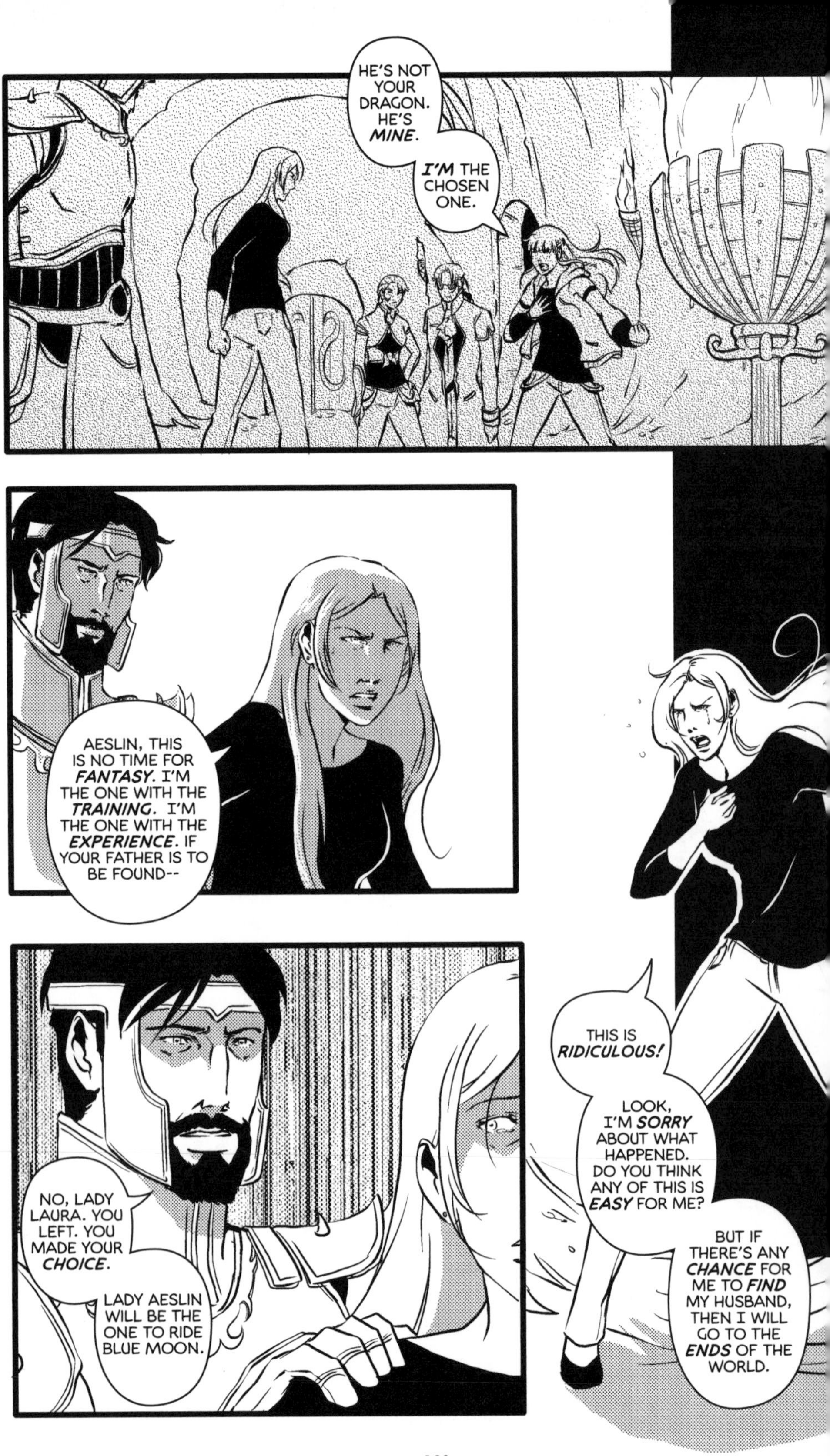
HE'S NOT YOUR DRAGON. HE'S *MINE*.
I'M THE CHOSEN ONE.
AESLIN, THIS IS NO TIME FOR *FANTASY*. I'M THE ONE WITH THE *TRAINING*. I'M THE ONE WITH THE *EXPERIENCE*. IF YOUR FATHER IS TO BE FOUND--
THIS IS *RIDICULOUS!*
LOOK, I'M *SORRY* ABOUT WHAT HAPPENED. DO YOU THINK ANY OF THIS IS *EASY* FOR ME?
BUT IF THERE'S ANY *CHANCE* FOR ME TO *FIND* MY HUSBAND, THEN I WILL GO TO THE *ENDS* OF THE WORLD.
NO, LADY LAURA. YOU LEFT. YOU MADE YOUR *CHOICE*.
LADY AESLIN WILL BE THE ONE TO RIDE BLUE MOON.

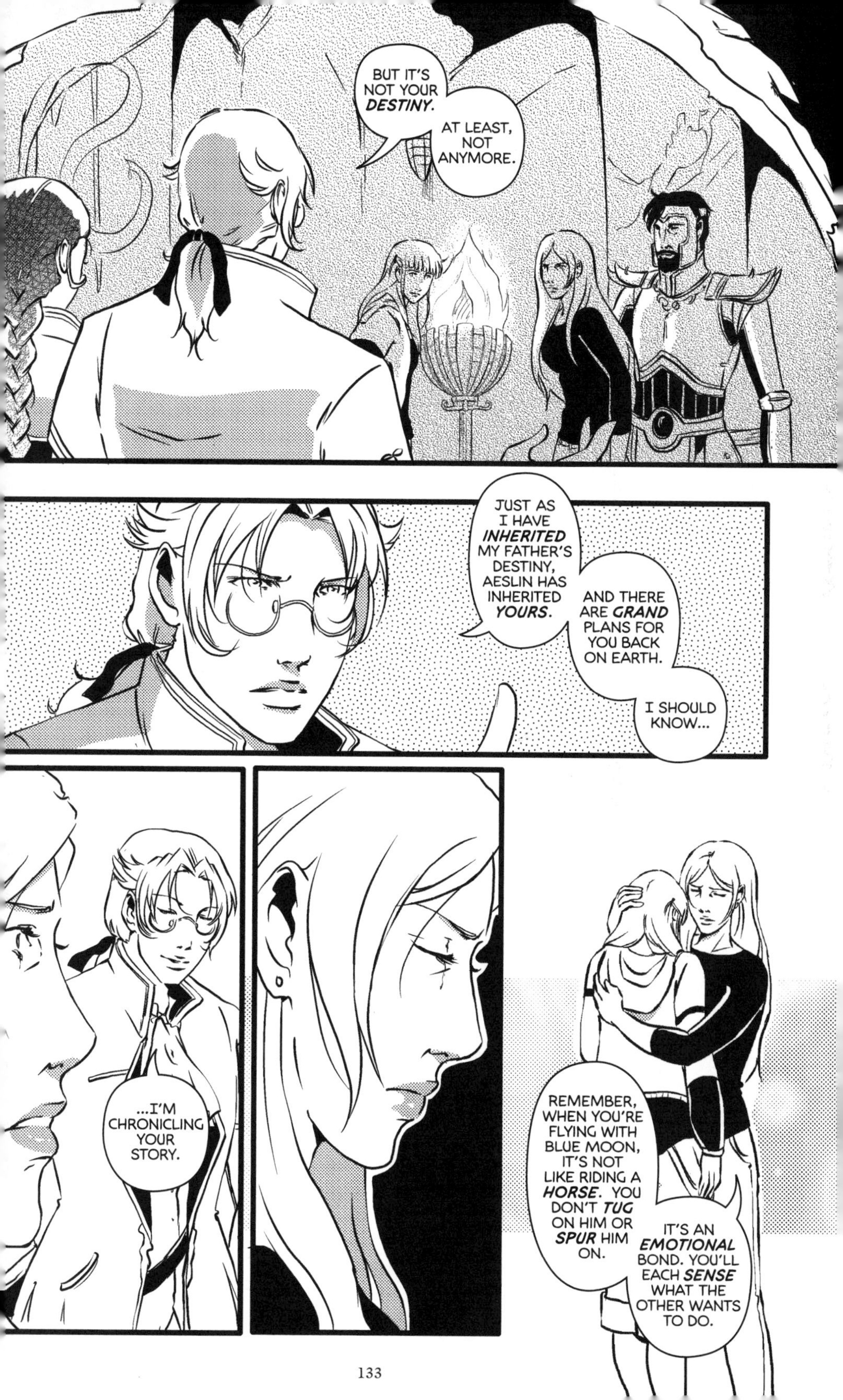

BUT IT'S NOT YOUR ***DESTINY***.
AT LEAST, NOT ANYMORE.
JUST AS I HAVE ***INHERITED*** MY FATHER'S DESTINY, AESLIN HAS INHERITED ***YOURS***.
AND THERE ARE ***GRAND*** PLANS FOR YOU BACK ON EARTH.
I SHOULD KNOW...
...I'M CHRONICLING YOUR STORY.
REMEMBER, WHEN YOU'RE FLYING WITH BLUE MOON, IT'S NOT LIKE RIDING A ***HORSE***. YOU DON'T ***TUG*** ON HIM OR ***SPUR*** HIM ON.
IT'S AN ***EMOTIONAL*** BOND. YOU'LL EACH ***SENSE*** WHAT THE OTHER WANTS TO DO.

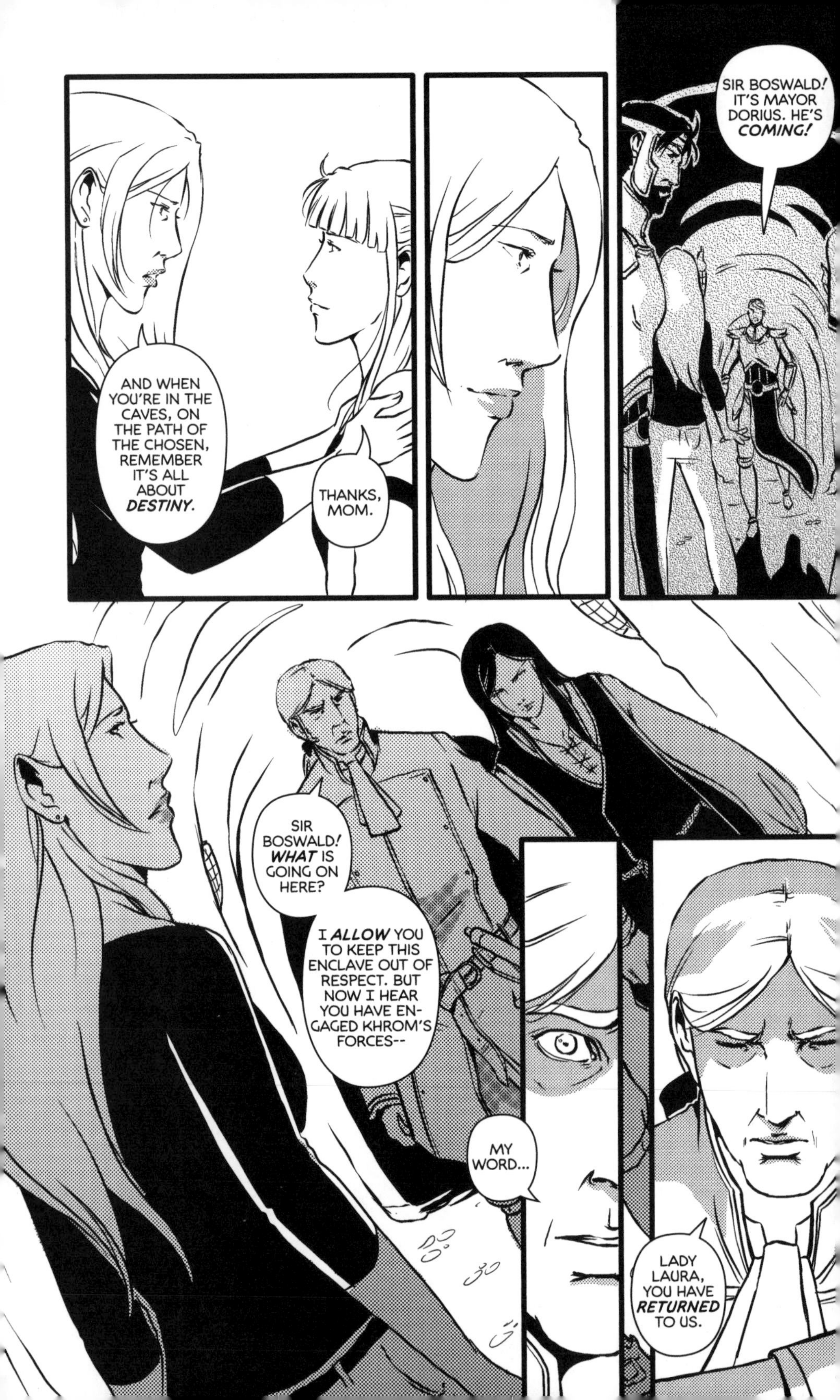
AND WHEN YOU'RE IN THE CAVES, ON THE PATH OF THE CHOSEN, REMEMBER IT'S ALL ABOUT ***DESTINY***.
THANKS, MOM.
SIR BOSWALD! IT'S MAYOR DORIUS. HE'S ***COMING!***
SIR BOSWALD! ***WHAT*** IS GOING ON HERE?
I ***ALLOW*** YOU TO KEEP THIS ENCLAVE OUT OF RESPECT. BUT NOW I HEAR YOU HAVE EN-GAGED KHROM'S FORCES--
MY WORD...
LADY LAURA, YOU HAVE ***RETURNED*** TO US.

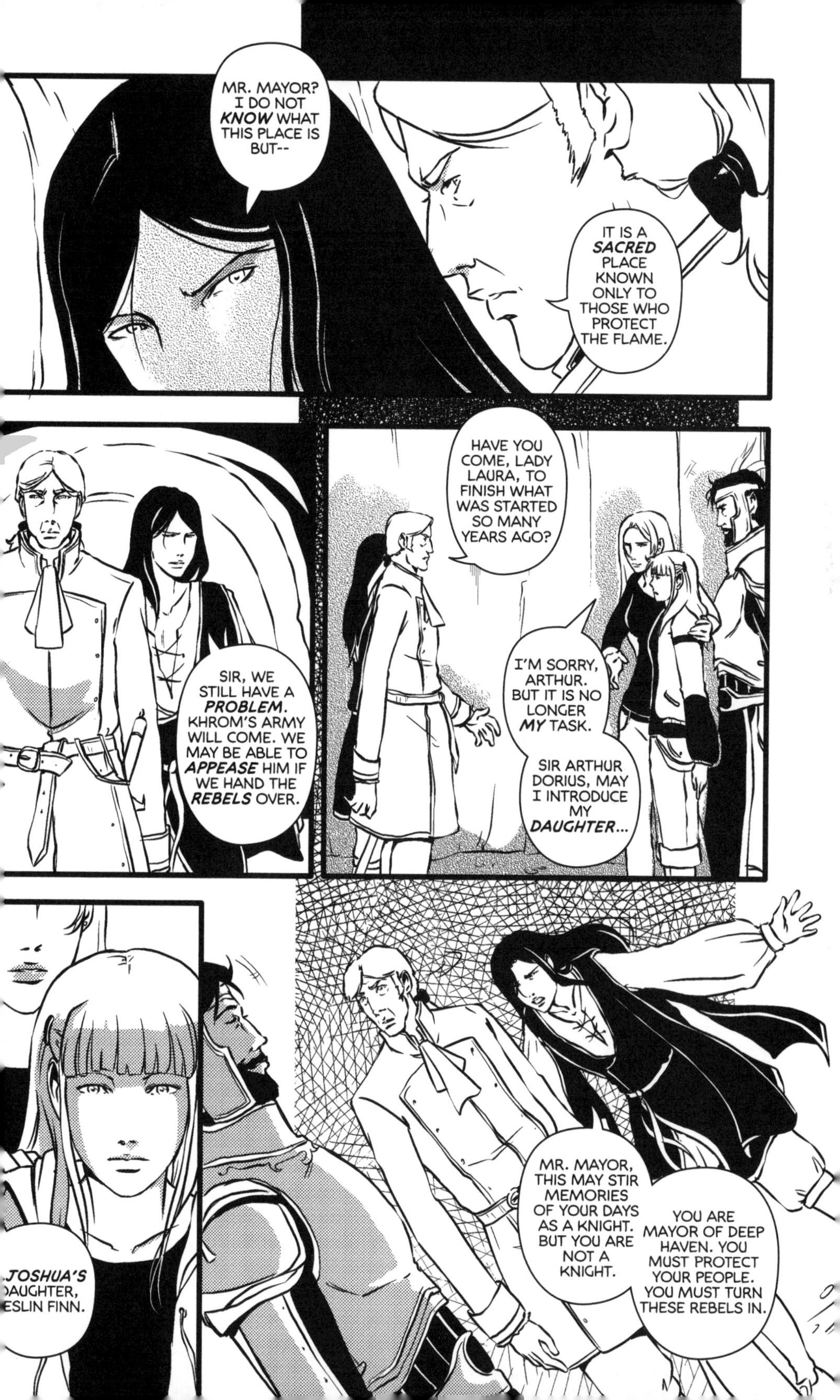
MR. MAYOR? I DO NOT KNOW WHAT THIS PLACE IS BUT--
IT IS A SACRED PLACE KNOWN ONLY TO THOSE WHO PROTECT THE FLAME.
SIR, WE STILL HAVE A PROBLEM. KHROM'S ARMY WILL COME. WE MAY BE ABLE TO APPEASE HIM IF WE HAND THE REBELS OVER.
HAVE YOU COME, LADY LAURA, TO FINISH WHAT WAS STARTED SO MANY YEARS AGO?
I'M SORRY, ARTHUR. BUT IT IS NO LONGER MY TASK.
SIR ARTHUR DORIUS, MAY I INTRODUCE MY DAUGHTER...
JOSHUA'S DAUGHTER, ESLIN FINN.
MR. MAYOR, THIS MAY STIR MEMORIES OF YOUR DAYS AS A KNIGHT. BUT YOU ARE NOT A KNIGHT.
YOU ARE MAYOR OF DEEP HAVEN. YOU MUST PROTECT YOUR PEOPLE. YOU MUST TURN THESE REBELS IN.

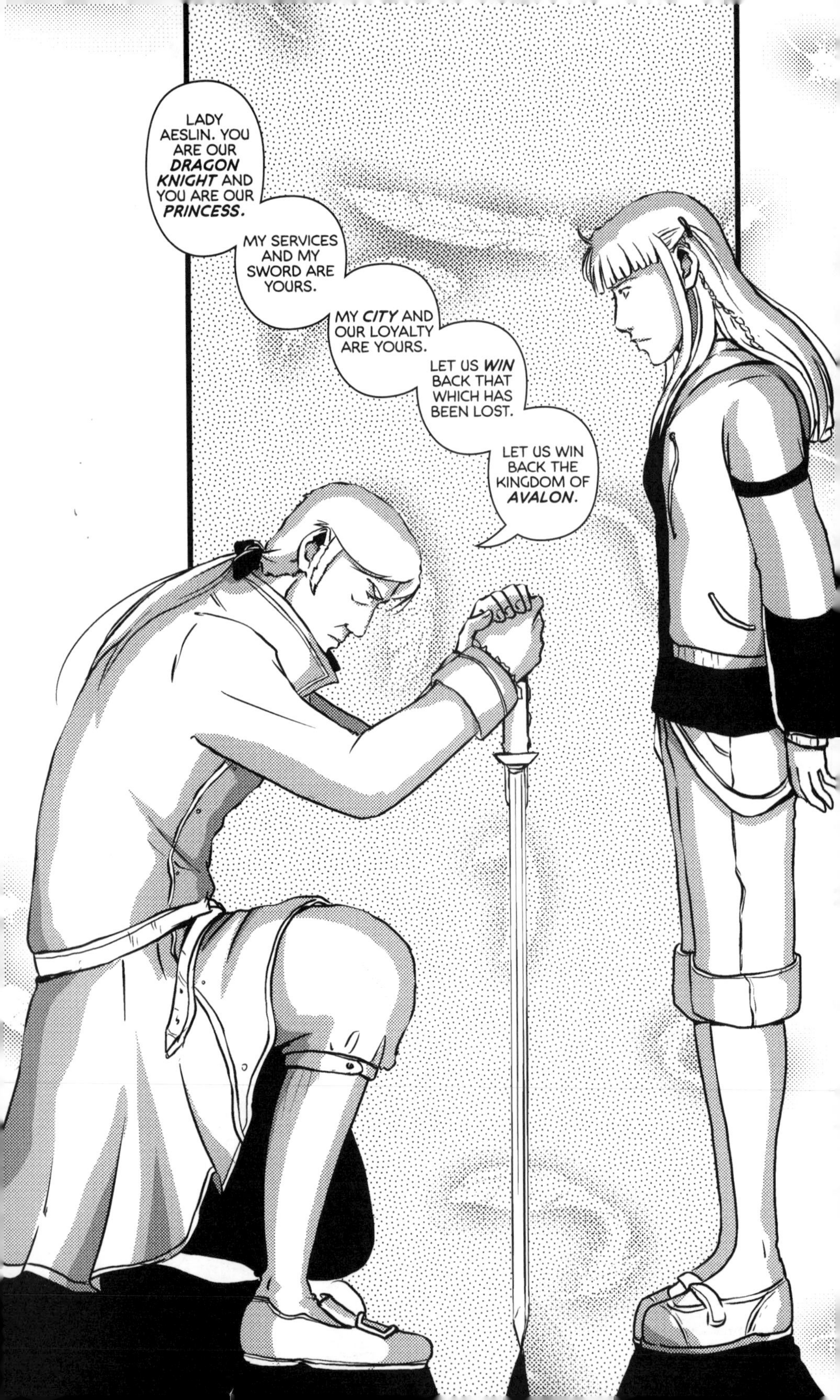

LADY AESLIN. YOU ARE OUR **DRAGON KNIGHT** AND YOU ARE OUR **PRINCESS.**
MY SERVICES AND MY SWORD ARE YOURS.
MY **CITY** AND OUR LOYALTY ARE YOURS.
LET US **WIN** BACK THAT WHICH HAS BEEN LOST.
LET US WIN BACK THE KINGDOM OF **AVALON.**

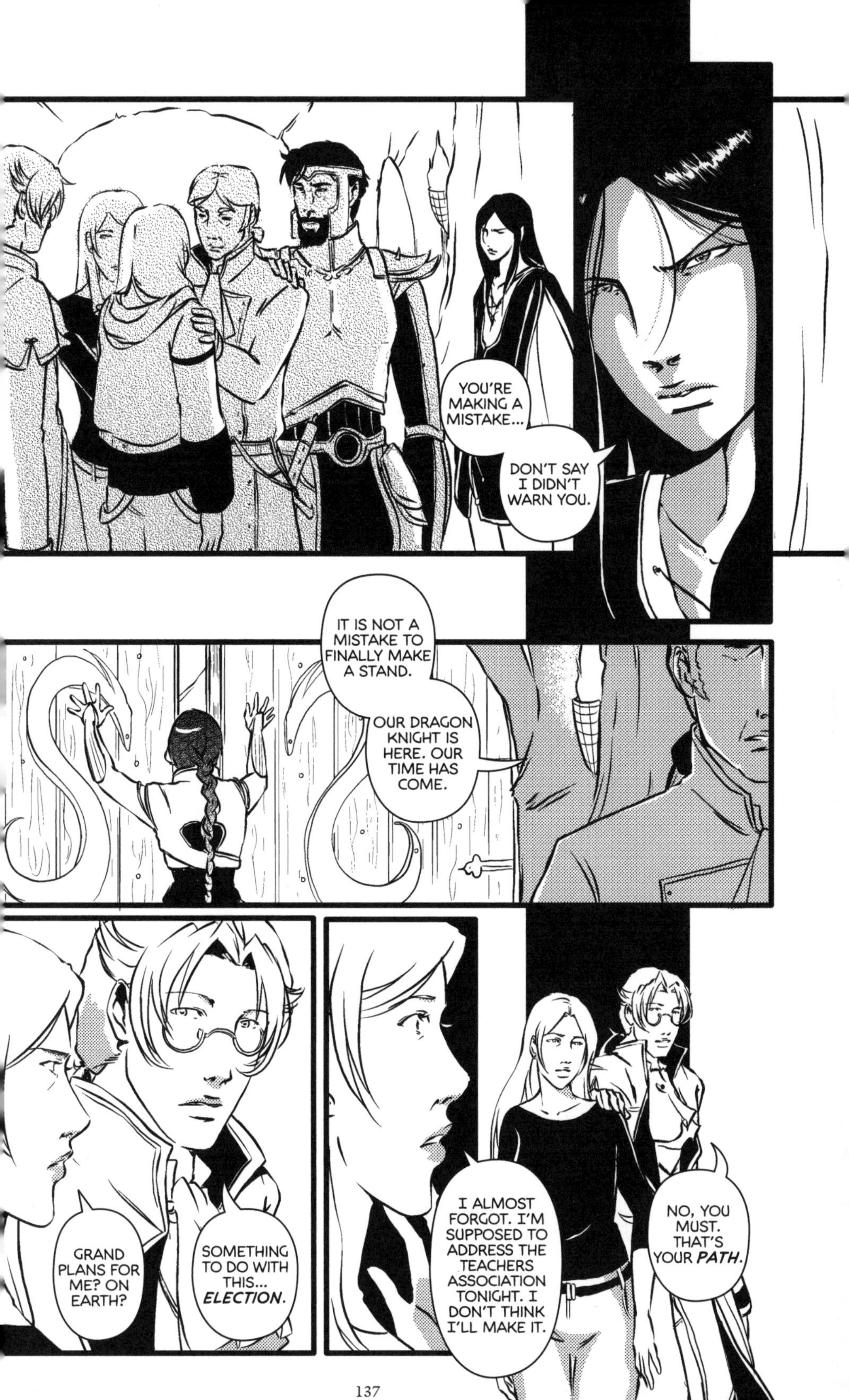

YOU'RE MAKING A MISTAKE...
DON'T SAY I DIDN'T WARN YOU.
IT IS NOT A MISTAKE TO FINALLY MAKE A STAND.
OUR DRAGON KNIGHT IS HERE. OUR TIME HAS COME.
GRAND PLANS FOR ME? ON EARTH?
SOMETHING TO DO WITH THIS... *ELECTION*.
I ALMOST FORGOT. I'M SUPPOSED TO ADDRESS THE TEACHERS ASSOCIATION TONIGHT. I DON'T THINK I'LL MAKE IT.
NO, YOU MUST. THAT'S YOUR *PATH*.

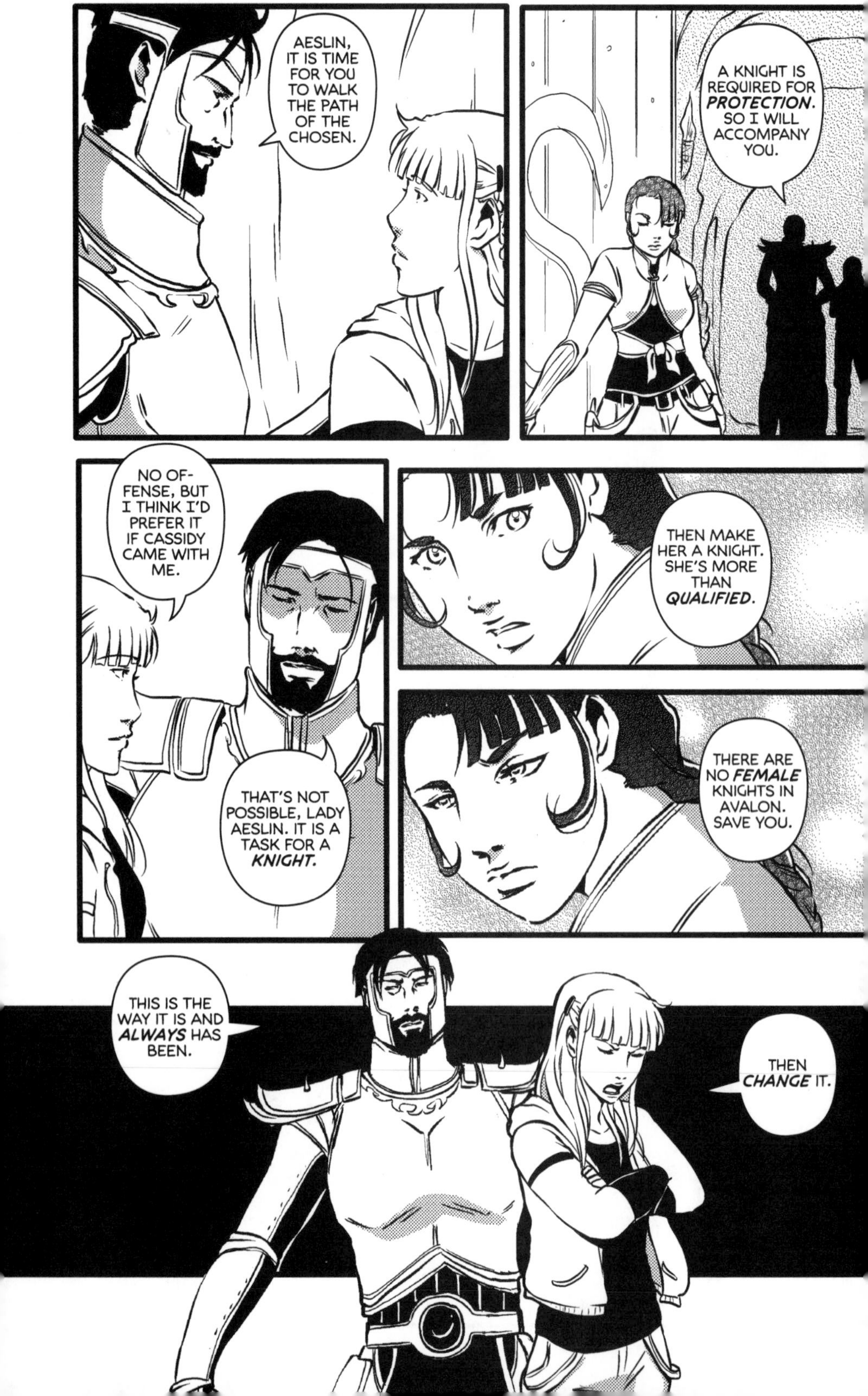
AESLIN, IT IS TIME FOR YOU TO WALK THE PATH OF THE CHOSEN.
A KNIGHT IS REQUIRED FOR PROTECTION. SO I WILL ACCOMPANY YOU.
NO OF-FENSE, BUT I THINK I'D PREFER IT IF CASSIDY CAME WITH ME.
THAT'S NOT POSSIBLE, LADY AESLIN. IT IS A TASK FOR A KNIGHT.
THEN MAKE HER A KNIGHT. SHE'S MORE THAN QUALIFIED.
THERE ARE NO FEMALE KNIGHTS IN AVALON. SAVE YOU.
THIS IS THE WAY IT IS AND ALWAYS HAS BEEN.
THEN CHANGE IT.

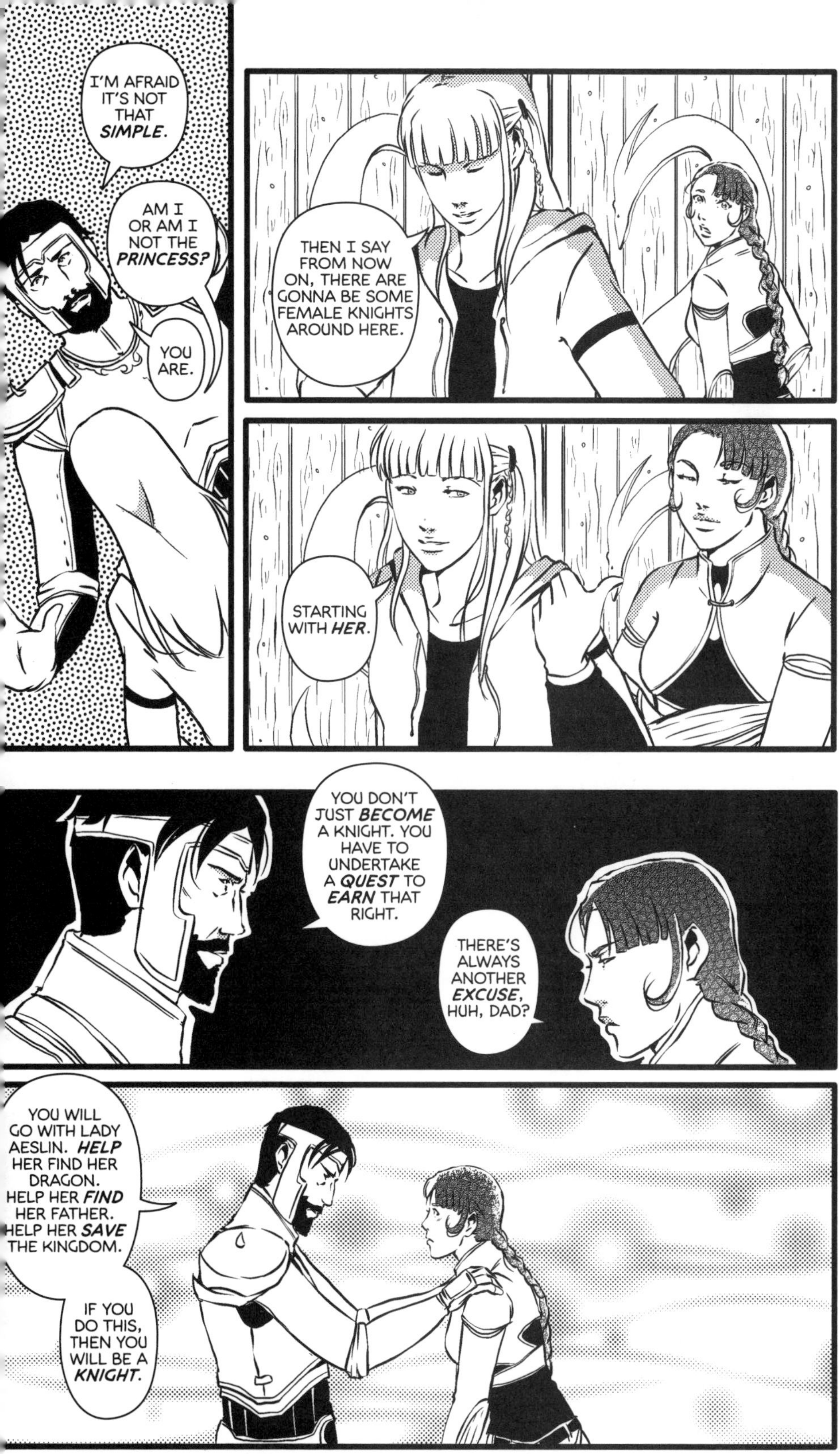
I'M AFRAID IT'S NOT THAT SIMPLE.
AM I OR AM I NOT THE PRINCESS?
YOU ARE.
THEN I SAY FROM NOW ON, THERE ARE GONNA BE SOME FEMALE KNIGHTS AROUND HERE.
STARTING WITH HER.
YOU DON'T JUST BECOME A KNIGHT. YOU HAVE TO UNDERTAKE A QUEST TO EARN THAT RIGHT.
THERE'S ALWAYS ANOTHER EXCUSE, HUH, DAD?
YOU WILL GO WITH LADY AESLIN. HELP HER FIND HER DRAGON. HELP HER FIND HER FATHER. HELP HER SAVE THE KINGDOM.
IF YOU DO THIS, THEN YOU WILL BE A KNIGHT.

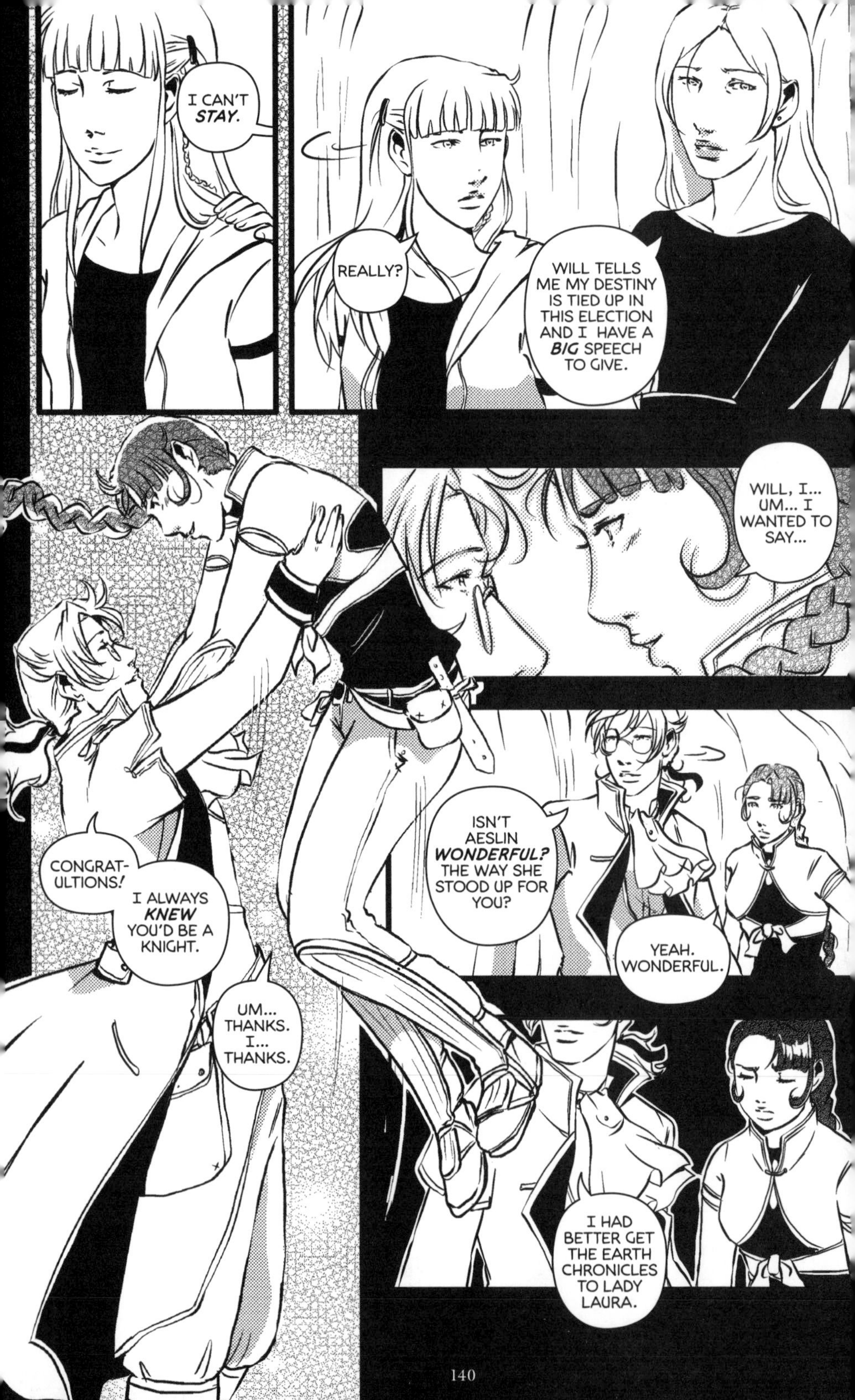
I CAN'T *STAY*.
REALLY?
WILL TELLS ME MY DESTINY IS TIED UP IN THIS ELECTION AND I HAVE A *BIG* SPEECH TO GIVE.
CONGRAT-ULTIONS!
I ALWAYS *KNEW* YOU'D BE A KNIGHT.
UM... THANKS. I... THANKS.
WILL, I... UM... I WANTED TO SAY...
ISN'T AESLIN *WONDERFUL?* THE WAY SHE STOOD UP FOR YOU?
YEAH. WONDERFUL.
I HAD BETTER GET THE EARTH CHRONICLES TO LADY LAURA.

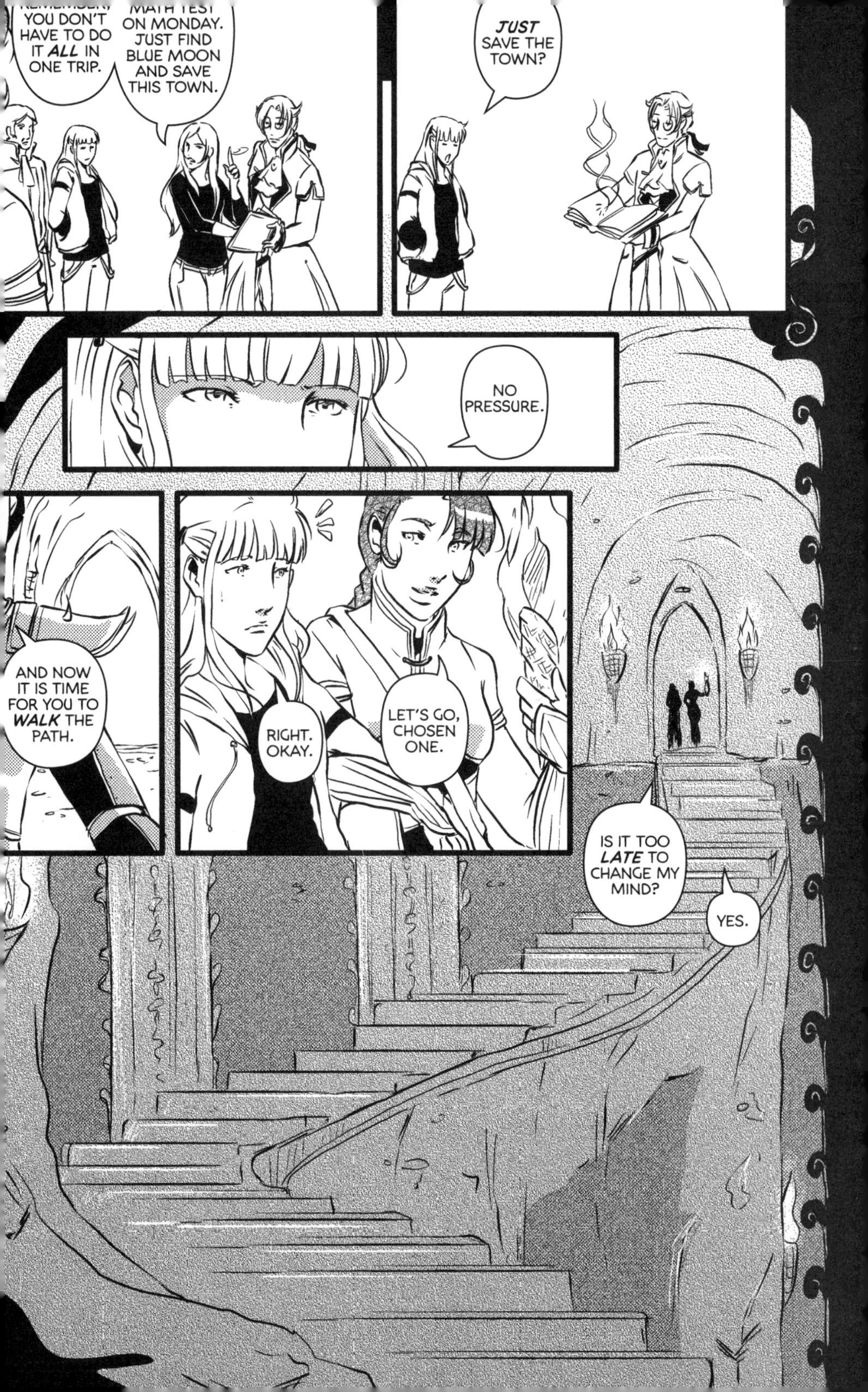

YOU DON'T HAVE TO DO IT *ALL* IN ONE TRIP.
ON MONDAY. JUST FIND BLUE MOON AND SAVE THIS TOWN.
JUST SAVE THE TOWN?
NO PRESSURE.
AND NOW IT IS TIME FOR YOU TO *WALK* THE PATH.
RIGHT. OKAY.
LET'S GO, CHOSEN ONE.
IS IT TOO *LATE* TO CHANGE MY MIND?
YES.

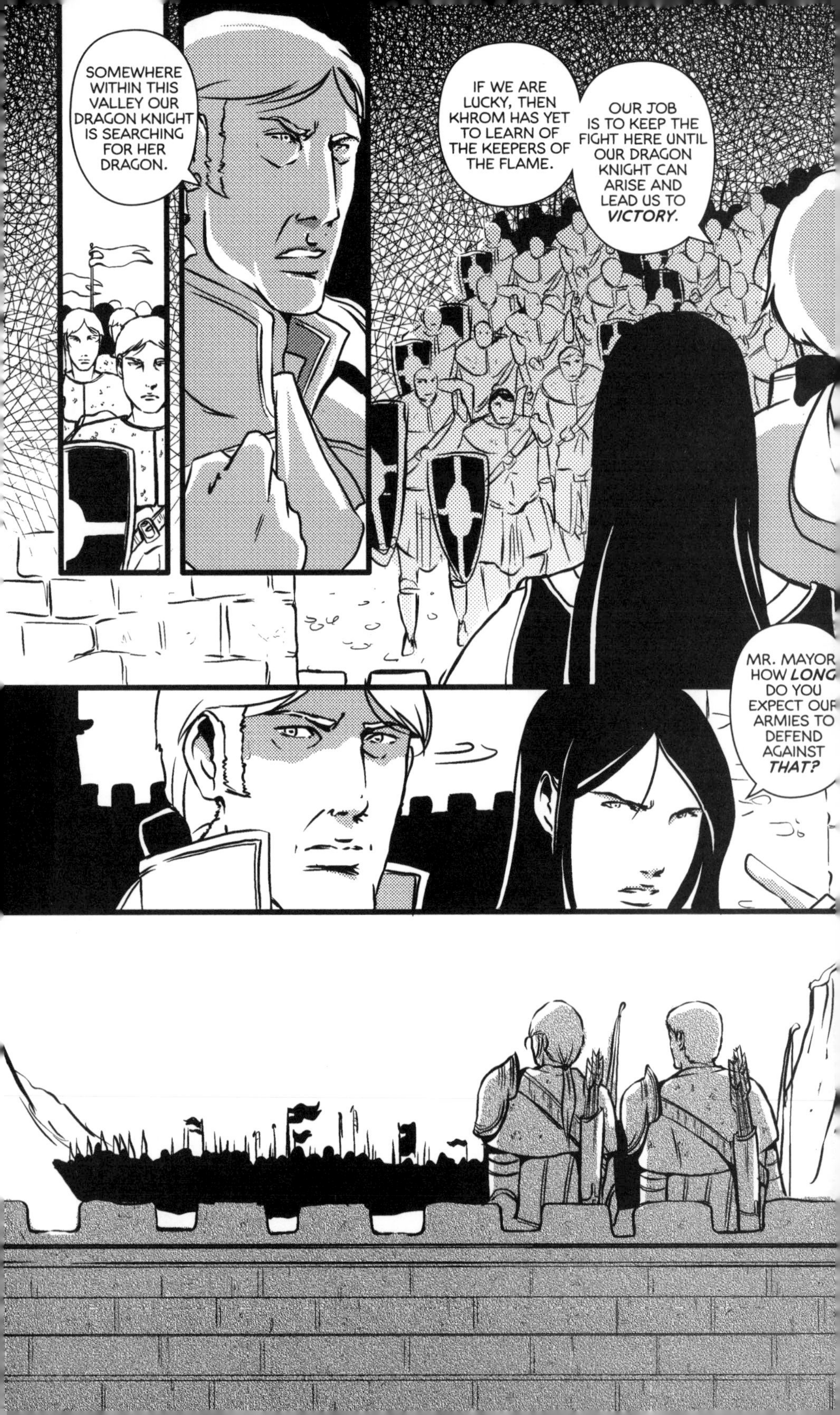
SOMEWHERE WITHIN THIS VALLEY OUR DRAGON KNIGHT IS SEARCHING FOR HER DRAGON.
IF WE ARE LUCKY, THEN KHROM HAS YET TO LEARN OF THE KEEPERS OF THE FLAME.
OUR JOB IS TO KEEP THE FIGHT HERE UNTIL OUR DRAGON KNIGHT CAN ARISE AND LEAD US TO *VICTORY*.
MR. MAYOR HOW *LONG* DO YOU EXPECT OUR ARMIES TO DEFEND AGAINST *THAT?*

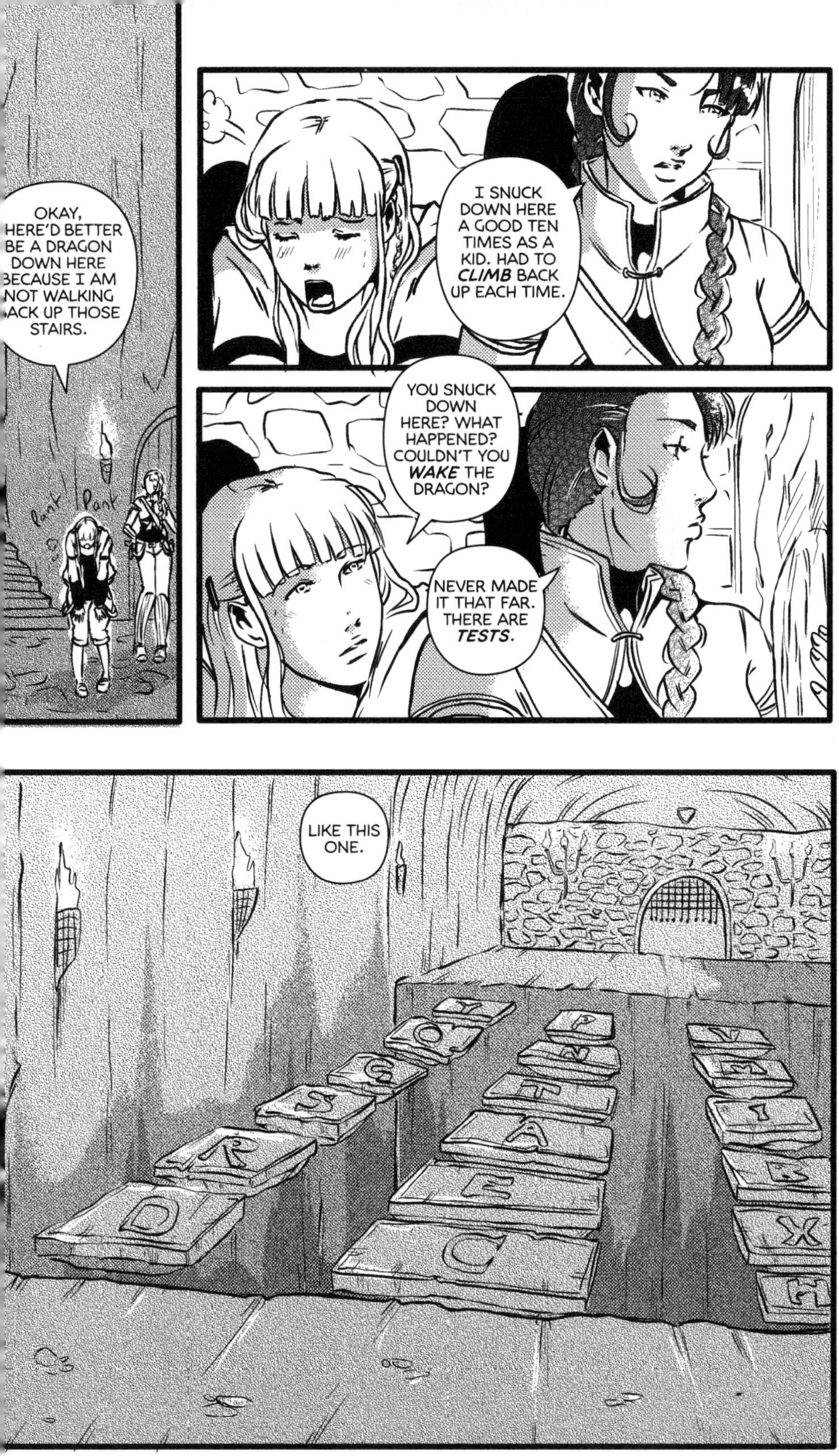

OKAY, HERE'D BETTER BE A DRAGON DOWN HERE ECAUSE I AM NOT WALKING ACK UP THOSE STAIRS.
Pant Pant
I SNUCK DOWN HERE A GOOD TEN TIMES AS A KID. HAD TO *CLIMB* BACK UP EACH TIME.
YOU SNUCK DOWN HERE? WHAT HAPPENED? COULDN'T YOU *WAKE* THE DRAGON?
NEVER MADE IT THAT FAR. THERE ARE *TESTS*.
LIKE THIS ONE.

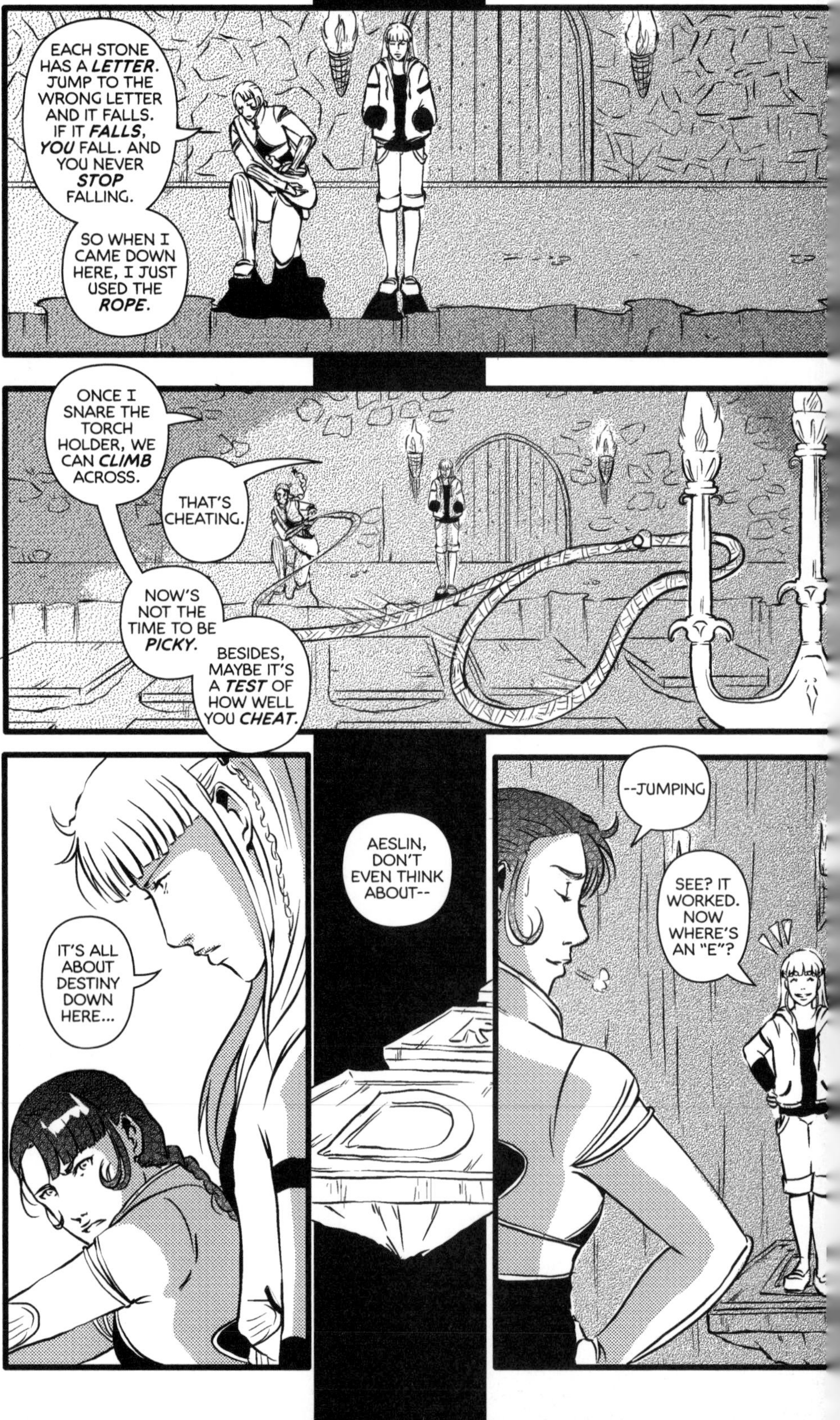
EACH STONE HAS A ***LETTER***. JUMP TO THE WRONG LETTER AND IT FALLS. IF IT ***FALLS***, ***YOU*** FALL. AND YOU NEVER ***STOP*** FALLING.
SO WHEN I CAME DOWN HERE, I JUST USED THE ***ROPE***.
ONCE I SNARE THE TORCH HOLDER, WE CAN ***CLIMB*** ACROSS.
THAT'S CHEATING.
NOW'S NOT THE TIME TO BE ***PICKY***.
BESIDES, MAYBE IT'S A ***TEST*** OF HOW WELL YOU ***CHEAT***.
IT'S ALL ABOUT DESTINY DOWN HERE...
AESLIN, DON'T EVEN THINK ABOUT--
--JUMPING
SEE? IT WORKED. NOW WHERE'S AN "E"?

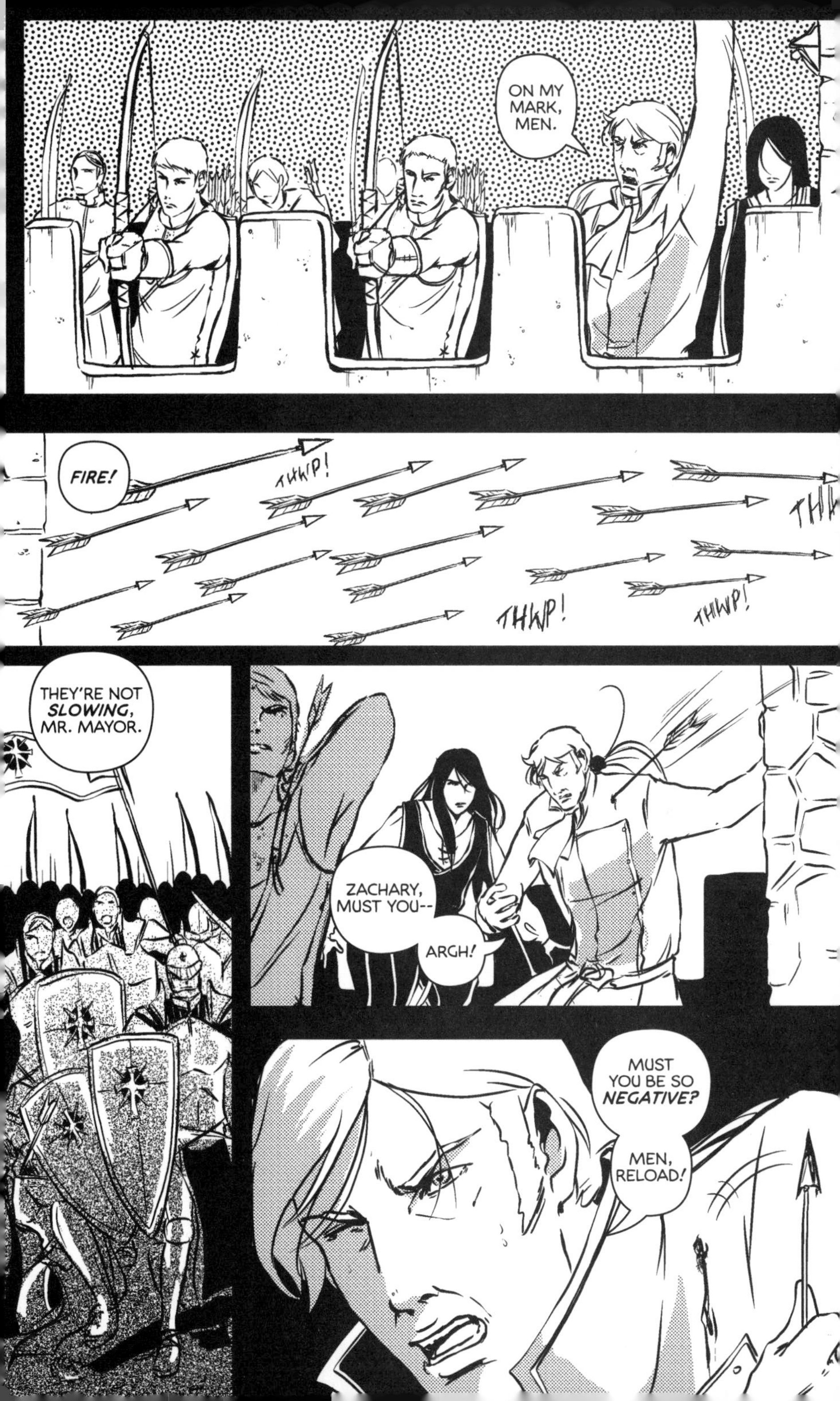
ON MY MARK, MEN.
FIRE!
THWP!
THWP!
THWP!
THEY'RE NOT *SLOWING*, MR. MAYOR.
ZACHARY, MUST YOU--
ARGH!
MUST YOU BE SO *NEGATIVE?*
MEN, RELOAD!

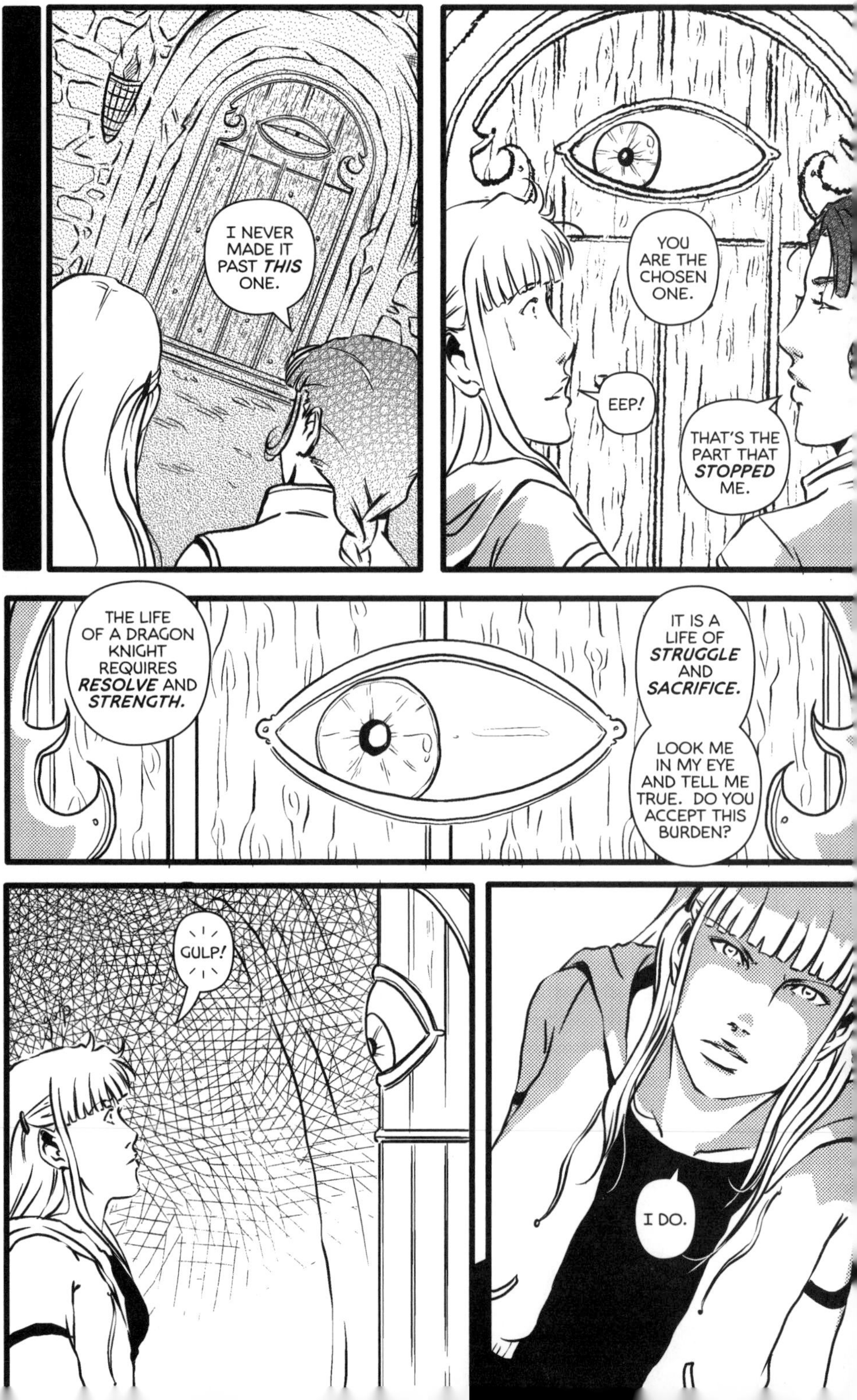
I NEVER MADE IT PAST *THIS* ONE.
YOU ARE THE CHOSEN ONE.
EEP!
THAT'S THE PART THAT *STOPPED* ME.
THE LIFE OF A DRAGON KNIGHT REQUIRES *RESOLVE* AND *STRENGTH.*
IT IS A LIFE OF *STRUGGLE* AND *SACRIFICE.*
LOOK ME IN MY EYE AND TELL ME TRUE. DO YOU ACCEPT THIS BURDEN?
GULP!
I DO.

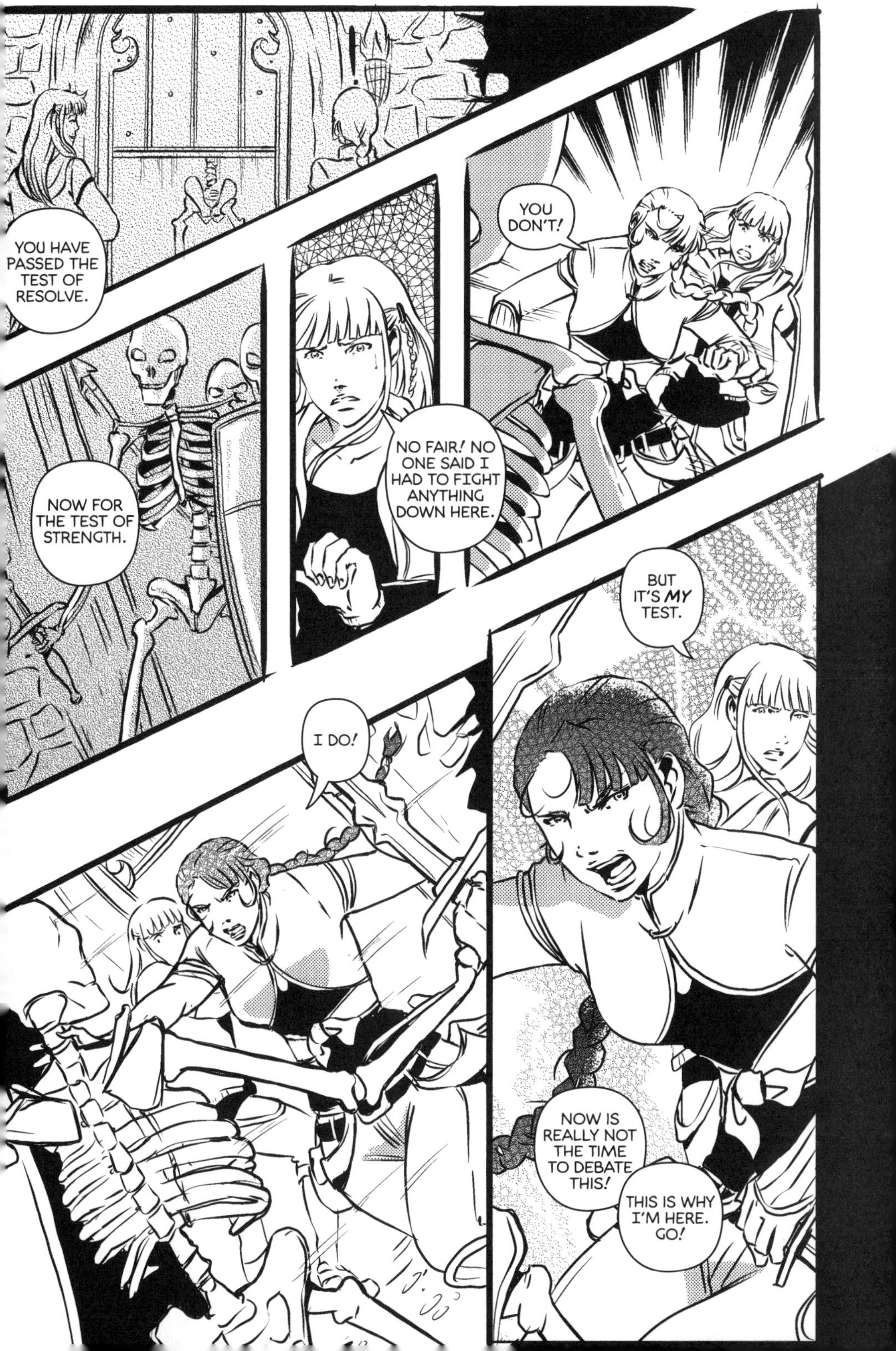
YOU HAVE PASSED THE TEST OF RESOLVE.
NOW FOR THE TEST OF STRENGTH.
NO FAIR! NO ONE SAID I HAD TO FIGHT ANYTHING DOWN HERE.
YOU DON'T!
I DO!
BUT IT'S *MY* TEST.
NOW IS REALLY NOT THE TIME TO DEBATE THIS!
THIS IS WHY I'M HERE. GO!

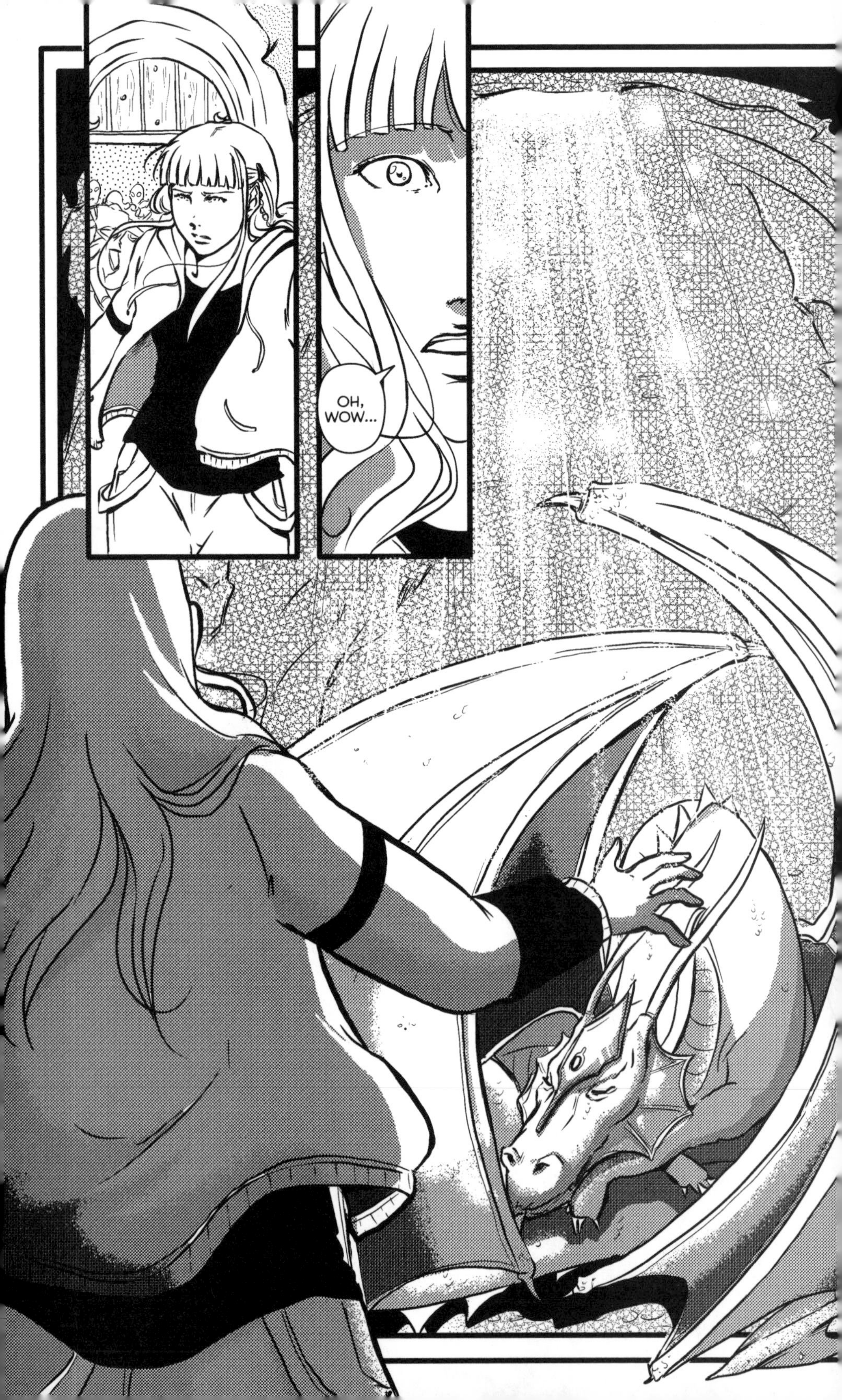
OH, WOW...

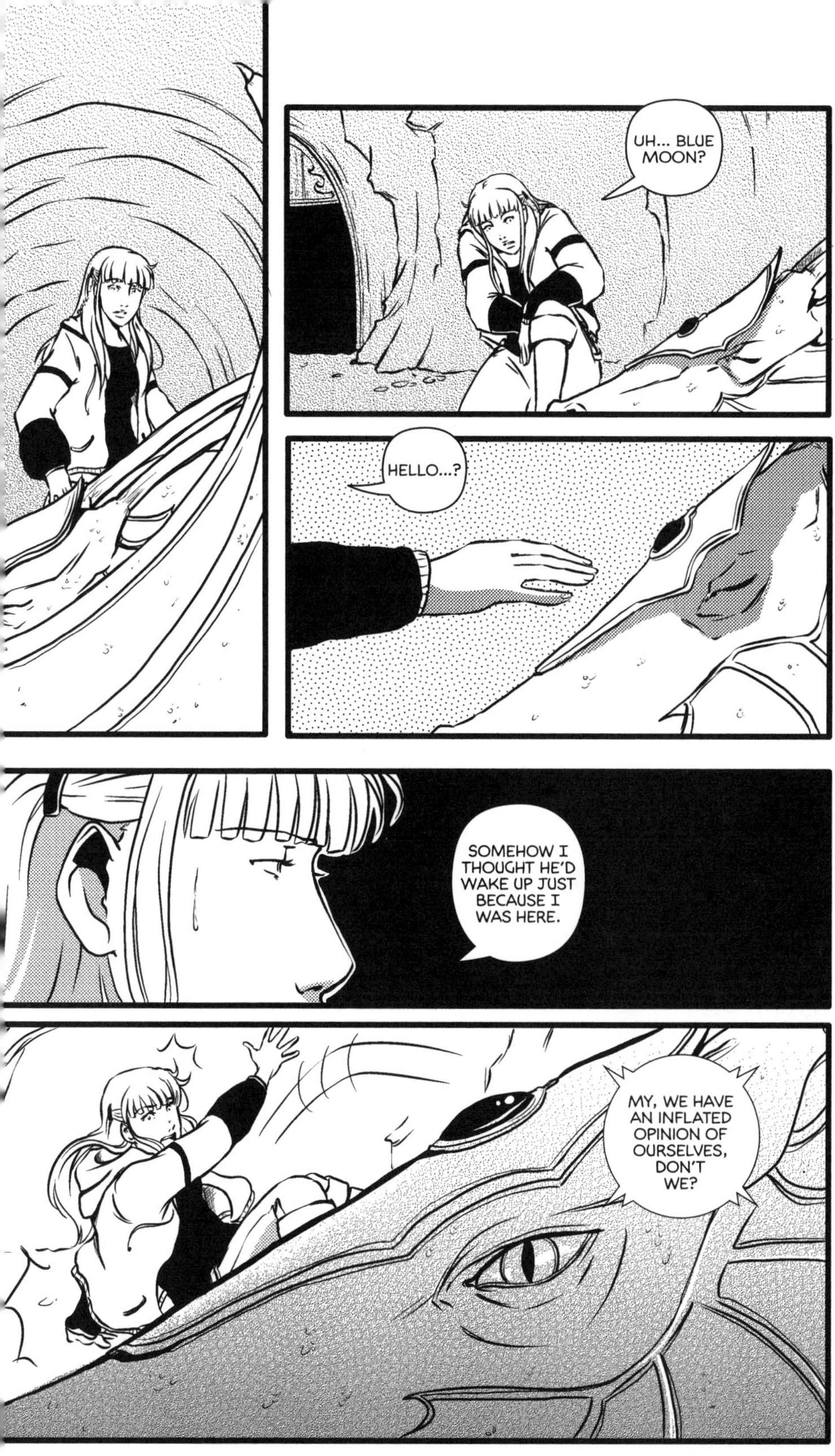
UH... BLUE MOON?
HELLO...?
SOMEHOW I THOUGHT HE'D WAKE UP JUST BECAUSE I WAS HERE.
MY, WE HAVE AN INFLATED OPINION OF OURSELVES, DON'T WE?

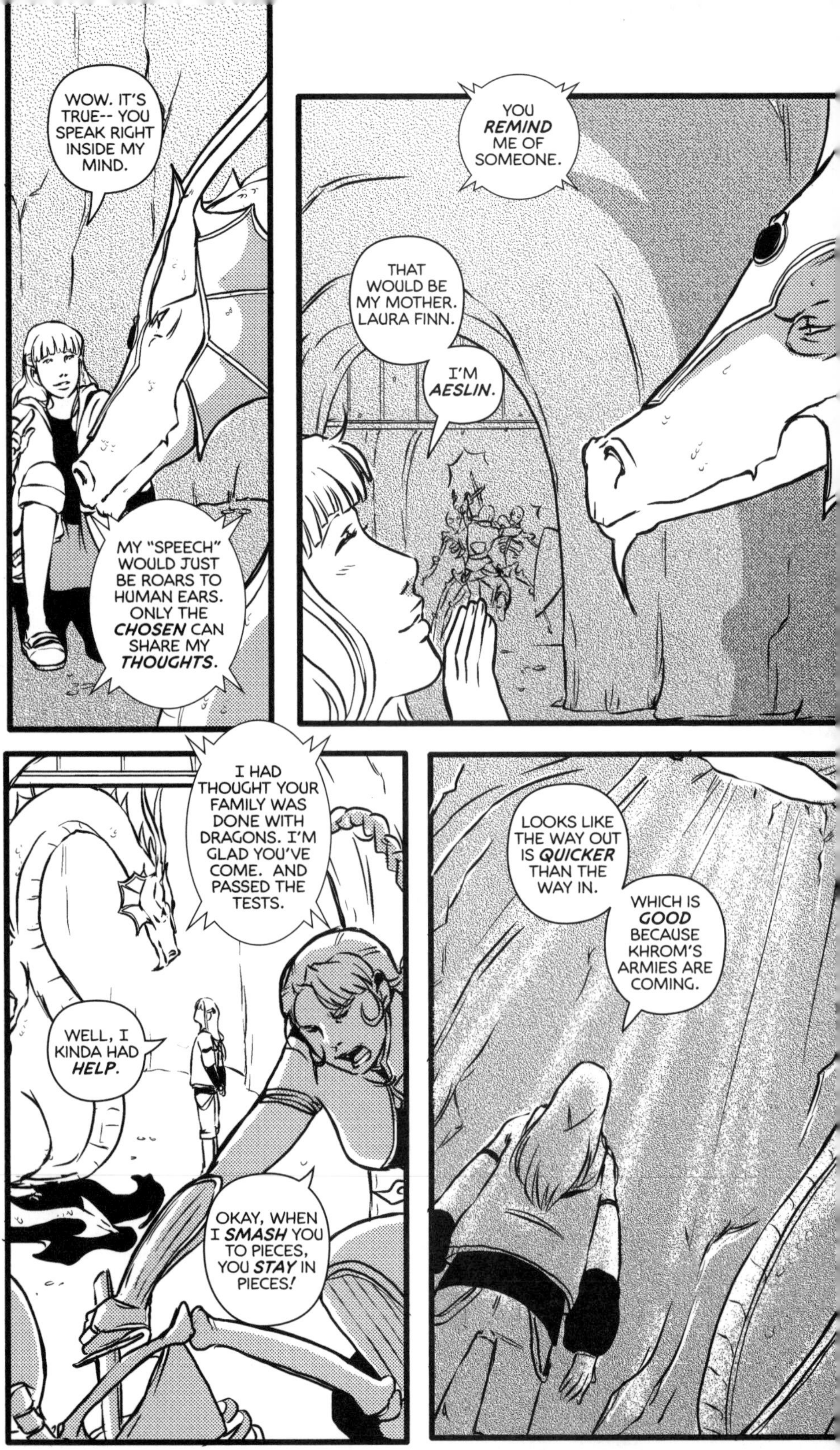
WOW. IT'S TRUE-- YOU SPEAK RIGHT INSIDE MY MIND.
MY "SPEECH" WOULD JUST BE ROARS TO HUMAN EARS. ONLY THE *CHOSEN* CAN SHARE MY *THOUGHTS*.
YOU *REMIND* ME OF SOMEONE.
THAT WOULD BE MY MOTHER. LAURA FINN.
I'M *AESLIN*.
I HAD THOUGHT YOUR FAMILY WAS DONE WITH DRAGONS. I'M GLAD YOU'VE COME. AND PASSED THE TESTS.
WELL, I KINDA HAD *HELP*.
OKAY, WHEN I *SMASH* YOU TO PIECES, YOU *STAY* IN PIECES*!*
LOOKS LIKE THE WAY OUT IS *QUICKER* THAN THE WAY IN.
WHICH IS *GOOD* BECAUSE KHROM'S ARMIES ARE COMING.

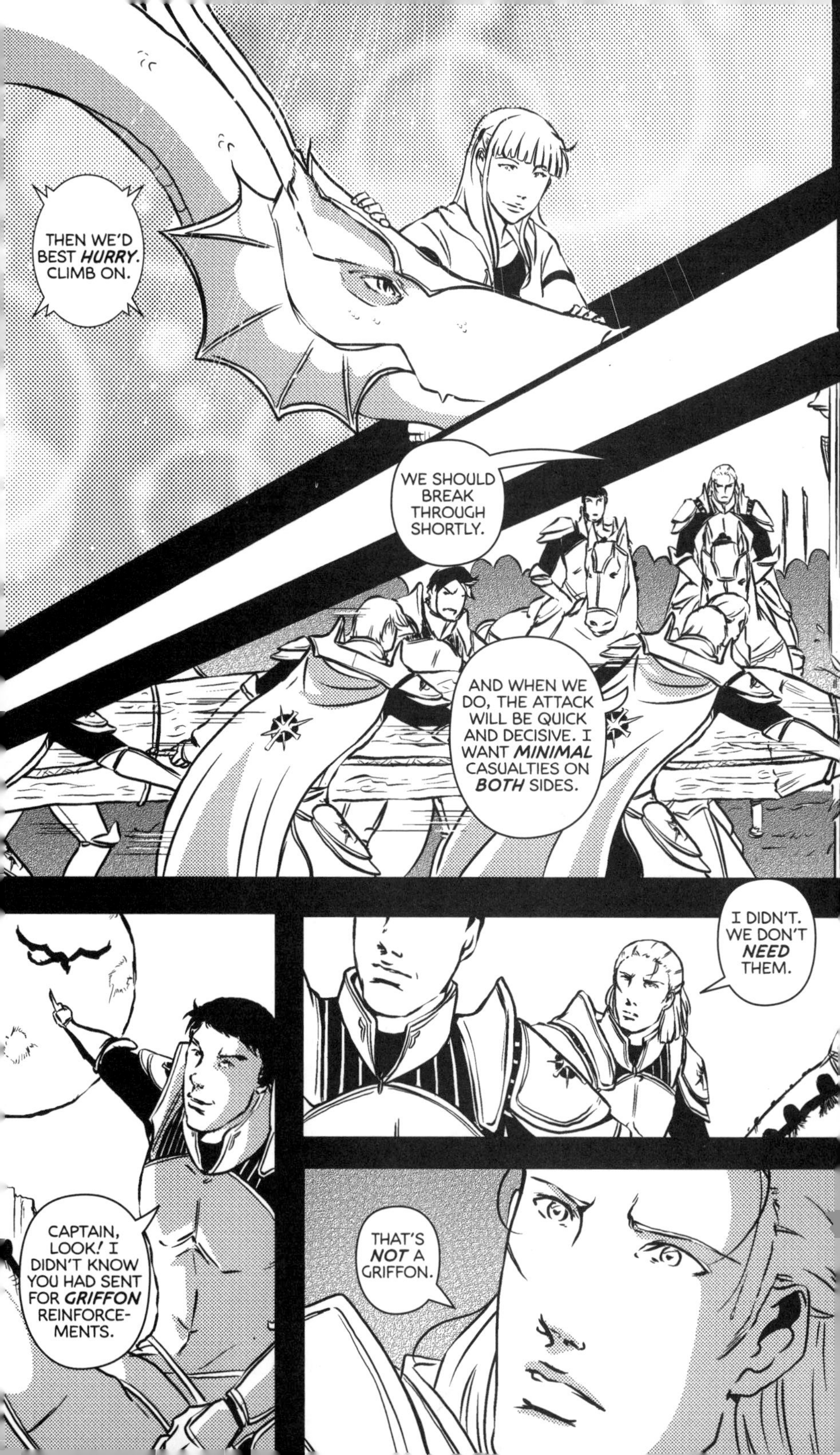
THEN WE'D BEST HURRY. CLIMB ON.
WE SHOULD BREAK THROUGH SHORTLY.
AND WHEN WE DO, THE ATTACK WILL BE QUICK AND DECISIVE. I WANT MINIMAL CASUALTIES ON BOTH SIDES.
CAPTAIN, LOOK! I DIDN'T KNOW YOU HAD SENT FOR GRIFFON REINFORCE-MENTS.
I DIDN'T. WE DON'T NEED THEM.
THAT'S NOT A GRIFFON.

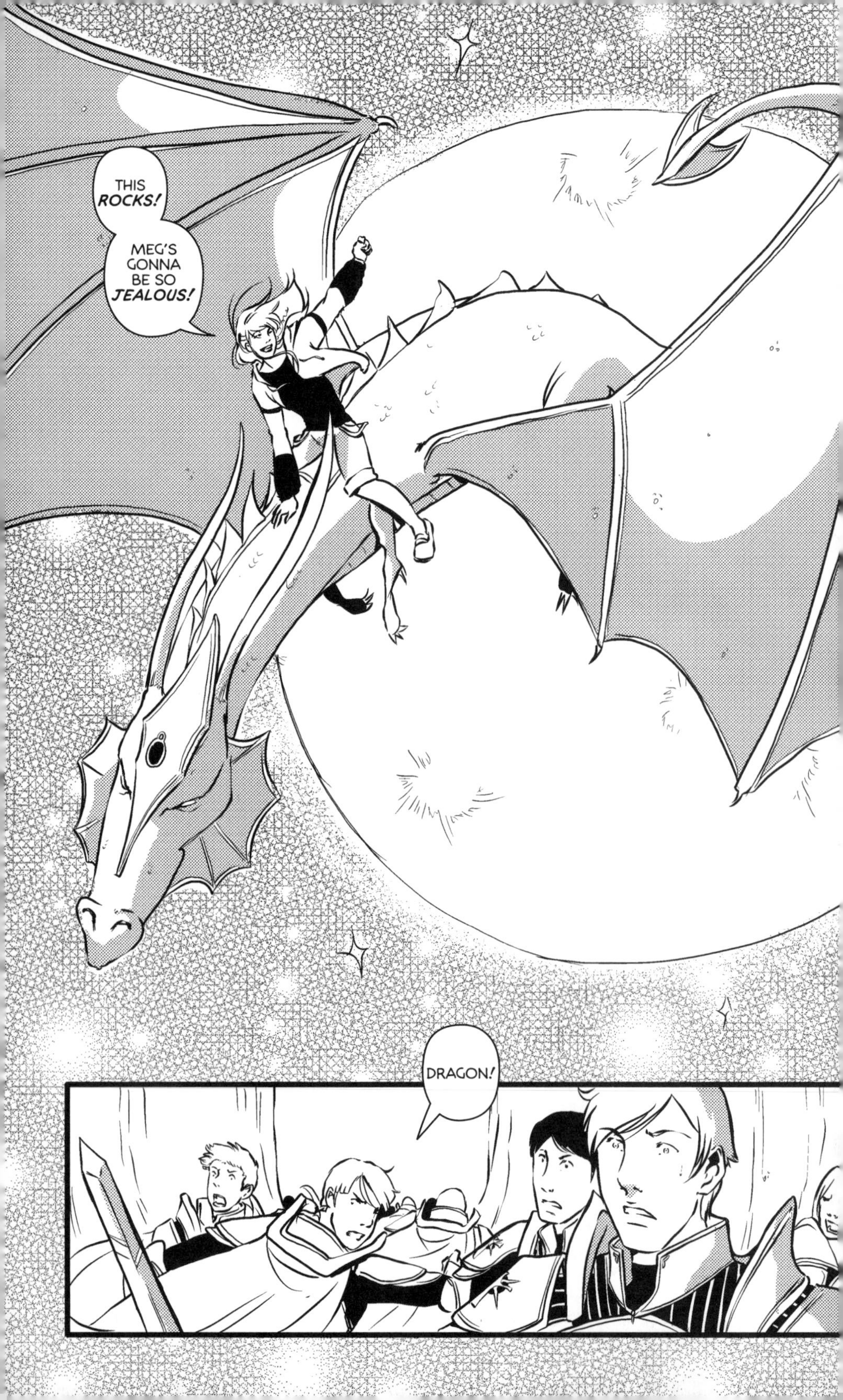
THIS *ROCKS!*
MEG'S GONNA BE SO *JEALOUS!*
DRAGON!

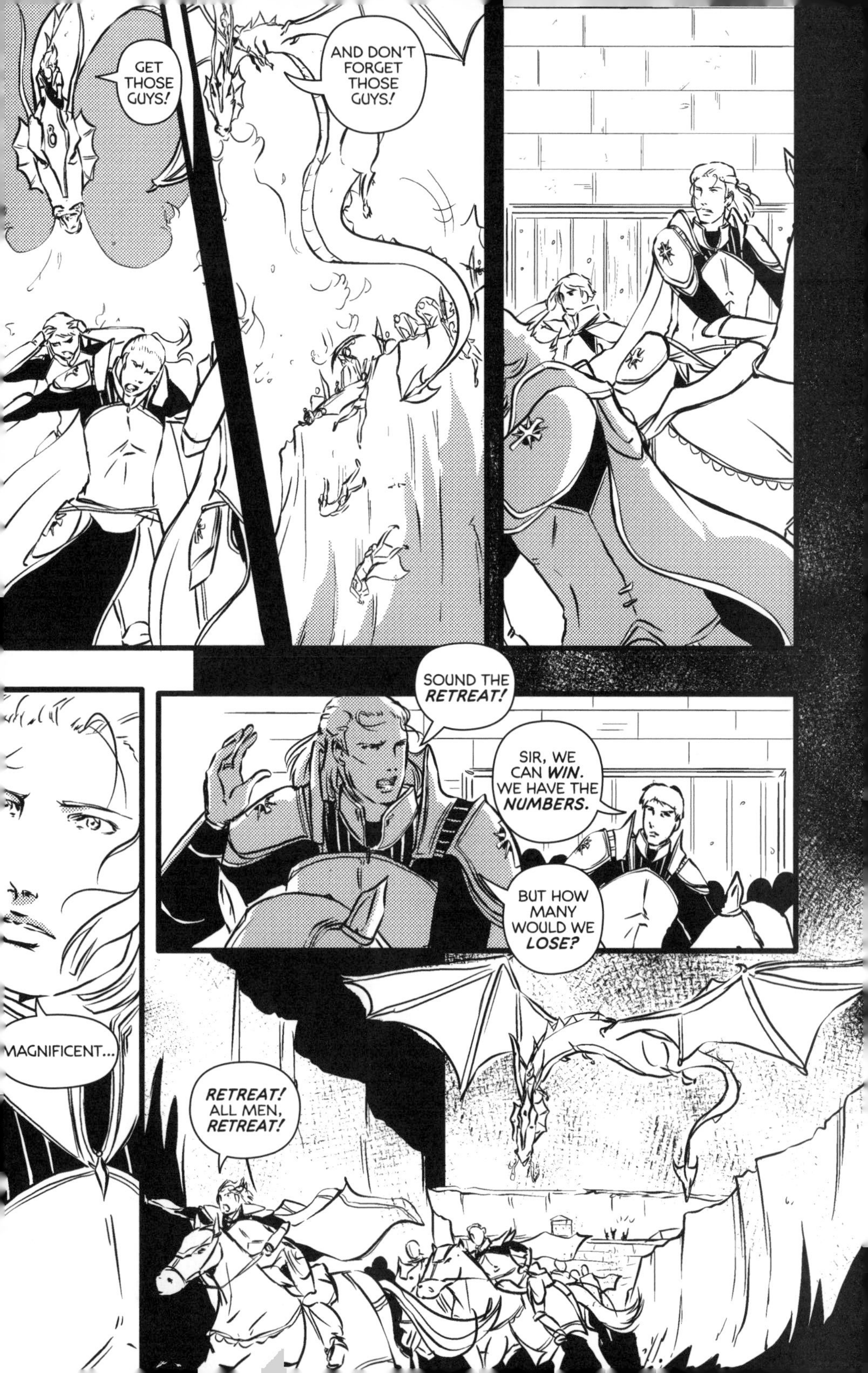
GET THOSE GUYS!
AND DON'T FORGET THOSE GUYS!
SOUND THE RETREAT!
SIR, WE CAN WIN. WE HAVE THE NUMBERS.
BUT HOW MANY WOULD WE LOSE?
MAGNIFICENT...
RETREAT! ALL MEN, RETREAT!

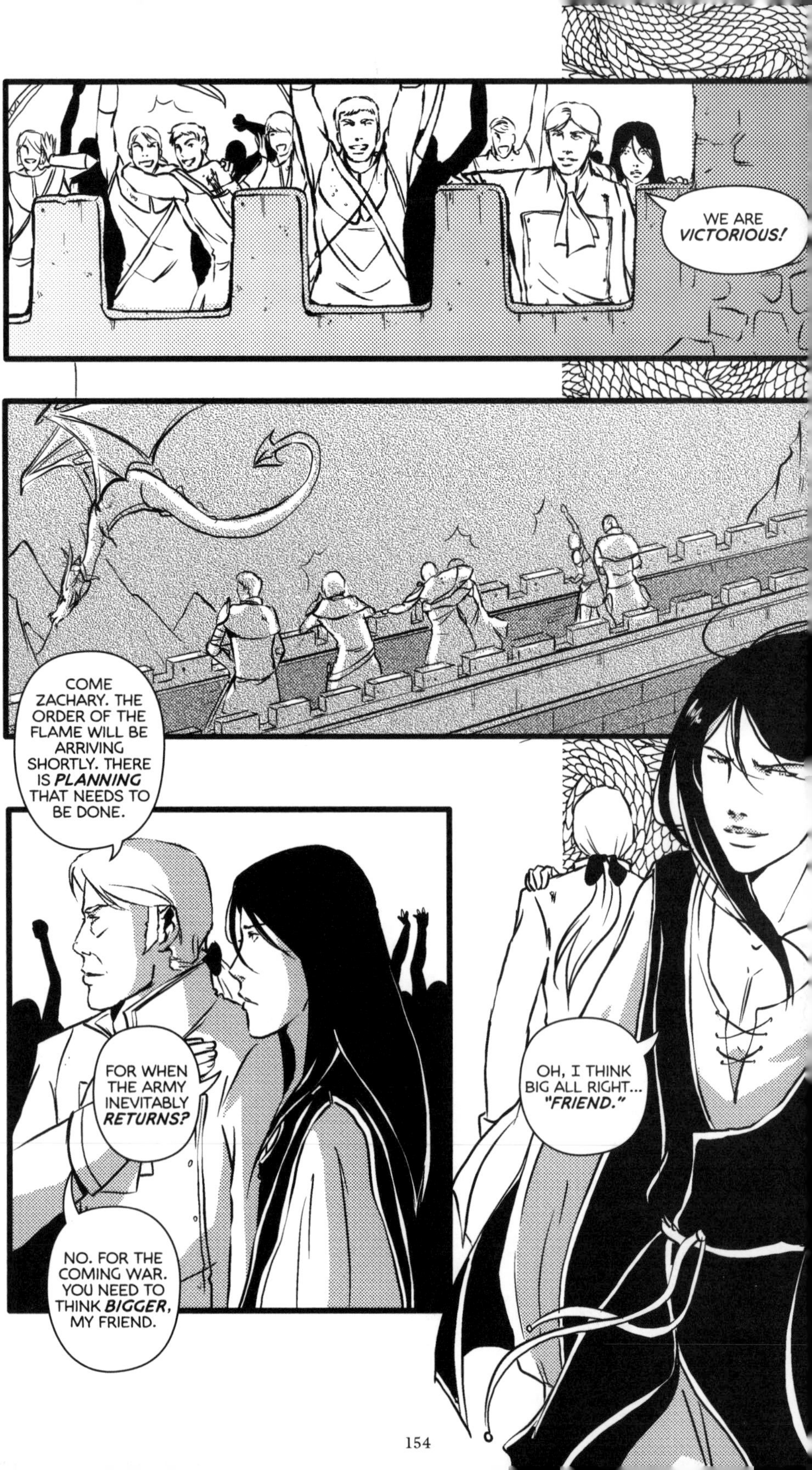
WE ARE *VICTORIOUS!*
COME ZACHARY. THE ORDER OF THE FLAME WILL BE ARRIVING SHORTLY. THERE IS *PLANNING* THAT NEEDS TO BE DONE.
FOR WHEN THE ARMY INEVITABLY *RETURNS?*
NO. FOR THE COMING WAR. YOU NEED TO THINK *BIGGER*, MY FRIEND.
OH, I THINK BIG ALL RIGHT... *"FRIEND."*

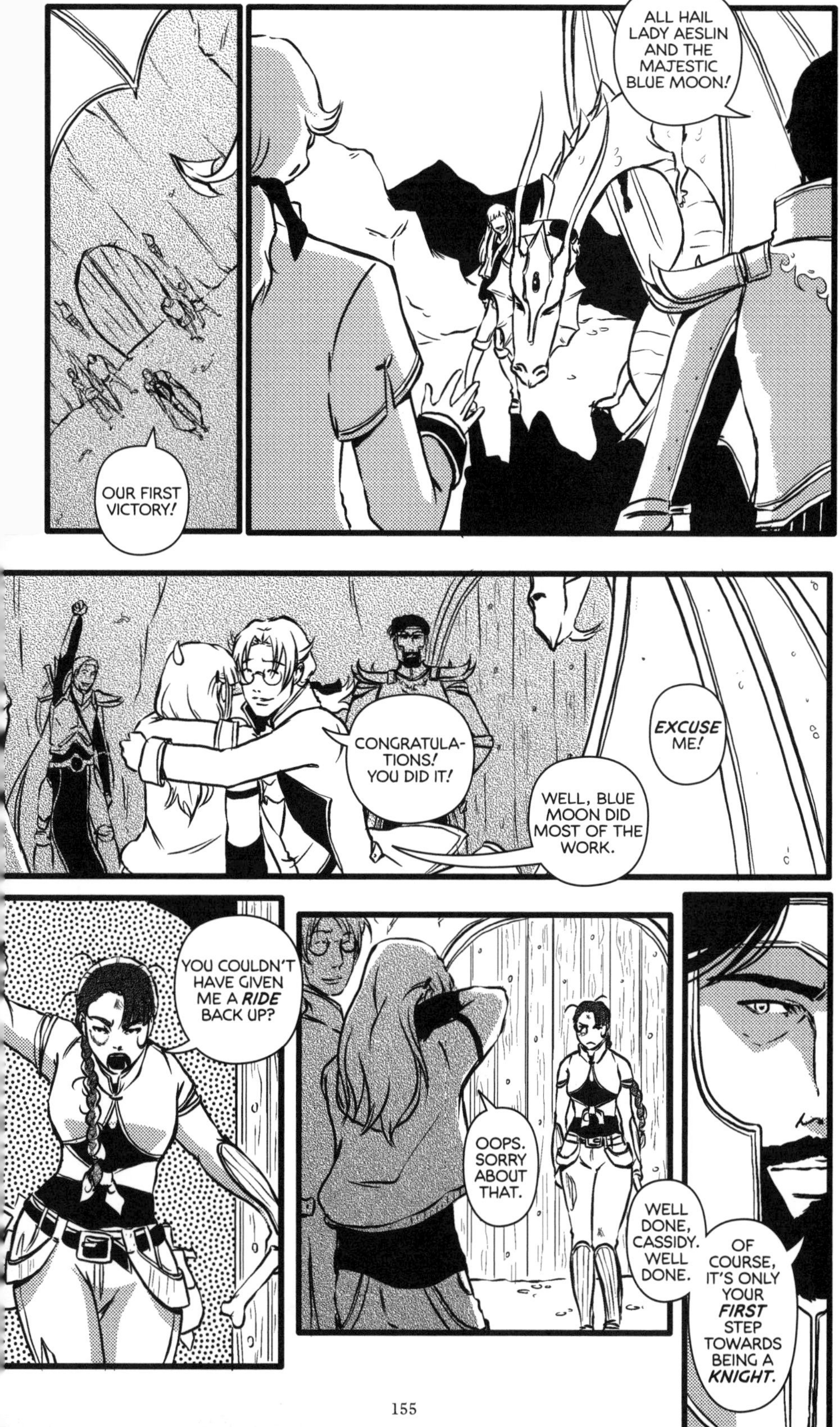
OUR FIRST VICTORY!
ALL HAIL LADY AESLIN AND THE MAJESTIC BLUE MOON!
CONGRATULATIONS! YOU DID IT!
WELL, BLUE MOON DID MOST OF THE WORK.
EXCUSE ME!
YOU COULDN'T HAVE GIVEN ME A *RIDE* BACK UP?
OOPS. SORRY ABOUT THAT.
WELL DONE, CASSIDY. WELL DONE.
OF COURSE, IT'S ONLY YOUR *FIRST* STEP TOWARDS BEING A *KNIGHT*.

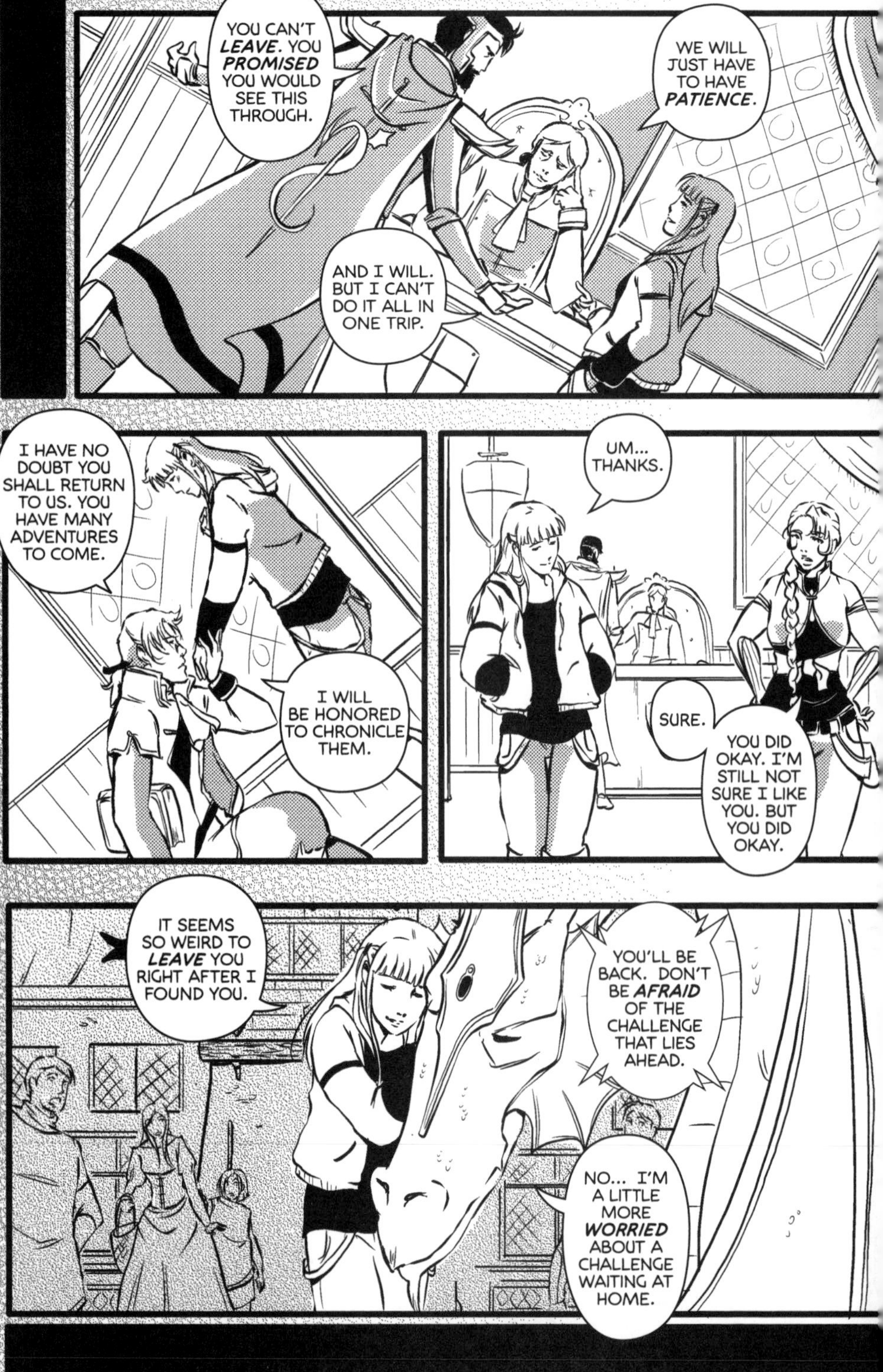
YOU CAN'T LEAVE. YOU PROMISED YOU WOULD SEE THIS THROUGH.
WE WILL JUST HAVE TO HAVE PATIENCE.
AND I WILL. BUT I CAN'T DO IT ALL IN ONE TRIP.
I HAVE NO DOUBT YOU SHALL RETURN TO US. YOU HAVE MANY ADVENTURES TO COME.
I WILL BE HONORED TO CHRONICLE THEM.
UM... THANKS.
SURE.
YOU DID OKAY. I'M STILL NOT SURE I LIKE YOU. BUT YOU DID OKAY.
IT SEEMS SO WEIRD TO LEAVE YOU RIGHT AFTER I FOUND YOU.
YOU'LL BE BACK. DON'T BE AFRAID OF THE CHALLENGE THAT LIES AHEAD.
NO... I'M A LITTLE MORE WORRIED ABOUT A CHALLENGE WAITING AT HOME.

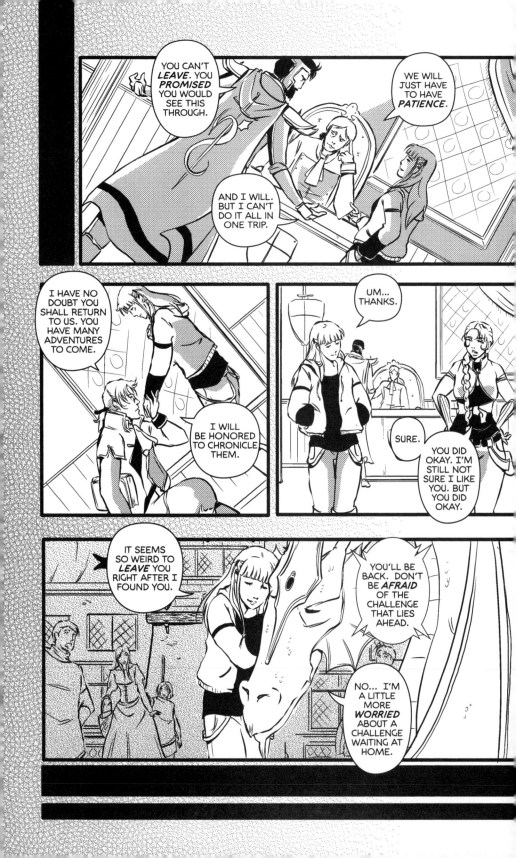

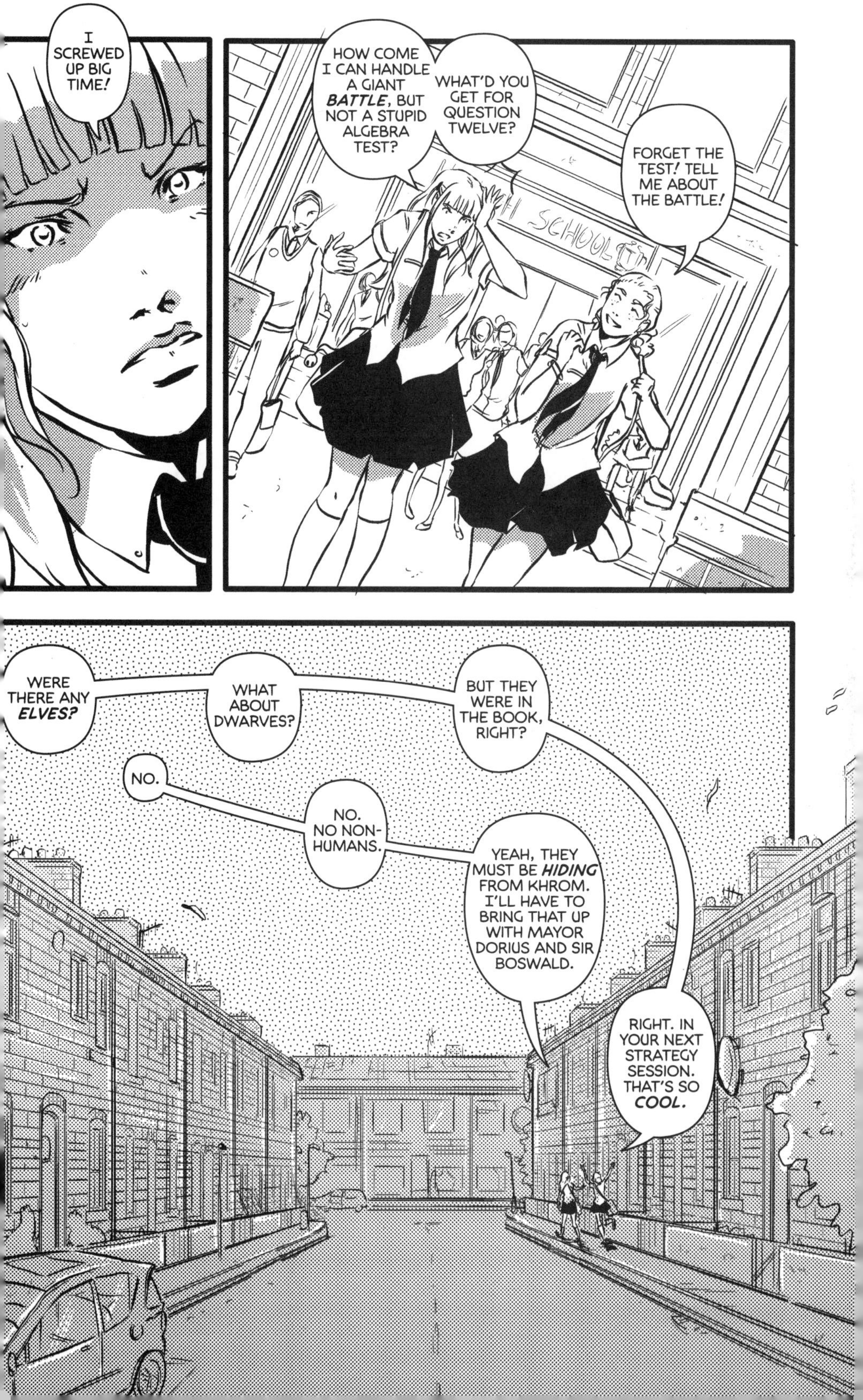
I SCREWED UP BIG TIME!
HOW COME I CAN HANDLE A GIANT *BATTLE*, BUT NOT A STUPID ALGEBRA TEST?
WHAT'D YOU GET FOR QUESTION TWELVE?
FORGET THE TEST! TELL ME ABOUT THE BATTLE!
SCHOOL
WERE THERE ANY *ELVES?*
NO.
WHAT ABOUT DWARVES?
NO. NO NON-HUMANS.
BUT THEY WERE IN THE BOOK, RIGHT?
YEAH, THEY MUST BE *HIDING* FROM KHROM. I'LL HAVE TO BRING THAT UP WITH MAYOR DORIUS AND SIR BOSWALD.
RIGHT. IN YOUR NEXT STRATEGY SESSION. THAT'S SO *COOL.*

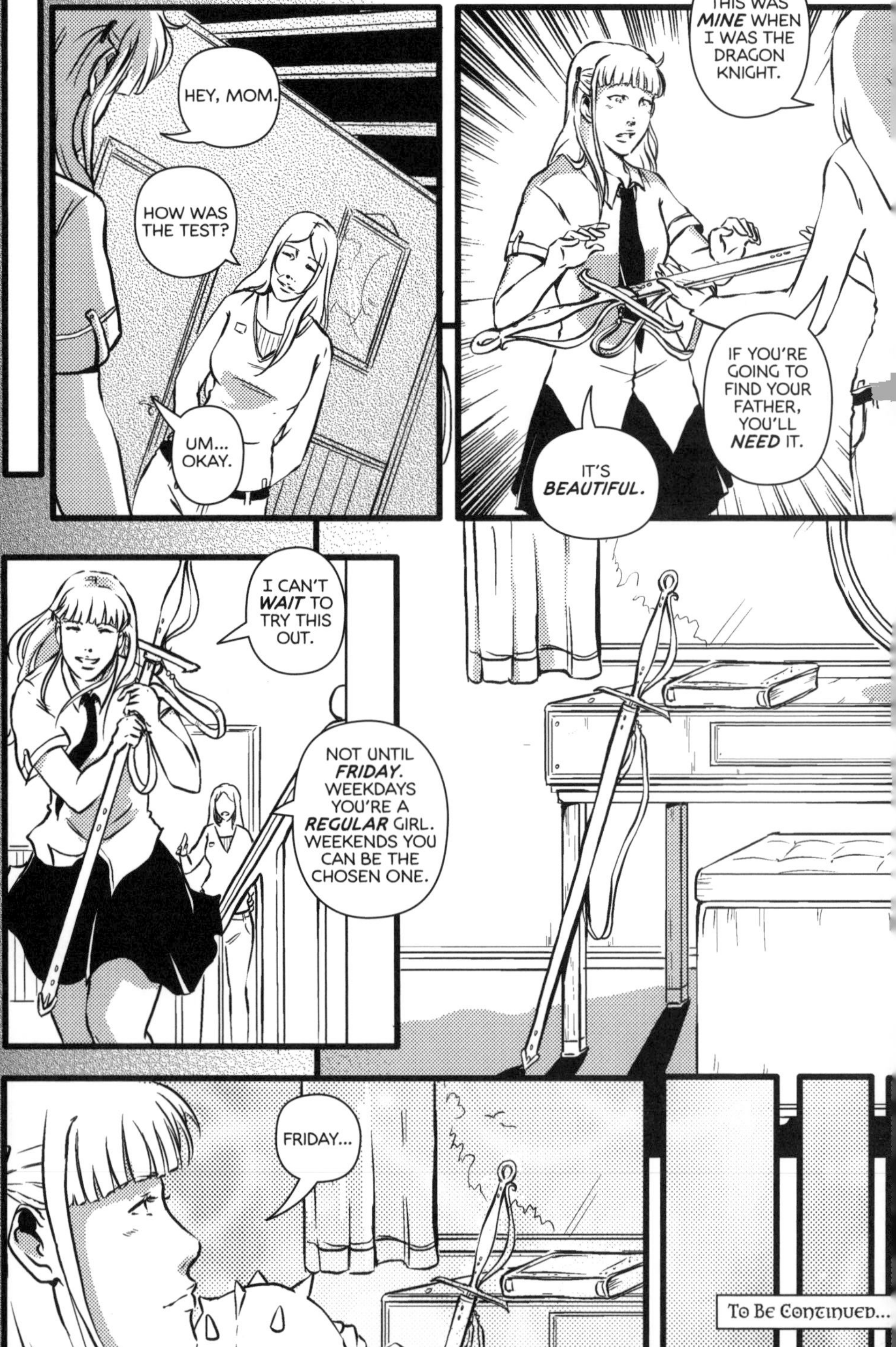
HEY, MOM.
HOW WAS THE TEST?
UM... OKAY.
THIS WAS *MINE* WHEN I WAS THE DRAGON KNIGHT.
IF YOU'RE GOING TO FIND YOUR FATHER, YOU'LL *NEED* IT.
IT'S *BEAUTIFUL.*
I CAN'T *WAIT* TO TRY THIS OUT.
NOT UNTIL *FRIDAY*. WEEKDAYS YOU'RE A *REGULAR* GIRL. WEEKENDS YOU CAN BE THE CHOSEN ONE.
FRIDAY...
To Be Continued...

ABOUT THE AUTHORS

 Nunzio DeFilippis and Christina Weir are a writing team trained as screenwriters. They have worked in television, on and off, for the last ten years. They were on the writing staff of HBOs *Arliss* for two seasons, and worked on Disney's *Kim Possible*. They have also written an independent film called *Paradise Springs* that is in development.

In comics, they have primarily made their home at Oni Press, who have let them write books in a wide array of genres, including *Skinwalker*, *Three Strikes*, *Maria's Wedding*, *The Tomb*, *Frenemy Of The State*, and *The Amy Devlin Mysteries*.

They have also written superhero comics like *New Mutants*, *New X-Men*, *Adventures Of Superman*, and *Batman Confidential*, and have worked in the field of manga, adapting numerous series for Del Rey. They created three Original English Language Manga series for Seven Seas Entertainment: *Amazing Agent Luna*, *Dracula Everlasting*, and *Destiny's Hand*, with a two-volume Luna spinoff called *Amazing Agent Jennifer* currently underway.

Currently, Nunzio and Christina have a graphic novel called *Play Ball* and an ongoing series called *Bad Medicine*, both set for release in 2012. Both projects are with Oni Press. They also just completed their first prose novel, a young adult thriller called *Mind Dance*, and are at work writing a second novel and a new screenplay.

www.weirdefilippis.com

 Emma Vieceli is a comic artist and writer based just outside Cambridge, United Kingdom. When she's not making comics, she's thinking about making comics. Her credits include work on the *Manga Shakespeare* series (Amulet Books), *Girl Comics* (Marvel), *Dragon Heir: Reborn* (Sweatdrop Studios) and she is the artist for the graphic novel adaptations of Richelle Mead's *Vampire Academy* (Penguin Razorbill). She is over the (blue) moon to be working with Oni Press.

www.emmavieceli.com

ALSO BY DEFILIPPIS AND WEIR:

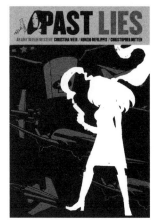

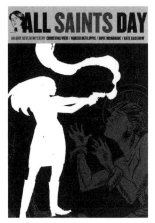

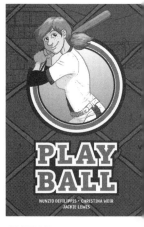

PAST LIES

THE AMY DEVLIN MYSTERIES:
PAST LIES
By Nunzio DeFilippis, Christina Weir
& Christopher Mitten
168 pages · Hardcover
B&W · $19.99 US
ISBN 978-1-934964-39-2

ALL SAINTS DAY

THE AMY DEVLIN MYSTERIES:
ALL SAINTS DAY
By Nunzio DeFilippis, Christina Weir,
Dove McHargue & Kate Kasenow
168 pages · Hardcover
B&W · $19.99 US
ISBN: 978-1-934964-23-1

PLAY
BALL
NUNZIO DEFILIPPIS • CHRISTINA WEIR
JACKIE LEWIS

PLAY BALL
By Nunzio DeFilippis, Christina Weir
& Jackie Lewis
152 pages · Hardcover
B&W · $19.99 US
ISBN: 978-1-934964-79-8

OTHER BOOKS FROM ONI PRESS!

Courtney
Volume One
Crumrin
The Night Things
Ted Naifeh

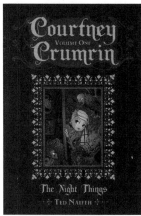

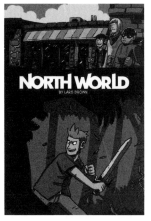

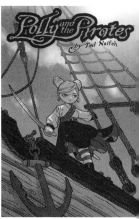

COURTNEY CRUMRIN, VOL. 1:
THE NIGHT THINGS
By Ted Naifeh
136 pages · Hardcover
Color · $19.99 US
ISBN: 978-1-934964-77-4

NORTH WORLD
BY LARS BROWN

NORTH WORLD VOL 1:
THE EPIC OF CONRAD
By Lars Brown
152 Pages · Digest
B&W · $11.95 US
ISBN: 978-1-932664-91-1

Polly and the Pirates
by Ted Naifeh

POLLY AND THE PIRATES, VOL. 1
By Ted Naifeh
176 Pages · Digest
B&W · $11.95 US
ISBN: 978-1-932664-46-1

ONI PRESS
REVOLUTIONIZE COMICS
www.onipress.com

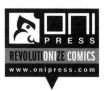

For more information on these and other fine Oni Press graphic novels, visit www.onipress.com.
To find a comic specialty store in your area, call 1-888-COMICBOOK or visit www.comicshops.us